LAUREL
EDITION

Plato's publications . . . constitute not merely the greatest philosophical work there is, but also one of the greatest pieces of literature in the world. They are philosophy par excellence; and if anyone asks what philosophy is, the best answer is: "read Plato."
—THE CONCISE ENCYCLOPEDIA OF WESTERN PHILOSOPHY AND PHILOSOPHERS

GEORGE KIMBALL PLOCHMANN has been teaching at Southern Illinois University since 1949. He received his B.A. from Columbia University and his Ph.D. with honors from the University of Chicago. Professor Plochmann was a Guggenheim Fellow in 1960 and has been Chairman of the Humanities Staff in General Studies at Southern Illinois since 1962. Editor and author of books in technical philosophy, he has written numerous articles and reviews for the professional journals and has been the consultant on philosophic terms for *American Heritage Dictionary*.

D1193756

Already published

ARISTOTLE

PLATO

George Kimball Plochmann

Published by
Dell Publishing Co., Inc.
1 Dag Hammarskjold Plaza
New York, New York 10017

Laurel ® TM 674623, Dell Publishing Co., Inc.
Printed in the United States of America
First printing—January 1973

CONTENTS

PREFACE

Let us be clear about one thing: We are dealing with one of the world's keenest, most inventive minds, one of the most original and refined artists. There is little reason to labor this point, for it has been agreed upon by the great majority of Plato's readers, even most of those to whom the philosophy of Plato is confusing, wrong, or irrelevant. Consequently, on artistic grounds, it is rewarding to read Plato, much as it is rewarding to witness the great tragedies of Shakespeare, or examine the drawings of Leonardo, or hear with a practiced ear the quartets or the sonatas of Beethoven. The dialogues are in that class of bold, intense, supreme art.

The aim of the present volume, however, is not to instill in the readers the impulse to offer fulsome praise for the philosopher, but to help develop the habit of careful, critical reading of his work. The love of Plato as an artist rests ultimately upon the understanding of him as a thinker. If art is to be less of an issue here than the patterns of concepts and their applications, then we should try to draw attention to significant features of his writing that constitute his special claim to soundness of comprehension of the world as it is. Plato needs to be understood as well as enjoyed, and of the two the understanding is the harder and more rare and more unshakable once it is gained. For this reason the introductory essay will stress the art of reading the dialogues, which in some respects is like that needed for the reading of other scientific treatises, or plays, or novels, or whatever, and in some respects is as unique as are the Platonic originals themselves.

What Plato was aiming at was nothing less than a charting of a new way of thinking that would reach to all corners of the intellectual globe and, either inconspicuously or radically, transform human thought. But whether it was to be in its content alteration or a major reversal of existing opinion and science, Plato was clear that only in part could it rest upon established habits of thinking. Not only was the method new but also the conceptions that were generated and put together as a system of ideas gave evidence of being formulated virtually for the first time. It was a bold effort, a mighty labor, as George Meredith would have said, and so far as any system of philosophy could be said to have succeeded, it has puzzled, stimulated, and instructed the Western world for two thousand years, and its day is by no means over.

I am indebted to a number of persons who have helped, perhaps without actually knowing it, and who have understood what I was trying to do in a general way without having been exposed to the typescript of this book. I owe much to Richard McKeon's analyses of a portion of the *Republic* and of the *Timaeus* in graduate classes at the University of Chicago many years ago; he and his other students will probably recognize this indebtedness, however dimly it may be manifested here. I owe to my own seminar students at Southern Illinois University the opportunity, always an excellent one, to try out a number of propositions being stated with more confidence here because of their very prodding, friendly disenchantments, their tooth-and-claw attentiveness. I owe to Ernest W. Dewey and his department of philosophy at the University of Toledo the chance to work (during the spring of 1970) in an atmosphere combining relaxation and eagerness in a way that Plato himself would have strongly approved. Dr. Steven S. Tigner of that department has made several very helpful suggestions regarding my translation of part of *Letter VII*, appearing in the section on dialectic. I owe to Philip B. Dematteis a close, competent scrutiny of my entire essay which leaves me with no one to blame but myself for errors or misproportions that may remain.

Mrs. Sheryl Ann Christenson has my gratitude for her typing and other skills in putting together this book.

Finally I owe to my artist wife, Carolyn, the chance to debate the merits, interrelations, and defects of our two callings, a debate which I shall regard as settled only because this happens to be a book of philosophy and not a painting.

GEORGE KIMBALL PLOCHMANN

October 1969—May 1970

PART ONE

PLATO AND
HIS PHILOSOPHY

THE LIFE OF PLATO

THE AIM and intent of Plato, we shall find, is nothing less than to explore in outline the structure of the world with its manifold contents, setting values upon them as the exploration proceeds, and to examine all aspects of the knowledge of that world as the human mind seeks to attain it. Plato is thus distinguished from the philosophers preceding him who appeared content to investigate nature, or parts of nature, but who left humanity to itself; and equally distinguished from many subsequent thinkers who have deemed it sufficient to treat of mind or spirit in its stages of self-development without much reference to a real universe.

To explain how Plato's philosophy could come about, we ought first to give an outline account of his personal life, conjunction of these two aspects of his career being a perfectly good Platonic practice. We may summarize his biography by saying that he was born into the fifth century, B.C., that he was an aristocrat, that he was versatile in his gifts, and so forth. These phrases will be our headings.

Plato was a fifth-century Athenian. According to our best records, Plato was born in 427 B.C., at a time when his native city, Athens, had barely passed her great prime, which is by custom entitled the Golden Age of Pericles. Athens had been ruled for over thirty years (463–431) by this Pericles, who by present-day standards could well be called a constitutional dictator—nothing that fits very closely our ordinary classifications of monarchic, republican, or tyrannical and dictatorial stereotypes. He assumed rule over a city just recently (490, 480, 479) victorious over the prolonged and repeated assaults of the far larger armies and naval units of the Persian Empire; the Athens that Pericles ruled was virtually bound for political and economic advance of its own and hegemony over its neighbor cities, but the canny and firm leadership of Pericles himself greatly contributed to the good fortunes of the city. And he brought his multiple political skills to bear in a way which would stimulate a great upsurge of artistic, literary, and scientific effort, as well as the mercantile supremacy which Athens was to enjoy almost uninterruptedly down to the commencement of a long and wretched war against Sparta (Lacedaemon), 431–404, a war which, after much seesawing, was thrown away by Athens and her craven or bumbling leaders.

So Plato's birth stands a couple of decades after the dividing point in the historical course of an Athens which escaped disaster at the hands of the Persians but which was about to suffer it from a sister state of Greece, a city-state far less formidable than the extensive empire that had been able to raise huge armies (Herodotus estimates that the Persian force mustered by Xerxes contained 1,700,000 men, more or less), and bring them hundreds and hundreds of miles by land and by sea to fight the Athenians. Sparta was less formidable—and far less cultured. She was ruled by a militaristically disposed dual kingship, and willingly sacrificed most other aspirations of private and public life to make her young men vigorous, courageous, and patriotic in their aggressive inclinations. Sparta was provincial, she lacked a body of intellectuals, she had no corps of artists, only artisans, farmers, and fighters who trained incessantly at gynmastics of a brutal sort. Had Persia won out against the Athenians in 480, the results would have been incalculable but probably not all detrimental to Europe, for by contrast with the Athenians the Persian Empire was a somewhat more advanced civilization. The victory of Sparta, however, was a cultural misfortune. Athens was the "school of Greece," in a happy phrase attributed to Pericles himself. But her pupils, the other city-states, often proved themselves independent, unruly, inattentive, and slow-witted students, and Sparta was their cold-eyed ringleader.

Plato was an aristocrat. He was born into a family of considerable political prominence, a family, moreover, that laid strong claims to intellectual distinction (the genealogy was traced back to Solon, a poet, lawgiver, reformer), and although Plato seems not to have possessed any great fortune, his family was comfortably well off and duly respected for its contributions to forms of administration that only by considerable extension of meaning could be termed democratic. As time passed, from Solon (early sixth century) to young Plato (late fifth), the strength of the common people gradually increased, giving the aristocrats a generally conservative and even autocratic role, if only by contrast. It is with no surprise, therefore, that we find Critias, an uncle of Plato, reviled by the democrats of the latter days of the war against Sparta (that city, being on a part of Hellas called the Peloponnese, the struggle has always been popularly referred to as the Peloponnesian War), then locked in combat against them, then executing some of them, and finally executed himself in a full-blown democratic revolt. Of Plato's own father, Ariston, there is little definite information, but the philosopher himself tells us of the keen minds of Ariston's other two sons, Glaucon and Adeimantus. The aristocratic life evidently meant for Plato a life of doing and thinking rather that of having and posing; but it was still a way of life that had become suspect in Athens, and after the eventual assumption of power by democratic elements, it was on the defensive, if not in actual retreat. Presumably it was Plato's activities as thinker and educator that gained him his great portion of acceptance and honor in his later career, rather than his family heritage.

Plato was versatile. His real name was Aristocles, but apparently quite early the nickname Platōn, meaning "broad," was given to him, in reference either to his shoulders (he was said to have been an excellent athlete in his youth), to his forehead (portrait busts show that nature had not scanted him in this regard), to his literary style (it is indeed sturdy, precise, yet endlessly suggestive and varied in its effects), and finally to his wide-ranging interests. If Athens was the school of Greece, then Plato is virtually the first man who gave evidence of having learned all that his city—and some others—had to teach, although evidence on earlier wise and well-traveled men is unfortunately insufficient, except in the case of Herodotus. Plato is the first, and perhaps next to the last, man to master the varied traditions of literature, for he quotes a wide variety of poets both epic and lyric, shows a grasp of religious history and mythology, gives us the first extant sketch of the history of rhetoric, uses Aeschylus, Sophocles, and Euripides, portrays and imitates Aristophanes; to master the lore of government, law, and politics in many Hellenic states; to master, at least in the way of an amateur, the chief arts

of the time, including music, painting, weaving, medicine,
and a number of others; and finally to master the sciences,
chief of them being mathematics, followed by astronomy, a
kind of blend of chemistry and physiology, and biology.
(His great pupil Aristotle is the only other Greek of whom
we have solid firsthand evidence of such mastery.) It is an
effort to grasp the whole, and to find a way of expressing
the ever-so-complex ways in which parts are related within
the whole and, in consequence, can be understood articu-
lately. One may disagree with every last thing that Plato
had to say; disapprove of his methods and their results;
find his problems trivial and his solutions arbitrary; but
it is hard not to admire him for having first noticed the
problems, first devised the methods, and first decided upon
his solutions. We are confronted with a unique phenomenon: this is the very earliest philosophic system of which
we have any more than a few hints and fragments remaining; and yet it is one of the most elaborate and subtle, a
system that has engendered the greatest frustrations in
its readers—and the greatest satisfactions. For want of
much documentary evidence, it would be idle to suppose
that Plato invented out of whole cloth everything that he
had to say; but we have the feeling nevertheless that nothing
went into his dialogues undigested, untransformed, un-
exalted by his power to rethink what he had learned.

Plato was a pupil of Socrates. It was said that in his
youth Plato wrote much poetry, and quite good poetry
at that; but evidently his taste turned to matters philosophical after he had associated with the remarkable and
baffling Socrates. This man, born of a poor stonecarver
and a midwife in 469, and executed in 399 by his beloved
city of Athens, is of such complexity that it would warrant
an independent study to deal fully with him; here our
main concern is to give some outline of his probable effect
upon Plato, far and away the greatest among his many
followers.

Unlike Buddha or Ludwig Wittgenstein, Plato did not
feel it necessary to discard all his worldly goods in favor
of philosophy. He was practical, and as a small example,
there is evidence that he offered to pay a fine for Socrates
when the latter was convicted of corrupting the young and
endeavoring to change the religion of the state. The contrast, however, between the wellborn young man of twenty
and the doughty old soldier, dedicated and destitute, already

in his early sixties when Plato joined him, was significant; but the exterior differences were doubtless more striking than their inner mental ones. Plato was apparently one of a number of pupils who received from Socrates no formal schooling but who must have done much reading and studying on their own, and who were guided, prodded, corrected, and enlightened by Socrates at critical moments in their individual development. Incidentally, our fullest information about Socrates comes, for good or ill, from Plato himself, and our evaluation of the relation of master to disciple must be based preponderantly upon Plato's own. We may assume, but with no real proof whatever, that Socrates directed the younger man's studies in the sciences (there is a tradition that Socrates himself in early life gave his chief attention to what we now nickname the hard sciences, only later turning his attention to ethical and political questions). We may also assume that Plato's extreme ethical conscientiousness—a term which again is not his but ours—was fostered by Socrates, although so strong a moral sense cannot be dropped into a man who has none already. And we may also assume that Plato's evident dissatisfaction with the world as it was in the closing years of the fifth century was sharpened by Socrates' teaching as much as it was by the fate that ended the life of this unusual master.

The major thrust of Socrates' life and teaching was to turn intellectual Athenians, or rather some of them, from the bare study of nature and of the arts to the investigation of man, his aspirations, obstacles, principles for finding truth, and the conditions of happiness and misery both when alone and in association with his fellows. Socrates evidently developed what we are going to call a dialectical method of inquiry, informal in its early stages but seeking greater and greater precision, directed to individual respondents to find its problems, yet seeking the greatest possible generality of application for its solutions; provocative and occasionally even polemical, yet seeking the fullest measure of agreement between himself and his respondents in the question-and-answer discourse he conducted endlessly in the streets and marketplace, in the public gymnasia, and in the homes of his friends and acquaintances.

The method that Socrates used was apparently one of stimulating a controlled doubt through the asking of pressing questions, which, if the search for knowledge happened to be successful, issued in sets of interlocking constructive propositions regarding the nature of man and his world. One must use such words as "evidently" and "apparently" because Socrates left no books, no manuscripts, no notes even, and all that we know of him is through the dialogues of Plato himself, through the soldier–author Xenophon, and through one or two other men. (These reports agree tolerably well in the facts they present, but not in spirit: Plato's is the only account suffused with creative genius, and Socrates would never have held an exalted position in history were it not for the dramatic dialogues of which he has been made the hero by his most brilliant follower.)

Whatever conversations or other types of instruction went on between Socrates and Plato, the effect upon the younger man was not forgotten by him, ever. Throughout the last years of the war with Sparta, years when the power of Athens was waning rapidly, Plato seems to have followed his teacher's fortunes; and he was permanently disillusioned by the execution of Socrates. In the last years of the war, control of Athens was given over to the so-called Thirty Tyrants, a junta, including Critias, whose needlessly cruel regime was brought to a close when a democracy—of sorts—was restored. Socrates was thought to have been personally friendly toward some of the Thirty (this was undoubtedly true), and in sympathy with their policies (this was probably quite false). His moral probings had, even by his own admission, been much resented by many of the Athenian citizens, and these not solely the wellborn and rich and conservative. A charge was prepared on behalf of the poets, orators, and artisans, the threefold terms of which alleged that Socrates corrupted the youth, that he denied the traditional divinities of Athens, and that he imported new ones. In a striking defense, Socrates attempted to show that stimulating the young to search for truth was scarcely corrupting to them, that if he alone harmed them while everyone else benefited them the youth could scarcely be in any danger. He flatly though briefly denied the other two charges. But his defense (if Plato's *Apology* can be trusted as even a remotely accurate report) was so worded as to cast doubt upon the men of Athens as citizens having more than a sham wisdom. Socrates pictured himself as a gadfly, stinging the great horse which was the Athenian public, stimulating it to thought and action when it wished to fall asleep, and causing it to reexamine the principles by which the city lived and worked. In consequence, opinion turned rather solidly against Socrates, and he was condemned to death by poison.

Plato was a traveler. Upon the death of his teacher, Plato, as well as several other members of the Socratic circle, left Athens for a time, fearing that the public hostility might be marshaled against them. Plato himself probably journeyed through the Greek mainland, and since he mentions Sparta quite often and describes her customs knowledgeably, we may assume that this recent conqueror of Athens was on his itinerary, perhaps more than once. He also refers to the cities of Thessaly (north of Athens) several times, though without much pleasure, and to a cave on the island of Crete. Although he may have learned of this at second hand, it is possible that his account is from immediate observation. And Plato has a good deal to say about the Egyptians, their inhospitality, shrewdness, love of money, and their persisting customs in music. Was he perhaps an unwanted tourist among them, or did he depend upon friends for reports?

Plato also traveled—and here the evidence is a little solider—to Sicily. More of this shortly.

Plato was a writer. Whether he first began writing down his dialogues before or after the death of Socrates cannot be decided, although a legend has it that the aged philosopher objected that what Plato had already written was misleading. If this remark was ever made by Socrates it might still have been in fun, and if in fun (or even if seriously) we do not know how to take it. Scholars have often talked as if they were sure that certain works of Plato were intended to be no more, or little more, than mere reports of what Socrates had actually said, though the evidence for this is so slim that if any such guess were true it would be so by merest chance. What *is* clear is that the figure of Socrates dominates something like two-thirds of the authentic works of Plato, and that the author expends much effort in making clear his conception of Socrates regardless of how closely the historical individual conformed to it. All the genuine writings of Plato, with the exception of one letter having quite good claims to authenticity, are cast in the form of conversations between personages, some of them historical, some of them imaginary or identified so vaguely (" slave boy," "a stranger from Elea," etc.) that it is impossible to discover any further information, and in these dialogues men speak and are silent, they come and go, they bicker and make amends. In addition, many of them enunciate, defend, and attack philosophic opinions. Not only that, but most of the participants in the dialogues are easily identifiable figures in Greek history—the cautious general Nicias, the reckless general Alcibiades, the successful and impressive sophist Protagoras, Gorgias the famed teacher of oratory, and many others whose identities can be traced with some ease. Those few who have resisted the labors of two millennia of scholars—such as Phaedrus, Crito, Aristodemus, and a few others of no special distinction—are probably not invented out of whole cloth by Plato, but we are at a disadvantage because so many records of Greek life and history have been destroyed.

At any rate, the dialogue form allows Plato the free ranging between fact and imagination, and between the abstract thought and the concrete embodiment, that would have been denied him had he employed pure history or conventional theater or philosophical treatise or psychological case-study as his mode of expression. (Such case-studies are not as remote from Greek thought as it might seem; a generation or two after Plato, Theophrastus and others were writing books of "characters" which were in spirit much like our modern psychographs.) The dialogue *is* history, it *is* theater, it *is* philosophy in a very tight-knit fabric, it *is* psychological analysis—and in a different sense it is *none* of them. It is restricted, there being many things that Plato does not allow himself to try when he uses the form; yet it is greatly varied, and is possibly the least monotonous of all the kinds of philosophical writing tried up to our own day. Moreover, it is unique to Plato. No one else, at least not in the general tradition of authentic philosophy, has ever succeeded in writing a work possessing the many special characteristics with which Plato endowed his glowing, glittering dialogues. And this is certainly not because no one has ever tried.

Plato was an educational organizer. Some while after he returned from his *Wanderjahren* to Athens (the old enemies of Socrates had by then been put down themselves), Plato, convinced of the ethical need and political utility of a system of higher education, apparently founded a school, the Academy. In this, several branches of learning could be pursued and communicated through expert teaching. We do not know exactly what all these branches were, except that they included mathematics and political sciences; the sciences of astronomy, of harmonics, of mechanics, of zoology, may or may not have formed a part of the curriculum, and there may or may not have been discourses on the theory of painting, of tragedy, epic, and musical art generally. It is pretty well agreed that rhetoric was a staple of the Academy, though the evidence is not much more substantial than it is for many of the other subjects. At any rate, Plato's skills as administrator are evident in this; the school, which was at the outset the only one of its kind anywhere, throve during the last forty years of the philosopher's life. The year 388 is frequently suggested as that in which Plato opened his Academy, an institution most closely approximating our colleges and post-graduate schools. It was in a period of intermittent decline of Athenian power and culture that the Academy first rose to its dominant position. A dozen years after Plato's death Philip of Macedon, father of Alexander the Great, put an end altogether to the independence of Athens. But the Academy still went forward vigorously, and indeed persisted in some form for nearly a thousand years. Its chief rival, the Lyceum, was set up by Aristotle, and another school, aimed primarily at imparting ability in rhetoric, was that of Isocrates, foremost teacher of oratory in that generation.

The dialogues offer a number of different divisions of knowledge, and it is tempting from some one of these to try reconstructing the course of study at the Academy. Music (i.e., the literary and what we would call the performing arts in general), gymnastic, mathematical sciences, and finally the philosophical reasoning known as dialectic are explained and evaluated at length in the *Republic*, most famous of all the dialogues; but the *Republic* is specifically oriented toward an ideal state that can never be realized upon this earth, and it is unlikely that this one classification of sciences would be used as an exemplar for a busy school of men being educated for the tasks of practical reform of the Greek city-states. The education of the wise ruler in the *Republic* is so long, so comprehensive, that it would scarcely be sensible to institute it for the young men of Athens who would wish and need to apply their learning

well before reaching their fiftieth year, the age recommended in the *Republic* for the conclusion of formal and
practical education and the assumption of political office.

*Plato failed in one important instance as a practical re-
former.* Either as part of his original period of traveling
(in which case the number of years assigned to this would
probably need to be given a slightly higher estimate), or
else shortly after he founded the Academy, Plato quite
likely undertook the first of his related but chronologically
widely separated missions to Syracuse. This was then the
leading city-state of Sicily, populated of course chiefly
by Greeks from the mainland, militarily successful, economically prosperous, politically agitated. Under Dionysius I the city became known for its pleasure-loving, its
divisions of classes and of privileges; but these were the almost inevitable accompaniment of an autocratic rule. As a
shortcut to the elaborate ethical-intellectual preparation of
the ruler suggested in the *Republic*, Plato evidently hoped
that advice to the king would be sufficient to initiate and
perhaps sustain an effective and just government. He was
unsuccessful, Dionysius I resisted his instruction, and eventually Plato left Syracuse, tradition having it that he was
sold into slavery on the way home to Athens and had to be
ransomed by friends. Many years later, after Dionysius had
died and his throne had passed to Dionysius II, Plato re-
visited Syracuse with much the same expectations as before.
The young king, however, had two drawbacks, the first
being that he felt himself already a capable philosopher,
the second that he had a continuing rivalry with Dion, a
half-brother. Dion was evidently the more able man, but
like Hamlet he lacked advancement, and his plots took the
place of his tenancy of the throne. Each time (367? and
361?) Plato returned to Athens without having achieved
anything like the reforms he had projected for Syracuse.
To the scoffers who have weighted these frustrated journeys
very heavily against Plato's efficacy as a man of affairs, one
can say only that Plato at least had the determination that
in better circumstances would have enabled him to persuade
Dionysius, father or son, to espouse more philosophical
principles of rule, and make Syracuse worthy of admiration, if possible, throughout that region of the ancient
world. For the second part, Plato himself—and this may
have been a reflex of his experience in Syracuse—was quick
to stress the combined unpredictability of human nature

and unwillingness to alter habits. He wished to see to it that new habits were formed by an intelligence which, abiding, could be persuaded and instructed to yield to an even more comprehensive intelligence.

Whether Plato lived an eventful life or an uneventful one is a matter of opinion. We may sum it up by confessing that we do not know how far he traveled (except to Sicily), we do not know from authentic contemporary sources how large and diverse the Academy really was, we do not know how much time was spent in writing or even when the writing actually began. But we do know that, well traveled or not, Plato was one of the first great cosmopolitans in his point of view. We do know that, large or small, the Academy was one of the tiny handful of the significant educational institutions in the classical world. We do know that, written early or late, the dialogues remain as an incredibly beautiful, varied, *thoughtful* monument to one of the best minds of his own time and of the long stretch that reaches up to ours.

PLATO'S WORKS

THERE ARE not quite thirty dialogues that appear to be authentic to the majority of the scholars and historical critics. Not every one of these works is thought to be genuine by all of the scholars, but a fair consensus has nevertheless been reached today. The numbers below refer to the total pages occupied in the famous three-volume collected edition published in the time of Queen Elizabeth by the French scholar Henri Estienne (otherwise known as Stephanus or Henry Stephens), and used even to this day for the page references to the dialogues. Letters a–e simply divide each page into five approximately equal portions. (The list here is alphabetized, and so does not follow the Stephanus order in his volumes.)

Apology 25 pages (17a–42a)	*Lysis* 20 (203a–223b)
Charmides 23 (153a–176d)	*Menexenus* 15 (234a–249e)
Cratylus 57 (383a–440e)	*Meno* 30 (70a–100b)
Critias 15 (106a–121c)	*Parmenides* 40 (126a–166c)
Crito 11 (43a–54e)	*Phaedo* 61 (57a–118a)
Epinomis 19 (973a–992e)	*Phaedrus* 52 (227a–279c)
Euthydemus 36 (271a–307c)	*Philebus* 56 (11a–67b)
Euthyphro 14 (2a–16a)	*Protagoras* 53 (309a–362a)
Gorgias 80 (447a–527e)	*Republic* 294 (327a–621d)
Hippias Minor 13 (363a–376c)	*Sophist* 52 (216a–268d)
	Statesman 54 (257a–311c)
Ion 12 (530a–542b)	*Symposium* 51 (172a–223d)
Laches 23 (178a–201c)	*Theaetetus* 68 (142a–210d)
Laws 345 (624a–969d)	*Timaeus* 75 (17a–92c)

In addition to these, there are several others on which general agreement has been reached that they are not, or not wholly, from the hand of Plato: *Alcibiades I* and *II*, *Hippias Major, Minos, Cleitophon, Lovers, Theages, Hipparchus,* and a few more. Most of these are quite brief, and generally speaking the elaborate study of them has not shown itself very profitable. There are also some letters, about which a word will be said later.

The only dialogue whose chronological placing in the group we can be quite sure of is the *Laws*; Aristotle, who evidently worked in the Academy for something like twenty years and who must have known what he was talking about, said that the *Laws* was the last work of his teacher, and that it was left not quite finished, or at least not polished up. Those who would find a biographical order, therefore, have examined the *Laws* mainly for its stylistic traits, and have attempted to date the works according to their closeness of resemblance to this last and longest dialogue. This is a perfectly proper task, it must be said, *provided* it does not interfere with the wise discrimination of methods and the demonstrating of their accommodations to the subject matter, or rather selection of subject matters, of each dialogue. Unfortunately, this interference has often shown itself, so much so that certain of the books most keen on chronology have virtually omitted discussion of the methods, and have thus misconstrued several of the doctrines as well.

There is a tradition of antiquity going back at least to an astrologer and grammarian, Thrasyllus, who died nearly 400 years after Plato, which rigidly classified the Platonic dialogues into sets of four. Thrasyllus asserted, we are told, that Plato himself published these works in these so-called tetralogies, and although almost none of the sets deal exclusively with a single subject, still there are other relationships, of common participants, or time sequences, etc., which *may* bind them in such groups. Some of the tetralogies hang together pretty well, for instance the one containing the *Euthyphro, Apology, Crito,* and *Phaedo,* each of which forms an episode in a continuous narrative of the last days of Socrates; but others, such as that of the *Parmenides, Philebus, Symposium,* and *Phaedrus,* have much less cohesiveness, certainly in respect to time sequence and other narrative and dramatic relationships.

In addition to this speculative grouping, there is an attempt by Thrasyllus (or his predecessors) to classify all the dialogues according to their types of argument and the topics with which they deal, as follows:

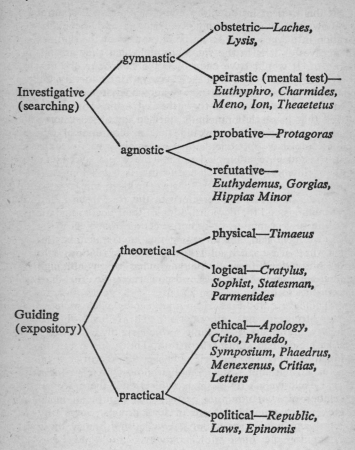

This mode of organization has a little more to recommend it, as methods and subject matters discussed are obviously of utmost importance; but it does not grow out of any similar classification set down in any of the dialogues by Plato himself. We have printed this catalogue simply to give a rough indication of some of the topics with which the philosopher deals, and as an indication of one direction in which Platonic scholarship moved. As we shall see, it is virtually impossible to pigeonhole any of the dialogues, as regards either methods or concepts.

As this present introductory essay on Plato will attempt to show, the difficulty with the tetralogies and the classification into types is not so much in the lists or the outlines themselves as it is in the rigidity with which they are adhered to. It would have been better to match up the dialogues in small groups, and then systematically to vary the combination and see what new insights develop. It would also have been better to try attaching each dialogue to different items on the branching chart, to stimulate what we might call experimental thinking. The *Theaetetus,* to choose one example, is obstetric, and remarks are made in the dialogue to support this; it is a mental test, and there are hints of this too; it is an attempt to prove certain notions about knowledge, but ends as a series of refutations of the positions adopted by the chief respondent to Socrates. And so for the rest.

To go back to the original list: the numbers just after the titles, we have said, are to pagings of the Greek text. Because that is a condensed language, the translations into English or German usually run somewhat longer, although many recent translated versions unwarrantedly introduce economies through excision. Plato was known for his rather fulsome style, yet a close examination of his seeming redundancies ends with the conviction that from his standpoint they are essential to the expression of remarkably rich and varied thinking. The two kinds of excess usually complained of are found first in his mythic and historical descriptions, in which qualifying epithets are laid on rather thickly, and second in his care to mark every step in an argument with an utterance of agreement or bland interrogation ("Why not?" or "How could it be otherwise?") by a partner to the conversation. Regarding the first we may say that even the most effulgent rhetoric of the *Phaedrus* turns out to have an exceedingly tight structure, in which every adjective is placed with a master hand in such fashion that the effects of rhetoric are served simultaneously with the purposes of a close-knit dialectic of the human soul. Regarding the second we remark that the interpolated comments and questions of respondents are an enormous help in making out the subdivisions in the arguments, in sounding out the difficulties, and in showing the degrees of certitude that Plato wishes to establish in the steps of the discussions.

There are in point of fact three components of the dialogue form as Plato conceived it, the first two always being present, the third usually: statements, persons, and exterior action together with its physical setting. The third supports and clarifies the second, which in turn supports and clarifies the first.

1. Statements of opinion and of reasoned conviction are, of course, cast into *sentences* (or propositions) consisting of individual words put in an intelligible order. These sentences (which are ordinarily assertions or denials) are put together in proofs or consecutive descriptions. Along with these there are questions, prayers, demands, and exclamations.

2. Different persons, whom we shall designate participants, speak in their own name or quote others. These persons are sometimes nearly equal in attitude and intellectual power, and are sometimes very disparate. Who says what is of great importance in the dialogues. I shall term this the *dialogic component*.

3. The *dramatic devices*, found over and over in Plato, but not universally, are the scene, the movements of the participants, their entrances and exits, their gestures. In some of the so-called later dialogues, these touches are almost absent. When present, they are of material importance in the dialogue, and when judiciously interpreted in the light of the whole they aid considerably in reading the work.

Most critics have come to the view that of these three components the first is of transcendent importance, and in this they are undoubtedly correct; Plato is first of all a man putting forward philosophical ideas, general notions meant to cover groups of like instances. Yet he has a purpose so significant that it can hardly be called secondary, which is to demonstrate the relation between what a participant says and what he himself is. In other words, philosophical concepts are not connected in propositions in a vacuum, but in a concrete context of human beings and their very complex interrelationships. It is not merely for the sake of parceling out ideas or enlivening the discussion with personalities, for Plato can often be heavy reading even when he has peopled his scene with half a dozen participants. What Plato is attempting to accomplish is nothing less than a union, little tried and very rarely succeeded in by other philosophers, of a drama and conflict of ideas and the similar but not quite parallel drama and conflict of persons. To both of these the "dramatic touches" provide vivid clues, but only clues, for they are not substantive statements and proofs.

The word "drama" as applied to Plato is a misnomer if we think of it as subject to the same analysis as a conventional comedy or tragedy or satyr-play (the three types with which the Greek audience was familiar). Occasionally, analyses of some of the dialogues have used the language of theatrical criticism, but this has generally obscured the nature of what Plato is trying to do, leaving out as it does the sentential aspects of the works and the special interrelationships of the drama and the statements. A sequence of events, a plot, going from good fortune to bad or from bad to good, is not strictly what Plato is trying to give us. Only in the sense that the transition from less clarity and self-knowledge to more is an important part of happiness, or indeed the unique feature of happiness, is it correct to say that a Platonic dialogue is a drama.

The question now arises whether dialogue makes the characters of men appear better or the same as or worse than they are in real life. (This was a point that Aristotle insisted was important in distinguishing tragedy from comedy; tragedy, he said, makes them seem nobler.) Here the answer is pretty certainly that whatever we may think of what Plato does to their *moral* characters, for their *intellectual* capacities he uses strong, bright colors, improving their arguments, heightening their metaphors, making the ambiguities in their statements more apparent, and clarifying the resolutions of these ambiguities. If, as someone in antiquity said, he has written up Socrates "grown handsome and young," it is no doubt in the power of his arguments, not his looks, that Socrates is restored. Now although tragedies make use of rhetorical declarations and reasonings of one sort or another, still these are not the most significant parts of the action represented on the stage. Consequently we should not think of a dialogue from Plato's hand as being a tragedy or comedy, even in those cases where we have several individual "comic touches," "tragic overtones," or the like. If Plato had thought of his writings as being dramatic and nothing else he would doubtless have been careful not to complain of the poets as often as he did.

So much for the dramatic features, at least for the present. The dialogic ones are more difficult to treat, because any discussion of the persons represented is likely to yank them out of the context of dialectic which Plato so painstakingly and abundantly provides; yet it is better to say a little something. As a rule the chief character is Socrates, usually functioning like an experimenter in a laboratory full of specimens or subjects, probing, testing, summarizing the results. When he is not in the scene as the chief interlocutor (the asker of questions and suggester of results), his place is taken by Parmenides, or Timaeus, or Critias, in the three dialogues named after them, or by an Eleatic Stranger in the *Sophist* and *Statesman*, or by a similarly unidentified Athenian in the *Laws*. These other five are also men of unexampled competence, in their very different ways, and they bear interesting contrasts and likenesses to Socrates. Lower on the scale are the respondents—the many inquirers, friends, hangers-on, or even set-jawed opponents, all persons of more ordinary stripe—Meno, young, rich, wooden in his flat questions; Euthyphro, pious, self-centered, self-righteous, indeed a wholly insufferable self-appointed keeper of public virtue; Clinias and Megillus (in the *Laws*), who are practical, well informed, but incapable by themselves of forming a plan for a new colony according to some fundamental principles of government; some obstreperous citizens (in the *Apology*) who merely shout their unconsidered hostility toward Socrates, on trial for his life.

Each man is given his say, but not necessarily his way. He is shown up for his intellectual immodesty, or vacillation, or downright confusion; witness the bewildered swain Hippothales in the *Lysis*, or the blushing young Clinias (probably no kin to the older one) of the *Euthydemus*, or Polemarchus in the *Republic*.

Here we have, then, a large array of intellectual types, with many combinations of native abilities and influences depicted, and with many emotional tendencies that emerge as prejudices and banners to wave in the winds of more serious doctrine. These carefully shaded personalities confront both each other and the most stringent tests of truth as proposed by the six chief interlocutors, and although much of the discussion is of questions we would call moral, still almost every facet of the scientific and literary works of the most stimulating race of the ancient world is in some degree explored.

When we set about discovering main features of the dialogic aspect of Plato's works, we notice certain factors

emerging almost at once. What causes the speakers to talk
as they do, no matter whether they are in control of the
argument or are subordinate to men of higher qualifications?

a. We must note the cities of origin of the participants
and their travel experience. Meno, for example, is from
newly rich Thessaly and Protagoras is from Abdera; the
latter is a seasoned traveler of the Greek world, he knows
dozens of city-states thoroughly, their men and institutions,
and this is as vital to the attitude he strikes regarding
knowledge and the art of teaching as the uncultured
background of Meno is to *his* insensitiveness and bluntness.

b. The callings, the vocations and avocations, and family
experiences of the participants are perhaps even more
central considerations. It makes a difference to Plato if a
speaker has an amateur or professional attitude toward
mathematics, toward politics, toward religion, whether he
is a good fighter speaking about war and soldiery or a
duffer clutching a weapon too heavy for him to carry. What
a man is, in relation to what he says, is not hard-and-fast,
but is a first approximation to the meaning of what he is
saying, an indication of what he will say. Deviations from
this approximation and this predictability are accounted for
by one of the other four factors being listed here.

c. The teachers of the participants are frequently indicated; sometimes they are famous men, such as Gorgias or
Parmenides, sometimes they are more ordinary. Sometimes,
too, they have given formal courses of instruction, sometimes they have been heard or even merely quoted in chance
encounters. These teachers furnish important parts of a
pupil's intellectual or moral equipment, and their function
in the dialogues is much the same as that of the callings
of the participants. Not only that, but they enter significantly into the theories that Plato develops regarding education and the transmission of virtue from one
generation to the next.

d. The native intelligence of a speaker is even more
crucial in determining the order of ideas that emerge in
a dialogue. The *Republic*, for instance, which ultimately
examines some of the highest principles that Plato dares
to consider publicly, leans heavily on the keen intellectual
perceptions of two of its subordinate speakers, both to
stimulate and to absorb this elevated account.

e. Beyond these questions of nature and nurture of the
participants of the dialogues, there is the question of what

happens to a man once he is put into the dialogue itself. The *Meno* would be a different work if young Meno had encountered Protagoras instead of Socrates. Most of the personages shift their point of view in accordance with the refutation and/or inspiration of Socrates, or of one of the other five chief regulators of the colloquies. Whether they are convinced and chastened at the end of a refutation (e.g., Theaetetus in the dialogue devoted to him, or Ion), or are left obdurate and smug (Callicles in the *Gorgias*, or Euthyphro), is a matter of much interest, and requires a thorough inspection of personal characteristics and philosophical reasons to be answered, but only with reference to a single dialogue.

Now to the question of interpreting these dialogues in respect of their complex arguments; this brings us first of all to the problem of how and when they were composed and published. Plato returned to Athens about 393 B.C. and the likelihood is that much of his published work was sketched in the immediately succeeding years. There is a tradition that he reworked many or all of these dialogues until the very end of his life, "combing and curling" them, as one ancient editor says, in order to impart the fullest richness and consistency to them. In spite of many scholars who have tried to discover a fixed chronological order to these most unusual works, the notion of near-simultaneous (should we say concurrent?) authorship has much to recommend it, for once the reader has begun to grasp the subtle devices of suggestion, explicit statement, and argument contained in the dialogues, the apparent discrepancies (which the biographical critics attempt to explain as changes of mind on the part of Plato) begin to dissolve away, and the so-called inconsistencies are seen rather as shaded differences in what is meant. In the many meanings which a single statement can have, one or more interpretations can be shown to be true in appropriate contexts, while the others deserve to be rejected as seriously wrong. No proposition is always and everywhere true, for Plato, simply because each time it appears it has a slightly different significance; and no real proposition is forever false. Hence constant *ad hoc* exegesis, by which is meant on-the-spot interpretation, is necessary, and the dialogues come as close as possible to a literary form in which Plato tries to make absolutely certain that this continuous interpretation will be carried out.

(To give a modern analogy: Almost any teacher of music would accept the response from a beginning student that a sonata-allegro movement consists of statement, development, and restatement; and almost any good teacher would disapprove this same proposition if it were to be uttered in a context of serious, knowledgeable discussion about musical form; there are very many riders and modifications to this rule. These levels of intellectual preparation are but one kind of determining factor causing the truth values of the propositions in dialogues to change, though the changes, as we shall later see, are not made at random.)

There is nothing intrinsically wrong with the biographical interpretation except that its practitioners so often substitute it for the philosophical construction of the dialogues, thereby missing a great deal of the unique message and the way Plato attempts to communicate it. If there is indeed a chronological order, we should attempt to reconstruct it only after a thoroughgoing effort has been made to settle the real meanings of the statements; outside confirmation of dates of the dialogues is almost wholly lacking, so the fixing of an order depends upon finding a supposed development of these meanings. Our strictures here bring us to considering the ways to expound Plato, and to the question why it is so difficult to discover any single way having no serious faults.

The first way is to review what Plato said, dialogue by dialogue, trying to make as much sense as possible out of each of them, partly by showing the interrelation of parts within the dialogue, partly by referring, however obliquely, to corresponding parts of other dialogues. (I refer the reader to Friedländer, *Plato,* Vols. II and III, to Taylor, *Plato, the Man and his Work,* to Voegelin, *Plato,* and, perhaps not quite so enthusiastically, to Shorey, *What Plato Said,* for samples of this kind of exposition; see Bibliography at the end of this book for fuller references.) This method has the disadvantage of seeming merely to copy Plato's own mode of expression, and of removing the literary attractiveness at the same time; but it can be defended by saying that it is least likely to distort the originals either by forcing some kind of rigid system upon Plato or—the opposite error—by taking away all cohesiveness whatever from the dialogues. They at least remain more or less intact.

The second method is to forget the dialogue form and

to take the work up term by term—to look up all that Plato said about *motion*, for example, expound it, then move on to *becoming* or *forms* or *justice* or whatever seems to come next. (See, as examples, the books by R. C. Lodge on Plato's theories of education, ethics, and the arts, or Demos, *The Philosophy of Plato*.) This has the merit of doing what Plato himself did not do, which is to focus upon one topic at a time, to deal with a subject matter presumably falling under one science. But it shifts the emphasis away from the manifold means that Plato used to help his reader follow the *exact* meaning—for instance, it is only with extreme rarity that a term means the same toward the end of a dialogue as it means near the beginning, so frequent and so deliberate are the shifts of context, and the devices used to bring out these shifts ought to be left in. This style of expounding Plato runs into either one of two opposite dangers: that of finding a bewildering confusion of words with no point of central tendency, and that of forcing some single signification onto a word that appears in many connections and hence in many meanings. Another danger, even if the first pair can somehow be avoided, is that the net result of a term-by-term perusal is bound to be a kind of glossary of Plato which leaves out the fact, almost peculiar to him among philosophers, that he attacks many problems at once, on a broad front. To take a famous example: Although the *Republic* is chiefly an effort to answer the question, What is Justice? (and therefore a glossary of the successive attempts at a definition of justice would be useful), nevertheless in the course of his answering that question he treats us to careful discussions of the purposes of the practical arts, the cultural arts, the political arts, and finally the mathematical and philosophical arts, with much else thrown in besides, in an array that in the hands of any lesser master would have ended in vapidity, irrelevance, and vagueness.

Third, the tracing of doctrines might be tried. A doctrine is an affirmative statement having philosophical character and intended to be applicable over a certain range of subject matters, or so I should define the word here. (Demos' book, mentioned just above, fits here as well, and so does Grube's *Plato's Thought* as well as Fite's *The Platonic Legend*.) If we assume that Plato can be reduced to a set of doctrines, we run the risk of being unable to account, save through some kind of adventitious developmental hypothesis, for the large number of doctrines which are enthusiastically put forth in certain dialogues but vigorously denied elsewhere. True, the method of the reading of Plato which seems right and best in light of his own thousand hints—the method that will be practiced and expounded in this present essay—can explain these apparent contradictions, without the need to invent a biographical account. But to reduce the teachings of Plato to a small set of propositions (as A. E. Taylor did in his book on Socrates) is to run the danger of impressing the reader with an image of a rigid, doctrinaire Plato that is very troublesome to erase. We may grant that it would be easy and pleasant to find a précis that would "take care of" large chunks of the dialogues; but Plato would seem to be at least partly in agreement with the German philosopher who said that if God were to offer him all truth in His right hand, and the search for truth in His left, he would choose God's left hand.

The fourth mode of exposition would be to discover— or invent—some enormously complicated chart, some schematic outline, upon which all of Plato's terms could be arranged, singly and in pairs (so that statements could be made, for all statements contain two such terms), filling this in with the representative notions from the dialogues. But this, tempting as it might be for a distilled treatment of Plato that would come at the end of a lifetime, would be of no great help to the reader just commencing his studies of the philosopher—or of philosophy in general! Such a scheme, even if headed with quite appropriate terms (truth, goodness, beauty, or wisdom, knowledge, opinion, ignorance, or soul, body, property, or indeed any similar groups of terms) would quickly deteriorate into an image as likely to harden one's conception of Plato as any other. It is quite true that Plato employs such schematic arrays in his dialogues, and with a little careful reading and a pencil one can easily re-create them from the prose text (the so-called Divided Line, coming at the end of Book VI of the *Republic*, is the most famous instance); but it is also true that there is almost no hint in the dialogues that this should be tried right off for all of the dialogues taken together, that a master outline ought to be made up. Indeed, what is so interesting and yet so maddening about the works is that they are kept quite separate from each other, literal "cross-references" being only sparingly supplied.

I shall try in this essay to employ good features in the first three of these methods, to combine them wherever possible, and yet at the same time admit that such a combination, being long, repetitious, and overly complicated, should only be sampled in what is, in essence, a beginning book on Plato's philosophy. Also, for reasons of simplicity, the fourth must remain quite hidden throughout. (Brumbaugh's *Plato for the Modern Age* and *Plato's Mathematical Imagination* exhibit fine instances of this schematic approach, the first fairly elementary, the second more difficult.) The Plato who emerges is a philosopher with a system, a man without glaring prejudices, with gaps in his knowledge occasioned more by his times than by his individual weaknesses, and with a prodigious capacity to excite not only himself but his disciples, of whom, if this book fulfills any of its intentions, the reader may eventually count himself one.

THE PLATONIC PHILOSOPHY

A. God and the Gods

There are many barriers to the sympathetic yet exact study of Plato as indeed of all the Greek philosophers, barriers such as the strangeness of the language, the imperfect condition of the texts we still have, and the very different laws and customs under which these men lived. Perhaps the chief barrier, however, is the quite foreign aspect worn by the Greek religion which, while it has many analogues to portions of Judaism and Christianity, is still a great way from them. Despite doctrines of sin and punishment and redemption to be found in some of the mystery cults, despite an insistence upon a chief divinity in the philosophies of both Plato and Aristotle—a chief one with lesser divinities in his train—despite insistence upon the working of divine justice and the need for moral uprightness which we encounter in the dramas of Aeschylus and Sophocles, despite hints of a future life offered by Homer and Plato—despite all this, we feel nowadays that Greek religion is simply strange, perhaps not a religion at all. Much of it appears to the orthodox Jew or Christian as immoral or silly, and he opines that its study does little to help us, except through an association by contrast, to understand the origins of our own objects and manner of worship.

Now it is tempting to say that in reading Plato we encounter none of this strangeness, that he is a Christian before Christianity; and of course there is a little something to be said for this point of view. He does oppose immoralism in the hitherto received stories of the gods, he does make his god a creator of the cosmos, he does conceive of god as a craftsman (not a carpenter, it must be admitted, but a fabricator of some unspecified kind nevertheless), he does insist upon the primacy of belief in a divinity. But the immoralism is opposed because it will have a bad effect upon the young; the god is not an all-powerful creator of the universe out of nothing, rather a mere arranger of the elements already existing, according to a pattern seemingly more eternal than the god himself; and the belief is not faith born in the heart but conformity for the sake of health of the state. (These three points are dealt with in the *Republic, Timaeus,* and *Laws,* respectively.)

Plato was a religious man, and he was a philosophical man, but we scarcely find in him what has come in the past couple of centuries or two to be called a philosophy of religion. He has something to say about the place of ritual in society, the force of religious law in the state, the general logical character of the proofs for the existence of God, the relation of moral goodness to the dictates of heaven, true enough; but some of these topics are discussed almost by indirection, and they are not laid down in any ordered account such as we find in philosophers from the seventeenth and eighteenth centuries onward. We do not find in Plato, as we do in Spinoza, any attempt to deduce a whole universe of moving bodies and their conjoined principles of intelligibility from a unitary God which is the substance of all things. We do not find in Plato, as we do in Immanuel Kant, any series of propositions designed to relate man's soul to a principle of radical evil. We do not find in Plato, as we do in Hegel, any effort to exhibit religion as a whole as one stage in the self-development of the spirit. The religion is prominent in Plato, but it is not marked off as a separate discipline with its own principles, nor is it made part of a vast deductive system, nor again is it the confirming yet rigorous examination of a single scriptural text.

Knowing what we should *not* look for, we are in a better position now to fix upon what Plato actually says, and to estimate its value in its own terms. Plato sometimes speaks of one god, Zeus, as father of all things, and sometimes of many gods; he speaks too of Muses, demigods, and still lesser beings. In some of the mythological passages of the dialogues, he speaks of the gods as superior, righteous personages guiding human beings, conferring gifts of wisdom, of the arts, or of certain moral virtues upon them. In the extraordinary myth of creation given expression by Timaeus, God is the supreme artisan, he is a principle of change, although himself unchanging, who orders many aspects of the universe according to a pattern of changeless forms. Yet God cannot quite overcome all of the innate resistance. The stuff of the cosmos (earth, air, fire, and water) originally lies ready to his hand, yet those elements tend to thwart his efforts to organize them for the best, most rational purposes. God makes the stars revolve in their orbits in imitation of a perfect form, he gives a spherical shape to the universe and places the earth at its center, he delegates much of the labor of constructing man to subordinate gods and goddesses; but none of them can quite overcome the inherent opposition of the bodily, three-dimensional medium.

There are two ways in which Plato deals with the lesser gods, the first through science, the second through literature, although, to be sure, these overlap. We shall have more to say about the scientific context in a section on the cosmos and the creation of the animal, and here we may speak of Plato's relation to the poets. The Greeks, as is well known, referred almost every art, every virtue, many passions and faults, to presiding gods and goddesses, and so up to a point Plato was able to make use of conventional religious teachings without himself running the risk of importing novelties. What was new in his treatment, and where he differed especially from Homer and Hesiod and indeed the entire epic tradition, was in his firm insistence that the tales of the gods must not display them as immoral—Homer, he said in effect, had almost persuaded the Greeks that the divine life is little more than an unparalleled opportunity to engage in squabbling, trickery, adultery, and carousing of the most unseemly kind (*Republic II*, 376e–383c). Plato clearly does not believe in such stories of gods and goddesses, although the expression of this disbelief rests on what we would call pragmatic grounds. In the *Republic*, badly trained soldiers brought up on wicked tales of the gods are the chief threat to the state, for we cannot trust them to defend us, and in the *Laws*, atheists are among the leading causes of disruption, because they do not fear legal sanctions; hence we must insist that the gods are good, and we must be prepared to demonstrate this fact, if we are to persuade the citizens that the gods are inherently virtuous and have a care for the welfare of man. All motion—so runs the

argument in Book X of the *Laws*—rests upon the power
of soul and divinity to cause change and to order it, and
this connection between the motion which is evident
everywhere in the cosmos and the divine is the ground
for persuading the partly unbelieving public that gods
exist. If the doubters persist in holding that the gods do not
exist, or, though existing, are not virtuous, or, though
good, have no interest in the fortunes of human beings,
then these atheists should be severely punished if the
official governmental persuasion after a certain time fails.

But in opposition to this hardheaded, political approach
to the religious life there is a very large measure of religious mysticism in the language of Plato, mainly in the
Socratic dialogues, though whether this is to be attributed
to the historical Socrates or to Plato's own predilections
is a moot point. Even though Timaeus and Critias speak
about the same topics as does Socrates, reference to the
mysteries, to judgment, and to purgation of the soul are
lacking in them, so that we may suppose Socrates himself to have had these interests and tendencies. But this
by no means proves that Plato did not. At any rate, there
are three great Socratic myths, coming at or near the end
of the *Gorgias*, of the *Republic*, and of the *Phaedo*, and
another one introduced in the very middle of the *Phaedrus*; each of these treats of life of the soul after death.
(References to this afterlife are to be found more briefly
stated in several other places, such as the *Symposium*
[176b–180b] and the *Apology* [40c–42a].) The burden of
each of these myths, regardless of marked differences of
geographic and other details, is that the fortunes of the
soul depend upon its choices, its actions, and that these
rest upon the dominance of reason, and more especially
upon its power to alter and subdue the demands of appetite and ambition.

In all four of these myths, Plato offers sweeping vistas
of a quasi-physical world, in which the soul can move
as if it were embodied, and there are also ample indications of levels of perfection and possibilities of passage
from one of these to another, in case a markedly right or
wrong choice makes it necessary to move from low to
high or, as is both more dramatic and more usual, from
high to low. The soul retains its functions that it had in
life; we know this because, for example, bad souls in the
Phaedo wallow in swamp and mud, and there would be

no point to this if the soul were deprived of sensation and pain. In the myth of the *Republic,* on the other hand, what is at issue is not pleasure or merely sensuous misery, but rather moral consequences. There the soul is made to choose, when it reaches a certain crucial stage in its after-life, a career which it will assume when born again on earth; there is a restriction of the fate of the soul to the direct consequences of one's moral decisions. The best life will be that of the private man who cuts no wide, deep swath among his countrymen, in a word one who minds his own business.

As regards state religion (and religion was far more closely bound up with government in Athens and in many of the other city-states than it is in most of the modern countries), Plato makes two different points. He recognizes (in the *Euthyphro* and *Apology*) that it can be invoked to hamper free thought and activity, yet at the same time (in the *Republic* and *Laws*) he sees clearly that it is an essential bond of individuals, families, and indeed of entire social classes in the state at large. Religion, true religion, does not come entirely from the heart, for its tenets can be communicated by proof (in *Laws X*) or by an indirect, metaphorical method appealing to the intellect as well as the passions (*Phaedrus* 246a–256d). Mere adherence to established dogma is insufficient, as we see from the very inconsiderable yet dangerous Meletus who, in the *Apology* (24c–28a), is counter-accused by Socrates of trifling with religious matters, and the only slightly more weighty and still dangerous Euthyphro, who evidently acts for selfish motives while pretending to himself and to the world that the very gods have decreed his action (*Euthyphro* 5a, etc.). On the other side we have many who are highly respectful of established religion, weaving it tightly into their conceptions of love (as do almost all of the speakers in the *Symposium*), of cosmogony (as do Socrates, Timaeus, Critias), and of the law and government (as do these same three men, plus all three participants in the *Laws*).

B. Cosmos and Animal

Plato is often represented as a "soft" philosopher who talks mainly about the values of this life—beauty, for one, and the virtues, and the place of the arts in society. But there is the "hard" aspect of Plato, too, closely bound with the other; he was a man of considerable scientific competence for his day, exact in the formulations of his own principles and strict in his appraisals of the work of his predecessors. As much as any philosopher, Plato sought to integrate the humanistic and the scientific sides of his nature and of his culture into a self-consistent whole.

The foundation of his view of the universe as a physical, perceptible unity rests upon three interests: first, the concern for mathematics as a knowledge of pure, perfect, eternal forms which can never be fully realized and made actual in a tangible body or collection of bodies (this is perhaps the dominating interest); second, the concern for small bodies themselves, their necessary, possible, and impossible combinations with each other under varying conditions—for Plato was an atomist in important aspects of his scientific philosophy; and third, his interest in the living organism and the way it maintains its identity, its oneness, in spite of its manifold parts and their functions, and in spite of the variety of unfavorable conditions often imposed by the environment. In other words, mathematics, chemistry, and biology were indispensable to his system, and though his speculations evidently far outran his own experimental enterprises, nevertheless his account is one of the first overall explanations of the physiological nature of man and his connections with the physico-chemical medium in which he lives. The medical treatises of Hippocrates and his followers were begun slightly earlier than the date when Plato commenced writing, i.e., perhaps about the time of the death of Socrates or shortly thereafter, and were doubtless based upon fuller observations of the human body and its ills, but they were, of course, the work of many hands and, moreover, less concerned with the origins and construction of the body and its relation to the universe at large.

Despite the fact that Plato's reputation as a biologist has been weak, especially when he is compared with the extraordinary Aristotle, we find traces of a theory of biology in the *Republic, Symposium, Statesman,* and *Laws*; brief suggestions, to be sure, but valuable nevertheless. It is for the *Timaeus*, however, to deal wholeheartedly with life in its widest possible context, the universe, and then to pass on to the particular living creature. This highly compressed and notoriously obscure dialogue moves dialectically from whole to parts, then to parts of parts, each single part at the same time being considered in its own limited wholeness. Because of this steady advance in the discussion, Plato does not give his terms their meanings exclusively with reference either to wholes *or* to parts. The terms are set up instead in an order giving their meanings in connection with pervasive traits in some measure common to both parts and wholes together. Plato uses three important principles:

1. The lesser imitates the greater. In more concrete terms, the man imitates the universe (*Timaeus* 42c). These two entities possess similar kinds of motions (43b), and they are composed of the same kinds of particles which have the shapes of regular geometrical solids (32a–c).

2. No one cause can account for everything. The *Timaeus* is a double explanation of the universe and its contents, first according to *reason* (29d–47e) and then according to an auxiliary cause called by Plato *necessity* (47e–69a), but which we might nowadays call *chance* instead; a third section of the discourse treats of the combined workings of the two causes together (69e–92c). The account using reason, suited primarily to the construction of the universe as a whole, sets up three notions: the creator (the god), the model (unchangeable forms or patterns in imitation of which the universe is made), and the copy or likeness (i.e., the cosmos itself, constructed by the divine maker). Under the heading of necessity as cause, we have an account of the four traditional elements of early classical physics, namely earth, water, air, and fire, as they move about in space and as their atoms join with or separate from other atoms; this leads to a description of the body of the universe as a whole, its rotary motion, and its joining with soul which is simply the rational principle of its motions and the awareness of

its parts. When reason and necessity are combined, the sole topic is the living human body and its own personal soul.

3. The presence or absence of soul determines whether a thing is alive, that is to say, life is not a mere set of mechanical motions, as it has come to be conceived by many leading modern theorists. Thus the greater animal, which is the universe at large, is no mere collection of pieces of matter set in locomotion; its rational plan and the motions it undergoes are its life; moreover it has intelligence as a whole and contains intelligences (associated with the heavenly bodies) to guide all its proper parts. If the cosmos *is* alive, then it must have motion, and this motion is what measures the time or duration of the cosmos. Time, says Plato in a memorable phrase, is the moving image of eternity (37e)—the eternity belonging to the forms of which the universe is a fairly good copy. The universe, then, is not quite eternal, it is only *like* the eternal.

The venerable philosopher and statesman Timaeus, who takes the place of Socrates as chief speaker—indeed his speech is a long monologue, uninterrupted after the first page or two—sets out to apply these alternate causes, reason and necessity. Reason is purpose, that which aims at the best, while necessity is blindness, aimlessness, what Mark Twain called the cussedness of inanimate things, often thwarting reason, but also quite frequently brought into line to subserve it. This is why we have said that in Plato's mind necessity is not essentially different from what we usually call chance.

The whole that Timaeus tries to explain is a universe with the earth at its center, fixed, circled round by the moon, the sun, then the planets (the "wanderers" of the sky), and lastly the stars. The orbits of the stars and planets are not substantial things, they are not like material rings carrying the celestial bodies around with them, they are simply the paths taken by regular circular motions, and they are caused by reason, for the bodies traveling by way of them always return to the same point, and the motion need never cease. Those motions, on the other hand, which are under the rule of necessity are rectilinear and, we might say, choppy by contrast. The perfect circular orbits of the heavens are imitated in smaller bodies; in the lesser animal, Plato wishes to

account for the cycles of breathing and of ingesting
foods, and the circular motion is constantly being inter-
fered with because air particles and food particles tend
to move in straight lines. Indeed, the only possible kind
of circle available to most bodily activities of such lesser
animals as human beings is a much distorted one, like a
traffic "circle" which may be a poor ovoid, because sections of it are nearly straight.

The interlocking of greater and lesser, of reason and
necessity, and of living and nonliving, makes the discussion
by Timaeus a most intricate one; in it astronomy, physics,
meteorology, chemistry, mathematics, and biology gain
strength from each other. Much, though certainly not all,
of what is said about the universe at large is inapplicable
to the motions of particles, which are themselves constructed with straight-line boundaries and move, as we
have said, primarily in straight-line directions. These motions cannot go on forever, otherwise bodies would forever be escaping from the universe, and in addition there
are many of them moving at random, not by a coordi-
nated plan such as controls the heavens, which means that
the terrestrial particles and clumps of particles which we
perceive are bound sooner or later to collide. The rebounding introduces even greater confusion. It is not
entirely random, however, because many of the particles
combine; they are limited by their mathematical shapes,
however, so that their compounds are of certain kinds
only—water and dye, for example, can remain in combination, but not water and oil, or water and most non-
ferrous metals.

Here we have, then, a cosmos at large which is live
and rational, and a many-faceted aggregation of atomic
bodies which are not alive, not rational, only partly con-
trollable. Man imitates the cosmos, as we have said, but
is also composed of the irrational, or nonrational, particles. Such stabilities as man possesses grow out of two
things, the orderliness of his basic form, and the comparative solidity of the particles composing him. But that
considers man's body alone; there is also his soul.

We have already hinted that the soul of the world
animal is the ordering system of motions that the heavenly
bodies will enjoy, and that soul in the cosmos is in the
first instance mere motion. But the soul, which is the
principle of life, is also intelligence, stable perception

of other things and their motions, and this stability matches the stability of what eternally exists. Hence soul is neither entirely in the realm of unchanging, eternal being, nor entirely in the realm of mere becoming and passing away: it is in both. In its role in becoming, soul has magnitude, so that, for example, the greater soul fills the body of the universe from center to circumference, in this way animating everything from earth to the outermost stars (35c–36d). The lesser soul is also distributed in the body of the lesser animal, though not quite uniformly (42e–43e). Part of the soul, which Plato also calls reason, is immortal, but anger and aggressiveness, and the appetites, are mortal, and do not outlast the body.

The body of the world always possesses visibility and solidity, and the god who made it wished it to be as much like the eternal forms or ideas as possible, so spared no pains to give it a body which would never fall to pieces. The only rub is that much of the world is brought about by necessity, which reason can but hope to overcome by persuasion, not force—Plato's way of saying that perfection in the universe would require everything to be made according to a plan for the best, but that there are constant partial frustrations of this plan. Plato's god, as we have said earlier, is not all-powerful, he does not create the world out of nothing, he cannot make the world all good. The best he can do is follow the ever-fixed plan, the ideas, the mathematical pattern lying even beyond himself and his universe.

Let us look, then, at the relation between human soul and human body. The first of these is compounded, says Timaeus, of the same materials as the cosmic soul, mixed in somewhat the same manner, but no longer of uniform purity (41d). Its immortal part is made by the god who makes the universe, but he delegates the construction of the mortal part to lesser gods—Plato was no monotheist. Reason as a divine cause is responsible for some of the shape and axes of the body—the spherical head (which is made to protect human intelligence), the elongated body, the four limbs (which keep the head well off the ground), the differentiation of front from back, and the eye (42e–46c). All other parts and functions of the body represent compromises with necessity. Each lesser function, in other words, subserves thinking and is in turn subserved by bodily organs of which necessity has been co-maker.

We must retrace our steps a little way in order to understand the physical basis of the human body. The motion of the atomic particles is a compound movement, arising out of their constant hitting and rebounding from each other. The atoms are bits of matter which existed even before the birth of the heavens themselves; but they were not differentiated fully and given precise and mathematically describable shapes until the god gave life to the world animal. Then, and only then, the atoms took on the shapes of four of the regular geometric solids: the four-sided figure or tetrahedron (fire), the octahedron (air), the twenty-sided figure or icosahedron (water), and the cube (earth). The fifth of these bodies, the twelve-sided figure or dodecahedron, was stretched like an inflated soccer ball to cover the entire universe. No other regular solids exist—Plato had a mathematical proof for this, apparently—and their use here explains why there are no more than four kinds, or better, four states of matter.

Any lesser body of a living creature, such as man, must possess many functions and therefore organs which it would not need were it not forced to interact with the greater animal and also with the persisting but not-always-controllable atomic milieu, parts of which are formed into that universal animal, parts into the lesser, the human. On earth we live in a medium supporting us on the one hand and interfering with us on the other, hence we need cognition, sensation, pleasure, and pain because we must always be ready to utilize or to cope with our environment, as the case may be (42a; 65a–b). The more restricted problems that Timaeus must solve if he is to grasp the complex nature of the body stem from the fact that he considers the overall human male body-plan in six different ways: (1) as consisting of supports and bearers of the head (44d–45a); (2) as subject throughout to the impingements of sense objects and their qualities, which subjection follows of course from the atomic basis of all bodies and their motions (65c–68d); (3) as body areas differentiated on a longitudinal axis (69b–76e); (4) as containing cyclic systems of intake and exit of materials (e.g., food, air) connected with the

outer world (76e–81e); (5) in relation to the balance of
functions, intellectual and physical, of the entire animal
(81e–90d); (6) as susceptible of differentiation into types
of functions found (as we move down the ladder from
man) in women, then mammals, birds, fishes (90e–92c).

Solutions to these six problems depend upon applying
reason and necessity and the principle of imitation. This
latter cannot be a simple one-for-one correspondence of
the body with the world body, yet we do find that man is
built upon concentric envelopes resembling to *some* degree
the concentric spheres and rings of the universe. Marrow,
bone, flesh, skin, hair—we move from within outward;
the generative substance is inside, that which is generated
lies outside, protecting the inner. The inmost marrow
is the fundamental living substance, the seat of the immortal part of the rational soul, and its own extremity
is the brain itself (73c–d); most of the Greeks, Aristotle
included, had very little notion of the brain's true function.

Not only is the lesser animal body part of the whole
living universe, (89d) but also there are parts of this
lesser body that are themselves animals, with lives of
their own, and similarly affections and diseases which
seem to possess independent existence, a kind of vitality
of *their* own (89b). Generation is taken up separately in
Plato's account, for in being able to make a new individual a man most closely resembles the god, the craftsman who makes the world. Through the very fact, however, that he works as a craftsman the god's power is not
identical to that of animal generation; so that parts and
products related to sexual generation are themselves living
creatures, animated in their own right, not entirely obedient to man as a whole (91b–d). Because they have a life
partly of their own determination, their participating in
the universal life is more through themselves than it is
through man, and man's unity is so far lessened through
their presence; man is an animal, as it were, containing
still lesser animals. For Timaeus the right control of the
sexual and, specifically, the generative activities is very
complicated. Plato supplements the *Timaeus*, therefore,
with a fuller discussion of Eros or desire in relation to
almost all branches of art and the sciences, as we see from
the fact that it turns up over and over in the *Symposium*,
the *Republic*, the *Statesman*, the *Laws*, the *Phaedrus*, and
elsewhere.

More than once (42e ff.; 69c), Timaeus is made to remark that one portion of the soul is immortal, and to a consideration of this we now turn, for Timaeus himself never offers any proof of this immortality.

C. Man's Soul

There are two quite distinct, yet significantly related, types of account of the human soul in Plato, the first being in discussions with various respondents, the second in myths delivered in long monologues, very often at the end of a dialogue after its chief dialectical aims seem to have been accomplished. There is ubiquitous mention of the soul in the dialogues; but the chief places where it is carefully treated are in the *Timaeus*, the *Republic*, the *Phaedrus*, and the *Phaedo*. These last three dialogues bear strong family resemblances to each other, but there are many differences as well. Each of the three has two rather different treatments of the soul, one in analytical discussion, the other in a myth—six accounts in all, for no more than a selection of which we shall have space.

Running through all four of the dialogues just named is the point that the soul consists of parts—generally three, and generally unequal in importance. The soul has an appetitive (or vegetative) portion, and this is merely the sum total of the entire range of desires, of drives, instincts—whatever we care to call them. In the *Timaeus*, Plato carefully locates this in the region of the trunk below the diaphragm. Second, the soul contains a part which for lack of a better translation we may call the aggressive or spirited, and this is the principle of ambition and the willingness to cope with a hostile world. Thus one would be hungry through the organs pertaining to the appetitive part, jealous of one's food in the spirited, which claims the chest region, between diaphragm and neck, for itself. The head is, of course, the precinct of the rational part of the soul, and the soul is in good order when this is the part that rules.

There is a remarkable discussion of immortality in the *Phaedo*, which depicts with gravity and the closest human sympathy the final hours in the life of the great Socrates.

He is cheerful and confident, and when his friends press him for a reason he offers four proofs, three of them rather tentative, the last one he feels incontestable, for the immortality of the soul. As we look further into the dialogue's meaning, we soon discover that this immortality is not claimed to be one carrying personal recollection, of "seeing one's friends and loved ones again," and in this sense very likely the proofs would appear to end in disappointment, just as the dramatic action of the *Phaedo* ends in Socrates' death, not his resurrection or even his promise to return.

The first proof (70c–72d) depends upon what we might call cyclic alteration, and is based upon the similarity between life and death on the one hand, and such phenomena as day and night on the other. Out of day comes night, but out of night also comes day, hence Phaedo and the other companions of Socrates are brought to admit that life springs from death.

The second proof (72e–78a), somewhat more stable, is based upon the notion of recollection of things previously known or experienced. Recollection is the sight of one thing bringing a perception (image) of another which is like it or else quite unlike. We know equality from two equal sticks, yet the sticks are not *really* equal, they fall short of the ideal equality they are supposed to exemplify, and which we somehow knew even without these instances. This knowledge of equality is therefore implemented in the soul earlier, without having any immediate sensory experience as its origin; but this must have taken place before birth, and recollection merely brings this to mind in our present life. If this does not prove that the soul survives death, at least it indicates that we have an earlier life that antedates the existence that we can remember on this earth.

The third proof (78b–84b) is an argument tending to show that the soul is more nearly akin to the eternal than is the body, for the latter is obviously dispersed at death. When the soul uses the body in any inquiry, Socrates claims, then it is dragged by the body toward the changing aspects of things: we look at a dog, and as we are looking the dog is altered in many ways, e.g., as the light changes on him. But when the soul inquires alone, for example into the nature of justice or mathematical equality, then the soul departs temporarily from the body and enters a

realm of purely eternal and changeless things, remaining
with them because akin to them. (It was for this reason
that earlier in the dialogue Socrates asserted that the philosopher is continually separating his soul from his body
and in that sense practices dying—67e.) Notice the shift
in emphasis: In the first proof, life springs from death
because it is like a changing thing—the day that comes
and goes. Now the soul is immortal because it is like unchanging things.

A series of interludes and objections now follows, for
although the friends sharing Socrates' last day are eager
to believe that in spite of his impending execution he will
somehow outlive it, still they want more security than
mere likenesses. Would not the soul, asks Simmias, resemble the harmony played on the lyre which is the body?
If the latter is destroyed, then what happens to the
harmony, which cannot exist without the taut strings?
And furthermore, asks Cebes, is our situation not like
that of the weaver who makes and wears many coats and
outlasts all of them—or rather, *almost* all, for the final
one is intact when the weaver, who represents the soul
which has made many bodies for itself, at long last
perishes? These objections by two young Pythagorean philosophers seem insurmountable to the company present,
and deepen the gathering gloom in the craggy little prison
where Socrates is waiting for his jailer-executioner.

Socrates himself is not afraid. The analogy between a
soul and a harmony is incorrect, he says, for one is not
more a soul than another, while a harmony admits such
variations of degree. A soul cannot have more discord
or harmony, hence all souls must be equally good. The
soul rules the body, and does not follow upon it, as
would a harmony dependent upon the plucking of strings.
So much for Simmias. To Cebes, Socrates replies that if
anything is beautiful besides beauty itself, it is beautiful
because it *partakes* of that beauty, just as a pair of things
are two by reason of their partaking in duality. This forms
a basis for the fourth proof (102b–107b).

Things differ, says Socrates, because of their forms or
what we might term their informing ideas, such as beauty,
duality, size, etc. The *thing* itself is not what determines
it to be beautiful, or part of a pair, or whatever. And
because the form of beauty is pure it is not ugly and will
never become so, nor will greatness become smallness.

Not only that, but the number 3 is not only an instance
of threeness but of oddness as well, and 3 will never
become 2 nor even. In the same way, death is always
opposite to life, and the immortal is the opposite of what
admits death. The soul does not admit this death. *Everything* would be destroyed if the immortal turned out to
be perishable. Hence when a man dies, death comes only
to his mortal part, but the immortal part withdraws from
death, and persists throughout eternity.

But Plato does not rescue Socrates from the death of
the body and the absolute and unequivocal departure
from his friends. There are no miracles, the hemlock
affects Socrates much as it has all other condemned men,
and the difference is in the classic equanimity with which
Socrates accepts the poisonous draft which he thinks of,
without any hint of cynicism, as the healer of life's ills.
"Crito," he says to one of those hovering over him as his
body is slowly cooled by the poison, "we owe a cock to
Asclepius." This is the bill to be paid to the inventor of
medicine. It is not a heavy debt, but one that even so
must be paid.

The four myths from the *Gorgias, Republic, Phaedrus,*
and *Phaedo,* though they differ greatly in structure and
detail, all agree that the soul is indeed immortal, and they
all provide some sort of afterworld for the soul's dwelling.
The *Phaedrus* and *Republic* myths take for granted and
to some extent describe the return to earth of the soul in
a new body and a new career, while the other two are
content to leave it in a world in which its fate is much
more clearly attached to the choices it once made in this
lifetime than would be true on earth. The *Phaedrus* assumes that the soul in another world sees much more of
reality than it does here, but that it retains some of this
as glimmerings of a truth it cannot acquire while in a
mortal body; in the *Republic,* in which learning is subordinate to choosing, the loss of memory of the afterlife
is rendered complete by a draft of the water of forgetful-
ness before the soul adopts its new cycle of pain and greed
and ambition and punishment, or of good sense which
helps obviate punishment. The myth of the *Phaedo* is a
fanciful geography which places the departed souls along
great rivers flowing in tunnels cored out of the earth's
interior. These souls are designated for their crimes and
passions, and the most severe wrongdoings are punished

in the ugly swamps and chasms in the center of the terrestrial ball. In the *Gorgias*, heavier emphasis is upon the actual judgment of the dead—they must appear with no clothes before their immortal judges, for clothing would hide the sins that must be accounted for. The afterworld is severe but just, serious but grim only to confirmed and inveterately wicked men. And it is all a story, or at least so Plato tells us many times.

The mere fact, however, that the soul's existence in another world is put into a mythical form rather than a closely reasoned argument is enough to warn us that although this is in each case an imaginative projection which may be like the truth, it cannot be taken as truth itself. Plato is careful to make the four geographies of the afterworlds differ markedly, and these hopeless discrepancies point up the fact that he is merely trying to project upon a wider screen (of the remote past or the distant future) a view of the relation between the soul, its capacity to learn, its memories, and the degree of improvement or deterioration it will undergo.

Men differ, according to Plato, very greatly in their native goodness and their abilities to benefit from experience, instruction, and persuasion, and these distinctions will show up given the longest possible stretch of time, even if one has to extrapolate into eternity to see this. The rewards and punishments of our actions take place in ourselves, but are frequently too subtle to be seen at work in a brief lifetime. Hence there is myth.

And yet we just may, in our purely intellectual soul which is firmly affixed to eternal things, be undying.

D. The Virtues

The question that Plato faces repeatedly is not whether there *are* any virtues, indeed, this question never arises. Nor is he so much concerned with a simple genus-and-differentia definition of each of the virtues, except to show that approach wrong. The virtues he usually names as wisdom, justice, temperance, and courage, together with a few others such as piety, grace, mildness, and the like, are often mentioned, sometimes described, and occa-

sionally defined. The two questions now arise: whether
these virtues are at bottom one or parts of some whole,
and secondly, how all these virtues, whether they be one
or many, are allied with certain other human capabilities,
chiefly knowledge and art.

Most of the dialogues dominated by a search for a
definition are concerned—one might almost say obsessed—
with the virtues. The *Laches* addresses itself to courage,
the *Charmides* to temperance (the word *"sophrosynē"* is
just as well translated self-restraint or self-control), the
Euthyphro seeks a formula for piety, the *Republic* defines
justice at great length and against the widest possible
canvas of the state, the soul, and finally, the cosmos. In
point of fact the many attempts to connect definitions to
names in those other dialogues come to a fruition in the
Republic, when countless appropriate separate images are
merged in one great image of the perfect state. Socrates
there shows, in an impressive analogy, that the three parts
of the soul which he differentiates, the appetites, spirited-
ness or aggressiveness, and finally reason, are connected
to temperance, courage, and wisdom, in that order, and
that the total balance of the parts of the soul is termed
justice. In the context of the *Republic,* Socrates little by
little takes his listeners and respondents from the account
of a primitive barter-community, devoid of culture, to
that of the state based upon a constitution in which the
ablest philosophers will rule by reason and a minimum of
partisanship and prejudice. It is only natural that in this
the social virtues loom large, justice most prominently of
all, as the chief virtues of man. Elsewhere, in a somewhat
corrupt Athenian society, friendship, which is not a virtue
but is closely akin to virtue, is the best of the social goods
on account of its benefits to the ordinary citizen. And love,
which includes erotic desire, but is mistakenly identified
with that desire by some men, is a blessing that takes a
man of wisdom above the common run of our society,
puts him in a world superior to the commonplace, and
gives him a synoptic view of the essential beauty lying
behind the constitution and customs of states (*Symposium*
210a–211a).

But love, with its intensity, can go wrong and, unlimited, can cause a man to act as a weakling and a fool
(*Lysis* 204b–206c); it might even seem better to be, or at
least behave like, a nonlover (*Phaedrus* 230e–234c; 237b–

242a). But the nonlover is not per se a virtuous man; lack of passion does not constitute control of passion. Yet suppression rather than control of all present feeling is also not a mark of goodness. The virtues generally require nothing other than the balancing of the passions (*Laws I* 631e–632c), not their exclusion. So anger, fear, love, and desire for fame are not eliminated but simply counter-weighted by their own opposites. The guide, however, must be reason, and it cannot remain only reason that calculates advantages and accommodates itself to the shifting tides of our desires and fortunes. It must instead be a reason that sees these advantages and changes of fortune (which may be good) in light of some eternal good, some standard, some prototype (which is good per se, that is, necessarily good in itself). Plato distinguishes (*Republic II* 357b–d) between things good in themselves, and things good as means to other goods, and things finally both good in themselves and good for other things; it would seem that only a general form of virtue or goodness would be of a sort that it would be good even if it did not lead to any other good. In the light of *this* good, the pure form of good, other goods become good by a kind of participation, a sharing of its preeminent quality.

What about the connections between the virtues and art, and again between the virtues and science? The arts show themselves in many guises, though they always involve some measure of reason, even if their processes and products allow, in some cases, for a sort of divine intrusion of inspiration. The arts are thought by Protagoras to be almost one with virtue, for though all men possess them, at least to some degree, not all men are capable of teaching art or virtue, because both are a sort of knowledge, and knowledge is in the hands of the few— the sophists (*Protagoras* 320c–328d). In his refutation of Protagoras, which does not involve denying the connection between art and the virtues, Socrates stresses the cognitive aspects of *all* of the virtues, inasmuch as courage, for example, without practical wisdom (we might say common sense) leads quickly to foolhardiness, and so with the others. For this reason Socrates, raising the level of virtue to a new plane, points out that true virtue is knowledge and that to do wrong is to act ignorantly, for no man voluntarily seeks evil (*Protagoras* 350c–360e). In the *Philebus* both the virtues and arts are relegated for much of the dialogue to the middle background, but the good for man is the topic for discussion: Is it pleasure or is it reason? The ultimate answer, seemingly strange to people whose reading of Plato is centered around the *Republic*, is that neither pleasure (which is infinite) nor reasón (which is finite) is good in itself without the presence of proportion, measure, moderation, and that consequently the best that we can hope for is a mixed (would "balanced" sound better?) life in which pleasure and reason have their proper places. Art would, in this context, be the pursuit of what is pleasant, or advantageous, or noble when making—creating—something; virtue would be the pursuit of the same ends but for the sake of doing, of acting, alone or in company with other human beings.

One of the important points to be insisted upon is the combination of general discussion with particular instances and the way the latter reflect the former. Thus Socrates, who talks at length about virtue, and who indeed turns almost every discussion into one about human good, is depicted as a good man, "of his time the best and wisest and justest" (*Phaedo* 118a), and the discussions are made to reflect back upón his choices and behavior. In the *Lysis* friendship is discussed with friends, and in the *Laches*, military courage is discussed with generals. This reflexiveness is, however, a two-sided affair.

In the search for knowledge, due concession should be made to the point that a certain kind of ignorance is of great importance. I do not know, says Socrates in the *Meno* (71b) and in the *Apology* (20c–23c), but I know that I do not know. This is of importance as a step in gaining positive knowledge, to be sure; but it can also be the final step in an inquiry whose subject matter does not admit of sure formulation, or whose methods are inadequate to the range of distinctions which need to be made. The end result of such an inquiry is not overall skepticism but the resolution to pause until something more satisfactory can be worked out, and one can come to know oneself better. Meanwhile one may suppose that at least the *habit* of asking and defining is instilled in the respondent, and that there will be a new and more critical approach, even to the questions of daily living. Socrates is aware, however, of the dangers of unrestricted "philosophizing," especially for the young; and the predicament in which he finds himself in the *Apology*, with accusers early and recent on every side, shows how he has antagonized the Athenians with his insistence upon precise statements of what their callings and functions are and how these relate to others of a similar kind.

Plato does not make the mistake of thinking that knowledge comes from sheer ignorance; rather he suggests that it may come from preexistent knowledge, properly altered when its consequences are made clear. The *recognition* of ignorance can also be a condition of knowledge. But when Socrates says that he knows that he knows nothing, he means that in the sphere in which he is searching, he does not have *knowledge*. That this does not mean that he is a total ninny is more evident in the Greek language, where the word for knowledge, *"epistēmē,"* is also translated as science. In the *Meno* the discussion is about the teachability of virtue, and it would be a foolhardy person indeed who would say that he had exact knowledge pertaining to *this* problem.

On the other hand, the mere awareness that one can have no more than an opinion—which is susceptible to change—is of some value, for it enables one to be on guard against elevating this variable opinion to the rank of unshakable science, which would do no more than turn it into brittle prejudice.

To sum up: Knowledge is best, but where knowledge is not possible opinion will have to do, provided it is accompanied with the knowledge that it *is* but opinion. After this comes opinion without an awareness of its limitations, and this is no better than outright ignorance, and may indeed be worse, for it impels the cold-hearted meddling of a Euthyphro or the unfounded self-confidence of Polus and many of the other sophists.

Closely related to this is the fact that a limited consciousness of ignorance is a moral good. Thus the soul needs some degree of humility, even after its greatest intellectual triumphs, for not only is it necessary to recognize that there are new worlds to conquer but also that the world has not been completely subdued either—that there are always better ways to explore the very same topics, coming to an ever clearer understanding.

The *Philebus* is one of the most comprehensive of the dialogues, one of the most concentrated and unrelenting. Aside from the fact that like all the others it relates itself at least in a general way to every aspect of the cosmos, it deals specifically, as we have said, with a principle of moderation that lies behind both wisdom and the purest of pleasures (66a–c). Second in the scale of goods is proportion and beauty, and only third is reason and wisdom. Science and art and true opinion rank fourth, then come the pure pleasures which accompany either knowledge or sensation. The sixth place—but we do not talk about that, for there we depart from what is exclusively characteristic of man among living things. This entire hierarchy is baffling for its apparent deposing of wisdom, until we realize that here Plato is first of all looking for goods that are wholly self-sufficient when taken in isolation. Although wisdom possesses *more* truth, measure, and beauty than does pleasure, still it cannot stand alone as a virtue, but must be conjoined with other things, even with pleasure itself.

In the *Phaedo* Socrates, who faces imminent physical death, points out that the philosopher desires death and in fact deserves it, because death is the separation of soul from body, and philosophy, which requires what we would call intense concentration upon things other than our own bodies, carries us thereby away from them, for the time being at least (64a–69e). How can we square this with the *Philebus*, which gives a place to wisdom partway down the list of goods? Should not wisdom or reason be the highest of human concerns, and should not man desire and love it for its own sake alone? In the *Phaedo*, we should reply, the wisdom of Socrates shows itself in the one kind of action which his imprisonment still allows him: his extraordinary moderation and self-control in the face of extinction. Thus moderateness becomes an ingredient in wisdom when we consider the latter as a practical way of life. The philosopher desires to be separated from his body, but not necessarily by putting an end to all his philosophical thinking; indeed, the joining of philosophy and death is only possible if one conceives of death to be a separation that *preserves* the soul, whatever it may do to the body which acts as a prison of this spirit that desires freedom. The *Philebus* puts intellectual pleasures far down the line; but what about the philosopher? Should he not seek out these purest of pleasures? Here again the answer would have to be that the philosopher does not think about eternal things in order to enjoy it, but the enjoyment is a side-issue, with understanding and wisdom itself the chief goal.

E. The Arts

Plato was an uncommonly acute observer of artists and their arts, and he offers us discerning descriptions of skilled men in the practices which give them the names—and the capabilities—of their calling: the weaver, the musician, the potter, the painter, sculptor, writer, interpreter, shepherd, teacher, and the ruler, all get their share of Plato's attention. To be sure his descriptions of individual artists are invariably not an end in themselves, for they are connected with descriptions of other artists which common sense might not connect. In addition one art is likened with another—music with literary authorship, shepherding with ruling, sophistic with angling, weaving with kingship, oratory with doctoring, and so forth. Again, Plato varies these combinations, likening oratory to kingship and to music. As with all the other subjects he touches, Plato sets these arts in a network dense or loose as the case may be, which relates these familiar artists—we might call some of them simply practitioners—to the arts and thence to the chief subjects of these arts—beauty, utility, justice, knowledge, or whatever is under discussion.

Similarly pertinent is Plato's conception of the arts taken as diverse aspects of the life of the city. Different communities receive the arts from different sources, some from the gods, some from demigods such as Prometheus and the Muses, and some through the hard and inventive work of much-honored men. Communities support the arts and use their many products in several ways, some favoring the soothsayer, some the man of science, some the tyrannical ruler rather than the wise one, some the sophist or the eristic, some the rhetorician, some the soldier.

In those dialogues in which the highest arts (those least workaday, those least dependent upon the mere exercise of the body) are concerned, Plato points out that the artists, insofar as they are artists, have knowledge: the doctor knows the organs and vital processes of the patient, the pilot knows the indications of the storms coming or the rocks submerged, the writer understands grammar. And yet precisely insofar as the artist works from rules and conventions, he falls short of the expression of truths higher than can be reached by the ordinary run of mortals. The finest works of art, Plato is saying, come not from art alone, but from something beyond art—the inspiration given to a few who already know their rules, by the gods generally and by the Muses (*Phaedrus* 244a–257b; one of the greatest passages in Plato). Art is not always the same as nature, for, if it were, all men would share it, and its processes and products would be in evidence everywhere, which unfortunately they are not. Nor is art mere chance, for otherwise the artist would be unable to decide when to practice his art and when not to—the pilot to steer, the physician to heal, the flute player to perform, and so for the rest. We may therefore say that although "art" signifies one of the most fundamental of all activities for Plato, he expends considerably more effort in telling us what it is not than in defining what it is. This paradox, simple in itself, is redoubled by the fact that art is also *identical* in important respects with knowledge, nature, and chance! With knowledge: the "artist" who does not know has no art (*Ion* passim). With nature: the art of God, by which the universe is made, is nature itself, its product is nature as well (*Sophist* 265e). With chance: the product of the fine arts cannot be fully predetermined or understood by insight drawn from everyday experience (*Ion* 533c–535a).

The artist who makes something is godlike, in a sense, for what he creates is chiefly by the exercise of compounding and dividing, i.e., putting together elements which were presented to him separate, and which require to be proportioned to each other, which in turn requires that they be measured, mixed, shaped, woven, and the resulting parts properly disposed (*Timaeus* 31b–46c; *Statesman* 279b–283a).

There is again a paradox, lying in the fact that although the work of art is a real thing, a thing having three dimensions, and hence (according to Plato) visible and tangible, it is also an imitation, and not only that, but the more perfectly it is made the more patently it is an imitation and hence at a further remove in degree of reality from the ideal form of which it is necessarily a copy. A bed is a copy of the perfect bed, but it is a poor copy. Every embodiment of excellent mathematical proportions is still only an embodiment of numbers which are eternal and hence totally real.

A common complaint against Plato is that he throws the poets out of his so-called ideal state outlined in the *Republic*. This exclusion might be defensible (at least to a modern experimental scientist!) were not Plato himself a poet in almost every sense of the term. Is he speaking as a philosopher, an apostate or, worse, a hypocrite?

There are two places in the *Republic* where Plato discusses the poets. In the first passage, in Books II and III (376e–398b), he is concerned with the education of young men for the task of guarding the city, which requires a delicate poise between solicitude for the citizens and ferocity toward the enemy. If these soldiers are poorly educated through having listened to immoral stories of the gods and heroes, then the poets who tell such tales are to blame. This may result in censorship in a state which is struggling to establish itself as a cultural center secure from outside enemies, but it is not wholesale dismissal of all poems and all poets whatever. The second passage is in Book X (598d–608b). Here Plato, having inch by inch raised the level of dialectical discussion so that he can talk meaningfully about justice not only in relation to the everyday world of transactions and professions but also in respect to eternity and being—here Plato says that tangible objects are but copies of reality, and that artistic representations of these objects are therefore copies of copies of the real. Consequently we must regretfully dismiss the claims of all poets who think they express what really and permanently exists. But this still does not reject all poets from all functions in the world; Plato is only saying that the poet is not the equivalent of the philosopher in his insights into the abiding aspects of the universe and of knowledge. The poet necessarily uses figures, images, of tangible and visible and audible things.

There is another complaint made against Plato and his attitude toward the literary arts. In the *Phaedrus*, Socrates shows that the spoken word is preferable to the written (275c–278b), and this too has been inflated by critics to mean that Plato the writer had turned his back upon his own art that he had practiced with such dexterity and stunning effect. But the remark is made not in a context that deals with poetry or science or dialectical exercises, but with speeches—speeches needing interpretation by the speakers to the hearers, to avoid the danger of misunderstanding. The speeches, however, are ethical and political in content, and are capable of causing much mischief if allowed to fall into the wrong hands. But otherwise there is no particular condemnation of philosophers, poets, mathematicians, and others simply because they have written down their reflections, images, or proofs. When Plato attacks his predecessors Protagoras and Anaxagoras, for instance, it is not because they have written books but because they have shown inadequacies or inconsistencies in the handling of their philosophical subject matter. Consequently, it is with more restraint than is generally realized that Plato alleges certain faults against writers of all sorts and against their works. He has, moreover, no intention of cutting off the limb upon which he himself is sitting; he looks upon his own dialogues, almost certainly, as correcting a number of the moral errors of Homer and the others, and as free from the mistaken identification of the absolutely real and the mere seeming.

In *Letter VII*, however, there is another remark, and if we may trust this letter to be genuine, it throws further light upon the question. There he says (341c–d) that there does not exist, nor will there *ever* exist, a treatise of Plato's dealing with the most general truths of philosophy. What this means in the context is that it is impossible to set down the principles of a philosophy that depends for its life-blood upon debate and discussion, opposition and correction, transcendence of one's own formulations. (Plato would no doubt be dismayed at the present essay which condenses so much, and the *only* justification is that I have tried to preserve something of the spirit of free discussion found in the dialogues at large.) Again, we have no blanket complaint against *all* philosophical writing.

To return by way of summary to the arts in general: We may say that in one sense these activities are the whole of our lives, for there is some smidgen of learning or conforming to a rational principle in the performance of every single task: cooking, eating, exercising, fighting, talking, and all the rest of what so abundantly fills our days. On the other hand, it is more than a smidgen in those arts in which not all persons engage: piloting, healing, weaving, and the other crafts. In the higher reaches of medicine (which is not a mere empirical knack but a thorough knowledge of the body and its workings), in astronomy, in musical theory, in grammar and some others, there is necessarily so much application of intellectual principles that it is hard in many cases to distinguish these arts from the sciences. Indeed it is not necessary to make this separation, because every art searches for that aspect of its material which is permanent. In these intellectual arts this feeling of permanence does not arise from the mere experimental stability of repetitions of similar acts (as in rowing a boat) nor from the hoped-for results of means known to have been efficacious very often in the past (as in empirical medicine), but from something better. That something is, of course, a recognition that what we see, hear, or touch is a copy of a more permanent, archetypal pattern to which bodies and events must in some degree conform, and which can be known once the receptive mind turns its full attention to things in relation to such an archetype. Finding these forms is itself an art, and speaking about them is doubly an art, for they are, however self-existent and awesome, as it were, obscurely understood by us and easily confused with their everyday embodiments, such as trees and men and courageous acts.

So much for what we find of the specifically human practice of the arts. But this must be supplemented by the consideration of divine practice. We have already said that Plato's account of the creation of the world involves a craftsman, a demiurge. His terms explaining the actions of this craftsman are drawn from the mechanical arts, not animal generation. Making the soul of the cosmos is done by mixing, measuring, splitting, etc., of what Plato calls indivisible being and divisible being (*Timaeus* 36b–c). God, the demiurge (this word means literally a worker for the people), is the maker, the cause. In this context art and nature are the same thing, namely any productive process (*Timaeus* 28b). "Art" here signifies what the god does in order to make something; "nature," the movement and change bringing an imitation of the form into what is made. Thus by art and nature the material is changed so that now it *almost* mirrors the pure form, the ideal pattern; but this form itself remains above the making, above the change, for if it did not, its purity and permanence would be destroyed.

To go one step further: the cosmos as a whole—what we

earlier termed the greater animal—is more like the forms
which serve as model for it than are the lesser creatures of
the world, which still imitate the forms but much less well.
And in having less perfection, you and I, we also have less
being, less of the everlasting in us.

F. The State

Over and over again, almost as frequently as he deals
with the good of the individual man, Plato returns to the
questions heaped up around the state, its types, its purposes,
its defects. Nearly every dialogue has something to say
about the state, either of its benefits or its shortcomings, and
eight of these works, including the *Republic*, the *Laws*
(these are the two most obvious examples), the *Gorgias*,
Apology, *Crito*, *Critias*, *Statesman*, and *Menexenus*, would
be reduced to next to nothing were all references to the
state to be untimely ripp'd from their pages.

There are several contexts in which the state is brought
into focus: in reference to the soul, its strengths and weaknesses, in the *Republic*; in reference to the art of government and a possible substitute for the exercise of that art,
in the *Statesman*; in reference to the power of speech to
rule or at least sway the conduct of political and legal
affairs, in the *Gorgias*, the *Apology*, and the *Crito*; in
reference to the technology of city planning in the *Critias*;
and so on.

First a word about the highest level of synthesis of the
state. Plato speaks from time to time about mankind in
general, and he refers occasionally to various nationalities,
principally the Egyptians and the Phoenicians, outside of
the Greeks. He speaks most often, quite naturally, of the
Greeks or Hellenes, whom he likens (*Phaedo* 109b) to ants
or frogs about a swampy pool. But he scarcely thinks of
anyone as being a member of a nation in anything like the
modern sense. Every string is tuned instead to the conception of the individual *polis* (a word whose untrans-
latability may make for a failure in understanding). A
polis is the compact-sized community which Plato and
Aristotle regularly consider, and it is thus both a city and
a separate principality, an independent governmental entity

subordinate to others only in cases of quite temporary federations. The Greek polis consisted of a central city and its surrounding farming villages and other subsidiary communities that supplied the city with food, timber, minerals, and other produce. In the very center of a good many of these cities was a hill or rocky eminence generally fortified, called the *acropolis*, the high city. Other fortifications were deployed in the surrounding countryside. Cities became overcrowded, and when wars and the disabilities of life in the ancient world did not keep the number of inhabitants within bounds, they were thinned by sending a portion of them to become colonists in other locations not already settled. A new polis was born, good or bad depending upon its internal regulations and government. Hence, as the *Laws* makes clear, there is an art of colonization, which is, among other things, the art of writing appropriate prescriptions for the constitution of the new city-state and the governing of its citizens.

This is the general historical setting for the Platonic analysis of the art of government (which Plato sometimes calls the royal art), of the constitution of offices and powers, of the various classes, of the distribution of rights and wealth, and of the often perverted and dangerous substitutes for a right ordering of these in society. Plato, however, goes beyond merely telling us of the current practices of the day, for in addition to many descriptions of the social and legal and cultural customs of the cities of his time (and, as we might suppose, his native Athens is far more often used as an example than are the others), he offers us three other sets of patterns of civic community, which have varying degrees of similarity to what the history books tell us about Greek life.

The first set is a group of cities having outlines deliberately clarified, simplified if you will, for the sake of our easier comprehension of the essential nature of right government in relation to the right balance of the soul; this set makes up the chief content of the *Republic*, which describes rather fully the leadership of the best possible city, but leads up to it by showing that it must develop as a third stage from two earlier ones, and then leads down from it by depicting four different degrees of degradation when the principles of the best state are no longer followed —seven cities in all. The second set has but one important member; in the *Laws* Plato gives an exhaustive account of the constitution of the second-best state; it is good relative to a set of economic conditions occasioned by a plan to colonize a new community on the island of Crete. The third set consists of a pair of opposites which appear as mirror-images of each other, or better yet as a photographer's negative and positive: a mythological Athens of 9,000 years past, and an equally hoary, storied Atlantis. Kallipolis, the "beautiful city" of the *Republic,* can never really exist except as an ideal; Magnesia, the Cretan colony, could exist if the right effort were made; and Atlantis and the ancient Athenian city are dimly remembered in an old legend, borrowed from Egyptian priests.

Contrasted to these three sets, there is of course a fourth and more random group, consisting of actual cities where Plato had lived or traveled or which he had been told of— contemporary Athens, Sparta, some towns of Thessaly, cities in Italy and Sicily, and so on.

In the first three of these sets, we have a kind of simplification of the extremely complex states with which history and daily experience provided Plato; he eliminates all sorts of extraneous variables so that what remains is relevant to one or another of the analyses, conducted respectively by Socrates (*Republic*), the Athenian Stranger (*Laws*), and Critias (in the introductory section of the *Timaeus* and in the dialogue bearing his own name). The purposes and styles of these simplifications differ in each case.

In the *Republic,* Socrates, in the course of a long search for the nature and value of justice, considers whether this virtue can be found in a very simple community of a handful of artisans brought together by the need to survive, and the common inability to do so without mutual aid. Justice being very difficult to locate here, he turns to a second and larger community which includes not only artisans but also purveyors of luxuries—merchants, lawyers, cosmeticians, and the like. Here again the principle of justice is not clear, for there is "fever," busybodying and confusion, in human transactions. It is a wealthy city, and as such, it needs protection, a defense which should be given over to a class of soldiers set apart from the moneymakers and consumers. These soldiers will need training, in body and soul, so that they will be able to recognize their friends and enemies and never attack the wrong persons. Thus begins their education, and a gradual transition to the best possible state, governed by the wisest members of the soldierly class, men selected and trained to be philosophers and rulers simultaneously.

The method of the *Republic* requires that an analogy be set up between the individual man and the city-state, the latter being primarily the former when writ large (*Republic II* 368d). Eventually the analogy is drawn between the soul of man and the constitution (i.e., order of offices and of classes) of the state. The parts of the soul that Plato distinguishes are, as we have seen, reason, high-spiritedness, and appetite. These answer respectively to the ruling class of the state, having the training proper to philosophers; to the soldiery, the guards of the state; and finally to the farmer and artisan class. The excellences, or virtues, of the three pairs are, in order, wisdom, courage, and temperance. But this ignores the unity, the cohesiveness, both of the soul and of the state, and justice is the principle of this balance in the soul and the state. To each faculty, to each class, belongs its own function; this is the essence of political justice, as opposed to busybodying or meddling, which is the principal meaning of injustice.

Plato, having sketched his state in outline, now gives further specifications of his ruling class; the account of justice, which is the center of discussion in the first half of the *Republic*, seems to give place to a treatment of the genesis and accoutrements of wisdom; more than once it turns out that lacking wisdom the other virtues are empty, unfocussed (see also *Protagoras* 349e–360e). The search in the *Republic* is for the wise *ruler*, however, not simply the man wise in theory; hence Plato must indicate certain bases for his selection, for his conditions of life, and for his nurturing. The first and third lie in the principles of education, which are massive and profound; the second lies in the fact that men and women of the ruling class should share all tasks (Plato was almost the first Greek of whom we have record who advocated the equality of women— under certain conditions), in the fact that women and children should, for the ruling class (actually a very small part of the state), be held in common, and in the fact that the philosopher must be given the authority of the king or the king must have the intellectual and moral powers of the philosopher. These are unpopular proposals, Plato recognizes, but they are essential; the last of them comprises the least change in the state that is likely to bring about general well-being. Usually there is one such excellent man, and when he is given the rule, we have a *monarchy*. If there should be two or more such men, an *aristocracy* would be the result. Either way, we would possess the best possible state, one in which justice is connected necessarily with the rational part of the soul. Now if the guardians of the law and education forget the proper regulation of the breeding and rearing of children, it declines into *timocracy*, a society primarily based on honor (part of which is status, we might say). If, again, some timocratic father does not receive the honors seemingly due him, the son revolts against his city, becoming the very type of the *oligarchic* man ("oligarchy" signifies, of course, the rule of the few, but it is the wealthy few whom Plato means here). If, after this, an oligarchic father should lose his fortune and become a mere drone in the hive, the son, attempting to scrimp and save money for himself, will turn into the democratic man in a *democracy* ("*dēmos*" is the word for tribe, throng, crowd), in a state in which there is full freedom and virtual equality for all persons, good and bad, wise and foolish. If, again, the democratic father is stingy with his son and fails to convince him of the need for careful economic management, the son falls prey to flatterers who play upon his desires, many of which are for evil things. And so he becomes a tyrant, repudiating his parents and even killing them, fomenting class wars and demanding a heavily armed bodyguard, stirring up wars outside in order to divert attention from his evil-doing at home. The tyrant does in waking what the rest of mankind do only in dreams: robbing, committing incest, and venting his rage upon all who cross him or do not contribute to his pleasures. *Tyranny* is slavery, of the many to the one; but the one most enslaved is the tyrant himself—enslaved to his worst appetites. State and ruler alike are terribly out of order.

The *Republic* envisages a society in which the preferences of ordinary men and women are, as far as possible, sublimated or transformed for the benefit of the state as a whole. The really good life for the state requires not that men become angels but that they live like men without mutual interference and consequent failure to develop their real potentialities. In the second-best state (which is a different sort of thing from any on the ladder of decline from monarchy to tyranny depicted in the *Republic*) Plato does not count on the philosophic wisdom of the ruler but rather upon a rigorous code of legal enactments. The aim

of constructing a code, as outlined in the *Laws*, prompts
Plato first to set down certain geographical requirements:
the city should be located away, but not very far away,
from the seacoast in a place where self-support of the
populace is possible but where natural resources are not
so plentiful as to lead to any luxury. The city is to be laid
out on a radial, wheel-spokes plan. The economic foundation of this city encourages a rather conservative, middle-
of-the-road dependence upon tradition rather than upon
fresh judgment. The laws can be changed only with great
difficulty, and are administered by a council meeting late
at night, hence less accessible to public pressures. The art
of government is an art of managing according to plan.
Whereas Plato says flatly that the city of the *Republic*
can never be realized on earth, he strongly indicates that
the city of the *Laws* might readily be founded and could
with a little luck survive. Plato recommends that the num-
ber of households be limited to $1 \times 2 \times 3 \times 4 \times 5 \times 6 \times 7 = 5040$, a very useful number because it is factorable
in a great many ways and can therefore be applied easily
to such apportionments as voting, military duties, political
representation, taxes, and so forth. The justice Plato envisages is in some cases completely even-handed, in others
it is proportional to responsibility or to need.

The *Laws* strikes one as more eminently practical than
the *Republic*, which it is, and at the same time as being
more "dated." No doubt it was Plato's intention that it
should appear this way. The "Beautiful City" of the
Republic cannot be realized except in the skies, although
it may be imitated on earth moderately well according to
how we approximate wisdom in the ruling class of the state,
courage and temperance in the soldiers and artisans, respectively. But the *Republic* has no particular trappings,
it says little or nothing about numbers of families, it has
no specification in regard to technologies, while the *Laws*
sets up multiple requirements, it is a finished blueprint, and
any one of its highly pragmatic expediencies will work only
if every other is put into operation.

Now for the third set, Athens of earliest days and her
enemy Atlantis, as depicted in outline in the *Timaeus* and
at greater length in the *Critias*. The mystery of the *Critias*
is a double one, first because the most casual reading shows
that it is unfinished—but by how much we cannot say, nor
can we say whether the portion we do have is as highly

polished as Plato would have liked or whether he would
have made alterations in the light of the completed whole.
The second mystery we encounter even if we can safely
assume that the dialogue is in substance perfected up to
its abrupt ending: the reason for the transfer of the war
between Athens and Atlantis back several thousands of
years, at the same time that Plato goes to some trouble to
"authenticate" the story through its transmittal by Solon,
greatest of Athenian lawgivers, is a matter of some puzzle-
ment. It may well be that with this odd mixture of history
and story—for Athens was obviously known to the other
Greeks, while Atlantis, regardless of what recent explorations have found about floor subsidence in the North
and Central Atlantic, was a tale made up out of whole
cloth by Plato, who after all was no oceanographer
equipped with sonar and other sounding devices—with
this odd mixture, Plato is seeking to remove the entire dialectical structure from the confines of Greek life. The
details he heaps up smack more of what he thought future
technology might become rather than what it was, either in
his own day or in the remote, suppositious past. Atlantis,
in contrast to the very ancient Athens he also describes,
is a grimly militaristic city, a mythical one to be sure, but
one whose physical characters are given a fuller account
by Plato than any other. The city of Atlantis rules an ill-
fated island west of the Straits of Gibraltar; it is a city of
mixed purposes, confused distribution of privileges and
property, whose public buildings are encrusted with gold
and other metals beyond the dreams even of Hollywood:
vulgarity which destroys harmony, blatancy which ruins
virtue. . . . In Plato's tale, Atlantis succumbs to a war with
Athens, followed by an earthquake and a tidal wave, and
lies forever in the mud shallows of the ocean. The purely
moral aspects of the story seem clear; but we cannot
properly jump from bad morals to inevitable submergence
under the sea, from low motives to negative mean altitude;
consequently it is the reader's privilege to fill in the gap
between the two in this extraordinary account, the first story
ever written of a kind of global warfare.

The *Republic* classified states according to the clearness
with which they exhibit, first, justice and, later, wisdom.
The *Laws* gives no overall classification of types, but sets
up a colony which is to receive laws conflating the best of
those of Athens, Sparta, and Knossos (the capital of

Crete), intermingled with many novel ones. The *Critias* reconsiders the political question not so much from the standpoint of virtue or of legal enactments but from that of town planning and technology and their influence upon civic and military affairs. But Plato also considers the condition of states in his own time, that is, actual communities of Hellas. There is a very strong pragmatic streak running through his account of these states, something we tend to forget if we read the *Republic* exclusively, or the *Laws*. As a kind of summary of what he finds about him, Plato is moved to classify the kinds of city-states in an entirely different way, not according to degrees of evil but rather a general schematism in terms of what might be called the legitimacy or constitutionality of rule. We find this in the *Statesman*, where Plato, anticipating much of Aristotle's famous classification, draws up a list of six states by conceiving the rule of one, of the few, and of the many, and multiplying each of these by two kinds, namely those with and those without law. Thus lawful rule by one man is monarchy; unlawful, tyranny; lawful rule by the few is aristocracy; unlawful, oligarchy; and lawful rule by the many is democracy, while unlawful rule is also called democracy, this time with a bad connotation. One of the purposes of the *Statesman* is to settle the question whether rule by persons is superior to that by custom or law. Plato points out that a pilot who steers entirely "by the book," by laws, is likely to run aground, and that it requires a person sensitive to shifting conditions to practice such an art. In the same way, human intelligence is required for the proper guiding of the state, and the philosopher adds that the larger part of this guidance is to be found in the correct interweaving of the stronger and gentler natures of the responsible men in the state, so that government is neither too harsh nor too soft. Thus the statesman is a person of insight, and in himself he demonstrates this intertwining of strength and sensibility.

In point of fact, the city-states that Plato observed around him mostly showed mixed constitutions, mixed virtues and vices, mixed cultures. Athens might be called a democracy for part of her career, for instance, but the democracy could not be called as "pure" as that which Plato described for purposes of illustration of his principles; at another time, Athens became an oligarchy, but not altogether for the reasons Plato indicated in the *Republic* and not with the essential characteristics envisaged for an oligarchy in the *Statesman* either. With his many references to the customs and beliefs of the Athenians, it is quite evident that Plato knew that he was not writing strict history in the four dialogues we have just noticed; his supplements are in the shape of observations of how men lived in the states of his time, contending not only with government edicts but with the winds of rhetoric and personal influence and differences of status conferred by wealth or family or accomplishment—things that cannot be entirely fixed once and for all because they are always in flux. Even the good man's position in society may change although he does not; in a good society, Socrates would succeed, would perhaps even become the ruler; in the Athens of his day, Socrates, who incorporates into justice the minding of one's own business, is condemned as a busybody, and charges about his religion are trumped up against him. And if we are inclined to blame Athens, we must remember that among the states of Hellas, she was—Plato is still talking—one of the more enlightened ones.

G. Education

It would be possible, we may suppose, to discuss and ask questions about virtually all of Plato's philosophy by completely tracing through the connections of any one of a dozen or two of its leading terms. *Justice, virtue, idea, good, nature, polis, eros, art, knowledge, soul, cosmos, animal, memory, being, imitation, becoming, dialectic, motion*— these and a few other terms would certainly qualify, and *education* would also have to be a member of the list. What we are also claiming is that a really comprehensive account of education would necessarily be an account of being, of virtue, of soul, and all the rest, together with their opposites, where such are possible. There is a sense in Plato in which *any* relationship of one man to a god, or to the cosmos, or to a fellow man is educational, as it has to do with the use of names and the formation of some kind of *logos* (definition) or of an image in the soul, or the breaking of some connection between these three interior furnishings, by refuting or by forgetting.

It follows that Plato was interested in practically every question having to do with education—with the methods and purposes of the transmittal of knowledge, with the institutions which foster education, with teaching and training in relation to age, with what people will do with their education once they have acquired it, with the selection of apt pupils and effective teachers, with alternatives to education such as experience and inspiration, with its content, with its sponsors, with its divine sanctions, and so on. Everywhere that the sophists, who are educators or would-be educators, appear in the dialogues, the process of education is given some examination; nearly everywhere that the military life is discussed, some educative feature of it is also mentioned, and there is, of course, no avoiding the topic when Plato is considering the relations of parents to children, as he often does.

The Platonic approach to education consists of three interests: the actual sciences and arts communicated by teacher to pupil; the moral virtues, if any, of the teacher and the student; and the political institutions in any way connected with the learning process.

1. In the *Hippias Minor,* the sophist Hippias evidently has no doubt of his ability to exhibit his skills, and in so doing to impart something of them to the viewers (368a–e). Prodicus, in another dialogue, gives courses in the art of words, costing either one drachma or fifty drachmae, and presumably the student must learn to drill and practice in order to put these to the best use (*Cratylus* 384b; a drachma was worth something like a couple of dollars in 1973 money, but fluctuations both in Greece and—alas— in the United States make this a risky estimate). In the *Theaetetus,* a great point is made of what mathematics the pupil has learned from his master Theodorus, and what he has been able to work out for himself. In the *Meno,* a slave boy said to be previously ignorant of geometry is led step by step through a demonstration in which, by judicious and helpful questioning, he turns out to be able to double a square, not the very simplest of mathematical tasks. For Plato, there is no doubt that at least under certain favorable circumstances, the arts can be taught—unless the soul is immortal and has learned everything in a previous existence, in which case the instruction is really a kind of reminding!

Where Aristotle seems to think of instruction as taking place in a rather restricted way, each new step being based

upon a small or large body of preexisting knowledge, and
then dealing with other types of communication under
headings such as orator and hearers, tragic playwright and
audience, etc., Plato looks upon all of these as merging,
and then as distinguishable only temporarily. The teacher is
the man who knows some subject matter that he is able to
impart to the pupil who does not yet know; he is the man
who persuades in the marketplace or in the privacy of a
small gathering; he is the person with a skill such as weaving or flute playing; he is the head of state who guides
his subjects; he is the person who discloses arcane mysteries
to the particular audience fitted to receive them. The words
he uses may be tightly organized demonstrations, the
apothegms of poets or rulers or the wise generally, the
sayings of ordinary people, or great florid, rolling and
thunderous speeches. The art of teaching takes on many
guises, and it is a delicate enterprise—one in which Socrates
is made often to engage—to estimate the beneficial and
the harmful aspects of each kind.

When Plato considers the equipment of the teacher and
pupil alike, he shows that one must accord a prominence to
memory, both as a subject for discussion and as an aspect
of the dramatic-dialogic presentation. This latter we are
inclined to dismiss as a mere "literary touch," but it is used
too often to be thus slighted. The entire account of the
Republic is narrated by Socrates to an audience never un-
ambiguously identified, but obviously thought to be as
capable of absorbing this long recital as Socrates is capable
of giving it. The *Parmenides* is an account by Cephalus,
who heard it from Antiphon, who got it from Pytho-
dorus, who was actually present when Zeno and Parmenides
both took the opportunity to teach the then-youthful Socrates what was wrong with his method of philosophizing
and what was right about theirs. The same degree of re-
moteness, bridged by phenomenal memories, is exhibited in
the *Symposium*; other examples turn up with a frequency
that makes us think either that Plato was simply unreasonable in his expectations or that considerable numbers of
Greeks actually met these hopes. Neither one of these
possibilities needs to be true, however; what seems likely
is that Plato had a firm conviction of the importance of
memory, inasmuch as knowledge for him is contained not
in individual propositions and isolated logical arguments
but in a whole dialectical sweep where later statements are

compared with and made to transform earlier ones. For the grasp of this, a good memory is essential, and Plato is simply stressing its value in his ascribing that gift to the participants or onlookers in the great debates.

For the grasp of skills or arts memory is not everything, however, and it must be supplemented by other capacities appropriate to the subject matter or exercise in question.

2. The teaching of virtue, on the other hand, is in a little different situation. Virtuous action is unlike the arts in this respect, in that while an artist molds the same sort of clay each time, a man acts justly now toward a weakling, now toward a child, now toward an equal, now toward a group of men, and so on, and the practices are all so different. The very transmissibility of virtue by instruction is in question, and indeed forms the center of interest in two important dialogues, the *Meno* and *Protagoras*.

The *Meno* begins abruptly with a question from a pampered young man: "Can virtue be taught?" Although Socrates demurs at trying to answer this question until the more fundamental one regarding what virtue is can be answered, he soon sees that the intellectual limitations and prejudices of the sporty and peremptory young Meno will force him to deal only with the subsidiary problem of teachability. Meno cannot, in three tries, satisfactorily define virtue, and he takes refuge in the famous accusation that Socrates is a torpedo-fish, a narkē, who stuns his respondents in such fashion that they are no longer able to speak of what formerly they could so abundantly articulate (80a). Restricted by Meno's weaknesses to a relatively superficial level, Socrates must go on to show that the hearsay that his respondent takes for knowledge is not firmly established in the soul and cannot be transmitted from generation to generation, either from professional teachers (the sophists) to their paying pupils nor from fathers to their own sons. The practice of virtue, Socrates concludes, comes from a divine dispensation, hence is not directly transmissible in our society. We can only hope (100b).

In the *Protagoras* the problem is again attacked, this time not from the viewpoint of Meno, who is supposedly a learner, but from the perspective of the greatly talented and experienced teacher, Protagoras himself. In this dialogue, Socrates is still young—chronology would suggest this, although Plato often shifted his historical events to suit himself—and the struggle with the older man ends in a peculiar kind of draw. Protagoras thought at the beginning that virtue was teachable (after all, was not he himself an effective teacher, making his pupils better the very first day of lessons, better still the second, and so on?), but now, at the end, he holds virtue not to be knowledge, hence not teachable. Socrates, in forcing this turn-about upon his opponent, is for his part required to change positions as well, for whereas he formerly held virtue to be nothing teachable—the claims of the sophist Protagoras seemed specious to him—he now insists that virtue really is a kind of knowledge, hence *must* be teachable.

This would seem hopelessly contradictory to the *Meno*'s conclusion until we remember that we are dealing no longer with the rough-and-ready formulas about virtue which Meno is prepared to accept almost on sight, and which may or may not be satisfactory (the gods will decide!) as a guide to action in the community. In the *Protagoras* the issue is between the sophist's day-to-day compound of instruction and persuasion which is evidently not based upon sound principles but which is aimed at getting "good results" quickly, and Socrates' more exact, thoughtful instruction which uses the most careful tests for all ideas at issue, and which is aimed at the reform of one's character.

We may look at this problem from a different point of view, namely the role that tradition plays in engendering virtue in the young and in nourishing it in the mature. Lest the reader be taking us to mean that Plato is nothing but a traditionalist—whatever that means—we should remark that although tradition in its varied relations to the state is a vital *topic* for discussion, this does not imply that he approves it unconditionally or would see innovation done away with. Education is partly identified with tradition, but is partly in opposition to it. Indeed the greatest of Plato's philosophical heroes, Socrates, is also an innovator in almost every department of moral and political reasoning.

The purpose of education, from this vantage point, is to ensure that the habits and aspirations of the older generation are transmitted to the younger—and then presumably to the next one after that. For this there are two human relationships that Plato emphasizes most, father-and-son and teacher-and-pupil; but beyond these there are others, such as mother-and-child, officer-and-soldier, court, priest-and-layman, speaker-and-audience, lawyer-and-law, which, though they are means of transmission of knowledge, turn up less frequently in the dialogues.

The transmission of virtue from father to son may come about, Plato concedes, in a number of ways. The first is biological heredity, which the philosopher admits is not a clear-cut affair, with all the characteristics of parents being made to reappear in the filial generation; mixtures and sports turn up, and a child is frequently quite unlike either parent. The second is example, and Plato wonders why it is that the sons of great men are not only lacking in greatness, but do not even seem to possess in lesser degree traits similar to those of their fathers (*Meno* 92b–94e). The third is word-of-mouth instruction, and about this Plato says not much in connection with parents and their children. (As an example, the sons of Socrates are mentioned in the dialogues only enough to show that Socrates hoped they would eventually turn out well after his execution.) The teachers are scarcely ever one's relations in everyday Athens, and it is only in Plato's imaginative projections that the question arises of combining successful pedagogy and family life.

Plato's great hope was evidently to reduce the effects of chance in these transmittals of habits and knowledge from person to person and to try to improve the traditions of virtue and culture through conscious sustained effort. Regulations affecting the marriage and procreation of rulers and others dot the *Republic* and the *Laws*; ordinances binding family life, so that the influence of elders upon their juniors can be firm and beneficial, are likewise abundant in the *Laws* (in the *Republic* little is said about the citizen-subjects, but for the rulers Plato vigorously proposes a kind of state community of wives, children, and property). And finally, education should be as carefully planned as it is universal, with subject matter, admissible candidates, age levels, examinations, and rewards being taken up as pressing considerations in state-supported and state-administered schooling.

Plato, then, is telling us that tradition is one of the fundamental factors required in *any* successful grasp of teaching, whether it be the dry and pedestrian arguments of Parmenides or the lightfooted treading by Socrates in his more prankish moods. The sense of time and of the past and change is of utmost importance to Plato, who evidently scorned those who thought they had been born yesterday (*Timaeus* 22b–c). For them the aim of education should be to give them a knowledge of their past, a realization that it had been rich and active, coupled with the awareness that what happened then had a direct bearing upon what is happening now. Tradition in *this* sense connects a man with his own past, and with the past of his city. What connects a man and his interests, his prejudices, and his calling with the greater world of which the timeless present is a slice, is philosophy, and the form that this takes is not so much history or poetry or the wise sayings of fathers, but dialectic. This dialectic is restless, it seeks and finds novelties, it moves constantly toward new problems.

3. The politics of education is perhaps that aspect with which Plato's name is most firmly associated. It is a topic that recurs many times, and is always introduced with great earnestness. This is true in the *Laches,* where the imparting of courage (as exemplified in the skills and duties of a soldier) is considered for its effectiveness and public utility. It is true in the *Gorgias,* where the power of the man who teaches rhetoric or who has recently learned it is subjected to an elaborate scrutiny. It is true again in the *Protagoras,* where the usefulness of the arts and virtues in society is balanced against the insecurity of their instruction in case they are not considered to be knowledge or at least connected with knowledge.

The effect that education will have upon the state is of course paired with the effect that the state will have upon it. Here Plato drops his criticism of the societies of his time and turns, projectively, to speculations about societies of a sort superior to the one known directly to Socrates and his colleagues.

By all odds the one most famous is to be found in the *Republic,* a work of incredible richness and depth. The interrelations of government and instruction are explored and exemplified at all levels from early adolescence to maturity, from simple skills to the most advanced mathematical and dialectical investigations. The earlier phases are described in Books II and III, and since this volume does not reprint them, something requires to be said. We might remark that the whole account in the *Republic* turns on the meanings of the word "guarding," for the educational enterprise is primarily to protect the polis, the city-state, in various ways from attacks from without and within.

Plato suggests that the formation of the state comes about through lack of self-sufficiency of the individual—no one man can practice all the arts required for providing him with the necessities of life. The minimal state, as we said earlier, is a handful of men each equipped with his own craft contributing to the support of living—farming, masonry, carpentry, etc. (*Republic II* 369b–371b). This is not a life with the amenities, and when purveyors of these *are* injected we have a second polis, no longer simple but "fevered," i.e., slightly out of balance. We must now set up guards for the wealth and the people, and to assist these guards we must train them properly, in mind as well as in body (*Republic II, III* 376e–417b).

Plato is certain that the only way possible to insure that the soldier–sheepdogs will fight the wolves and not mistakenly attack the sheep is by training their souls as well as their bodies, the latter by gymnastic, the former by what he calls music, i.e., by the arts presided over by the nine Muses, and which we often term the liberal arts. Even here Plato would introduce certain restrictions, for the existing stories of gods and demigods and heroes have been cluttered up with many immoralities and would have a corrupting influence upon the uncritical young. So Plato would delete Homer's less savory accounts of the gods and goddesses, together with certain other legends, and would instead celebrate virtuous actions—a proposal that has given rise to the mistaken assumption that Plato is somehow in favor of a universal censorship, without reservation.

Gymnastic is for the body and music is for the soul, true enough; but it is also true that the real purpose of training these guardians of the people and of material goods is to give them a certain stability of judgment; thus gymnastic too nurtures the soul (*Republic III* 410c). Plato discusses music in the narrower sense (i.e., what *we* would call music), and opines that the instrumental and vocal scales fit for the guardians are restricted in kind, some scales or modes being far too unmanly, tied to luxurious living, others being too exciting. The right education of these guardians must be a blend of the soft and the rough, so that they will have a degree of aggressiveness tempered with gentleness, and will, as watchdogs, fight against the wolves and not devour the helpless but friendly sheep, i.e., the rest of the city over whom they are set to guard. To speak in psychological terms, their courage must be mixed with a

kind of self-restraint, or temperateness, and on a lower
level this is accomplished by the right course of training,
but in the more able members of the soldier class, it
must be brought about through wise choices in the selection
of the individuals. Thus the best guardians are not really
ordinary soldiers at all, for these latter are virtuous through
the habits instilled into them from outside; rather the
prospective guardians are self-controlled, self-disciplined,
in a way that shows incipient wisdom. It is for this reason
that the philosopher who should become king, and who
is the real guardian of the state, having a care for its laws
and customs, is selected out of the soldier class. The curriculum envisaged in Book VII of the *Republic* is one designed both to educate the best of these soldiers so that
they eventually become truly philosophical (wisdom-loving,
as opposed to philodoxical, opinion-loving) and at the same
time separating out those not quite fit for the intellectually
and morally taxing course of studies and their practical
applications; examinations held at intervals will automatically exclude those of insufficient capacity from going any
further.

The educational program of Book VII of the *Republic* is
seen as the very capstone of a reorganized state; in Book
VIII and a small section of Book IX the educational decline
is held to be as important as the political descent—from
monarchy or aristocracy through timocracy, oligarchy, and
democracy to the final collapse into tyranny—to which it
gives rise. Chiefly what happens in each of the steps is that
more attention is paid to economic and political aspirations
than to the acquisition of real knowledge; and the gaining
of political sagacity gives way to mere love of talk, then
drops even that and eventually aims first for money and
then for the satisfaction of all manner of private desires
—the very essence of the undisciplined despotic man.

The educational system planned in the *Republic* is state-
controlled. This is part of the best state, and is restricted to
the very few who can qualify. That planned for the colony
to be called Magnesia (in the *Laws*) is not so restricted,
since legal justice rather than wisdom is the touchstone of
this second-best state. The education begins even before the
birth of the child, for the mother must exercise properly to
ensure the health of the baby. Early (but carefully controlled) exercise is prescribed for the very young child and
this must be supplemented by various means that will

keep it from becoming frightened or otherwise emotional. Supervised play is the next stage, arranged for in a general way by the state, and this is followed (at the age of six) by instruction for both boys and girls, who although they should learn the same disciplines and sports, must be segregated. Dancing and wrestling are the two chief kinds of gymnastic to be pursued, and of music in the narrow sense choruses (which must be seemly) are to be allowed and encouraged; in poetry all must be respectful, indeed prayerful. Since peace rather than war is the proper condition of life, the arts taught in school must be conducive to peaceful life even though the citizens must become hardy and strenuous.

In addition to works of prose selected by a ministry of education, all students should, in the later reaches of the educational curriculum, learn arithmetic, geometry, and astronomy so far as individual aptitudes permit, and especially should they be taught that the heavenly bodies, including the planets, are not irregular in their motions, in spite of appearances to the contrary. (The purpose of this becomes clear later on, in Book X, where Plato makes regularity of movement one of the fundamentals in a proof of the existence of the gods, a doctrine he considers so essential to the stability of the state that atheists should be first admonished and then, if persuasion fails, severely punished, ultimately with death.)

These are proposals for state education. Plato had ready to hand methods of private education in plenty, for in most major cities of Greece there were sophists who plied a trade in wisdom or, rather, its sham substitutes. Plato's attitude toward these itinerant teachers, who picked up as much information and technic as possible in one town and moved on to the next to purvey it, who usually lacked any firm commitment to truth, and who were happy to sell what they had picked up in rather expensive packages of private or semiprivate instruction, is a mixed one. In the *Sophist*, a fairly long and very difficult dialogue, Plato subjects these features to elaborate analysis, using a method that sets up a series of definitions at the end of multiple groups of successive bifurcations, narrowing down the account of art in general to that particular kind of artist which is the sophist. He is (a) a person having an art of hunting after young men; (b) a salesman who has acquired his wares by exchange; (c) a retail seller; (d) a maker of commodities for the soul; (e) an eristic, i.e., a fighter with words; (f) a producer of catharsis (purification) in the soul; (g) a semblance-maker or counterfeiter employing mimicry, without knowledge, and insincere. Lest the reader should think that this is Plato's only or even final word on the matter, we should point out certain facts about this dialogue.

The *Sophist* opens with the question, put by Socrates to an unidentified philosopher from the southern Italian town of Elea, of how the sophist is considered there—whether he is thought to be the same as or different from the states-man and the philosopher. The stranger replies that he knows well the arguments by which the three are dif-ferentiated; he will, in other words, run through a set piece which is accurate but more inflexible than the method of Socrates. Using the Eleatic Stranger instead of Socrates, we should remark in passing, reveals Plato's sensitivity to a problem of method. From Socrates' point of view, there is a vast difference between his own method and the sophistic, while from the viewpoint of the sophist him-self (or of the public who are accustomed to sophists but not sympathetic to Socrates), there is relatively little dis-tinction between the two: they are both handy with words, being happy to argue endlessly with and over them. On the other hand, the Eleatic uses a method which begins not from the statements of sophists themselves (as Socrates does in the *Protagoras,* the *Gorgias,* the *Theaetetus,* etc.), but descends from above. It begins from the general term, art, dividing it into kinds and sub-kinds and thus narrowing as it goes. It is not Socrates' method of face-to-face friendly discussion, but instead strikes an Olympian attitude which approaches the sophist as a kind of exterior fact, a third person who never enters the immediate conversation as a participant, and who cannot therefore defend himself or affect the outcome. The unknown Eleatic's method has the great advantage of objectivity; but it must be supplemented by the Socratic involvement.

It cannot be said that Plato's philosophy as a whole is simply a reaction against the sophists, any more than it can be said that the philosophy of Aristotle is nothing but a reaction against Plato. At no point did Plato take over any doctrine of the sophists lock, stock, and barrel, nor did he totally discard any. The sophists were, after all, the nearest thing to an institution of higher education current in Hellas between approximately 430 and 380 B.C., and their very independence from official ties and from each other gave them a freedom that Plato must have found encouraging in cities often beset with officialdom and provincialism. The need for advanced teaching and for the interchange of ideas between persons and between communities was as great then as it is now, and only the founding of Plato's own Academy, of the great school of rhetoric by Isocrates, and of the Lyceum by Aristotle ushered in a system more in harmony with the real needs of the public than were the hit-or-miss procedures of the sophists. These traveling teachers of a rather hard-headed practical wisdom were many of them trusted men who cannot be regarded as cheap carpetbaggers of dubious honesty. Protagoras was apparently a famed teacher for nearly half a century, and Gorgias ran a school of rhetoric whose intellectual roots were in some of the more distinguished philosophers of the generation just before him, and whose results could be seen in many enthusiastic and successful pupils. Prodicus was one of the first to make a systematic study of language, and Hippias was reputed a polymath who mastered not only arts of discourse but fabricative arts as well. (These thumbnail sketches are taken straight from several of the Platonic dialogues, which are our only close-at-hand evidence, in most cases, for the activities and accomplishments of these and other men.)

But all in all, these sophists were not the best channels of education, or even second-best, being motivated by desire for money and fame rather than knowledge. Some of them were keen to appreciate the order of arguments, but in practice their order was garbled, nor did they perceive the order of sciences, i.e., the *overall* discipline that should take care of the apt pupil from the time he first begins to learn until the time he is put at the head of the great city-state, with all its problems and perplexities.

H. Mathematics

Not only does a respect for mathematical method run through virtually all Plato's writings, but we can assemble from them a reasonably comprehensive account of most of the leading concepts of that science, as developed in his day. Numbers, magnitudes, irrationals, and the properties of these—all have so important a place that the old story that an inscription, "Let None Ignorant of Geometry Enter Here," was carved over the door of one of the Academy buildings carries much plausibility. Whether this was the principal building, and whether the decree applied therefore to students in all phases of the Academy work, is hidden in the darkness of our very incomplete history of that rather shadowy institution. The legend should not, of course, bury the other sciences under a myth that all thinking, for Plato, must be strictly mathematical. Indeed, that "rigorous discipline" which we think of as mathematics because it deals exclusively with abstract quantities and their orders is only one facet of what Plato termed *mathēsis*. The fact is—this can be heavily documented— that mathematical discipline is *almost* coterminous with dialectic, for it deals not only with quantities themselves but also with things that *have* quantities and can thus be measured.

These things are essentially everything, not merely bodies. The identification of a thing marks it inevitably as one, and this unity is a basis of measure, a kind of number. Otherness of any sort, whether it be opposition and contrast or simply a difference of like objects, implies duality; and threeness arises as a mean between any two extremes, e.g., lukewarm between hot and cold. Thus definition, statement, and mediation form integral parts of a mathematical analysis as well as a dialectical one. Or perhaps we should say that mathematics is that aspect of dialectic which concentrates chiefly upon the permanent patterns in being, yet without inquiring why they are permanent. If one seeks to use mathematics, for example, in astronomy, or military logistics and tactics, or in legal and constitutional regulations, all well and good—one thereby introduces an aspect of being into the changing, and stabilizes what is otherwise unstable.

Mathematics appears, then, as an ideal, as an ordering principle, and as a tool, but these three aspects of it are not sharply separated when Plato talks about the origin of the heavens. Mathematics then emerges very clearly as a set of perfect relations which can only be approximately realized, even by a god creating these heavens, but little by little the discourse of Timaeus, who is describing this act of creation. descends to the level of the human body, which ma ife-ts very imperfectly the circles and spheres of the he ve s and of mathematics itself.

In the *Meno*, regard ess of the psychological reasons offered for the ultimate success of the slave boy in grasping the right way to double any given square, we see mathematics presented as an inflexible order in which the proofs of one's conclusions are absolutely at one with the right counting of parts—to double a square (1) quarter it into four squares and then try doubling a side, giving us sixteen smaller squares, which is wrong because we need just eight; then (2) try three rather than four of the small squares, which multiplied by another three will give us nine, still the wrong answer; and finally (3) cut our four little squares in half with a diagonal and erect a new larger square upon it, thus giving a figure with four of our small squares in it plus eight halves, i.e., the equivalent of eight complete small squares in all. Taking this to be typical of a huge array of separate problems collected into plane geometry, and assuming, as Plato assumes, that arithmetic, solid geometry, astronomy, and harmonics provide many other problems, we may look upon this kind of mathematics as being close to modern textbook theory. But Plato ordinarily connects it with discussions of other topics, such as learning theory, the plan of the state, the heavens, etc. This connection makes us think of mathematics as an instrument of psychology or morals or politics, and in some important respects this is true. Just as Plato's remarks about the nature of discourse never occur in isolation from that about which the discourse is being held, so the exercises in geometry and number theory do not occur unrelatedly. The promising young mathematician Theaetetus expounds a classification of so-called square and oblong numbers (*Theaetetus* 147d–148b), and then Socrates takes sixty pages or so to try to connect Theaetetus' suggestions about the nature of knowledge with his own exhibition of this surest kind of knowledge.

That Plato does not imagine that the entire range of experience needs to be cast into mathematical formulations in order to be known, is proven by the long list of dialogues where scarcely any explicit mathematical formulation is offered. Thus the *Apology, Charmides, Crito, Euthydemus, Euthyphro, Ion, Laches, Lysis, Menexenus,*

Phaedrus, Gorgias, Protagoras, Symposium, Hippias Minor
are all works in which quantities, measures, numerical
propositions make brief though often important appearances; from these alone a reader would scarcely guess the
close affinity which Plato sometimes finds between dialectic and mathematical science. It is not easy to general-
ize regarding the characteristics of dialogues in the list we
have just offered, in order to find a common reason for
their failure to include accounts of mathematical knowledge, although many of them are oddly inconclusive
dialogues. Also we note in most of them the strong presence of sophists, either as participants or as topics of discussion. On the other hand, the *Republic* is full of mathematical devices but there are also sophists present; and the
Sophist itself discusses these travelers but even so has
much to do with certain concepts lying at the heart of
mathematics, such as unity and plurality. These are two
leading exceptions.

A reason sometimes offered by Plato for the pursuit of
mathematics is much the same as that offered by a dozen
other philosophers; there is a stability in numbers, also a
clarity in our apprehension of them, which serves to
eliminate the misunderstandings and disagreements that
dog most discussions concerning good and evil. Number-
ing and measuring, whether with "pure" numbers that
have no direct relation to tangibles or with numbers which
are represented in ordinary bodies, can be carried out
with sureness.

Because of this stability, Plato makes numbers the
ground for the fourth and probably the most convincing
proof of the immortality of the soul—we have mentioned
it earlier—offered by Socrates in his final hours (*Phaedo*
102b–107b; this is one of the most tense and crucial passages of dialectic in all of Plato, even apart from the
dramatic circumstances of the discussion). The facts that
a thing has size by its participation in an idea of size, and
that nothing can be its own opposite, have already been
established, and now Socrates wishes to find out whether
a thing is identical with its chief form or idea. Thus 3 is
called *odd* in addition to *three*, though to be *called* odd,
i.e., to have "odd" predicated of it, is not the same thing
as *being* odd, simply because other numbers are called
odd too. Oddness and evenness exclude one another, and
things which are respectively odd and even also exclude

or repel one another, so that three will be destroyed
before becoming even, even though two, which is even,
is not the opposite of the odd number three. A fraction,
in the same way, repels the form of the whole. What
causes a number to be odd is not (the obvious answer)
oddness, but (the more intelligent answer) the number
one, when it is added to an even number. In the same
way what causes the body to be alive is the soul, not life.
The soul, while not being an opposite to anything, still
does not admit the opposite of life, namely death, any
more than three admits evenness. The soul which is thus
immortal does not perish when death comes, any more
than fire will become cold; hence when death does come
to a man, his mortal part (the body) dies, but the immortal soul repels death. Thus Socrates argues from a
class of mathematical things to a class of living things.

As an appendix to our little account we should at least
take note of the dreadfully obscure passage occurring at
the beginning of Book VIII of the *Republic* and thus
included in the present volume. This is most often called
the Nuptial Number, because it is described by Plato as
having to do with the breeding of the philosophers who
are rulers of the state. The number seems purposely to be
left obscure, the reason for that being most likely that
Plato thinks of it as a concern of the very best minds who
have undergone the most rigorous mathematical training,
thus in part fitting them for the rulership. The most
satisfactory discussions of this "number" (it does not seem
in the end to be one unique number but a set of proportions stated in quasi-mathematical terms) are probably
those by J. Adam in his edition of the *Republic,* and
Robert S. Brumbaugh in his *Plato's Mathematical Imagination.* Some phrases are almost untranslatable, so ambiguous is their rendering—no doubt Plato left them
ambiguous deliberately, though he could hardly have fore-
seen that the British and American scholars would have
special difficulties! Suffice it to say here that in the central
part of the passage a triangle is mentioned having sides
of three, four, and five units, respectively, and that these
may represent the three parts of the soul (or classes of
the state), the four virtues (or subsections of the divided
line of cognition), and the five kinds of mathematical study
(or major respondents to Socrates and their dialectics),
all of these having been expounded at length earlier in

the *Republic*. The rest of the passage apparently deals with the cycles of birth and death.

I. Types of Cognition

In Plato's writings we come upon several devices lending strength to each work. These devices are often thought of as mere dialogic touches, ways of catching and holding the reader's attention until Plato can set before us some sentence or group of sentences that he wants us to believe. This of course is a misapprehension, for the dialogues amply illustrate through these devices distinctions between the types of cognition which these same works expound and explain. Not all of the dialogues employ all the devices, but since the *Republic* is fairly representative, it would be well to list what we find there: *description of the scene* (which helps determine what will be said); *casual banter* (which nevertheless reveals much in the temperaments of the participants and often sets the direction that the fuller and more serious discussion is going to take); *citations from the poets* (for Socrates is made to show that while the poets have a considerable poetic wisdom, they must be interpreted carefully, and ultimately are not to be trusted without many previous reservations); *definitions* proposed and rejected for the meanings their upholders have intended (for what is found to be false in one context turns out to be most satisfactory and true in another); *refutations* (for it is the individual proposition that must be studied, and agreement must be secured if the participants are to be sure that they are speaking the truth, and if this agreement cannot be reached it is high time for a reformulation); *myths and tales* and other images (for here again these can be examined for the kernel of truth they may contain, and indeed they may be able to suggest truths that more sober discussion misses); *mathematical images and formulas*, often difficult, even paradoxical, but intended to suggest relationships between concepts that are statable in this way more economically than in any other fashion; *flat propositions or statements* (which are acceptable in certain contexts as things to be taken for granted, but which elsewhere must be looked at skeptically); *proofs* (for the dialectic cannot afford to drift on a river of suggestions and allusions and plays upon words): and finally, *groups of definitions, proofs, and images* assembled in the light of some unitary principle in order to deal concentratedly with various types of inquiry.

What we notice most of all is that these devices illustrate different levels of what we ordinarily call abstract or generalized thought. Thus the description of the scene is directed, if we read a dialogue naïvely, at our senses, whereas the citations from the poets are a kind of hearsay unless and until we can give them a proper interpretation. Propositions, proofs, refutations, mathematical formulas—all these, arbitrary as they may seem, are at least stepping-stones on the way to knowledge and truth. Now if these latter do in some way exist, and if they have real objects, and if knowledge is permanent, e.g., if we do not change our convictions about relations between numbers or about the movements of stars once we have grasped them, it follows that there is a permanent realm of things truly known. The nature of this realm must be postponed for a moment; all we need to grasp here is the difference between the sensory faculties and the intellectual, together with the corresponding difference between their proper objects. Plato illustrates this by his two most famous images, the Divided Line (*Republic VI* 509d–511e), directly followed by the Image of the Cave (*VII*, 514a–518b). If we can agree for the moment that not all the cognitions we have are of sensuous objects, this will allow us to suppose that some things can never be seen and touched, yet may still exist. We know perfect circles, yet they are never presented to the senses.

The line is further subdivided. The entire lower portion of the line marks the realm of sensation, but that is the realm of opinion as well. We may think about what we see, but our mere thoughts following along upon sensations come into being and pass into nonbeing; they are fleeting, no matter how strongly they may affect us at the moment. Having no real stability, they are not the direct basis for any knowledge of real things, but at least they can be subdivided into belief and conjecture. Conjecture is simply our awareness of fake visible things in the world, shadows, mirror reflections, and so forth, which we mistakenly believe to have the existence of solid,

three-dimensional objects. No doubt the objects and even
the shadows do have *some* reality, but it is a reality infected with constant change, and it raises paradoxes. Our
middle finger is long, our last finger is short, but the
fourth finger is both long and short—this is reported by
our eyes—yet nothing can properly be both long and
short at the same time (*Republic VII* 523c–e). Here
is where the intellect must step in to make a distinction. The intellect gives us precisely the stability for
which we seek through the lower one of *its* two subdivisions which is termed *hypothesis* and which is the basis
of the method geometers employ, that of arbitrarily setting
down assumptions and then reasoning from them to conclusions. But this third level still falls short of seeing the
truth whole. This view of the whole results, in Plato's
philosophy, from being able to trace back all arbitrary
hypotheses (as well as beliefs and conjectures) to a final
unity, a single idea in which all the partial existences and
arbitrarily grounded fragments of truth could take their
places and thereby show all their interrelations one with
another. Call it reason or mind. Our thinking requires to
be integrated into a totality. Dante speaks of his own
ultimate vision of God, "wherein I saw the scattered
leaves of the universe in one volume composed," and
this is not far from Plato's conception, though a single
Judaic or Christian God is not the unifying principle for
him, but rather a form somehow superior to all other
forms: the *form of the good*.

One of the seemingly ineradicable difficulties facing
Plato is that we must employ the same language—even
the very same words, to some extent—in communicating
both the intellectual and the sensuous. Thus the "I" in
"I think" and "I see" remains the same, as does "clearly"
in "He reasons clearly" and "He hears clearly." "He sees
clearly" can be out-and-out ambiguous—we say that a
man could see the road sign clearly, and also that he can
see clearly the advantage of coming to a political compromise. But this ambiguity can be an aid to a philosopher such
as Plato, who though he may occasionally show that there
are sharp divisions between the two "levels," nevertheless
deliberately sets up instance after instance (e.g., the three
fingers in the *Republic*) that apparently contravene such a
distinction. Thus sense and intellect can report differently,
but both can report on the same objects.

It is often said that an idea, a conception, is general while a sensation is individual. I may see *this* beautiful flower, but I *think* beauty in general, of which the flower at hand is only one instance. But Plato himself is well aware that the notion of a unified form or idea, that which is conceived, must exist even when there is no single instance which bears its characteristics (*Timaeus* 27c–29a), and consequently that that form (of beauty, or goodness, or twoness, or whatever) would not be a universal, i.e., would not cover a host of individuals similar to itself and similar to each other. If something is eternal (and such ideal forms as beauty *must* be eternal, or so Plato holds in *Phaedo* 105e–106c), then the coming-to-be of individual instances would be of no consequence. Again, an individual flower is not so barely, uniquely singular that it is devoid of all qualities that can be shared with other things. To be able to know the flower—and by that we shall mean *this* slightly wilted daisy clutched in my hand at *this* moment—we must know it in its relations of likeness and unlikeness with other daisies, with marigolds, hollyhocks, and others. And these likenesses are common features, e.g., the possession of petals, corolla, and odor, color, etc. This is not just a happy convenience so that we may identify and know this daisy as daisy, flower, living thing, and perceptible body, but it is also implicit in the very nature of the thing, the daisy itself.

We have already indicated that what is permanent is the object of knowledge, while the transitory is the object of opinion. We cannot say something is *known* by opinion because that would be a contradiction in terms. Although there is a clear distinction in Plato's mind between knowledge, taken in its most important or essential aspects, and opinion, taken in *its* most essential aspects, still there is a rapid shift of movement from one to the other when we come to consider examples. In a fairly typical dialogue, Plato begins with an interchange of opinions, and then moves from this through a sifting of them, a testing of them (in order to produce agreement among the participants on the real natures of the things discussed), to the exact statement of the knowledge that is gained through this dialectical process of testing, and hence a statement of the known. Such a final statement, however, *still* cannot be allowed to stand, and must be supplemented by new approaches to what is generically the same problem.

In the most conspicuous example, the knowledge gained
in the *Republic* in the last five books must be supplemented by at least three kinds of discourse: (1) a myth
capping Book X of the *Republic*, to show the relations
between justice and cosmic destiny; (2) a more exact
account (in the *Timaeus*) of the cosmos into which human
life and action can be carefully fitted; (3) a casting of
the good city of the *Republic* into a historical role (in
the *Critias*) which allows for the application of its constitution—after a fashion—in ordinary human strife.

Other readers of Plato might object that there is no
good reason to believe that the *Republic* is actually followed, in dramatic sequence, by the *Timaeus* and by the
Critias. This is not especially germane, however, since
even if the dialogues were not planned as a sequence we
can still read them together, just as we habitually connect
the *Meno* and the *Protagoras* in our thinking, though
there is rather less dramatic and dialogic relation than
between many other pairs. If indeed the *Republic* really
is meant to be followed by the *Timaeus*, it simply becomes
a little easier to chart the rhythm of succession of political wisdom, myth, science, and history, and so back, presumably to practical political wisdom. In the succession
and mutual replacement and transformation of these we
have knowledge; if any one of them is allowed to stand
alone we risk falling into mere opinion. This opinion is
whatever is taken for granted and made rigid, without
an active movement of the mind through *all* the steps
required to make the knowledge fully correspondent to,
commensurate with, its objects. Such fluidity in knowledge is got by continually refining terms through juxta-
positions with other terms in statements, and through
definitions; and it is also got by expanding the applications of these terms through a variety of dialogic and
dialectical means, in other words, by characterizing and
shifting the persons of the dialogue and by putting their
opinions in sharp contrast one with another. Ultimately,
what is known can be seen to take its place in a universe
well mapped by description, myth, and formula in co-
operation each with the other.

J. Ideas or Forms

Many philosophers, of whom René Descartes, George Berkeley, and Immanuel Kant are good examples, have expounded a group of doctrines and then gone on to record objections which other men have raised or might have raised to these teachings, refuting the objections in the light of the positive doctrines already established one by one, as if knocking off clay pipes in a shooting gallery. Plato's attitude toward objections and their authors is not so simple as that. He is impartial in the sense of presenting more than one side—even the wolf, he says, deserves a hearing (*Phaedrus* 272c)—but he is as likely to begin with views apparently hostile to his own as he is to end with them after he has built what seems to him to be impregnable fortifications. The method of Plato is built around the varied character of objections, some of them mere misunderstandings, some of them journeys into the very heartland of philosophy, but all of them based upon points of view narrower than they should be to give a clear presentation of what can be considered true.

Thus it may not startle us to discover that in order to show what an idea is in the various senses Plato gives to the word "*eidos*" (it could be translated as form, or even as type or species, just about as well), he must go to extraordinary lengths to show also what it is *not*. Indeed, his dialogic device may be understood as a way of exhibiting ideas rather than merely telling about them. In talking about them the language used often becomes highly figurative, as when one special idea is likened to the sun which illuminates all things, or else it veers the other way and becomes overly precise, leading to objections based upon taking the ideas or forms too rigidly. It is because of this that we are so hampered in trying to make what is at bottom intuitive, such as beauty, or good, or justice, into something discursive. Ideas are seen by the mind's eye, so to speak, and are the unspoken and ineffable *results* of philosophizing about experience rather than structures that can be exactly described in conscious, highly verbalized formulas. The formulas are necessary as a preliminary discipline, no doubt, but they do not exhaust the subject of ideas, and should be used for putting the mind into a condition where a glimpse of a great truth will later be granted.

The word "idea" or "form" has a great variety of meanings for Plato, and they emerge in many contexts, some of which relate to the mere shape of a figure or body, some of which relate to the common notion subsuming many separate individuals, some of which refer to a kind of model imitated by copies which are themselves more or less faulty, some of which group around general quantities and kinds and qualities (e.g., "two," "tree," and "good"). The so-called Platonic Theory of Ideas, an expression used in histories of philosophy and elsewhere and carrying two more capital letters than are necessary and proper, is pretty much an amalgam of some of Plato's remarks bearing chiefly on the last two groups, hardened—calcified, so to speak—because it seems nobler to talk of high imponderables, and it is much easier to speak of a single doctrine than to expound a carefully graded set of meanings.

Let us summarize and juxtapose the two points just made: (1) Plato often entertains objections to ideas; indeed the fact that it is the young Socrates himself who is made to propose the view of the ultimacy of these ideas (in the *Parmenides*), and who is defeated by Parmenides in his attempts to uphold it, is a hint to us that of its simpler versions, chiefly those in which the ideas are made into topics of a rigid doctrine with one, two, three-step proofs, the refutations are easy. (2) "The Theory" does not exist as Kant's theory of the internality of space and time exists, set forth in a separate section, complete with statements, proofs, summaries, objections, and refutations of those objections. Rather it is put forward mostly in brief glimpses, often as premises to prove other kinds of conclusions. Some scholars have thought it possible to trace this so-called theory right through several of the dialogues, but this requires considerable forcing of the texts; in point of fact only about six or eight dialogues really take up aspects of the relations between individual things and their perfect and essential realizations (these are instances and ideas, respectively) in any careful way.

Timaeus speaks of the distinction between what is ever changing but never really exists, which is apprehended by our senses, and what never changes and always is, which is known by the intellect. Mark these as *becoming* and *being,* respectively. Plato's problem, however, is not so much the drawing of this distinction and its elaboration into a complete account of two mutually exclusive spheres or worlds, as it is the finding of a partial fusion of these two, or at least a set of bridges crossing over, so that he can talk of the relevance of each one to the other. Yet the very means by which the bridges are created and upheld are themselves akin to forms known rather than to objects touched or seen; such means are based upon the active exercise of the intellect rather than the senses alone. The fullest account of being provides for itself and for becoming as well.

The *Parmenides* has as the first of its two parts several pages on what Socrates, still very young, has said about ideas; Zeno and his teacher Parmenides assume these remarks to have been erected into a theory. Zeno asserts that multiplicity is in effect self-canceling, that there cannot exist a many, hence all that is is one, the absolute unity. Socrates, on the other hand, apparently thinks of forms as a mediator between what always changes and what never changes—that is, between becoming and being. Becoming, for Zeno, must be identified with nonbeing because it is self-contradictory, i.e., it always passes away, while for Socrates becoming can in some fashion be shown to be related to being, instead of to nonbeing. Socrates is thus beaten from the start in his effort to uphold forms, *if* Zeno and Parmenides are allowed to use their framework. Even if forms could be shown by Socrates to exist and to relate to changing things, these forms would be forms of nothing. So when Socrates proposes that the members of any given class of things, such as beautiful objects, just acts, or well-regulated cities have their character simply because of their resemblance to a form or idea which is single and knowable and pure, Parmenides, a venerable demon of dialectic, trounces him easily. If we have forms of beauty, goodness, and so forth, then what about forms of hair, mud, and filth? Do sense objects *imitate* forms, do they somehow participate in them, or what is the relation? Does the form "cover" individuals as a sail covers things lying on the ground? At the conclusion of this section, during which forms are successively treated in terms of whole and part, of interrelations between parts and wholes, of absolute and relative, of fictions of the mind, patterns, essences, and of entities held in the mind of the god, Parmenides commends the youthful Socrates for making a good try, and then shows him a sample of method more satisfactory. What Parmenides now exhibits is a method based upon working out the consequences of an assumption, and then working out those of the *opposite* of that assumption; his method, while intended to be thoroughly rigorous, is also meant to avoid final commitment to any one proposition.

The Platonic Socrates is on the side of Marcus Aurelius, Voltaire, Rousseau, John Dewey, Jean-Paul Sartre, and all others who feel that wisdom, however abstract in formulation, is preeminently wisdom of life or is at least adaptable to life's problems—indeed one notes from *Republic VII* that the full training of the philosopher who is fit to rule the state must be through dialectic which seeks out these inexpressible forms. There must be a conviction of truth which, however broad-minded it may be, is never wholly impartial. It makes a difference to man whether ideas exist; the only thing is, they exist in many senses, but to assert that they also exist in certain other senses winds up in nonsense. Socrates is not impartial, but he is highly selective. We might say that all beautiful girls are beautiful, for example, not because of certain details of nose, eyes, hair, etc., but because they imitate or participate in an idea of beauty—this is Socrates' proposal, and Parmenides misses the point in thinking that there must be a part-by-part or whole-by-whole correspondence between thing and idea. How can we say of a pair of hands, a pair of ducks, a pair of stars that they are each of them two unless we allow that they are, numerically, instances of twoness? And how can we say that we *know* of them as being such pairs unless we look beyond the pairs to the abstraction, the twoness, from which as individual instances they have sprung?

Plato distinguishes between the understanding of hypotheses, which takes them at face value as arbitrary starting points, and the reasoning back to some unitary principle which of itself generates these assumptions (*Republic VI* 510b; this passage is included in the present volume). The assumptions of Parmenides thus turn out to be on a lower level than the sustained effort to find a principle lying back of all other "principles." Parmenides, with his carefully conceived pairs of contradictory assumptions, never gets behind them, for all his skill. Socrates does get behind them, but at the cost of having to lapse into figures of speech, of having to put aside discursive reasoning temporarily and to count on his intuitive awareness of the unity abiding behind all assumptions. Both these men are spokesmen for Plato, and we cannot resolve the differences between them nor can he, for the discrepancies are part of being and knowledge.

Knowledge, Socrates has established earlier (*Republic V*, not in this volume), deals with unqualified being, while ignorance relates to nonbeing pure and simple. Opinion is a mean between the two, and treats of things which partly are and partly are not, hence opinion is untrustworthy. That which knowledge grasps cannot be this changing, evanescent world of pluralities, but must be proportioned to what exists of itself and for itself; but this enters as a kind of cause into the generation of created things. Being is the source of whatever becomes.

1. In order to make this clear, Socrates introduces (*Republic VI*) the likeness of the sun, which both confers existence upon all creatable and destructible things on earth and also furnishes the light by which these things are made evident to our eyes; the idea or form of the good confers existence upon everything else and is also the prerequisite for real knowledge in the soul. The form of good is higher than all else in the intellectual world, just as the sun is supreme in the sensory world. Socrates avers that the idea or form of good confers the power to know truth; that truth and knowledge resemble it; that truth and knowledge do not fully possess it; and that the idea of good is not essence but is above this essence, i.e., the inmost nature of some kind of thing as distinguished from some other kind. Plato wishes to set up not only a goal for knowledge, that which is itself most intelligible, but also something to explain particular good actions by making intelligible the nature of goodness inhering in such actions. The form of good causes the existence of good action, and causes the essence of them as well, what it means to be a good action whether or not there happens to be a given instance of such an action at any particular time.

If we keep in mind this absolute supremacy of the form or idea of good, we may attain to a reasonably clear view of other features of these forms. We cannot, however, state *literally* what relation things or acts bear to forms (it is not partaking of a form as a piece of cloth partakes of blue color, or participating in a form as a bridesmaid participates in a wedding ceremony, or copying a form as an art student draws a plaster head). Neither can we make sharp delineations between different forms and the relations that *they* would bear one to another.

2. Plato also speaks of manifold forms, as we have seen. If they exist as individual things then they must be related to the idea of good much as objects are related to *them*. Thus the form of justice, for example, must be a kind of intermediary between just acts and the highest form, that of the good. A form is thus supreme in one sense and subordinate in another. There is little point, however, in trying to make out a fixed list of forms.

3. There are also passages in which Plato describes what we think of as quantitative notions, "mathematicals," such as "three," "line," etc., much as he does ideas, and it would seem for the moment strange, since ordinarily he lists only qualitative notions as ideas. But whatever is permanent and can be put into abstract relations with another similar being is somehow a pure entity, uncontaminated with change and capable at best of being only approximated by individual changing things. We should say that the idea of the number three, which is different from the number two, is permanent in the sense that whatever is two will never become three, what is even will never become odd (*Phaedo* 106b), and what is intelligible in this way will never become unknowable. Moreover, the threeness and twoness are also similar in kind to pure unity, the unity that lies beyond all plurality and every alteration and movement in the cosmos. The point that Plato seems to be making here has to do not so much with the exact status of numbers, but rather with the fact that as we look to what is above mere sensory experience we find a pattern. With the help of dialectic and the insight of a good man there will come about an awareness of an order, or many orders, in bodies, acts, and feelings and in the whole world in which we live.

K. Truth and Being

Truth, in its most general sense, is unchangeable being taken as it is intelligible to the mind. As a man comes closer and closer to the apprehension of what is really unchangeable, he comes closer and closer to possession of the truth.

To be rightly aware of the flux of things, to "know" that *this* event occurs after *that*, and afterward still another event occurs, is to have both sensation and true opinion, no doubt two steps in the direction of knowledge and truth. In spite of the fact, however, that the capacity to describe the order of changing events is better than an incapacity, it still leaves the connection of events in reasoned causes out of account. Hence to "know" *why* things happen as they do is certainly better than to be in the dark about causes, but to stop there wrongly assumes that what we perceive sensuously—an event of some sort, causally related to another event—is the most real kind of thing to be known. (This is the negative lesson of the *Theaetetus*.) To account for the changeable gives us more perceived changeable events, in which case it affords us no more than what we began with, no fixed point of reference, or else, if we use a sound method, it gives us patterns of changing things.

It is at this latter point, however, that knowledge is generated, for the basis of the pattern is fixed, it is a form, an idea, and we can at least approximate it with a mathematical rule that will aid in grasping this comparative regularity of astronomical and even terrestrial bodies. In the *Timaeus*, very many such rules are sketched in rough outline. On the other hand, even this is not the highest knowledge, is not real truth. The problem of that dialogue is the explanation of change, and though the most unchangeable kinds of discourse, the mathematical formula or physical definition, are invoked to make this explanation, still the grasp of absolute being is no better than partial, and is mingled with a concern for passing events. Again this has been an essential stage, and it is the highest one we can reach by direct, discursive,

rational means. The great myth of Timaeus is an exploration of being immersed in becoming, hence it is no more
than something *like* the truth—a likely, probable story.
But the sure truth, unalloyed with anything else, is got
only *after* this kind of science has been acquired and run
through, it is the spark kindled in the soul that is never
extinguished, if we are to believe *Letter VII*. We cannot
look directly at the idea, the form, in itself, and communicate it to others as if we were examining a tree and
telling of its parts, their distinctive marks, and the causes
of their reciprocal organic interactions. Nor will rhapso-
dizing about the ineffable confrontation of mind and
form be understandable; we may be able to mention it
briefly, but even this can best be done in some sort of
figurative, poetic way (*Phaedrus* 246a–b).

It follows that we can scarcely read Plato successfully if
we take him to hold that all true statements are equally
true. In brief, each true, accurate account is improved
upon, clarified, as it is transformed in terms of later
accounts that raise the level of discussion to higher stages,
until finally—but here speech and discursive reason break
off and we are left with a perfume but no tangible flower,
we are left with a sound but no instrument to give it
resonance, we are left with incredible light, but no source
and nothing visibly illuminated. There are many, many
shades of validity in the arguments by which the participants in the dialogues express themselves, just as there
are many meanings of the individual words used, and for
this reason no single formulation may be finally accepted
and held ultimate in the array of our knowledge. A cor-
relative of that in the dialogues, which are the embodiment of Plato's system, is this: Not everything is of equal
weight in assuring the unity and coherence of a dialogue,
not everything is of equal weight in forcing a correct
interpretation upon us. The "seeing" of truth which the
dialogues in some measure afford us is contingent upon
our being aware of the sources of the unity of each work;
this is a far cry from happening across some impressive
passage and pulling it out of the dialogue and merely
agreeing with it, for such a reading, however sympathetic,
is really a dismemberment, and plunges us back into the
particular, the episodic—into becoming.

Perhaps enough has been said so that the reader will
conclude, as he is meant to conclude, that although being

and becoming are in essence distinguished, we cannot find and talk about unalloyed examples of either one. Thus the usual "two-worlds," being-becoming interpretation of Plato is overly simple, and neglects the fact that there are certain permanent aspects of the tangible and visible, and that our understanding of the purely intelligible is at best indirect and at worst quite momentary. And when it is momentary even the forms become matters of opinion.

Both the system of Plato and its embodiment, the dialogues, bespeak a complex world, a very complex world, and reflect it in the great difficulties besetting everyone who reads his philosophy. The cosmos—or whatever term we select to designate the totality that is the ultimate subject matter of Plato's widest focus—requires a subtle philosophy to keep pace with it:

1. If there were *no* changes, only static being, then a system could be set up as a series of flat statements in which, without fear of self-contradiction, we could put down principles together with what followed from them regarding reality in whole or in part. This is the world of Parmenides.

2. If there were only *uniform* change, with no other being, no fixity, we could put down a series of propositions in which the numbers signifying amounts of change would have perfectly clear and instant application—there would never be any possibility of individual variation in the way things conform to law, and all science would be nothing but logistic, i.e., computation. This is the world of a number of atomistic philosophers.

3. If only *random* change existed, with relation neither to stable reality nor to uniform motion, then we could do no more than suggest a series of propositions which, because of their fleeting nature, could never be explained. We might as well wag a finger as try to speak, for whatever we named would be "frozen" and not fluid, as life and the universe really are. This is the world of Cratylus.

4. If, on the other hand, the world at large is made up of *all* of the first three, not necessarily parceled out in geographical parts of the universe, then what we have is a vastly complicated set of adjustments as being, uniformity, and randomness rule, now in one way, now in another. There is, to be sure, the same blind march of the atoms that Bertrand Russell writes about, but it is endlessly in collision (and partial collaboration) with

rational causes on the one side and with bare chance on the other. And our knowledge, however extensive, however secure, is for that very reason subject to comparable collisions.

In the same way, the dialogues themselves display this threefold "layered" aspect: there are structures in them that are fixed, such as the necessities of proof and classification and the divisions of subjects into parts; there are events that are transient but predictable, such as the actual execution of Socrates after sentence had been passed and after he had refused to escape from prison; and there are chance occasions, such as unforeseen meetings, interruptions, misunderstandings. These three are not easy to reconcile, but they must be reconciled, or we miss what is most important in Plato. Nor is it easy to tag a single incident or personage with a single designation: we are tempted to think of Socrates, the man having wisdom, as representative of being, of stability, of permanence. But at the end of the *Symposium*—a colossal masterpiece, by the way—he is not deified, he is not revealed as anything more than a man who is somewhat baffling to his admirers: and he goes about the business of the day, which is to say he is again taken up with becoming. In the *Phaedo*, which can well claim to be the literary equal of the *Symposium*, Socrates really dies and is not resurrected, as we have already pointed out. So in any literal sense we cannot assume for him any special privilege of a higher cosmic rank, a divine nature. On the other hand, there *is* a relation between wisdom and being, indeed, the two are in some sense identical, and clearly Socrates has wisdom; he is one of the few characters in the dialogues to be concerned with being as it is in itself. Polus, a talkative, impulsive respondent in the *Gorgias*, is coltish— the Greek pun on his name makes what is already obvious still more so—and we might attach him to motion or chance or becoming, so wayward seem to be even his best points. (We might just as well have instanced Polemarchus in the *Republic*, Anytus in the *Meno*, Clinias in the *Euthydemus,* as blurters, arguers who have not thought through their arguments.) But there is, even so, a structure in the discourse of Polus, and in its own way all his talk concerns problems eternally confronting the human mind. Consequently he cannot be consigned to a mere locus in the impermanent, all the more so because his own utterances are taken up and transfigured by Socrates, and made part of a solider view of man.

Let us return to the point at which we began. A text-book of wisdom, or even of philosophy which is not wisdom but the love of wisdom, cannot be written, according to Plato. As we set out to use the intellect—and try to use it we must!—we find that there is a limit beyond which we cannot carry it, that intellect merely puts us in a position where we can receive knowledge; where, to express it in more Platonic terms, we come face to face with the ideas or forms which represent real being. The ideas make up a world, but that world is in our own world of dimensional, sensible objects, and the two interact, so to speak, so that in knowing one we know at least something of the other. Being and becoming, we might say, are not precisely the same, but neither are they so different that they do not communicate with each other.

In the course of showing how that which becomes possesses many aspects of that which really is, and how what exists informs what becomes, Plato makes use of a double overarching analogy—but it is still an analogy, no more! The parts and whole of the human soul are somehow like the parts and whole of the city, which Plato takes to be the most advanced and inclusive of the associations of men; and the city and its parts are somehow like the parts and the whole of nature, that is, of the cosmos. These are the three chief subjects in which being and becoming are traced, and the tracing is best accomplished when one is able to analogize from a man to a city-state, thereby finding those aspects of permanence in him by this comparison; or when either man or city are analogized to the cosmic system as a whole, thereby giving either or both of them something of *its* stable reality. The forms, the ideas, turn out to be the patterns of these more and more fundamental existences. True, the reference in Plato is often to becoming and change in this chief trinity of man, state, universe, but even in the most frequent, rapid, and erratic changes he thinks he can detect some trace of order, and where there is this order we find number, formula, intelligibility, and some reference, thereby, to the unchangeable. We can best comprehend becoming through being, total permanence; but to be able to arrive at a conception of this permanence, to be able to grasp an idea or form, we

must be fully aware of the universe as sensible, as corporeal, hence as generable and destructible. To open our
minds we must first open our eyes and our other senses
wide, and then, by the intellectual process of constant and
permuted pairing-off of names, definitions, and images
in which our own thoughts are couched, we reach the
outer limits of intelligence, and beyond that there is only
the real, which cannot ever be literally named and communicated.

L. Dialectic

Thus far we have neglected the Platonic letters, of
which there are supposed to be thirteen. Of them the
second and the seventh have perhaps the best claim to
authenticity, and even large parts of these appear suspect;
there is a whining, cantankerous tone in much of the narrative sections of *Letter VII* that seems out of keeping
with the self-confidence and freedom of the dialogues.
For the most part the letter relates episodes in Plato's
earlier life, culminating in his trips to Syracuse in his
(eventually disappointed) efforts to help establish a better
government in that city. But there is also a remarkable
central section in which Plato speaks of the obstacles to
educating the impetuous know-it-all Dionysius II in the
intellectual habits of sound philosophy. What the author
of the letter offers in place of the cut-and-dried notions
of Dionysius is of utmost importance, and there seems no
very good reason to think of it as a forgery, so ultimately
consistent is it with the methods practiced in the dialogues. It runs thus:

Indeed, I know that some other persons have written
about these same things, but what sort they are even
they do not know. This much I can assert of all
these writers or would-be writers, who say they know
about what I earnestly pursue, whether as listeners
of mine or of others or as discoverers on their own;
these, in my view, cannot have any real understanding of such matters. There is nothing written
down by me, nor will there ever be, dealing with these

things; for it cannot be a subject of speaking, like other kinds of learning; but out of great intimacy with the things known and of communion with them it is, like light kindled by a leaping spark, generated in the soul, and forthwith it nourishes itself. Even so, this much I know, that a written or spoken rendering would best be done by me, and that if it were badly written I would be the one most pained. And if I had thought that those things could be written down or adequately stated for the many, what nobler act in my life could there be than that of writing what is of great benefit to men, bringing the nature of being to light for them. But I do not think that doing this would be a good thing for men, save for a few able to discover the truth for themselves with a little teaching. . . .

But I have in mind to say more, for what I speak about may be clearer after I have spoken. There is an important truth which confounds anyone who wants to write anything about these things, which I have often spoken of in the past, and which seems to need stating again now.

There are three things necessary to generate a knowledge of each real entity; a fourth is the knowledge itself; and as the fifth, one must put the entity itself which is intelligible and true. First is the name (*onoma*), second the definition (verbal account, *logos*), third the image (*eidólon*), fourth the knowledge (*epistēmē*). If you would grasp what is now being said, take one thing and realize what holds for all. A "circle" is something of which we speak, whose name is that just mentioned. The definition, second, is composed out of names and verbs; for "what is everywhere equidistant from the extremities to the center" is the definition of what is "round" and "spherical" and "circle." Third is what is drawn from life and obliterated or turned on a lathe and destroyed; but the circle itself never suffers these— they are related to it, but are different. Fourth is knowledge and intuition and true opinion about these entities, all of which we must take as one in not being in speech or in bodily shape but in souls. So it is plain that it is different from the nature of the circle itself and from the three things mentioned.

Of these intuition is most like and akin to the fifth, and the others are more removed.

The same is true of both straight and spherical shapes and colored surfaces, of the good and beautiful and just, and of all bodies whether manufactured or generated by nature, fire, water, and all such as these, all animals and habits of the soul and actions and passions. For unless a man grasps these four, he will never have perfect knowledge of the fifth. Moreover these try to express the quality of each thing no less than the reality, because of the inadequacy of the verbal account (*logos*). For this reason, no one having intuition will ever want to commit its insights to a verbal account, especially when this is unchangeable, as it is when in written form.

Again it is necessary to understand what was just said in terms of our previous example. Each circle drawn in exercises or turned on a lathe is full of what is opposite to the fifth, since it touches the straight everywhere; but the circle itself, I assert, contains neither less nor more of the opposite nature. And none of these has any fixed name, nor is there anything to prevent what are now called round from being called straight, or straight round, and no one will find transposed names less fixed when they are used thus oppositely. The same holds true of the definition too, since because it is composed of names and verbs, nothing is fixed with sufficient fixity. One might go on endlessly concerning the unclarity of each of the four; but the most important point, as stated as little while ago, is that although each is twofold, what the thing is and of what sort, and the soul seeks to know not its sort but what it is, each of the four offers in definitions or in the actual thing what is not sought. Since what is spoken of or exhibited is always subject to refutation by sensations, nearly all men are filled by them with all sorts of perplexities and uncertainty. . . . Going through all of these stages, up and down, one to another, barely engenders knowledge, even when the man is like what he knows, well-formed. . . . To put it in a single statement (*logos*), neither aptitude nor memory will ever engender knowledge in someone lacking affinity with the thing to be known; it cannot even begin in an alien habit of mind. To come to an understanding of these things it is necessary at the same time to understand what is false and true of all reality, after hard and very time-consuming labor, as I said at the beginning. It is only with great difficulty, by the rubbing of each of these against the others, names and definitions, visual images and sensations, putting them to the test in a friendly manner, and engaging in the exchange of questions and answers without jealousy, that there bursts out the light of wisdom and insight regarding each object in him who exerts the utmost in human power. (341c–344b)

It *may* be that the last paragraph is intended to explain why Plato cast all his written work in dialogue form—that by putting thoughts into the mouths of other persons, especially of historically real ones, he could evade responsibility for what is said and could in one sense preserve his silence while in another sense speaking at great length. This is an oft-proposed theory of his procedure. The interesting observation on this is that the dialogues, despite their many differences of structure, of detail, of mood, can be shown to have an underlying unity of themes, of purposes, and of purport, so long as we are willing to keep our interpretation free of dogmatism. So long, that is, as we do not light upon some passage and say, "*This* is what Plato is really driving at, *this* is what we are going to use as a criterion for everything else he says on the same topic." The dialogues seem to be merely the long way round, making use of hints, statements, explorations, and more, that will clearly suggest an open philosophic system that cannot directly be stated in language, but lies, as it were, at the outer limits of a language. The dialogue form, were it to have been used in the absence of the dialectical method, would have been Plato's way to cover his tracks; but the dialectic is there, to bind everything together, to bring out resemblances between apparently unlike things and the differences between things apparently alike, and consequently to show each thing in its true colors both as a separate entity and as interrelated with the rest of the universe.

Dialectic and dialogue overlap, and indeed they are partly the same. It would be handy to think of dialectic simply as the method used in dialogue, but of course it cannot be as easy as that; indeed, dialectic is such a massively protean thing that it can scarcely be reduced to any one definition, and certainly Plato, in the many passages in which he speaks of it, makes no attempt at such a reduction. At certain points he treats it rather lightly, as a kind of game; but elsewhere he accords it an almost religious respect. How can this be?

The best way for us to expound dialectic is to introduce it in eleven successive guises, showing how these are interrelated with each other. The first few of these, by the way, are close to dialogue, but later we see how different dialogue and dialectic can become.

1. Dialectic is conversation. The two aspects of such conversation interesting to us here are its casualness and its cooperativeness. Dialectic may be quite rigid, in the sense of being planned in advance, but so long as there is another voice, another person who is serving as party to the discussion, there is bound to be some degree, however small, of unexpectedness in the responses. In the *Sophist, Statesman,* and *Parmenides,* the three dialogues in which there is some approximate anticipation of what is to come, the responses are most nearly mechanical, but even so there is still room for error, for backtracking, and for requests for further explanation. Second, conversation requires some kind of joint contribution, some sort of agreement, even if the conversation be quarrelsome, for at least the subject matter has to be jointly explored though in opposite ways. There is a reference in the *Parmenides* (137b) to the need for a respondent in order to rest the voice of the principal speaker. In that dialogue this request must be taken seriously, the reason being that the respondent contributes little or nothing to the progress of the argument, briefly marking divisions in the proofs with his expressions of agreement. Parmenides himself sees philosophy as a way of looking at the consequences of various assertions followed by the consequences of their denials—an impartiality in his method which, as we have said earlier, is both inferior to the more nearly partisan Socratic method and also superior to it. But this objectivity of Parmenides and the preestablished plan of its exposition all but reduce any other participant to silence.

On the other hand, casual, open-ended conversation by itself is nothing more than common opinion, ill-digested, ill-assorted, without order, and would doubtless bring us no nearer to truth, and scarcely nearer to real agreement, which is agreement not so much in speech as in thought. In conversation clear meanings are rare, and no two persons really understand one another. Hence we need a means of improving, of elevating this ordinary colloquy.

2. Dialectic is question and answer. The two chief kinds of interrogation are (a) that in which the questioner does not know the answer but hopes that the answerer does know, and (b) that in which the questioner knows the answer but is not sure that the respondent will. These two are motivated by inquiry and instruction, respectively. In Plato these two sometimes merge, Socrates, the chief instructor, frequently saying that he does not know the answer to his own or to someone else's question.

The fact that there are indeed questions and answers, however, gives both a sharpness to the inquiry and a persuasiveness to the instruction, for the questions serve to mark off stages of a connected discussion, with each new problem developing out of the preceding ones; and it persuades in this peculiar and important sense, that it is necessary to secure agreement at each step before going on to the next. The agreement rests upon understanding in this regard, that when one has grasped the meanings of the constituent terms at any given stage of the discussion, then associating them into pairs which are the basis of statements becomes inevitable (e.g., "Virtue is difficult," "Poetry lacks truth"). Consequently the teacher who uses dialectic is the best persuader, and this is exemplified by the victories of Socrates, Parmenides, and the Athenian and Eleatic Strangers. Socrates does not, we must concede, always win; but he is confronted with some of the most recalcitrant men in Athens, and is at least able to show them that in thinking they know they are very likely to be wrong, that their confidence is due to faulty judgment, a little knowledge mixed with ignorance; in a word, opinion.

3. Dialectic is an art. There is an art of using language at *any* level, no doubt, because words are only partly natural (see the *Cratylus* for an extended account of this). Secondly, most men who have arts also possess the art of using words pertinent to their skills. Thus the doctor knows how to talk to his patient about health and disease, the astronomer knows how to describe constellations, the statesman proposes laws and policies, and so forth. Thirdly, there are certain persons whose whole art rests in the use of words, for example the poet and the rhetorician, and fourth is an *extra* art of language, call it grammar or rhetoric or what you will, beyond the bare use of sentences to ask for, describe, question, or deny matters of common everyday opinion. Over and above this, however, the dialectician is revealed as the man who uses an art of language which ranges universally over all the other arts and their concomitant arts of language, examining their principles, their purposes, and their interrelations.

We can approach this from another viewpoint: the potter who tells us how to throw a bowl on a wheel, or the general who tells us how to deploy troops or how to distinguish courageous from cowardly soldiers, is speaking from experience. He cannot go beyond his experience (the potter does not teach us how to make shoes or command soldiers), because his art grows out of his special experience and not merely out of grasp of the principles underlying *any* practice, *any* work, *any* experience. But dialectic is an art because while it implies that some experience has already been had, it goes beyond the range of any individual experience, discussing pottery and shoemaking and generalship with impartiality and insight. For this reason, dialectic may be called an art of arts, an art of *all* arts, for the man with dialectic, while he may still be unable to use his hands to throw a pot or perform a surgical operation, nevertheless knows the manipulatory steps required and also the importance of the pot or the operation, and also the relative importance of each of the arts. Thus the physician is shown by the dialectician to be related to the gymnast and the cook, and in some respects he is dependent upon these, yet in one sense he dominates them both. This interweaving of men of various arts, and of their functions, which goes beyond any single art, is a problem of special interest for the dialectician. Mere conversation and mere questioning, without art, cannot do this.

4. Dialectic is an art of enumeration. One of the reasons that mathematics ranks so high in Plato's estimation is that in certain cases we may be sure of what we are counting, and that our counting is complete. Thus if we grasp the fundamental difference between even and odd, or between straight and curved, we can be sure that each of these is an exclusive and exhaustive enumeration, and moreover we can be sure that if we are asked to list the even numbers between 1 and 15, then 2, 4, 6, 8, 10, 12, 14 is the definitive answer. If, on the other hand, we must know all the different sexes of mammals, it requires some study to be certain that male–female is the complete and necessary answer, simply because the fact that all dogs are either male or female does not of itself assure us that all members of the cat family are, or all ruminants—we must examine representatives of many species. To find out if all species of roses have thorns, or if all swans are white, is to seek information of still more doubtful character. Dialectic cannot, obviously, become a substitute for the travels of an ornithologist who takes up swans kind by kind to see if they are all white; but on the other hand, *this* is the topic for a dialectical question itself, a question resting upon distinctions between characteristics purely incidental to the diverse species and diagnostic features essential to them. It is the dialectician or the biologist who assumes a dialectical function who inquires whether a grouping into species is a fruitful and justifiable procedure in science.

Dialectic contributes to the drawing of necessary distinctions, so that our enumerations are not merely random bits ending with a weak "etcetera," but have some scheme, some rationale, that in any case is more ordered, closed-ended, and essential. This rationale cannot always be found in early stages of scientific inquiry, but when it is it helps give us the proper form to our knowledge.

These enumerations in popular science are not, as a rule, based upon distinctions of better and worse. The enumerations we find in Plato, on the other hand, are of many kinds, but nearly all of them turn out in the end to be based upon judgments of value. Some, and perhaps the most typical, are straight hierarchies running from inferior to superior (e.g., the so-called ladder of love in the *Symposium* 210a–211d), or the reverse (the list of more and more degenerate states, *Republic VIII–IX*), some are lists that initially give little hint of lower and higher (as in the account of the limited, the unlimited, the mixture, and cause of the mixture of limited and unlimited, an important enumeration in the *Philebus* 23e–27b, which only later shows itself to be a hierarchy). Some are of everyday things (such as the stages of weaving, *Statesman* 279b–283a), while others are of gods and lesser souls in their heavenly flights (*Phaedrus* 246a–248e). The purpose is always unique to each hierarchy, though it may bear some family resemblances to the purpose of another such list, and Plato's justifications cannot be transported wholesale from one part of the corpus to another.

The art of enumerating, simply because it must enumerate things, cannot proceed independently of experience.

5. Dialectic is a means of statement, proof, and refutation. Dialectic always has an axe to grind, there is always some statement that is to be upheld (if only temporarily) or refuted (even if not finally and forever). Dialectic is restless in the sense that it moves from statement to statement, testing to discover what is true and what is false in each formulation, and this it does by imposing a meaning upon the constituent words. The meaning, however, is not arbitrarily imposed by an omniscient philosopher, but in some cases by the ordinary-minded respondent (Euthyphro, Crito, Charmides, Polemarchus, and a swarm of others). In some cases it is by the cooperative conclusion of such respondents and the master dialectician, Socrates, for instance, who is refuting them and leading them beyond their own conceptions by successively introducing new images and arguments.

Substantiation, or affirmative proving, and refutation, which points to a negative end, possess another character, one which could never be seen except in a dialogue: the defeat or victory of points of view and with them of persons. Refutation even more than substantiation is aimed at the soul, and it is morally as well as intellectually educational. In extreme cases it is an outright humiliation, as with Thrasymachus (*Republic I* 344d–354d), who yet becomes friendly and docile, even if he no longer actively participates (*VI* 498c–d); in other cases the personal element is no more than hinted at by Plato, and the purpose of refutation is simply to establish and underline dialectical impossibilities. In either case, however, the finding of refutations depends upon enumeration, and this, as we have seen, depends upon experience, at least experience of an everyday sort. Consequently the proving of a propo-

sition right or wrong hinges not upon a naïve readiness
for combat, but upon the awareness of what lies in the
nature of things. Dialectic, says Plato in a famous simile,
must cut at the natural joints, and should not, like an
awkward butcher hacking away, break any part (*Phaedrus*
265e).

6. Dialectic is self-revelation. As a person speaks, he
reveals something of himself, and this speaking is least
self-revelatory if it is a mere word, more so if it is a
sentence or definition (the word *"logos"* in Greek does
for both), and still more so if it is an extended proof
or myth. Thus Protagoras, in the dialogue bearing his
name, embarks upon a tale of the gods and demigods in
order to explain a paradox connected with the view that
all men possess the arts yet only a few men are able to
teach them. In so doing the formidable old sophist shows
himself in the professional and personal attitudes he has
developed over a long career in semi-public life. The
statements and arguments proposed in a dialectical discussion are, though seemingly impersonal, yet of such a
kind that the character of the men putting these forward
is revealed, sometimes in spite of the speaker's desire to
keep himself wholly in the background. If this is not
obvious to a reader at the moment when a participant is
speaking it will have become obvious later on, after the
proposals have been taken up, rejected, or accepted outright, or transformed in the course of discussion with
Socrates or one of his colleague master-dialecticians. Every
speaker has a dialectic, but generally it is a dialectic of
sorts only, an enfeebled expression of what a dialectic
ought to be. In that sense, the self-expression, the self-
revelation, is incomplete, and only Socrates can make *himself* fully clear as a man through what he says. This self-
revelation and the doctrine support each other when both
have been satisfactorily laid out before the reader, and
are used in two ways. (a) Together they show what a
good, self-consistent, honest philosophy has been developed, all the more because a noble exemplar of that
philosophy has expounded it; (b) together they also show
what an excellent protagonist is on hand, all the more
because he has elicited and expounded such a profound
and valid sequence of thoughts. If you object that this is
circular reasoning, the reply can only be that of course

it is, but the intimate attachment of a man's real nature
to what he articulates in his philosophy is exactly what we
want. It is hard to find sham battles in the dialogues of
Plato.

This throws some light upon the famous refutations that
Socrates hands his respondents in case after case—Polemarchus and Thrasymachus in the *Republic,* Euthyphro,
Protagoras, Gorgias, Lysis, Theaetetus in the dialogues
named after them, and many others. If what we really are
is revealed in what we say, even when we try to dissemble,
and if our general intellectual formulations are tied to
our personal natures, then it is improbable that we can
divorce our experience from our theories and speculations about the world. Even our reading—of which the
Greeks could not as a rule do much, so scarce were
books—is taken up into our stream of personal thought
and made part of our own mental life. Hence when a
respondent is attacked for his foundations it is not a
game—*he* is being attacked, along with what he says. But
as Plato makes clear in *Letter VII,* there can be no bitter-
ness, no jealousy, in dialectic; the attack looks to reform
of a person's thinking and character, not to his discom-
fiture. If a respondent is disgruntled at being refuted
(Thrasymachus is very huffy, for instance, and so is Anytus in the *Meno,* and so in his own small way is Euthyphro), that is because of some flaw in his own character
which makes for a misconception of the nature of dialectic and the intent of Socrates. The just penalty for
being out of tune, says Critias, is to be put in tune (*Critias*
106b).

7. *Dialectic is impersonation.* Part of the excellence of
Socrates' dialectic rests upon the fact that he can enter
into the points of view of other men, both those at hand
in the dialogue and those absent or even long since dead.
The dialogues in which Socrates dominates are all dotted
with allusions to remarks others would have made, proofs
they would have given (e.g., a passage in which Socrates
reconstructs a long argument, putting it into the mouth
of the now dead Protagoras and making it as coherent
and persuasive, no doubt, as that celebrity could have
made it himself). The presumption is that if Socrates can
reconstruct a point of view at variance with his own, it

means that he is the one who can refute or transform it most successfully.

This impersonation, as we have called it here, is not a gift which is exercised at the expense of revealing oneself. But Socrates never forsakes his own convictions, yet having a wider dialectical framework, he can readily fit into this the rather narrower views of other men. Thus Agathon is easily understood by Socrates, who quickly shows him that if one holds parochially to a simple opposition between beauty and ugliness one cannot explain satisfactorily the nature of love; but if one widens the frame, to include an intermediate between the two opposites, the explanation of love becomes much more satisfactory, even if more complicated (*Symposium* 199c–204a). The impersonation rests, then, upon a grasp of the respondent's thought structures, his patterns which he habitually and probably unconsciously uses in relating his chief terms to each other, seeing the consequences of these relations. Then one must make explicit in a refutation or transformation what is needed to clarify the patterns so that they fit the real state of affairs they purport to define or describe.

8. Dialectic is the art of definition. A definition is primarily a statement of what it is to *be* something, consequently a definition requires also that we make clear what a term means. A definition is a direct confronting of the speaker with a kind of thing, and the man's art, insofar as he has any, is to express what his experience of that thing has forced him to think about it. Not only is this expression extremely difficult, but also the resulting definition quickly becomes a target for refutation, on the ground that it is untrue to the experience it supposedly reflects (e.g., in the *Charmides* and *Laches*), or on the ground that it does not sufficiently delimit the nature of what is being defined— separate it from other things (*Gorgias* 449d), or that it neglects those aspects of things under definition which give them stability and being (*Republic I* 331d–334b). In the dialogues not featuring Socrates, the uses and kinds of definition alter considerably, so that the Athenian Stranger, whose purpose in the *Laws* is to set up a working model of a new city-state, stresses origins rather than definable natures; Timaeus thinks of definitions as incidental to a complete formal construction relating natural things to each other and to an eternal pattern; Critias describes and measures but does not define, for that is the direction which a historical-mythical account must take; and the Eleatic Stranger enters into a string of definitions that would floor Socrates himself—almost—except that each definition is proposed and justified by the Stranger, and is not refuted even though it may be modified or further explained. Socrates himself rarely offers definitions but instead elicits them from his struggling respondents.

9. *Dialectic is a science.* Science is often distinguished from art by being termed more secure, more unshakable, more concerned with changeless being. It is typified, as we have hinted, by mathematics, which is accurate, self-checking, and unvaried. Astronomy and harmonics are two sciences lying closest to arithmetic and geometry, Socrates treating the former pair as superior because more complex and inclusive, Timaeus regarding them as inferior because they deal with things that partake of becoming. The earth sciences begin from a different set of mathematical principles, according to Timaeus, and introduce some measure not only of change but of chance. The biological sciences, again, combine all the principles of the others, but in a much less exact way, so that ideal proportions are rarely if ever met with, and so that perfect circles in the heavens are only loosely imitated by mere cycles of nutrition, respiration, and the like. In all these, dialectic emerges as the common structure of inquiry binding together and finding the shared principles and formulas applicable to all or at least to many of the disciplines. In a sense it is more exact than mathematics, which deals with equalities and inequalities of quantities; dialectic is able to range freely into comparisons of qualities and their intensities and their complex evaluations—whether, e.g., justice is a virtue, and whether virtue is a good, and if a good what kind of good, or indeed whether good is divisible into kinds at all.

As a science, dialectic makes full use of observation, enumeration, testing (refutation and defense), and definition. These devices can achieve their full stature and justification only when they are put together in the context of a complete scientific inquiry. Dialectic, which appeared so random and unorganized at the outset of our little account, now reveals itself as an integrated inquiry into what is most permanent, even when the subject matter of the explanation is changing: man or animals or the state; for dialectic, even though it makes every allowance for change, defines the permanent essence.

10. Dialectic is the search for and demonstration of truth. In a sense truth is very easy to reach, being contained in ordinary combinations of words following the thoughts in the soul which attribute reality to things that are, or deny it of things that are not. At the same time, truth is exceedingly difficult to find, because reality or being has no basis in the changing, the merely apparent, the imitative. To grasp truth, to know the reality of something requires first a long search into the permanent aspects of a thing, and then the setting of it into relation with other things similarly permanent. To cut a thing off from the rest of being would mean to give it limitations which it does not actually have, to constrict it, and thus to remove from it the very permanency which we are seeking.

The search *for* truth, however, is also the same thing as instruction, teaching *of* truth. This is one reason why Socrates says several times—in the *Apology, Meno, Republic, Theaetetus,* etc.—that he does not know anything except that he does not know, which implies that he cannot teach when he cannot inquire. What we examine in any successful inquiry is a self-consistent whole, an unchanging whole, and this is exfoliated, leafed out, into unchanging aspects (which Plato calls ideas or forms) that can be viewed all together or each separately, depending upon how far we have moved in the inquiry from the individual changing, accidental, fleeting appearances of daily life. But this final grasp of being is at the same time its orderly exposition. Such an exposition, Plato admits, is not altogether accessible to rational thought or reducible to strict language. For this reason knowledge of the real is kindled as a spark, and the object of knowledge—the unitary form of good which lies behind all other forms, behind all changing things as their ultimate cause—is like the great bright sun, upon which no man can ever gaze directly.

11. Dialectic is being. Plato does not make the same large claim that Hegel makes, that the progress of dialectic and the structure and progress of the world are identical. For Plato dialectic is far more supple than that, and the universe would reel and shudder were it required to keep up with what is said by human beings, even philosophers. But since the end of dialectic is the grasp of being and its fixed forms, it should follow that if such forms are uniquely neither in an outer world—as they are not—nor in an inner world of thought—as again they cannot be—then the reality of things is indifferently physical or mental; dialectic is not at all a happy chance that brings to a congruence mind and universe. So we must also assume that it is irrelevant to ask whether the world moves dialectically—dialectic in its highest, purest form is no movement at all, but rather fixity; in its lower manifestations dialectical movement is identical with movement in the world only in the very loose sense that the literary account written into a dialogue imitates the behavior of characters as they really think and speak and act. But this is no more than history, and falls short of finding any permanency in change, any formula in flux, any constitution in a welter of desires and habits. To look for an identity of reality and dialectic anywhere below the very highest level is to degrade both of these, making them servants of impermanence and of chance.

M. Nine Impostor Methods

All this has been very high talk, of course, and to accept these characterizations as being true of dialectic alone, with no accord shown to any other candidates, is to make Plato appear unnecessarily dogmatic. What we need, therefore, is to show what is wrong with the other methods claiming to share equal privileges—methods, by the way, that Plato takes full account of in the dialogues, both by description and by example.

It seems natural that something would try to creep in and occupy the honorable place of dialectic, unseat it, shame it, and dismiss it as being of no consequence. To accomplish this such an impostor would be required either to look very much like dialectic—so that only a close dialectical examination could show up the differences—or else be able to refute dialectic, or both. We trust that in the hands of Socrates, or the Eleatic, or some of the other great interlocutors, there will be someone keen and strong enough to hold up the impostors for what they are, pretentious, imperfect, bogus, false. Now Socrates challenges, without much help from anyone, all of these envious adversaries, which we may list as common opinion, the special sciences, history, rhetoric, sophistic, eristic, myth, poetry, and grammar. Without much help: Neither his own respondents nor the other master-interlocutors battle these substitutes in quite the same way. The Eleatic Stranger thoroughly discredits the sophist, but does so only by talking *about* him, not *to* him; only by defining him, not refuting him. (Along with the sophist, the eristic, who is a mere scrapper with words, is put down for good.) In the *Laws* the Athenian Stranger speaks slightingly of dialectic, terming it the harmless amusement of old men (*VI* 769a; *VII* 820c). This same Stranger makes use of myth and history combined with political science in order to account for the institution of good laws. Timaeus, in some ways the most impressive of all six interlocutors, including Socrates, expresses himself in a fascinating blend of myth and science. And so on. It should come as no surprise, however, that the impostors are simply methods which when taken *by themselves* have not the ring of truth which they do possess when they take their places in a dialectical framework. Myth, science, and the rest regain their dignity once they are absorbed into a more all-embracing method. The substitutes, then, for genuine dialectic are false in the hands of anyone thinking they are *not* substitutes, not mere *parts* of the true method. The grave difficulty is that when they do turn false, it is likely to be so subtly that it is next to impossible for anyone short of a Socrates to detect their phoniness. So we shall if possible hold up to view what is so dangerous about their disguises.

1. Common Opinion. In most of the dialogues, with certain obvious exceptions such as the *Parmenides* and *Timaeus* and *Critias*, Plato commences with a voicing of common attitudes, common sentiments, everyday wisdom, usually phrased in a pedestrian and even commonplace fashion. This is so frequent, and the refutations or improvements of these attitudes are so often partly unsuccessful, that the reader may easily conclude that because dialectic is in part simply conversation, its ultimate aim is to communicate a sort of rough-and-ready wisdom of life, a common folk bond. This is to some extent true: Plato proscribes the teaching of dialectic to the young, for it will make them unduly contentious (*Republic VII* 539b). At worst, the intellectual elevation of the youth turns them combative, and at best the indulgence in such games of method, as described in the *Laws,* fritters away their hours. So it would seem that all that is left must be horse sense, agreed-upon aphorisms, wisdom lacking in pretensions.

Looking deeper, we see that a mere airing of, or battle over, common opinions is no more than a first step in a dialogue. The very fact that refutation is brought against dogmas of ordinary life is enough to make us suspect that Socrates is unsatisfied with these dogmas. The additional fact is that as refutations pile up against the original proponent, Socrates attempts, albeit often unsuccessfully, to climb into a purer region of more nearly universal and permanent and interrelated values. This should point to the insufficiency of views stemming from habit, custom, popular hearsay, and approval. In accord with this, we recognize that the character of Socrates is without affectation, and he ironically notes that Ion (and others) do put on airs (*Ion* 530b–c; *Euthydemus* 271c–272b). One of the great charms of a Socratic dialogue is that it escapes from the burden of jargon and technicality. In spite of this, however, Socrates' main effort is to lift a discussion from the low grasslands and swampy ground of popularly accepted rule-of-thumb conceptions to the plateau of a more clear-headed and self-conscious appreciation of moral good and evil, regardless of the simplicity of the language in which this appreciation is to be couched. Socrates talks to experts many times, but his disappointment with them is usually owing to their use of their own expertness as a way of merely disdaining the commonplaces of *hoi polloi*—the many. The only worse thing would be to try leaping into philosophic knowledge without any common thinking, practical sense, daily rote; we must not try to give form to our cognitions without the substance of experience. It is for this reason, also, that dialectic is not for the young—they may be lettered and bright, but they lack contact with life itself. Socratic dialectic, then, lies in the reform of experience; but experience alone, and the shared opinions of the many which go hand in hand with this, are no substitute for philosophy in its properly developed form.

2. Science. Socrates ventures quite often into the so-called special sciences, showing competence in mathematics (*Meno, Theaetetus,* and *Republic*); in astronomy (*Republic*); and there are many briefer references to other sciences as well, and many more accounts, showing interest in a kind of mythological variant of current Greek knowledge. Thus the *Phaedo* has some very peculiar geology and geography in it, the *Cratylus* expounds some odd etymologies. Strange biological references abound in the dialogues, though most of them are referred to as legends, not facts.

The gift of any special science is precision, and the fault is rigidity. If the conclusions follow necessarily from principles clearly stated, even so the principles are in some measure arbitrary, and—if we are to believe the second part of the *Parmenides*—as much follows from negating these hypothetical starting points as from asserting them. Not only that, but the exclusive use of any one science tends to warp the interpretation of *any* subject matter in the direction of the presuppositions of the science. This seems to be the lesson of a well-known passage in the *Phaedo* (97b–99d), in which Socrates tells of his disillusion with Anaxagoras (a philosopher of the previous generation who apparently had much influence upon Pericles) for having promised to explain all things using mind as his principle of explanation when in fact he gave a purely mechanical account of the heavenly bodies and all other things. In the *Symposium* the doctor Eryximachus tries to interpret the nature of love by way of medicine, but the spoofing of that science in the speech by Aristophanes directly following shows the weakness of that one-sided approach. In the *Republic* there is a kind of science (or even wisdom beyond science) belonging to the ruler, but this arises out of mastery of a carefully ordered *set* of the special sciences, coupled with much other training in dialectic and experience in practical applications: If there exists any political science at all, it is only because it is inclusive of the other sciences, not exclusive.

The upshot is that dialectic must be placed above the sciences, for it includes their methods, it grasps the principles and conclusions of all of them, it sets them in their proper relationships one to another, and it justifies them by tracing their hypotheses back to some unitary principle. Dialectic says in effect that to have any fully explicit scientific knowledge one must transcend it and see it whole, which implies seeing it from outside, which in turn implies the seeing of all reality.

Not only this, but much is to be gained from poetry, history, and the other substitutes for dialectic; yet the sciences taken by themselves tend to exclude the positive assets of each of these. What scientist as scientist can make use of poetry as poetry? What scientist could tolerate a sophist? Again we return to this point, that if any of these other deputies and impostors are to be properly understood and evaluated, assimilated and profited from, dialectic will be the one to make the assessment.

3. History. Plato offers many instances of history in many forms. Thus in the *Laws,* the three participants are careful to set their discussion of future plans in the context of past and current practices in their own states. In the *Republic,* there is frequent reference to the musical styles of Hellas, and reference also to the ways in which the mathematical sciences have been pursued. In the *Apology, Crito, Phaedo, Charmides, Symposium,* there is some biography and autobiography. The *Ion* makes abundant use of poets of the past, in particular Homer, and the *Menexenus* contains an account (though oddly distorted) of the history of Athens. The *Sophist* interrupts a lengthy argument to display a tightly classified list of previous philosophers who have had something to say about being. This last might give us a clue to the proper formulation of history, for the *Sophist,* as we have already pointed out, uses repeated dichotomies in its method, and the thumbnail history of philosophy is outlined in precisely the same way—the philosophers are divided into two camps, and these in turn are subdivided. History as a recounting of individual events must be invested with a kind of structure by a dialectician—some principle of separation or of collection of elements in a list. Otherwise history, for all its show, can teach us nothing, can give us no real knowledge, can lead us to no forms helping us to comprehend human life and action.

There is a further point: Even if it is given some formal

structure, even if a coherent method seems to have been at work on it, history falls short of giving us truth, because it plays up a succession of events in time, rather than a series of levels reaching, at the top, being itself. The closest that Plato ever comes to using history as a dialectical lesson complete in itself is in the *Critias*, but this is a very special case, for history is here interwoven with many other strands, the chief one being myth. Critias' account explains present circumstances in terms of a remote past which was better—the present is a deterioration from antiquity. But what constitutes the best possible age is laid down dogmatically, not dialectically.

4. Rhetoric. The *Phaedrus* makes it clear that when left to itself rhetoric is just as likely to lead the soul to error and grave moral fault as it is to lead to virtue; and that not only are professional and amateur rhetoricians (Lysias and Phaedrus, respectively) susceptible, but also the philosopher himself when he puts his philosophy aside for the moment. The *Gorgias* makes it clear that in spite of the fact that the rhetorician believes he has a greater control over other persons than has anyone else, his power is really quite limited. It is implied that, at bottom, only when the orator has knowledge can we concede that his is a power wielded by the soul rather than by mere circumstances upon which no one can depend. The *Crito* makes it clear that despite the strongest possible rhetorical plea from a suffering, supplicating heart, the common arguments of personal interest and safety must not be allowed to prevail against truth and the welfare of law and philosophy. The *Symposium* makes it clear that only when we praise a thing (love) actually knowing *what* it is, i.e., grasping its essence, and possessing the truth about it, do we avoid running into confusion and self-contradiction even if praise is our modest aim. The *Apology* makes it clear that the choice of ends must not be made or defended upon grounds of the attraction these ends may possess for us, and that the successful use of rational defense may in fact defeat the best and noblest purposes dominating our lives.

Rhetoric, like history, must be guided by dialectic, then, but the reasons are different. Rhetoric has to do with action, action springing from moral choice, so that lack of dialectical insight in rhetoric may lead to vice and shame;

history, on the other hand, has to do with our information about what has existed, and lack of dialectic here is a lack of insight into the patterns which are the only valid causal explanations of what has come to be. Rhetoric practiced by the everyday orator may be very effective in gaining its immediate purpose, such as voting down a measure or convicting a suspected criminal, but these purposes may turn out to be the ruin of hearer and speaker alike, if the ends of belief and action have not been carefully examined. It is its very unreliability as a moral weapon that makes rhetoric so dangerous to society, and the only control is not counter-rhetoric, which suffers of course from the same defect, but that other, much more deeply penetrating and self-conscious instrument of knowledge.

5. *Sophistic.* We have already said that sophistic and the sophists are treated very differently in the dialogues dominated by each of the six interlocutors, beginning with virtually total neglect in the *Parmenides* (where change and chance are disallowed and the reduction of all things to these would be proscribed). In the many Socratic dialogues there is a strong preoccupation, on the other hand, with sophistic methods, doctrines, and the men espousing these. If sophistry is an outright evil, one of the advantages of a Parmenidean dialectic would be that it steers clear of sophistic questions (however much its impartial examination of both sides of an assumption may resemble sophistic); the disadvantage is that sophistic is apparently not amenable to any dialectical analysis by Parmenides at all, thus will not be refuted by him. Exactly the opposite two points hold for Socrates, and it is therefore a measure both of weakness and strength that so many pages of the dialogues led by Socrates are occupied with comparison, alliance, extrication, contradiction, and even invective with reference to the sophists. The two methods, sophistic and Socratic dialectic, are alike in their using pairs of contrary terms such as justice and injustice, motion and rest; in their reduction of separate ideas; in their unwillingness in many cases to start from opinions held by the multitude; in their falling back upon myth when strict accounting is not profitable; in their readiness to call up lines of verse or wise saws. The two sets of teachings are allied in their emphasis upon the need for more trained intelligence in

public affairs, for more education and culture generally and for more connected argument in discourse. Socrates takes pains to divorce himself from the sophists in their habit of charging fees—large fees—for their instruction, from their willingness to make the worse appear the better part, and from their readiness to accept coincidental features of things as leading to knowledge. Socrates contradicts the sophists in their assertions that nature and law (or custom) form the two opposite bases of all human behavior and that when one cannot explain action by one, then one may, indeed must, use the other.

The truth is that to the many, Socrates appears indistinguishable from the sophists, either because he seems bad along with them, resembling those traveling salesmen of manufactured wisdom, or else because they seem good along with him, and appear genuinely to be cultivating arts useful to society and the gaining of wisdom. Socrates, on the other hand, views himself and the sophists as being worlds apart, not only in personal attitudes—he gains no outward personal advantage from his mission—but also in method. In him there is a surge of the intellect toward the upper reaches of knowledge and being, something with which none of the sophists are concerned. In him there is a moral earnestness of speech and practice which far outstrips their inch-deep sincerity. In him there are multitudes of distinctions which intertwine subtly, and are applied with a sureness and flexibility that makes the sophists appear hard and doctrinaire.

There is a paradox here: A Socratic philosophy, which is built around literally hundreds upon hundreds of distinctions, is not readily distinguished by other men who are its opponents. These antagonistic sophists profess what is at best a weak and mutilated theory of man and the state, in spite of their natural abilities, and they are largely ignorant of mathematics (at least in the higher mathematics of that day) and most of the other sciences, and are really only clever, nothing more, in keeping up with what ambitious men are doing to succeed in their city-states. If one may express it so, a Socrates needs another Socrates to see him in proper perspective; or, to phrase it in more abstract terms, the Socratic philosophy must be examined by the Socratic method itself in order that its nature may be fully manifest. Not all of the sophists, either historically or as presented by Plato, were men of exactly the same stripe; as we have already pointed out, Hippias is a polymath, with many arts and crafts on call (see the *Hippias Minor* 368b–369a), Prodicus is a quick man with synonyms (*Protagoras* 337a–c), Gorgias is apparently not only an eloquent speaker but an impressive teacher of rhetoric and its theory (*Gorgias* 447a–449b, *Phaedrus* 267a, etc.). Then there is Protagoras, the best and best-known of them all, with his political insights (he was lawmaker to the Athenian colony at Thurii in southern Italy), his literary erudition, his subtle legalisms. But if Socrates really were a sophist, then he was by all odds the greatest of them. On the other hand, *he* knew that he was *not* one.

6. Eristic. Most critics lump the sophists and the eristics together in the dialogues of Plato. There are many passages, however, in which the two are separated, in essence if not in person. Sophistic aims at instruction—of a sort; eristic aims at victory. Both are arts of words, but eristic is the pugilism of colloquy, and puffs up the victor at the expense of the vanquished. Socrates frequently has an audience, though he does not need one; the sophists evidently prefer some silent witnesses; but the eristics would languish without applause and the derisive laughter they engender when they have trapped some helpless boy. Socrates plays upon words, but only to decorate his discourse; the sophists pun and invent conceits based upon changing meanings to illustrate a point; the eristics play upon words as an essential part of their strategy. The sophists are relatively able, in their question-and-answer episodes, to change tack and alter their proofs or fend off an adversary coming at them from a new standpoint. (The ability of Socrates to do this because of the flexibility of his dialectic needs no comment. Not even in the instruction of the slave boy ignorant of geometry, *Meno* 82b–85b, do we feel that Socrates would be without resource were the boy to demand more and more explanations.) The eristics Dionysodorus and Euthydemus, for their part, have a thoroughly rehearsed program, a routine that they even boast about, though it is in truth but a weak caricature of the *Parmenides*.

Eristic, then, is argument for argument's sake, a battling for the mere love of fight, a war of words unrelated to truth and instruction or even to persuasion and belief. The

word-tricks—of which we find many witty examples in
the *Euthydemus*—are rooted in no real distinctions of
nature, thus separating it even further from dialectic than
is sophistic. Where the sophist alters words in an effort
to persuade the hearer to an end personally advantageous
to himself—to hell with the city at large!—the eristic com-
batant intends merely to humiliate and overcome his victim. But it should also be made plain that all three—
dialectic, sophistic, and eristic—are still bound to employ
the same *tactics* of method (e.g., dichotomy: e.g., the
division of mammals into male–female; trichotomy: e.g.,
a division into being, becoming, and nonbeing) except that
the words have different meanings in each of the three different arts.

7. *Myth.* This handful of substitutes for dialectic, substitutes which in spite of the fact that they each resemble
dialectic and contain bits and pieces of it incomplete and
confused, are not arranged in a single hierarchy. Thus we
do not flatly say that myth is higher or lower than history
or eristic. Myth is primarily a device of persuasion rather
than proof—it is a device that permits the speaker to
project a state of affairs which both he and his hearers
know does not factually exist, but which still suggests a
structural arrangement *similar to* one that the speaker is
pushing the hearer to accept. When the speaker is a man
of science and the hearer is at least conversant with the
sciences as an enlightened amateur, as Timaeus and Socrates are, respectively, then the myth takes on the character of scientific discourse, only excepting the fact that what
is a formal causal sequence is described *as if* it were a
temporal order (*Timaeus* 29d–47e), or what happens
within the soul is described *as if* it were a spatial movement (*Phaedo* 108c–114c). When, on the other hand, the
hearer is a speech-struck young man, as is Phaedrus, and
the talk is about the advantages and disadvantages of love,
then the myth by which Socrates explains the nature of
the soul in relation to ordered and disordered passion is
cast in a religious mold, the language is highly colorful,
and the analogies become much more remote—indeed
become more like consecutive metaphors, with the soul
taking on the quality of a chariot and winged horses
(*Phaedrus* 246a–d). Myth does not necessarily contradict
dialectic, but it runs the risk of becoming a delightful rest

from real philosophizing, and is less easily made firm in
interpretation. Because myth is cast in the form of long
speeches, the speaker cannot assure himself that he is
completely understood at every step; he must deliver his
goods in a cart, so to speak, and dump them all at once
upon his listener. For this reason, again, there is no check
upon and control over the mythmaker till after he is
finished with his tale.

The primary difference between the sophistic use of
myth and the Socratic is that in the former the myth is
given first, as in the *Protagoras*, where a myth is offered
as answer to the very first question, and by Socrates it is
ordinarily given last, after all the distinctions have been
made and all questions answered (*Phaedo, Gorgias, Republic*; the *Symposium* and the *Phaedrus* are rather different kinds of dialogues, being at least in part concerned
with the reform of rhetoric from within rhetoric itself.)

8. *Poetry.* The art of poetry (and its inspiration too,
for it possesses this as well) is easily associated with myth,
but it also has ties with science and the rest; Plato frequently quotes lines from the poets in support of scientific formulations (as when Homer and Hesiod are used
to buttress a perceptional theory of knowledge in the
Theaetetus), and he refers constantly to such lines when
the discussion turns to ethico-political questions. A myth
can be embodied in a poem, indeed it is a kind of poem,
with a movement of thought and a succession of images
close to the heart of poetry. Oddly enough, however, when
Plato is thinking primarily of what the poets *mean*, he
quotes at best no more than a line or a short passage; both
in the *Republic* (331e–336a) and in the *Protagoras* (338e–
347a) Simonides is cited, but at no great length, and the
stress is upon what an individual line could possibly
signify. In the *Ion*, the emphasis is upon whether the
rhapsode or the man of a particular art—charioteer, doctor, general—is better at interpreting passages of Homer
devoted to racing, healing, and warmaking, in that order.
The difficulty Plato finds with the poets is that the very
inspiration making them so admirable is a kind of irra-
tionality, or supervenes upon an irrational state, and thus
is not subject to dialectical checking and proving by the
poets themselves, and can only be examined from outside.
Poetry, unlike sophistic and eristic, aspires—one might

say *constantly* aspires—to an insight into true being; but it does not do so by reference to principles or by the use of the closest reasoning that dialectic commands. Consequently Plato finds a waywardness in poetry that brings him to condemn (on more metaphysical grounds) its inability to reach the very reality toward which it looks so hopefully, only to construct an imitation of an imitation of the forms which are, collectively, true being.

9. *Grammar.* The Greek word "*stoicheion*" meant both a letter (of the alphabet) and an element or simplest part of anything. Plato frequently uses the letters of the alphabet as points of analogy for philosophical propositions which he wishes to clarify. In the chief passage exemplifying this practice (*Sophist* 253a–259c), the Eleatic Stranger likens the "greatest classes," which are absolutely general notions predicable of all things, to letters which can form various combinations, though not entirely indifferently. Thus "being" can be used as a predicate for "same" ("the same exists") and of "other," of "motion" and of "rest" as well, but "motion" cannot be predicated of "rest." This, he remarks, is similar to the way some letters combine while others do not. On the other hand, there is no attempt on Plato's part to find a one-to-one correspondence between *specific* letters and the greatest classes; other philosophers who have attempted this have thought that a general alphabet of concepts could be manipulated in such fashion as to produce all possible philosophical truths and eliminate automatically those combinations that would be meaningless or self-contradicting.

Plato's admiration of grammar is cool and temperate. The sophist Prodicus makes several distinctions between near synonyms, but his suggestions, which are for interpreting a poem, are largely bypassed or even satirized (*Protagoras* 337a–342a). A species of grammatical analysis is carried on at length in the tortuous and almost eccentric *Cratylus*, a dialogue which like the rest in the corpus ultimately connects with all others, but which confines itself mainly to what may be called the appropriateness of names. Hermogenes holds that all names are conventionally applied to things, but is presented by Socrates with many counterinstances, while Cratylus, a follower of the philosopher Heraclitus, is convinced that all names naturally corre-

spond to the things they name. He too is refuted, mainly
with counter-instances, and the upshot is that we are unable to conclude *any* principle of exact correspondence
between the name as sound or mark and the name as
designating a thing. For this reason we must abandon hope
that grammar, in spite of the attractive analogies it bears
to dialectic, can in any detail furnish us with precise
answers to philosophic questions, except as these questions spring up in a context of dialectical debate on other
matters, and are dealt with individually. Letters combine,
words combine, but in the one case it is owing to rules
of pronunciation, in the other it is because of meanings
hopefully correspondent to the nature of things. In the
same way, a word reflects through its origin something of
the way things exist or are related, and so does a statement. But the former merely hints at it, and its history
can never make us certain, while the latter, if arrived at
dialectically, is secure because tested rather than established by a kind of etymological good fortune.

In summary, it is a mistake to think of these nine impostors—which in the hands of a Socrates or a Timaeus take
on authenticity—as being locked in nine blocks of Pentelicus
marble, hard-faced, with no interconnection between them.
There is much intermingling of each of these with almost
every other one, and of each of them in turn with dialectic,
so that *aspects* of myth are dialectical, or scientific, or historical, and so on. We find, moreover, that myth is explicitly paired off with science, with history, with poetry,
and so for the rest. The possibilities are large, but not
endless. Eristic and science have so little affinity for each
other that it is hard to find a place in the dialogues where
they are played in concert. There is no arbitrary or a
priori way of settling what combinations are justified,
hence the only recourse is in the actual study of the dialogues, in the dialectical rejection or transformation of them
all. But that would appear to be good news.

PLATONISM AND THE HISTORY OF WESTERN THOUGHT

SOONER OR later almost everyone writing an initiatory book on our philosopher feels that he must quote Alfred North Whitehead's famous remark, buried in the depths of the great but obscure *Process and Reality*:

> The safest characterization of the European philosophical tradition is that it consists of a series of footnotes to Plato. I do not mean [this sentence the historians usually leave out] the systematic scheme of thought which scholars have doubtfully extracted from his writings. I allude to the wealth of general ideas scattered through them. (p. 63)

In the rather informal way in which Dr. Whitehead meant this to be taken, it is no doubt true; and only when we come to examine countless instances which could confirm or disconfirm it, do we begin to see any limitations upon the dictum. Plato's effects upon Western civilization have been overwhelming, even though he is by no means the only mind, or even the only Greek philosophical mind, who has had much part in forming the subsequent discussion of philosophical and scientific problems. His own pupil, the mighty Aristotle (384–322 B.C.), has been the source and occasion of an amount of speculation no smaller, and the work of many other Greeks, maimed though it has been for us because of the loss of almost all their books, has given form and content to traditions of intellectual inquiry ever since. It is hard to think of Plato, however, with his blend of powers of observation and abstract reasoning, with his passion for the sciences and his equal passion for the arts, with his rare literary gifts, with his humane insight into the aspirations and degradations of men, as anything but a thinker unique.

Hence we ought not to conclude this little study with-

out a nod to some characteristic shapes that occidental
thought has taken, with reference to what may be called
its Platonic elements. Such a summary is perforce superficial in the extreme, and the reader is invited to fill out
these sketches with his own citations and analyses. We
may devote a paragraph or two—it should be a book or
two—to each of the topics already treated in his philosophy. Some remarks are directed to trends and thinkers of
long ago, some to thinkers of our time.

a. *God and Gods.* Plato's influence upon New Testa-
ment and all subsequent Christian doctrine has been argued
by many scholars. The Gospel of St. John, especially, with
its hierarchies, its dialectic of spirit and body, Word and
thing, was very likely written with the dialogues in mind,
or at least with intermediate interpreters of those dialogues
in mind. The substance of the ministry and passion of
Jesus belongs to the historical personage, of course; but
the peculiar character of its rendering in the hands of
John and Paul was probably affected in general outline by
Plato, their predecessor by nearly 500 years.

Beginning with Plotinus (A.D. 205–270) and St. Augustine (354–430), the Platonic dialectic becomes more
formal, less personal. Although the One of Plotinus is
neither the forms nor the demiurge of Plato, and the God
of Augustine is more awesome, more *total* than Plato's
god among gods, still the hierarchies that these two men
propose are not very different in form from those in the
Phaedrus, *Symposium*, *Ion*, and *Republic*. Plato is apparently the first man to try to prove the existence of God
(*Laws X*), and although Augustine uses a far different
proof, still the enterprise remains essentially the same.

The doctrine of the living, omnific, infinite God of
St. Augustine persisted essentially unchanged for almost
1,500 years in the writings of the Christian theologians—
some Jewish writers, such as Moses Maimonides, evidently
took over aspects of this theology—but even the challenge
to this during the past century or so has its antecedents
alike in Plato's readiness to challenge all our presumptions,
and more particularly in his expressed notion of the vain
struggles of the god against necessity, the arrogant intrac-
tability of matter that can never be made utterly to yield
to reason. The contrast of finite and infinite, a staple of
the religious reflections of Søren Kierkegaard, is an oppo-

sition endlessly treated in the Platonic dialogues. Consequently we may assume that the two versions of Christianity, the positive and the hesitant, can be seen as antithetic phases of what in their background was a single Platonic whole.

It is hardly necessary to add that the conception of a host of lesser divinities and demigods which we find in the *Timaeus, Republic, Phaedrus,* and elsewhere, is transmuted into the Christian doctrine of the angels, principalities, and powers, levels of goodness and semi-divine strength. In contemporary thinking, however, the heavens have become progressively depopulated, and doubt has climbed upward, denying first the angels and other divinities, until finally God himself has been declared dead. This does not mean that the issue is settled, but we should point out again that the struggle in the pulpits mirrors exactly the dilemmas which Plato's Socrates had to face, both within himself and in the court of his accusers.

b. *Cosmos and Animal.* The great world systems of the seventeenth century—those of Descartes, Spinoza, Newton, Leibniz, and others—heralded, in good part, a return from the Aristotelianism flowering in the later Middle Ages and early Renaissance to a more decisively Platonic view. This showed itself in their common emphasis upon a method that would bring the sciences to some kind of unity, and their effort to find a few simple principles in light of which one could explain the universe and its multifarious contents. Plato's atomism is joined with his theory of an active soul in the monadic centers of spiritual force that are forever associated with the name of Leibniz (1646–1716), and his atoms, deprived of their ability to develop spiritually, are again found in the "hard, massy particles that never wear" of Sir Isaac Newton (1642–1727).

The attempts of Hegel (1770–1831) and Schopenhauer (1788–1860) to exhibit the universe as an outgrowth of idea and of will, respectively, have their clear and acknowledged beginnings in Plato's cosmos, and much of the nineteenth-century speculation in biology reflected his notion of the uniqueness of the living organism—together with its irremovable attachment to the environment. Mechanism, a doctrine for which Herbert Spencer (1820–1903) was a leading spokesman, is an exaggeration of

Plato's account of the workings of necessity; a theory popularized by Hans Driesch (1867–1941) and certain embryologists, called vitalism, is a simplification of what Plato
says concerning the primacy of reason and soul.

In his biology, Plato attempted to relate the living body
first to the very great, the cosmos (also alive) and to the
very small, the atoms. He attempted, moreover, to relate
the organism here and now to the past of the species and
to the future, through what we would today call genetics.
Balanced against the first of these there is, of course,
Aristotle's approach, in which the connections to great and
small are less important than the discrimination of functions and the classification of parts and kinds of animals
performing these functions, and against the second a conception of genetics which is in large part made to revolve
about methods of reproduction. In such a distinguished
anatomist as the seventeenth-century William Harvey
(1578–1657), the Aristotelian ideal clearly prevails; and
Harvey's brilliant success with the vexed question of circulation has had a standing influence right through to our
day. On the other side, the interactions between inheritance and practice which Lamarck (and many neo-Lamarckians) noted are more Platonic in their affinities. As
we have just mentioned, mechanism and vitalism are both
rather one-sided versions of two doctrines that Plato sought
to integrate. A recent development in biological theory
which has its origins in Plato is that of Sir D'Arcy Thompson (1860–1948) and his many followers who have tried
to demonstrate that life forms are embodiments of mathematico-physical formulas.

The greater animal and the lesser animal are combined
in what A. N. Whitehead (1861–1947) calls his philosophy
of organism, in which eternal objects (such as the color
blue, etc.), answering roughly to Platonic forms, enter
("ingress") into actual occasions, which are the events of
our tangible, visible world that taken together make up
the sum-total of changing things. Each occasion is aware
of ("prehends") all others in the universe, which is therefore like a great animal all of whose parts have organic
relations to all other parts. Framing this gigantic system
of mutual dependencies, says Whitehead, are mathematical
laws. Whitehead repeatedly acknowledges his obligation to
Plato, and although his departures from his Greek progenitor are often striking, nevertheless he is one whose world

view has been of outstanding importance in reasserting the conception of a limited togetherness of all things that Plato tried to establish.

The popular debates in psychology and sociology nowadays include the question whether life has purpose, and this very Platonic query is answered on the one side by those holding that the universe is a lifeless assortment of particles and collections of particles, and on the other by those who cannot admit this. Up to a point, Plato was with the latter group, his declaration of rational ends in the universe being a foreshadowing of the doctrine, embraced by many scientists, that the universe is fairly hospitable, that it manifests living forms scattered here and there throughout its endless bulk, and that it would be foolish to say that this was all quite pointless and silly.

c. *Man's Soul.* For Plato the soul is essentially immortal. This does not mean that *all* of it is immortal—he specifically says that parts of it are not but that its intellectual operations which bind it fast to an ideal object, an object of knowledge, are undying. This has been part and parcel of the Christian faith virtually since its inception, and although not every Church Father has been equally convinced that it is easy to prove such immortality, the conviction that there is eternal life *itself* has animated the adherents to the faith. Man is a wayfarer upon this earth, his mortal life is very brief when compared with what is to come (and what may have been past), and what he learns but sketches in the details of what his soul has known long before he arrived here. Yet brief though this life may be, it is not morally insignificant, and exerts great weight in determining the soul's career, i.e., its rewards or punishments in the afterworld. . . . These propositions might be paraphrases from either several of the Christian Fathers or the *Phaedrus* and *Gorgias*.

For Plato the difference between a really good man and a really bad one is enormous, as great as in the Christian morality, though differently described; Socrates would doubtless have made out poorly in any church (except some small, heretical sects) before the twentieth century. But the Christian conception of man as god insofar as he puts aside earthly concerns and separates himself from his senses is in the main a Platonic one also, and gives point to the conviction that the reward of virtue, which is virtue itself, is an eternal one; all the other satisfactions are of the here and now, and many of these bring pain and misery in their train.

One interesting sidelight on the influence of Platonism in the twentieth century, especially in the United States, is the tremendous upsurge of enthusiasm for the art of astrology. Plato himself appeared to have had a mixed attitude toward this art, for on the one hand he thinks of man's soul as undergoing motions that both resemble and are affected by the motions of the heavenly bodies; but he is skeptical of being able to discover precisely what their effects upon the soul would be. The proponents of astrology nowadays base their conclusions upon at least two points that a philosopher such as Plato would be bound to make: that there are forces partly shaping human destiny and lying far beyond the human range of direct tangible experience, and these forces can scarcely be contravened. Whether Plato himself would have had the slightest respect for the very literal interpretations of these, and the calculations based upon them, remains a wholly different question.

d. *The Virtues.* The list of virtues that Plato offers his readers varies in number and composition from time to time, but for the most part it can be standardized as containing at least the familiar four—courage, temperance, wisdom, and justice. These four virtues, through the writings of Aristotle and Cicero (106–43 B.C.) are taken into the Neoplatonism of Plotinus and thence into Augustinism, where they become the "cardinal virtues" so important to the Middle Ages. St. Thomas Aquinas (1225–1274) subjects them, along with others suggested by Aristotle, to a searching analysis, weighing them one with another. Much later, they are taken into Protestant theology, but not, as a rule, intact: some one of them is usually stressed at the expense of the others, and often all four are placed well behind faith, hope, and charity in importance.

The vast number of psychological descriptions and remarks in the dialogues are borrowed and translated by Aristotle into a classification of passions and intellectual traits of the soul (in his *Rhetoric,* Book II, and *Nicomachean Ethics,* Book VI) and into a theory of friendship (VIII and IX of the *Ethics*), and these also find their way into the writings of St. Thomas and others in the thirteenth century. As common coin, though with peculiarities in each fresh minting, they are adopted by Descartes and Spinoza and Hobbes, and remnants are still to be found in the works of present-day psychologists, who may not always be fully conscious of their forebears.

In somewhat the way that St. Augustine's account of the virtues set a mold for the Middle Ages, so the new analysis of the virtues by Thomas Hobbes (1588–1679) became the type of much of the modern discussion. For Hobbes it is not the virtues themselves that become paramount, but the passions: fear, anger, etc., and it is little exaggeration to say that virtue and social values generally are a thin cover for a hot cauldron of emotions, many of which are in conflict with other emotions, and most of which are likely to put one man into conflict with others, unless there is a common power over all men to enforce a peace through fear. The virtues are understood in terms of the passions (e.g., courage is defined as aversion, with a forewarning of hurt or harm from some object, together with the hope of avoiding that hurt by resistance), and, quite the reverse of Plato and the medieval writers, the virtues in consequence become wholly secondary to those passions.

A still lesser importance is granted to the virtues in the work of Jeremy Bentham (1748–1832), an English social reformer and legal theorist who greatly expanded what he had seemingly borrowed from Plato's suggestion for a calculus of pleasures and pains (which we find in *Protagoras* 354a–355a), i.e., a way to estimate the relative strength of pleasurable and painful feelings as they cause, or result from, various kinds of activities. Thus the virtues would reduce merely to the estimation of probable effects from certain lines of action.

Bentham's calculus tended to reduce all men to the same level, by weighing all kinds of pleasures against all kinds of pains. The distinctions between faculties enjoying those pleasures or suffering those pains almost disappeared, hence the differences in men, so clearly dramatized by Plato, needed restoring. Arthur Schopenhauer and Friedrich Nietzsche (of whom more shortly) seemed ready to attempt this restoration, but Schopenhauer, at least, ended on a gloomy note that denial of one's nature is the best way to assert it. A German, he acknowledges Plato as one of his three great philosophic forebears (the other two being Immanuel Kant and the ancient Indian *Upanishads*), but he builds his entire system upon the primacy of the will. Because individual wills (which are expressions of a more general force· throughout nature) are in everlasting conflict, the best that we can do is to divert our attention to the timeless beauties of art and to thwart, if possible, the strength of our own will in the control of our actions. For Plato, the good comes from a turning of the intellect from sensuous and temporary objects to eternal things; for Schopenhauer, it is a "turning of the will" which, in denying itself, leads to a kind of salvation, if one may call a mere diminution of pains a salvation at all.

The more recent trends in ethical theory have in the main taken the shape of exhaustive studies of leading terms used in setting up standards of right and wrong. The so-called Oxford Analysts, powerful in many universities after World War II, have scrutinized the uses of the words "good," "wish," "need," "desire," and many other expressions, believing that by settling what these mean we can discover the "real" nature of good and evil and whatever is connected with them. This conviction that the philosophic task is performed with language recalls Plato's efforts, especially in the briefer dialogues, to arrive at satisfactory definitions of the virtues, though Plato also tried to move from there to the discussion of good acts themselves, good men, and finally goodness. For him, nouns and verbs and adjectives were but a first step.

e. *The Arts.* To Plato's way of thinking, one could arrange hierarchies of the arts, based upon their degrees of intellectual content, or again upon the kinds of advantage they afforded to their practitioners or to mankind at large. But the divisions in any one list, though sharp enough for the time being, are healed over by the other hierarchies, so that what is separated in one way become joined in another. So "music," or culture, lies well below mathematics for Plato as an intellectual discipline, and there is a split between them; but "music" is a good of the soul, along with mathematics, and both are split off from gymnastic, which trains the body. This is not always the way that philosophers since Plato have dealt with the complex interrelations of the arts. We find during the Middle Ages some hard-and-fast distinctions between the liberal and the servile arts, the arts, that is, of a freeman and those of an auxiliary or even a slave. In our own day we have had technological arts sharply divided from the humanistic ones, giving rise to the doctrine of the inevitable split between two cultures just as with the earlier there was a division between two social classes. On the other hand, the distinctions between kinds of arts and their effects in society have, although quite opposed to Plato in points of detail, remained in a general way much the same. His full-bodied respect for the arts has carried over, if not always by all of the people, at least by prominent groups of them. Today we are seeing a shift from trust to distrust of the technological disciplines, and perhaps this will soon be followed by a shift back, perhaps not. The fine arts come and go as objects of affection and even veneration—today we are admiring them for the wrong reasons, certainly for reasons different from those of the Middle Ages or the early Renaissance. Plato stated some of the reasons why we should admire them: they embody real beauty; they imitate (even if at some remove) the good or the real; they engage one's highest efforts. The career of our great cities proves, however, that we do not view these goals of art in the same way. Patrick Geddes and Lewis Mumford would say that we move from the early neopolis, with modest wants and attainments, through successive stages to metropolis where the art shows itself in the good measure and proportion of the city, to the final puffed-up, moribund megalopolis, in which the will to make something bigger loses its restraints, and our needs and satisfactions are in continual disproportion—the very antithesis of the rational planner's art.

Another topic is the political control over the arts. Plato's suggestion that certain types of music (in the narrower sense in which he sometimes uses the word) should be encouraged and certain others forbidden in the best state has not been followed, certainly not in our time; popular ragtime gave way to jazz, jazz to swing, swing to rock music, rock to acid rock, and beside harmonic novelties and rhythmic eccentricities all along the way we have gained new instruments, new levels of amplification, startling aural sensations. In literature and the theater, on the other hand, censorship, official or unofficial, has until lately been strong, and the morality of describing or showing the body and what pleases the body has been debated, endlessly, hotly, and not always fruitfully. The issue is at bottom a Platonic one: Does a certain subject matter in the imitative arts do good or harm to the state, and what action should the state now take to foster or prevent such artistic practices? Plato's answer is no simplistic one, and the multiple ratings of moral acceptability recently adopted by the motion picture industry are rather mist-enshrouded images of his complex conclusions.

f. *The State.* The complaint is often made that Plato's conception of the state at large is too tightly fixed, and it leaves little room for development, improvement, freedom. Plato has anticipated this criticism by carefully describing events and characters in everyday, real-life cities, giving them in their full context of the flux of passions and opinions and public praise and blame. It is well enough to say that Plato is the spiritual father of utopias written by Sir Thomas More in the sixteenth century, and by Tommaso Campanella and Francis Bacon in the early seventeenth, and by their successors in this kind of science fiction, but the fact is that he would consider all these as *images*, not dialectical analyses of government in its immediate relation to human character, and not descriptions getting at the heart of any societal processes.

A more pertinent charge is that Plato is a fascist, a charge balanced by an equally prevalent assertion that he is a communist. The accusations of his dictatorial tendencies attach to his proclivity for discovering principles that would closely regulate and perhaps control the city-state; and the other charges, making him a socialist of more or less extreme persuasion, stem from the fact that for Plato there was nothing especially sacred about private property or—in certain restricted contexts—the family. The limits of this authoritarianism and of this attack upon personal enterprise and possessions have already been marked out in our section on the state, and anyway the reader had best consult the *Republic IV–V* to make sure just what Plato was advocating. But the existence of the two different interpretations that are foisted upon the philosopher points either to his inconsistency or to his guarded subtlety; and if the present account is at all correct, then the latter is the right explanation.

At any rate Platonism (rather secondhand) enters as an ingredient in the thinking of St. Augustine with his two cities, one of God and the other of Satan; of those fourteenth-century writers who argued the questions revolving around the separation of state and papal authority over men; of Thomas Hobbes, who rebuilt the state upon a social contract rather reminiscent of one described in *Republic II*; of Jean-Jacques Rousseau (1712–1778), who distinguished the will of all, which the people want or think they want, from the general will, which is that course which would actually be best; of the framers of the Constitution of the United States, who desired to secure a more perfect union by means of a division of functions similar to one suggested in the *Laws* so many centuries before; of Hegel and his pupil Karl Marx (1818–1883), who set up a dialectic of social classes and economic functions having its inspiration in the *Republic* and *Laws,* and resolving the contrasts between opposed interests either by history (Hegel) or revolution (Marx). None of these men, of course, is a very good Platonist in the sense of trying to carry through the same involuted dialectic handled with such virtuosity by Plato himself. On the other hand, the resemblances between the overall dialectical structures of many of these men and Plato are fairly unmistakable (here I would go a trifle farther than Whitehead). Then, too, there are a host of particular points in each of these men that seem to reflect Platonic sources (here I would agree with Whitehead's assertion about the wealth of ideas in the Greek master).

The so-called welfare state of the past few decades, with its constant though frequently bumbling care for the livelihood of the people, is in some few respects like the Magnesian city described in the *Laws*. The great difference between the two, of course, is in point of size; to make a state work effectively, Plato would hold it to something we would call a large town or small city, whereas there is virtually no limit to expansion of most nations except what war has decreed. Plato's effort was to correlate civic benefits with civic obligations, but with our own urban and national gigantism this now seems impossible. With proliferation so rapid, even the most successful attempts at reform of social institutions barely hold to workable arrangements of the past.

g. *Education.* The historian who perversely attempted to deny Plato's overwhelming importance to the history of culture would probably be hardest put to prove his case when speaking of the theory of education. Quintilian (35–95), author of the *Institutes of Oratory*, which is primarily about the training of speakers, makes use of line after line of Plato's own reflections on the learning and employment of rhetoric. Medieval rhetoricians—and there were many, though their names are as a rule less prominent in our histories than those of the theologians—codified, or so they thought they were doing, the aims and devices distinguished in the *Gorgias* and *Phaedrus* and *Symposium*. Indeed the seven liberal arts (grammar, rhetoric, and dialectic or logic, and also arithmetic, geometry, astronomy, and music) can with a bit of ingenuity be teased out of the dialogues. Especially can the last four, the quadrivium, which is plainly derived from the five mathematical sciences of the *Republic VII*.

In the Renaissance even the irrepressible François Rabelais (1494?–1553) set up a program of learning very comprehensive in its intended effects upon the individual and society. In the sixteenth century Roger Ascham not only used the dialogue form on occasion, but also attempted to strengthen English education on principles explicitly referred back to Plato. He was not the only Englishman so inclined, for we find similar attempts to put teeth and what is nowadays called "relevance" into education both public and private in the extended writings of John Milton (1608–1674) and John Locke (1632–1704) in the seventeenth century, of J. S. Mill (1806–1873) and Herbert Spencer and Matthew Arnold (1822–1888) in the nineteenth century, and of Bertrand Russell (1872–1970) and Whitehead himself in the twentieth. Continental philosophers as well have busied themselves with revising Plato: Immanuel Kant, Rousseau, Kierkegaard, Schopenhauer, Nietzsche, and many more. Nor should we forget such Americans as William Torrey Harris (1835–1909), William James (1842–1910), and John Dewey (1859–1952), all three of them consciously dialecticians, and all three of them seeking for a way of integrating what can be communicated in words from outside with what is native, inborn in the mind.

In the history of thought, Plato's reputation has fared best as a philosopher of education. In the latter half of the twentieth century, the question plaguing all educators has been how to do justice to the very process that Socrates is made to exemplify so brilliantly, and yet take charge of the millions needing to participate in this. Socrates' method seems to require individual attention, penetrating insight, and many gifts of patient and inspired explanation and interrogation. Where does one get a chance to practice this? Perhaps in the best graduate colleges or tutorial systems, but certainly nowhere else. Consequently the educators have proposed that machines supplement live teachers, and do the drilling. This overlooks the fact that the drilling is not always a matter of bare repetition, which thus far is all that a computer can perform. On the other hand, computers are barely three decades old, and perhaps some day a little part of the Socratic ideal might be realized in them.

h. *Mathematics.* Mathematics differs from the other topics we have dealt with in being more cumulative. We get more and more metaphysical theories with the passing of the years, but they are in opposition to each other, while the elements, technics, and theorems of mathematics are added to and in spite of divergent interpretations seem to fit reasonably well into a new and more comprehensive whole. Hence the positive contributions of Plato to mathematical discipline itself grow smaller in perspective with the passing of time—the five regular solids have for long been viewed, and properly so, as covering only a very small patch of solid geometry. But Plato's conception of mathematical *method,* and its bearing upon the discovery of truth, is of greater value.

In the seventeenth century the pressures for a reform of science which had been building up since the fourteenth century, or thirteenth, if you include Roger Bacon (1210?– 1295), were responsible for breaking apart many older categories and proofs. What took their places is primarily a mathematical method, which we find in René Descartes (1596–1650) as the prototype for the attainment of clear and distinct ideas and then, these having been found, the drawing of necessary deductions in chains of reasoning; in Benedict Spinoza (1632–1677), for whom the geometrical order gave promise of demonstrating, as decisively as for lines, planes, and solids, the existence and essential nature of God, of man's body and mind, and the interweaving and superseding, one by another, of human emotions and virtues; in Gottfried Leibniz, who hoped by constructing an alphabet of clear ideas to be able to reach by irrefragable calculations the most indisputable

conclusions. It must be owned that David Hume (1711–
1776), with his view that geometry is an inaccurate science
because it distorts and departs from sensation, is an opponent of Plato's, but with Kant's theory that mathematical equations are universal, necessary, and thus independent of experience, and are furthermore models for all
scientific knowledge, we arrive back at a conviction that
resembles much of what Plato teaches of our inquiry into
numbers and figures.

Not long after Kant, Karl Friedrich Gauss (1777–1855),
Nicholas Lobachevsky (1793–1856), and others set a new
style in mathematical research by denying at least one
principle (concerning the possibility of drawing but one
line parallel to a given line from a point outside that given
line) which had been thought fundamental to the plane
geometry (and all the rest of the geometry, too) of Euclid
(about 300 B.C.), and indeed to all subsequent geometrical
reasoning. Euclid, probably a pupil of Plato's, incorporated
some Platonic and also some Aristotelian features in his
Elements. In any case, the denial of Euclidean geometry
opened the way for a host of new geometrical systems in
which the starting points were held as mere assumptions;
where Euclid took the surface on which the figures were
drawn to be rigid and homogeneous throughout, the nineteenth-century thinkers took their chances, so to speak,
with surfaces and indeed spaces of many shapes and properties, thus allowing their figures to be of more and more
kinds—not only flat triangles, but triangles whose lines
have positive curvature (as if drawn on a sphere) or even
negative curvature (as if drawn on a saddle), and so on.

For Plato, mathematics commences with arbitrary assumptions (e.g., unit, number, etc.), which he called hypotheses created by the power of understanding; higher
than this was reason, a faculty for going behind the
hypotheses and finding their strictly unitary bases, i.e.,
discovering their ultimate truth and unity. Most of the
nineteenth and early twentieth-century mathematics had
assumed that the very best we can hope for is hypotheses,
that one system of constructions and proofs is not better
than another except in point of consistency and convenience of formulation. Mathematics for David Hilbert (1862–
1943) is a game played with largely meaningless marks on
paper; mathematical theories, according to other formalists
and to such positivists as Rudolf Carnap (1891–1970),

are formulas which can be interpreted to fit as many diverse models as possible, so there can be no unique set of meanings to the terms of any formula; the right method of mathematical physics, according to Albert Einstein (1879–1955), is to set up explanations that are simply convenient and fruitful ways of accounting for our sensations but are not necessarily "true"—whatever that word might mean. The varieties of approach in different men resemble collectively the flexibility of Plato's dialectic, but the effort to attach number and extension to something ultimately real is lacking; and as we say, the diversified approaches are not the work of any one man, as they were with Plato, but of many, working independently and without much thought of harmonizing with others.

i. *Types of Cognition.* The primary teaching of the *Republic* (and several other dialogues) in regard to our modes of cognition is that science or knowledge is of the unchanging, or at any rate the unchanging aspects of that which changes, while belief or opinion relates to change, becoming. The early Christian Fathers, hopeful as they were to show that Scripture was the first and final resort of the human soul seeking truth, generally reversed this, putting faith or belief above reason or knowledge and then showing that faith is that which brings us to the understanding of fixed and eternal things: the trinity, the incarnation, immortality, and other matters. In the twelfth century some theologians began cautiously to reinstate reason as a way to Christian salvation, but the ultimate result of this, in the fourteenth, was to make reason supreme in all matters of direct awareness of things logical, physical, and ethical, and to make faith a kind of repository of ignorance and dilemma. In the seventeenth century, again, reason was often united with faith, so that in Descartes, for example, we could prove the existence of God, but only after our everyday beliefs had been ridded of nonsense by an act of reason that steadfastly refused to accept any product of hearsay and common opinion and relied instead on supposedly self-evident proposition: I think, therefore I am. In Spinoza what he calls intuition is the highest kind of cognition, and is primarily the knowledge of things self-caused, i.e., things which we cannot conceive of as not existing; but this knowledge is not to be had from reading or ordinary reasoning processes, only from the closest attention to the natures of things and the two attributes through which we conceive all things, namely thought and extension. The grasp of the divine nature, a nature which is self-caused but is in turn the cause of all other things, comes about only if we love God by an intellectual love, which at the same time seeks understanding of Him.

The status of reason vis-à-vis faith was also debated by an informal group of men who for want of a better name are nowadays almost always called the Cambridge Platonists, although they were nicknamed the Latitude-men in their own time. Mostly followers of Benjamin Whichcote (1609–1683), they included Henry More, Ralph Cudworth, Nathaniel Culverwel, and half a dozen others. In Whichcote's lectures and sermons there was a fervor, but it was a fervor with reason as its ground and inspiration. Reason is "the candle of the Lord," and must be used to vanquish both empiricism and superstition.

Immanuel Kant (1724–1804) in the next century alters this vocabulary and this conception to frame a philosophy in which understanding is restricted to objects that we may experience through our senses. Reason, which ordinarily seeks to speculate upon totalities that far transcend objects, totalities that we as finite selves with limited powers of sensation cannot possibly experience, is severely curtailed. Indeed reason, which must in effect bypass the senses in an effort to know reality, is restricted to knowledge of moral good and evil, which Kant thinks are real and absolute as principles of our actions. Religion is for the most part to be kept within the limits of our (moral) reason, though in point of fact some aspects of it are matters of faith not penetrated by our intellectual powers. (Reason, understanding, and sensation appeared on Plato's Divided Line, but with considerably different meanings, as a reading of the final portions of *Republic VI* will assure anyone.)

In Friedrich Nietzsche (1844–1900) we find a partial overturning of Platonic method and doctrine. Reason is no longer at the top of the hierarchy, or indeed any out-and-out cognitive faculty. Instead we have moral strength, courage, will, independence, as the guides not only of action but of knowledge as well. The work of reason is as suspect as the work of Christian faith, for both alike have placed restraining shackles upon force of individual character and have allied themselves with the interests and obligations of the slave, not the master. The world of t' ordinary "thinking man" is an insane world, and only by elevating ourselves to a stage where we can consistently choose that which is most difficult to do, even impossible to do, can we be certain of attaining a truly human stature. But that is at the same time superhuman.

In a very different direction a recent school which calls itself Phenomenology (its founder was Edmund Husserl, 1859–1938) has sought to confine the chief problems of philosophy to knowledge, and the chief problems of knowledge to a description of what actually happens in our perceiving of an object. A characteristic method of Husserl's was to rivet attention upon the act of perceiving the object as phenomenon, and provisionally remove from consideration the object itself and also any analytical thoughts that we might be entertaining concerning the object and its reality. This method, called "bracketing," reminds us of Plato in one respect, for the Platonic dialectic aimed always at focussing upon some one aspect of the world with utmost concentration and clarity; but it also departs from the equally strong Platonic conviction that the very clearness also depends upon a grasp of the whole context, or group of varied contexts, in which the subject of our attention can be shown to appear.

Ralph Waldo Emerson (1803–1882) represents yet another side of Platonism, this time tinged—some would say plastered—with romance. The insistence upon an over-soul, the need for self-analysis, the stress upon independent thinking, the subtle delineation of psychological types—these and other traits of Emerson's essays and journals are reminiscent of aspects of Plato's dialogues, though in Emerson the emphasis is upon the primacy of imagination and poetry and religion rather than the interlocking of these with sense-experience on one side and reason on the other.

We live in an age which generally speaking mistrusts reason, certainly mistrusts it if it is not closely bound to experience that will prevent it from becoming "speculation." Crystallized by John Dewey, the doctrine of the priority of experience has filtered to the totally inexperienced, who often look to this justification of "seeing for oneself" as a formula for doing what seems wholly natural, for living free—for unreflective experience merely for the sake of unreflective experience. This attitude, which represents a long move away from the actual teachings of Dewey, has in itself the great advantage of stripping away

shams along with rigid social conventions; and there is no
doubt a greater air of reality in one's thoughts and emotions if one can judge for oneself. On the other side,
it discards reason, also implanted in us by nature, and
whose exercise is—so Plato thought—the surest way, possibly the only sure way, of avoiding the confusions and
calamities of our hectic past.

j. *Ideas or Forms.* While there has been a little controversy
over almost everything Plato has ever dramatized, discussed, or described, including the famous hiccoughs in
the *Symposium,* still, some parts of his writings have been
much more the occasions for embittered polemics against
him or his interpreters than have others. The sections on
education have generally been allowed to pass, but Plato's
attitude toward the poets has for reasons not hard to supply
been attacked and defended, generally in terms rather wide
of the mark either way. What Plato has had to say about
forms is in this latter category: it has set brother historian
or commentator against brother, and often both against
Plato himself.

The history of logic and metaphysics, two disciplines
which Plato neither named nor separated from others
nor distinguished from each other, is shot through with
discussions of the ways in which it is possible, if at all,
for things universal to exist apart from things singular.
On all hands it has been agreed that the objects we touch
and see are in themselves singular; but apart from proper
names, which after all constitute but a small portion of
our language, we use terms of quite general designation.
If one may pin the original formulation of a problem upon
any one man, then we might look to a disciple of Plotinus
named Porphyry (232–304?), who composed what he took
to be an introduction essential to understanding the *Categories* of Aristotle. Porphyry places near the beginning
three famous questions:

> Now I shall not say anything concerning genera and
> species whether they exist or whether they are simply
> placed in the bare understanding, or whether existing
> they are corporeal or incorporeal, and whether they
> are separated from sensible things or are placed in
> the sensibles and in accord with them. Such questions

are very exalted and require great industry to inquire into them.

These genera and species are simply broad and narrow classes or universals, and although the three questions Porphyry asks concerning them are probably not closely pertinent to Aristotle's logic at all, still they exerted enormous weight during the early part of the Middle Ages, for among other things, if God is threefold in any sense, then He is a universal, and if universals should turn out to exist in bodies or even *be* such bodies, the whole of religion would be threatened. Those believing that universals are real over and above bodies were referred to as *realists,* those thinking that they are mere names were called *nominalists,* and those holding an intermediate position, that they are only thoughts entertained in the mind, were called *conceptualists.* No clear-cut and lasting victory was ever won by any side, though in the fourteenth century more of the ablest philosophers joined the nominalists. The bearing this all has upon Platonism is, of course, that the universals can (in a context such as that of many of the medieval discussions) be loosely identified with the forms of the *Republic, Phaedo, Phaedrus,* and other dialogues. (Later, when Plato's works became better known in the Western European Renaissance, this identification was actually made.)

The problem of the universals is raised differently every time it appears, and more than once it has been dismissed almost as soon as it has been raised, as for instance by David Hume who, writing in the eighteenth century, said:

A very material question has been started concerning abstract or general ideas, whether they be general or particular in the mind's conception of them. A great philosopher [George Berkeley, 1685–1753] has disputed the receiv'd opinion in this particular, and has asserted, that all general ideas are nothing but particular ones, annexed to a certain term, which gives them a more extensive signification, and makes them recall upon occasion other individuals, which are similar to them. As I look upon this to be one of the greatest and most valuable discoveries that has been made of late years in the republic of letters, I shall here endeavour to confirm it by some arguments, which I hope will put it beyond all doubt and controversy.

In the twentieth century the problem has been parceled out among the logicians, who by and large have quit talking about genera and species but who ever since George Boole (1815–1864) have had much to say about the existence of classes; among philosophers such as George Santayana (1863–1952), who posits a realm of essences; among the social psychologists, some of whom, like William McDougall (1871–1938), have suggested a "group mind" set over against the individual minds of persons in that group; among historians who follow Oswald Spengler (1880–1936), in thinking that each culture is a kind of entity in itself having a life—and a decline—of its own; among such sociologists as Vilfredo Pareto (1848–1923), who finds a list of "residues" left over, irreducible, after we have done away with fine language but which are common emotional denominators of all thinking; and among psychoanalysts such as C. G. Jung (1875–1961), who thinks of universal archetypes as underlying all the symbolism and other common behavioral manifestations of our mental-emotional life.

Because devices of persuasion of the masses have received so much suspicious attention in the past four decades, we have become highly sensitive to the use of universal expressions. Thus, "glittering generalities" is a term of disapproval, and indeed one need do little more than charge an opponent with using one of these in order to discredit him. By coincidence, we have in these same decades seen the decimation and even the disappearance of species after species of animal, owing to the befouling of earth and atmosphere, and this too has shaken the belief in any kind of type or form more permanent than the individual. At the moment, then, the existence of the species as anything more than a word is generally held up to doubt, if not to scorn.

k. *Truth and Being.* The discussion of the nature of truth has often, and over simply, been stated as the rivalry between two mutually exclusive theories. The correspondence theory holds that there are verbal propositions (or verbal judgments) that must correspond part for part with the facts they allege. Any given proposition, by this theory, could be true or it could be false, determinately. The coherence theory, on the other hand, speaks of truth as a development, not a property of an isolated proposition; truth emerges from a systematic framework which reflects the whole, and if we wish to speak correctly of a part of the universe, we can do so only if we somehow imply the remainder of all existent things. Determination is negation, i.e., we mark out what a thing is by contrasting it to what it is not, but truth must be positive. (A special case of this is the pragmatic theory, which holds that truth is added later to ideas, that no idea becomes true until it is shown to be workable in experience, that the test for an idea against its opposite is always to find which of the two is the more useful.)

Perhaps enough has already been said about Plato to indicate that this would be an unreal distinction to make in his philosophy, and that he puts each of these into practice and moreover combines each with the other (or two others, if you prefer). The subsequent history of philosophy, on the other hand, has seen many thinkers (Aristotle is distinctly *not* one of them, if he is read through carefully) of whom it is much easier to say that they adopt one or other of the theories. Thus St. Thomas Aquinas holds that truth is the adequation, the bringing to equality, of thing and understanding, whereas St. Augustine had thought of truth as the gradual unfolding of successive connected realizations in the mind of the individual; Christ, the Truth, says Augustine, teaches us within.

In the Renaissance, the doctrine of Francis Bacon (1561–1626) that knowledge is power colors the notion of truth: truth, when it is determined by inductive examination of instances similar and dissimilar to each other, is valued as a way of gaining control over nature. For Thomas Hobbes, on the other hand, truth is a property of speech, and is to be had when the predicate of a proposition signifies all that the subject signifies. In the next generation of philosophers this leads to the distinction between synthetic and analytic propositions, made in several ways, but generally amounting to this: that a synthetic proposition is one in which the predicate and subject are originally concepts independent of each other, while the analytic joins two terms of which the predicate is already implied in the subject, or, to put it differently, the subject is contained in the predicate. "Man poisons the atmosphere" is synthetic, while "Man is an animal" is obviously analytic, for it would be impossible to be a man without being an animal as well—animality is implied in man, though man is not implied in animal. For the next couple of centuries, and indeed throughout most of our own time, the problem of how we are able to frame these two kinds of propositions, and the related question of whether we can frame synthetic propositions that are universal and necessary (all analytic propositions are of that sort) are highly significant. In the philosophy of Kant, these are the keys to the broader question, What can I know? which together with What must I do? and What may I hope? is one of the three roots of all philosophic inquiry. In recent logic, Kant's distinctions are frequently pushed to one side, and very often what is left is a syntactic organization not of concepts but of arbitrarily assigned symbols.

Plato, as we have seen, sets up a range of meanings for both "being" and "becoming." He is also greatly concerned over what distinctions might exist or be communicated between the thing itself and the properties it may have, or the aspects it may wear, or the circumstances in which it finds itself. These two pairs of terms, "being" and "becoming," and "thing" and "property," are joined by a third, which distinguishes the nature of the thing itself, i.e., what it means to be that thing, from the question whether the thing actually exists. We know what a unicorn is, but does it exist anywhere? Can we say that it can have an "essence" without an "existence"? On occasion Plato joins "essence" with the forms, with being, with what can never change. On the other hand, the essence of certain things, such as this pencil, is precisely to change, to be used up.

The terms and their interrelations have concerned philosophers ever since. Aristotle treated them in a separate science, which he called first philosophy or wisdom and which his followers have termed metaphysics. In the Middle Ages the essence and existence of God were usually not treated in quite the same way as the essence and existence of transient things. Thus God's essence was held, as by St. Anselm (1033?–1109), to be His very existence, or put differently, the existence of God necessarily followed from

His essence. Others in a long list of critics opposed this with an argument that usually took this form: Even if I have a conception of a being whose existence is implied by its essence, this is no ground for supposing such a being to exist, and the question therefore of whether God really does exist is only elbowed back one little step. The seventeenth century, in many ways so eager to break with the past, consistently made use of these arguments current in the Middle Ages, and was content to push its more significant inquiries into quite different fields.

The main tenets of existentialism have been with us almost from the beginning of the history of philosophy, but have flowered vigorously in the past three or four decades, first on the Europen continent and then in the United States. The chief point of existentialism in all its myriad forms seems to lie in a reversal (probably not a conscious one) of Plato: existence takes precedence over essence, essences (particularly the essence of man) can change, in fact must change. What we are in the present is a sort of crystallization of the conditions of our actual existence; and man makes and remakes himself with every fresh decision. We are born into a situation permitting complete—and fearful—freedom to us, and the only real goods are our own commitments to belief and, of course, to action. This leaves the rest of the universe as rather less than indifferent; for many philosophers it is disgusting, nauseous. This is a kind of Platonism-in-reverse: the demiurge, we recall, made a cosmos having reason, and he made it as nearly perfect as he could. This confidence in the existence, let alone the goodwill, of a divine creator is hardly in style as we enter the last three decades of our own century, and in a way pessimism has replaced it—not universally, but in most of the articulate and popular movements. We cannot say that such a confidence necessarily declines only in hard times. The Middle Ages had seemingly boundless faith, and this seeped away in the Renaissance, when life took a better turn for nearly everyone. Consequently no one can predict what will happen to Plato's abiding though not obtrusive optimism.

l. and m. *Dialectic and Impostor Methods.* As if we had not already made enough indefensibly large jumps over the history of thought, we would need to make still more were we to embark upon the history of methods subsequent to Plato's own pioneering use and self-examination of the ways to philosophize.

Aristotle sought to restrict the term "dialectic" to knowledge merely based on probable premises, that was not really knowledge firsthand, but founded upon authority. The sciences as separate disciplines, each with its own subject matter, principles, and method, loom very large for Aristotle, so large in fact that it is impossible to disentangle them from the roster of sciences. History in Aristotle is relegated to a specific, but secondary, function.

The position of dialectic in the seven liberal arts of the Middle Ages is usually one that combines Plato's notion of a method able to attain truth with Aristotle's notion of its limited scope and devices. Eristic—which aims at victory solely for the satisfaction of winning—was not explicitly recommended in the Christian church teaching, although what has taken place behind closed doors has no doubt been at variance with approved principle. Sophistic was obviously the method of the heathen and the heretics, to be opposed by the light of truth in dialectic, the strength of authority, or (after the advent of the Inquisition in the thirteenth century) the heat of a fire. The Middle Ages is much more technically minded and empirical than is ordinarily supposed, at least after the rise of the church schools and universities in the twelfth and thirteenth centuries, respectively, and the sciences occupied an ever more prominent position in the scheme of human knowledge. But science was not, in general, conceived as merging with philosophy, and certainly not as a serious rival to it.

Dialectic in the early Renaissance turns from Plato's conception of a universal method by which to investigate all things and all shades of opinion to a distinctive, precise way of enumerating, interpreting, and classifying. Most of the outstanding thinkers of the seventeenth century write short books (or even mere chapters) on method, and these are aimed at directing or reforming mental habits. A hundred years later Kant equates dialectic with what he calls the logic of illusion; this mere appearance of knowledge arises when man oversteps the limits of what can be experienced through the senses, and begins to speculate upon the constitution of the world (or the self) as a whole, something which we can never apprehend sensuously. Dialectic ends in error, in self-contradiction and total frustration.

Not so, said G. W. F. Hegel, who tried to restore the dialectic to its original pinnacle as the highest activity of reason. No one since Plato had possessed this vision of a method not only most excellent but all-embracing. All being is nothing but the progress of the Idea taken first as it is in itself, then as externalized in a new manifestation in nature, and finally as it brings these two opposed phases together into a new unity. Being is restless, and forms itself into carefully linked modes of change. Thus Hegel.

The philosophy of Karl Marx is founded on a modified version of this restlessness, but here the dialectic centers more specifically upon the practical aspects of human life, and it is materialistic in the sense that it takes the purely physical and economic conditions as being prior to the cultural and spiritual aspirations of mankind. It has had a thousand variants, some of them taking a more dogmatic stance than Marx himself apparently intended, dogmatic, that is, in offering few alternative frames of reference or courses of action.

A severe opponent to Hegel is found in quite another kind of dialectician, Søren Kierkegaard (1813–1855), who wrote his master's thesis on Socratic irony and who, more than any other, followed Plato in being able to combine an interest in theory with the keenest observation of human psychological types. Many literary features of the dialogues are to be found in his work, even though Kierkegaard did not regularly employ the dialogic form, and although Kierkegaard's range of topics is considerably narrower than Plato's, being restricted chiefly to the question of what it means to be a Christian in Christendom, nevertheless it is to a man such as he that one must look for a revivified Platonic spirit. It is indeed harder to find Plato in the literal-minded historians and scholars, valuable though their digging and probing in the text has been for the reconstruction of details.

But the best place to become familiar with Plato is still the dialogues. They are individually jewels of philosophic analysis and speculation, and collectively they are a gigantic monument to the labors and insights of a great man, an extraordinary genius. At the end of *Seven Pillars of Wisdom*, T. E. Lawrence speaks of the broad scheme he himself had formed quite early in life for the remaking of a greater Arabia. Lawrence had much to do with the im-

plementing of parts of this plan—just how much is nowadays in dispute, but that is little to the point—and he concludes his long tale, with its crises and losses and heady
victories, by a reference to his projects for the future:
"Fantasies these will seem," he remarks, "to such as are
able to call my beginning an ordinary effort." Plato left
a plan for the instauration of all wisdom in his time, and
could well have trusted that we would never call his beginning an ordinary one.

PART TWO

SELECTED DIALOGUES

PRELIMINARY NOTE TO THE DIALOGUES

THE SELECTION of dialogues is arbitrary, but at least I have tried to make it representative. Two of them, the *Protagoras* and *Symposium*, are usually cited as the dramatic masterpieces of Plato, although philosophically they are of course much more than just that. The *Apology* can hardly be omitted from any collection, being a courageous, ringing declaration for philosophy and the search for truth in spite of conflicts that it may engender. The *Ion* is possibly the best dialogue with which to begin the reading of Plato, for it is very short, yet contains samples of the friendly irony associated with Socrates, also a tiny mythlike figure of speech to explain poetic inspiration, and it contains several pages of refutation by which Ion is finally shown the untenability of his view of himself and his calling. The *Timaeus* as a whole is probably unsatisfactory for the beginner in Plato, for it is quite difficult—everyone agrees with this estimate. Consequently we are including no more than the introductory section, which only hints at the difficult universal science that follows, but which is indispensable to the understanding of the *Critias*, a dialogue much more intimately connected to its predecessor than are most dialogues usually paired by tradition. The *Critias* is the easiest and most colorful of the dialogues not dominated by Socrates.

Joined (through the *Crito* as intermediary) with the *Apology* is the great *Phaedo*, a somber rendering of the last hours of Socrates in prison. The *Republic* must not be omitted, but it is too long to be printed in its entirety here, so two books which are central to its development of educational, moral, and political themes are included, together with a few pages essential to complete them.

The outlines that precede each dialogue are intended as

mere guideposts; they have no philosophic content in themselves, and they might be altered, perhaps to better effect. As outlines they are more full than most that have been offered in print, but simply to say, as most outlines do, that a dialogue has three parts, or four, or whatever, is to assist the reader very little over a rocky road. Much of the misunderstanding of Plato arises out of failure to discover the joints and their proper articulations, to change our metaphor. Longer, much longer, outlines have been made, indeed the present ones are for the most part condensations, but we have included only as much detail as seems necessary under the circumstances. If these points are in line, then it should be no great task to fill in the further details.

Incidentally, the reader will hopefully not feel irritated that the outlines in some cases use slightly different renderings of the Greek terms from those in the translated text. There is no one way of translating them all, and it may even help to bring out new meanings if one is to strike an average between two different versions.

Perhaps this is a good place to remind readers that the Stephanus numbers printed in the margins are regularly used for the references to Plato, similar to the chapter-and-verse citations of the Bible. Stephanus (or Henry Stephens, or Henri Estienne) divided each of the pages of his collected three-volume edition into five portions, lettered a, b, c, d, e. These letters have been removed from most editions of the Jowett translation, including this one, but it merely means that one must search a page for a reference rather than a fifth of a page.

Outline of the Ion

I. Introduction: possibility that Ion has an art (of exposition) (530a–532c)
   A. Ion has won a prize at Epidaurus and may win at Athens (530a–b)
   B. Socrates: I envy rhapsodes for adornment of body and being in company of fine poets, especially Homer; a rhapsode should understand poet's thought, and interpret it to audience (530b–c)

C. Ion: I speak of Homer better than anyone, and will display this to Socrates (530c–d)

D. Examination: Is Ion clever about Homer only? (531a–532c)

    1. subject matter of poets: one who speaks with art can expound where poets talk differently as well as the same (531a–b)

    2. manner: since Homer has same subjects as all other poets, they can be differentiated only in manner; but knowledge of better and knowledge of worse are in same person (531c–532b)

    3. Socrates' conclusion: Ion must be equally skilled in speaking of Homer and others (532b)

    4. Ion: but when other poets are talked about, I pay no attention, offer no remarks of value, and fall asleep—why? (532b–c)

II. Ion has no art (532c–542b)

A. [Rational] art of poetry is a whole (532c–533c)

    1. examples: painting, sculpture, flute playing, etc. (532e–533c)

    2. Ion: but I still speak of Homer well, though not of others—why? (533c)

B. Magnet and rings as an image of divine power (533c–536d)

    1. Muse (533c–e)

    2. poets (533e–535a)

    3. rhapsodes (535a–d)

    4. spectators (535d–e)

    5. summary and explanation (535e–536d)

C. Proof that this applies to Ion (536d–541e)

    1. Ion: I am not convinced that I am mad when speaking of Homer (536d)

    2. proof that Ion speaks without art but with inspiration (536e–542b)

        a. on what in Homer does Ion speak? On all things (536e)

        b. but Homer speaks of many things of which Ion has no knowledge (537a–539d)

            i. separation of charioteer from doctor (537a–c)

            ii. separation of other arts (537c–d)

            iii. conclusion: what we know by one art we cannot know by another (537d)

            iv. reason: arts are differentiated in terms of

ION

Socrates. Welcome, Ion. Are you from your native city of Ephesus?

Ion. No, Socrates; but from Epidaurus, where I attended the festival of Asclepius.

Soc. And do the Epidaurians have contests of rhapsodes at the festival?

Ion. O yes; and of all sorts of musical performers.

Soc. And were you one of the competitors—and did you succeed?

Ion. I obtained the first prize of all, Socrates.

Soc. Well done; and I hope you will do the same for us at the Panathenaea.

Ion. And I will, please heaven.

Soc. I often envy the profession of a rhapsode, Ion; for you have always to wear fine clothes, and to look as beautiful as you can is a part of your art. Then, again, you are obliged to be continually in the company of many good poets; and especially of Homer, who is the best and most divine of them; and to understand him, and not merely learn his words by rote, is a thing greatly to be envied. And no man can be a rhapsode who does not understand the meaning of the poet. For the rhapsode ought to interpret the mind of the poet to his hearers, but how can he interpret him well unless he knows what he means? All this is greatly to be envied.

Ion. Very true, Socrates; interpretation has certainly been the most laborious part of my art; and I believe myself able to speak about Homer better than any man; and that neither Metrodorus of Lampsacus, nor Stesimbrotus of Thasos, nor Glaucon, nor any one else who ever was, had as good ideas about Homer as I have, or as many.

Soc. I am glad to hear you say so, Ion; I see that you will not refuse to acquaint me with them.

Ion. Certainly, Socrates; and you really ought to hear how exquisitely I render Homer. I think that the Homeridae should give me a golden crown.

Soc. I shall take an opportunity of hearing your embellishments of him at some other time. But just now I should like to ask you a question: Does your art extend to Hesiod and Archilochus, or to Homer only?

531

Ion. To Homer only; he is in himself quite enough.

Soc. Are there any things about which Homer and Hesiod agree?

Ion. Yes; in my opinion there are a good many.

Soc. And you can interpret better what Homer says, or what Hesiod says, about these matters in which they agree?

Ion. I can interpret them equally well, Socrates, where they agree.

Soc. But what about matters in which they do not agree?—for example, about divination, of which both Homer and Hesiod have something to say—

Ion. Very true.

Soc. Would you or a good prophet be a better interpreter of what these two poets say about divination, not only when they agree, but when they disagree?

Ion. A prophet.

Soc. And if you were a prophet, would you be able to interpret them when they disagree as well as when they agree?

Ion. Clearly.

Soc. But how did you come to have this skill about Homer only, and not about Hesiod or the other poets? Does not Homer speak of the same themes which all other poets handle? Is not war his great argument? and does he not speak of human society and of intercourse of men, good and bad, skilled and unskilled, and of the gods conversing with one another and with mankind, and about what happens in heaven and in the world below, and the generations of gods and heroes? Are not these the themes of which Homer sings?

Ion. Very true, Socrates.

Soc. And do not the other poets sing of the same?

Ion. Yes, Socrates; but not in the same way as Homer.

Soc. What, in a worse way?

Ion. Yes, in a far worse.

Soc. And Homer in a better way?

Ion. He is incomparably better.

Soc. And yet surely, my dear friend Ion, in a discussion about arithmetic, where many people are speaking, and one speaks better than the rest, there is somebody who can judge which of them is the good speaker?

Ion. Yes.

Soc. And he who judges of the good will be the same as he who judges of the bad speakers?

Ion. The same.

Soc. And he will be the arithmetician?

Ion. Yes.

Soc. Well, and in discussions about the wholesomeness of food, when many persons are speaking, and one speaks better than the rest, will he who recognizes the better speaker be a different person from him who recognizes the worse, or the same?

Ion. Clearly the same.

Soc. And who is he, and what is his name?

Ion. The physician.

Soc. And speaking generally, in all discussions in which the subject is the same and many men are speaking, will not he who knows the good know the bad speaker also? For if he does not know the bad, neither will he know the good when the same topic is being discussed.

Ion. True.

Soc. Is not the same person skillful in both?

Ion. Yes.

Soc. And you say that Homer and the other poets, such as Hesiod and Archilochus, speak of the same things, although not in the same way; but the one speaks well and the other not so well?

Ion. Yes; and I am right in saying so.

Soc. And if you knew the good speaker, you would also know the inferior speakers to be inferior?

Ion. That is true.

Soc. Then, my dear friend, can I be mistaken in saying that Ion is equally skilled in Homer and in

532

other poets, since he himself acknowledges that the
same person will be a good judge of all those who
speak of the same things; and that almost all poets
do speak of the same things?

Ion. Why then, Socrates, do I lose attention and go
to sleep and have absolutely no ideas of the least
value, when any one speaks of any other poet; but
when Homer is mentioned, I wake up at once and am
all attention and have plenty to say?

Soc. The reason, my friend, is obvious. No one can
fail to see that you speak of Homer without any art
or knowledge. If you were able to speak of him by
rules of art, you would have been able to speak of all
other poets; for poetry is a whole.

Ion. Yes.

Soc. And when any one acquires any other art
as a whole, the same may be said of them. Would
you like me to explain my meaning, Ion?

Ion. Yes, indeed, Socrates; I very much wish that
you would: for I love to hear you wise men talk.

Soc. O that we were wise, Ion, and that you could
truly call us so; but you rhapsodes and actors, and
the poets whose verses you sing, are wise; whereas I
am a common man, who only speak the truth. For
consider what a very commonplace and trivial thing
is this which I have said—a thing which any man
might say: that when a man has acquired a knowledge of a whole art, the inquiry into good and bad
is one and the same. Let us consider this matter; is
not the art of painting a whole?

Ion. Yes.

Soc. And there are and have been many painters
good and bad?

Ion. Yes.

Soc. And did you ever know anyone who was skillful in pointing out the excellences and defects of
Polygnotus the son of Aglaophon, but incapable of   533
criticizing other painters; and when the work of any
other painter was produced, went to sleep and was at
a loss, and had no ideas; but when he had to give
his opinion about Polygnotus, or whoever the painter
might be, and about him only, woke up and was at-
tentive and had plenty to say?

Ion. No indeed, I have never known such a person.

Soc. Or did you ever know of anyone in sculpture, who was skillful in expounding the merits of Daedalus the son of Metion, or of Epeius the son of Panopeus, or of Theodorus the Samian, or of any individual sculptor; but when the works of sculptors in general were produced, was at a loss and went to sleep and had nothing to say?

Ion. No indeed; no more than the other.

Soc. And if I am not mistaken, you never met with anyone among flute players or harp players or singers to the harp or rhapsodes who was able to discourse of Olympus or Thamyras or Orpheus, or Phemius the rhapsode of Ithaca, but was at a loss when he came to speak of Ion of Ephesus, and had no notion of his merits or defects?

Ion. I cannot deny what you say, Socrates. Nevertheless I am conscious in my own self, and the world agrees with me in thinking that I do speak better and have more to say about Homer than any other man. But I do not speak equally well about others—tell me the reason of this.

Soc. I perceive, Ion; and I will proceed to explain to you what I imagine to be the reason of this. The gift which you possess of speaking excellently about Homer is not an art, but, as I was just saying, an inspiration; there is a divinity moving you, like that contained in the stone which Euripides calls a magnet, but which is commonly known as the stone of Heraclea. This stone not only attracts iron rings, but also imparts to them a similar power of attracting other rings; and sometimes you may see a number of pieces of iron and rings suspended from one another so as to form quite a long chain; and all of them derive their power of suspension from the original stone. In like manner the Muse first of all inspires men herself; and from these inspired persons a chain of other persons is suspended, who take the inspiration. For all good poets, epic as well as lyric, compose their beautiful poems not by art, but because they are inspired and possessed. And as the Corybantian revellers when they dance are not in their right mind, so the lyric poets are not in their right mind when they are composing their beautiful strains: but when falling under the power of music and meter they are

534

inspired and possessed; like Bacchic maidens who
draw milk and honey from the rivers when they are
under the influence of Dionysus but not when they
are in their right mind. And the soul of the lyric poet
does the same, as they themselves say; for they tell
us that they bring songs from honeyed fountains,
culling them out of the gardens and dells of the
Muses; they, like the bees, winging their way from
flower to flower. And this is true. For the poet is a
light and winged and holy thing, and there is no invention in him until he has been inspired and is out
of his senses, and the mind is no longer in him;
when he has not attained to this state, he is powerless
and is unable to utter his oracles. Many are the noble
words in which poets speak concerning the actions of
men; but like yourself when speaking about Homer,
they do not speak of them by any rules of art: they
are simply inspired to utter that to which the Muse
impels them, and that only; and when inspired, one
of them will make dithyrambs, another hymns of
praise, another choral strains, another epic or iambic
verses—and he who is good at one is not good at any
other kind of verse: for not by art does the poet sing,
but by power divine. Had he learned by rules of art,
he would have known how to speak not of one theme
only, but of all; and therefore God takes away the
minds of poets, and uses them as his ministers, as he
also uses diviners and holy prophets, in order that we
who hear them may know them to be speaking not of
themselves who utter these priceless words in a state
of unconsciousness, but that God himself is the
speaker, and that through them he is conversing with
us. And Tynnichus the Chalcidian affords a striking
instance of what I am saying: he wrote nothing that
anyone would care to remember but the famous
paean which is in everyone's mouth, one of the finest
poems ever written, simply an invention of the
Muses, as he himself says. For in this way the God
would seem to indicate to us and not allow us to
doubt that these beautiful poems are not human, or
the work of man, but divine and the work of God;
and that the poets are only the interpreters of the
gods by whom they are severally possessed. Was not
this the lesson which the God intended to teach

when by the mouth of the worst of poets he sang 535
the best of songs? Am I not right, Ion?

Ion. Yes, indeed, Socrates, I feel that you are; for
your words touch my soul, and I am persuaded that
good poets by a divine inspiration interpret the
things of the gods to us.

Soc. And you rhapsodists are the interpreters of
the poets?

Ion. There again you are right.

Soc. Then you are the interpreters of interpreters?

Ion. Precisely.

Soc. I wish you would frankly tell me, Ion, what
I am going to ask of you: When you produce the
greatest effect upon the audience in the recitation of
some striking passage, such as the apparition of Odysseus leaping forth on the floor, recognized by the
suitors and casting his arrows at his feet, or the description of Achilles rushing at Hector, or the sorrows of Andromache, Hecuba, or Priam—are you
in your right mind? Are you not carried out of yourself, and does not your soul in an ecstasy seem to be
among the persons or places of which you are speaking, whether they are in Ithaca or in Troy or whatever may be the scene of the poem?

Ion. That proof strikes home to me, Socrates. For
I must frankly confess that at the tale of pity my
eyes are filled with tears, and when I speak of hor-
rors, my hair stands on end and my heart throbs.

Soc. Well, Ion, and what are we to say of a man
who at a sacrifice or festival, when he is dressed in
holiday attire, and has golden crowns upon his head,
of which nobody has robbed him, appears weeping
or panic-stricken in the presence of more than twenty
thousand friendly faces, when there is no one despoil-
ing or wronging him;—is he in his right mind or is
he not?

Ion. No indeed, Socrates, I must say that, strictly
speaking, he is not in his right mind.

Soc. And are you aware that you produce similar
effects on most spectators?

Ion. Only too well; for I look down upon them
from the stage, and behold the various emotions of
pity, wonder, sternness, stamped upon their coun-
tenances when I am speaking; and I am obliged to

give my very best attention to them; for if I make them cry I myself shall laugh, and if I make them laugh I myself shall cry when the time of payment arrives.

Soc. Do you know that the spectator is the last of the rings which, as I am saying, receive the power of the original magnet from one another? The rhapsode like yourself and the actor are intermediate links, and the poet himself is the first of them. Through all these the God sways the souls of men in any direction which he pleases, and makes one man hang down from another. Thus there is a vast chain of dancers and masters and under-masters of choruses, who are suspended, as if from the stone, at the side of the rings which hang down from the Muse. And every poet has some Muse from whom he is suspended, and by whom he is said to be possessed, which is nearly the same thing; for he is taken hold of. And from these first rings, which are the poets, depend others, some deriving their inspiration from Orpheus, others from Musaeus; but the greater number are possessed and held by Homer. Of whom, Ion, you are one, and are possessed by Homer; and when any one repeats the words of another poet you go to sleep, and know not what to say; but when anyone recites a strain of Homer you wake up in a moment, and your soul leaps within you, and you have plenty to say; for not by art or knowledge about Homer do you say what you say, but by divine inspiration and by possession; just as the Corybantian revellers too have a quick perception of that strain only which is appropriated to the God by whom they are possessed, and have plenty of dances and words for that, but take no heed of any other. And you, Ion, when the name of Homer is mentioned have plenty to say, and have nothing to say of others. You ask, "Why is this?" The answer is that you praise Homer not by art but by divine inspiration.

Ion. That is good, Socrates; and yet I doubt whether you will ever have eloquence enough to persuade me that I praise Homer only when I am mad and possessed; and if you could hear me speak of him I am sure you would never think this to be the case.

Soc. I should like very much to hear you, but not

until you have answered a question which I have to ask. On what part of Homer do you speak well?—not surely about every part.

Ion. There is no part, Socrates, about which I do not speak well: of that I can assure you.

Soc. Surely not about things in Homer of which you have no knowledge?

Ion. And what is there in Homer of which I have no knowledge?

Soc. Why, does not Homer speak in many passages about arts? For example, about driving; if I can only remember the lines I will repeat them.

Ion. I remember, and will repeat them.

Soc. Tell me then, what Nestor says to Antilochus, his son, where he bids him be careful of the turn at the horse race in honor of Patroclus.

Ion. "Bend gently," he says, "in the polished chariot to the left of them, and urge the horse on the right hand with whip and voice; and slacken the rein. And when you are at the goal, let the left horse draw near, yet so that the nave of the well-wrought wheel may not even seem to touch the extremity; and avoid catching the stone."[1]

Soc. Enough. Now, Ion, will the charioteer or the physician be the better judge of the propriety of these lines?

Ion. The charioteer, clearly.

Soc. And will the reason be that this is his art, or will there be any other reason?

Ion. No, that will be the reason.

Soc. And every art is appointed by God to have knowledge of a certain work; for that which we know by the art of the pilot we do not know by the art of medicine?

Ion. Certainly not.

Soc. Nor do we know by the art of the carpenter that which we know by the art of medicine?

Ion. Certainly not.

Soc. And this is true of all the arts;—that which we know with one art we do not know with the other? But let me ask a prior question: You admit that there are differences of arts?

[1] Il. xxiii. 335.

Ion. Yes.

Soc. You would argue, as I should, that when one art is of one kind of knowledge and another of another, they are different?

Ion. Yes.

Soc. Yes, surely; for if the subject of knowledge were the same, there would be no meaning in saying that the arts were different—if they both gave the same knowledge. For example, I know that here are five fingers, and you know the same. And if I were to ask whether I and you became acquainted with this fact by the help of the same art of arithmetic, you would acknowledge that we did?

Ion. Yes.

Soc. Tell me, then, what I was intending to ask you—whether this holds universally? Must the same art have the same subject of knowledge, and different arts other subjects of knowledge?

538

Ion. That is my opinion, Socrates.

Soc. Then he who has no knowledge of a particular art will have no right judgment of the sayings and doings of that art?

Ion. Very true.

Soc. Then which will be a better judge of the lines which you were reciting from Homer, you or the charioteer?

Ion. the charioteer.

Soc. Why, yes, because you are a rhapsode and not a charioteer.

Ion. Yes.

Soc. And the art of the rhapsode is different from that of the charioteer?

Ion. Yes.

Soc. And if a different knowledge, then a knowledge of different matters?

Ion. True.

Soc. You know the passage in which Hecamede, the concubine of Nestor, is described as giving to the wounded Machaon a posset, as he says,

"Made with Pramnian wine; and she grated cheese of goat's milk with a grater of bronze, and at his side placed an onion which gives a relish to drink."[2]

---

[2] Il. xi. 638, 630.

Now would you say that the art of the rhapsode or the art of medicine was better able to judge of the propriety of these lines?

Ion. The art of medicine.

Soc. And when Homer says,

"And she descended into the deep like a leaden plummet, which, set in the horn of ox that ranges in the fields, rushes along carrying death among the ravenous fishes—"[3]

will the art of the fisherman or of the rhapsode be better able to judge whether these lines are rightly expressed or not?

Ion. Clearly, Socrates, the art of the fisherman.

Soc. Come now, suppose that you were to say to me: "Since you, Socrates, are able to assign different passages in Homer to their corresponding arts, I wish that you would tell me what are the passages of which the excellence ought to be judged by the prophet and prophetic art"; and you will see how readily and truly I shall answer you. For there are many such passages, particulary in the *Odyssey*; as for example, the passage in which Theoclymenus the prophet of the house of Melampus says to the suitors:—

"Wretched men! what is happening to you? Your   539
heads and your faces and your limbs underneath are shrouded in night; and the voice of lamentation bursts forth, and your cheeks are wet with tears. And the vestibule is full, and the court is full, of ghosts descending into the darkness of Erebus, and the sun has perished out of heaven, and an evil mist is spread abroad."[4]

And there are many such passages in the *Iliad* also; as for example in the description of the battle near the rampart, where he says:

"As they were eager to pass the ditch, there came to them an omen: a soaring eagle, holding back the people on the left, bore a huge bloody dragon in his talons, still living and panting; nor had he yet resigned the strife, for he bent back and smote the bird which carried him on the breast by the neck, and he in

[3] Il. xxiv. 80.
[4] Od. xx. 351.

pain let him fall from him to the ground into the midst of the multitude. And the eagle, with a cry, was borne afar on the wings of the wind."[5]

These are the sort of things which I should say that the prophet ought to consider and determine.

Ion. And you are quite right, Socrates, in saying so.

Soc. Yes, Ion, and you are right also. And as I have selected from the *Iliad* and *Odyssey* for you passages which describe the office of the prophet and the physician and the fisherman, do you, who know Homer so much better than I do, Ion, select for me passages which relate to the rhapsode and the rhapsode's art, and which the rhapsode ought to examine and judge of better than other men.

Ion. All passages, I should say, Socrates.

Soc. Not all, Ion, surely. Have you already forgotten what you were saying? A rhapsode ought to have a better memory.

Ion. Why, what am I forgetting?

Soc. Do you not remember that you declared the art of the rhapsode to be different from the art of the charioteer?

Ion. Yes, I remember.

Soc. And you admitted that being different they would have different subjects of knowledge?

Ion. Yes.

Soc. Then upon your own showing the rhapsode, and the art of the rhapsode, will not know everything?

Ion. I should exclude certain things, Socrates.

Soc. You mean to say that you would exclude pretty much the subjects of the other arts. As he does not know all of them, which of them will he know?

Ion. He will know what a man and what a woman ought to say, and what a freeman and what a slave ought to say, and what a ruler and what a subject.

Soc. Do you mean that a rhapsode will know better than the pilot what the ruler of a sea-tossed vessel ought to say?

Ion. No; the pilot will know best.

Soc. Or will the rhapsode know better than the physician what the ruler of a sick man ought to say?

Ion. He will not.

540

[5] Il. xii. 200.

Soc. But he will know what a slave ought to say?

Ion. Yes.

Soc. Suppose the slave to be a cowherd; the rhapsode will know better than the cowherd what he ought to say in order to soothe the infuriated cows?

Ion. No, he will not.

Soc. But he will know what a spinning-woman ought to say about the working of wool?

Ion. No.

Soc. At any rate he will know what a general ought to say when exhorting his soldiers?

Ion. Yes, that is the sort of thing which the rhapsode will be sure to know.

Soc. Well, but is the art of the rhapsode the art of the general?

Ion. I am sure that I should know what a general ought to say.

Soc. Why, yes, Ion, because you may possibly have a knowledge of the art of the general as well as of the rhapsode; and you may also have a knowledge of horsemanship as well as of the lyre: and then you would know when horses were well or ill managed. But suppose I were to ask you: By the help of which art, Ion, do you know whether horses are well managed, by your skill as a horseman or as a performer on the lyre—what would you answer?

Ion. I should rely, by my skill as a horseman.

Soc. And if you judged of performers on the lyre, you would admit that you judged of them as a performer on the lyre, and not as a horseman?

Ion. Yes.

Soc. And in judging of the general's art, do you judge of it as a general or a rhapsode?

Ion. To me there appears to be no difference between them.

Soc. What do you mean? Do you mean to say that the art of the rhapsode and of the general is the same? 541

Ion. Yes, one and the same.

Soc. Then he who is a good rhapsode is also a good general?

Ion. Certainly, Socrates.

Soc. And he who is a good general is also a good rhapsode?

Ion. No; I do not say that.

Soc. But you do say that he who is a good rhapsode is also a good general.

Ion. Certainly.

Soc. And you are the best of Hellenic rhapsodes?

Ion. Far the best, Socrates.

Soc. And are you the best general, Ion?

Ion. To be sure, Socrates; and Homer was my master.

Soc. But then, Ion, what in the name of goodness can be the reason why you, who are the best of generals as well as the best of rhapsodes in all Hellas, go about as a rhapsode when you might be a general? Do you think that the Hellenes want a rhapsode with his golden crown, and do not want a general?

Ion. Why, Socrates, the reason is, that my countrymen, the Ephesians, are the servants and soldiers of Athens, and do not need a general; and you and Sparta are not likely to have me, for you think that you have enough generals of your own.

Soc. My good Ion, did you never hear of Apollodorus of Cyzicus?

Ion. Who may he be?

Soc. One who, though a foreigner, has often been chosen their general by the Athenians; and there is Phanosthenes of Andros, and Heraclides of Clazomenae, whom they have also appointed to the command of their armies and to other offices, although aliens, after they had shown their merit. And will they not choose Ion the Ephesian to be their general, and honor him, if he prove himself worthy? Were not the Ephesians originally Athenians, and Ephesus is no mean city? But, indeed, Ion, if you are correct in saying that by art and knowledge you are able to praise Homer, you do not deal fairly with me, and after all your professions of knowing many glorious things about Homer, and promises that you would exhibit them, you are only a deceiver, and so far from exhibiting the art of which you are a master, will not, even after my repeated entreaties, explain to me the nature of it. You have literally as many forms as Proteus; and now you go all manner of ways, twisting and turning, and, like Proteus, become all manner of people at once, and at last slip away from me in the disguise of a general, in order that you may escape exhibiting your Homeric lore. And if you have art, then, as I was saying, in falsifying your promise that you would exhibit Homer, you are not dealing fairly with me. But if, as I believe, you have no art, but speak all these beautiful words about Homer unconsciouly under his inspiring influence, then I acquit you of dishonesty, and shall only say that you are inspired. Which do you prefer to be thought, dishonest or inspired?

Ion. There is a great difference, Socrates, between the two alternatives; and inspiration is by far the nobler.

Soc. Then, Ion, I shall assume the nobler alternative; and attribute to you in your praises of Homer inspiration, and not art.

Outline of the Protagoras

I. Frame narrative: Socrates, instead of chasing Alcibiades, has been seeing Protagoras, who is a foreigner and an object of admiration and affection; he is the wisest of living men. The wiser is the fairer (309a–310a)

II. Principal narrative (310a–362a)

  A. Preliminary account (310a–316b)

    1. the news: Protagoras has come to town; it is a rare event, and Hippocrates is excited (310a–d)

    2. Hippocrates expects to become wise, if he pays and makes friends with Protagoras, the most accomplished of speakers. Protagoras lodges with Callias, a rich young man (310d–311a)

    3. what is Protagoras, and what will he make of Hippocrates: a sophist, a wholesaler or retailer of food for the soul (311a–314c)

    4. Slave at Callias' house door is told that Socrates and Hippocrates are not sophists (314c–e)

    5. description of Protagoras, the other sophists, and listeners, most of whom are foreigners (314e–316b)

  B. Protagoras on the nature of goodness (316b–328d)

    1. Hippocrates has native ability, and aspires to political eminence, hoping to achieve this through conversation with Protagoras (316b–c)

    2. the art of the sophist is of great antiquity, but was formerly disguised as poetry, prophecy, gymnastic, music. But Protagoras acknowledges himself to be a sophist, for running away is folly to him. Protagoras would therefore rather speak about his profession before the company (316d–317e)

    3. effect of Protagoras upon a pupil (317e–319a)

      a. Hippocrates: what will happen if I associate with Protagoras?—You will be a better man each day (317e–318b)

      b. Socrates: analogies between Zeuxippus, Orthagoras, Protagoras; association with him makes one better in what? (318b–d)

      c. Protagoras: to have prudence in private and public affairs; ordering his own house, and speaking and acting for the best in the state.

Thus I teach the art of politics, and make men good citizens. I have a noble art (318d–319a)

4. Socrates: but can the art of politics be taught? (319a–320c)

   a. analogies between building, shipbuilding, politics: this sort of knowledge cannot be taught (319a–e)

   b. the same thing holds true of individuals such as Pericles and his sons. What is the answer? (319e–320c)

5. Protagoras' reply (320c–328d)

   a. Protagoras arbitrarily chooses to give a part of his answer as a myth (320c–322c)

      i. natural protection supplied to animals by Epimetheus (Afterthought) (320d–321c)

      ii. mechanical arts and fire supplied to men by Prometheus (Forethought) (321c–322a)

      iii. reverence and justice supplied to all men by Zeus (322a–c)

   b. men who confess dishonesty are thought mad but men who confess lack of skill are not. People think any man must have some degree of honesty (322d–323c)

   c. people do not conceive honesty to be given by nature, or to grow spontaneously, but to be a thing which may be taught. We do not punish those ugly because good and evil are the work of nature and chance; but if a man lacks qualities attained through study, exercise, and teaching he is punished; mankind thinks virtue can be acquired, and tries to deter men from future wrongdoing (323c–324d)

   d. if there is one civic virtue, it is strange that good men do not teach it to their sons (324d–328d)

      i. family, teachers, and laws instill virtue into young

      ii. children of the great turn out badly because virtue is not any man's private possession. If flute-playing were common, sons of good flute players would be no better than sons of bad ones. All men are teachers of the virtues, each according to his ability

C. Unity of the virtues (328d–334c)
   1. Socrates: is virtue one whole, of which justice and
       temperance and holiness or piety are parts, or are
       these only the names of one and the same thing?
       (328d–329d)
   2. Protagoras: the virtuous qualities are parts of a
       whole, as the parts of a face are related to the
       face as a whole (329d–e)
   3. Socrates' examination of this (329e–333b)
       a. the parts are independent of one another (329e)
       b. courage and wisdom are also parts; wisdom is
           the noblest part (329e–330a)
       c. the parts differ in their functions (330a–b)
       d. justice is a thing, and is itself just; the same is
           true of holiness (330b–d)
       e. if justice is not like holiness, it is unholy, and
           vice versa; in some point of view everything is
           like everything else; yet things alike in some
           respect should not be called alike altogether
           (330d–331e)
       f. but what is done in the same manner is done
           in an opposite manner by the opposite. Every
           opposite has but one opposite (331e–332d)
       g. summary of previous argument, showing contra-
           diction: folly appears to be opposite to both
           wisdom and temperance, hence temperance and
           wisdom appear to be the same, as before justice
           and holiness appeared nearly the same (332d–
           333b)
   4. continuation of the argument (333b–334c)
       a. some men are temperate but unjust. Temperance
           is good sense, i.e., good counsel in committing
           injustice if one succeeds (333b–e)
       b. goods are both expedient and inexpedient for
           man and for things. Goods are all relative
           (333e–334c)
D. Character of discussion (334c–348c)
   1. dialectical form of the debate: Protagoras makes
       speeches too long for Socrates to remember but
       objects to speaking more briefly. Socrates is about
       to leave (334c–335c)
   2. protestations by the group (335c–338e)
       a. Callias: hearing Socrates and Protagoras debate
           is a pleasure (335c)

E. Resumption of argument, whether virtue can be
   taught (348c–360e)
   1. recapitulation (348c–349d)
      a. summary of character of Protagoras (348c–
         349b)
      b. summary of earlier argument (349b–d)
   2. criticism of this view (349d–350c)
      a. courageous are bold and impetuous
      b. all virtue is good, it is the whole
      c. but some men, like fighters and divers, act boldly
         through wisdom, others through madness
   3. objection by Protagoras and preliminary reply; re-
      lations between courage and wisdom (350c–352d)
      a. objection by Protagoras: all courage is boldness,
         but not all boldness is courage, which comes
         from constitution and nurture of soul; analogy
         with power and strength (350c–351b)
      b. preliminary reply (351b–352d)
         i. Socrates: men living well live pleasantly,
            those living badly unpleasantly
         ii. Protagoras: some pleasant things are not
             good, some unpleasant things are not bad,
             and some are indifferent
         iii. Socrates: but is not pleasure itself good?
   4. reexamination, in light of opinion of the many that
      knowledge is weak, and that a man is ruled by pas-
      sion, pleasure, pain, erotic desire (352d–358a)
      a. Protagoras' view that wisdom is the highest is
         not agreed to by the many, who must be con-
         sidered (352d–e)
      b. Socrates' reply to the many (352e–354e)
         i. the pleasures cause diseases and poverty and
            pains later on
         ii. some pains later result in health and other
             goods, hence we pursue pleasures as goods
             and shun pains
         iii. even lesser pleasures are thought evil if
              if they rob us of greater ones
      c. objection and reply: why Socrates speaks at such
         length (354e–358a)
         i. to know what is meant by "overcome by
            pleasure" is difficult, and on this all our
            conclusions rest

ii. if one can live pleasantly, without pain, it is absurd to say that a man does evil knowingly, when he might abstain, simply because he is driven by pleasures

iii. if we reduce terms to good and evil, the absurdity becomes clear of saying a man cannot do evil because he is overcome by good. The good is unworthy

iv. but in what sense is the good unworthy of the bad, or the bad of the good?—When one is greater and the other smaller. Hence "being overcome" means getting greater evil in exchange for lesser good

v. we now add pleasant and painful: what unworthiness can there be in pleasure as against pain, except in proportions?

vi. objection and reply: the immediately pleasant is different from the subsequently pleasant or painful.—But only in pleasure and pain; we can weigh the pleasant against pleasant, and prefer the greater

vii. but distant things appear smaller to us, and we judge by appearances. We need an art of measurement, as against appearances, and this art is knowledge, the salvation of life. It chooses between the more and the fewer, the greater and lesser, the nearer and remoter

viii. the man overcome is not overcome by pleasure but by ignorance, and the many do not gain knowledge, even from the sophists

5. appraisal of problem by three sophists (358a–359a)
   a. summary (358a–b)
   b. new relations established between virtue and knowledge (358b–359a)
      i. all actions tending to make life painless and pleasant are honorable and useful
      ii. nobody does anything thinking that some other thing would be better and also attainable
      iii. inferiority of a man to himself is ignorance, superiority of a man to himself is wisdom

     iv. ignorance is false opinion and being deceived about important matters

     v. hence no man voluntarily pursues an evil, or the greater of two evils

     vi. fear or terror is expectation of evil. A man does not pursue what he fears, unless compelled

6. revision by Socrates and Protagoras of the formulation of argument about courage (359a–360e)

   a. summary (359a–b)

   b. four respects in which courage can be viewed (359c–360e)

     i. *toward what*: the courageous do not go to meet dangers which they consider dangers, since to be overcome by oneself makes men rush into dangers, and this is ignorance. Courageous man and coward both go to meet that about which they are confident, hence meet the same things. If courageous man goes to battle while coward does not, it is because battle is honorable and good and pleasant

     ii. *what sort of men*: the courageous man goes to meet what is better, pleasanter, and nobler

     iii. *with what feeling*: courageous man has neither base fear nor base confidence, while coward has both

     iv. *causes of feeling*: these base fears and confidence originate from ignorance and lack of instruction, and cowards act from ignorance of what is and what is not dangerous. So men cannot be ignorant and courageous at the same time

F. Conclusion (360e–362a)

   1. summary of the argument: it has been necessary to ascertain the nature and relations of virtue in order to know whether virtue can be taught. Socrates and Protagoras have worked around to opposite positions

   a. Socrates began by assuming virtue cannot be taught, and now proves that all virtues are knowledge, hence can be taught

   b. Protagoras started by saying virtue can be

taught, but now insists virtue is other than
knowledge, hence cannot be taught
2. Socrates prefers Prometheus to Epimetheus
3. Protagoras: Socrates will be eminent in philosophy.
The argument should be resumed later

PROTAGORAS

SOCRATES	PROTAGORAS
HIPPOCRATES	HIPPIAS
ALCIBIADES	PRODICUS
CRITIAS	CALLIAS

Companion. Where do you come from, Socrates? And yet I need hardly ask the question, for I know that you have been in chase of the fair Alcibiades. I saw him the day before yesterday; and he had got a beard like a man—and he is a man, as I may tell you in your ear. But I thought that he was still very charming.

Soc. What of his beard? Are you not of Homer's opinion, who says[1] "Youth is most charming when the beard first appears"? And that is now the charm of Alcibiades.

Com. Well, and how do matters proceed? Have you been visiting him, and was he gracious to you?

Soc. Yes, I thought that he was very gracious; and especially today, for I have just come from him, and he has been helping me in an argument. But shall I tell you a strange thing? I paid no attention to him, and several times I quite forgot that he was present.

Com. What is the meaning of this? Has anything happened between you and him? For surely you cannot have discovered a fairer love than he is; certainly not in this city of Athens.

Soc. Yes, much fairer.

Com. What do you mean—a citizen or a foreigner?

Soc. A foreigner.

Com. Of what country?

[1] Il. xxiv. 348.

Soc. Of Abdera.

Com. And is this stranger really in your opinion a fairer love than the son of Cleinias?

Soc. And is not the wiser always the fairer, sweet friend?

Com. But have you really met, Socrates, with some wise one?

Soc. Say rather, with the wisest of all living men, if you are willing to accord that title to Protagoras.

Com. What! Is Protagoras in Athens?

Soc. Yes; he has been here two days.

Com. And do you just come from an interview with him?

Soc. Yes; and I have heard and said many things. 310

Com. Then, if you have no engagement, suppose that you sit down and tell me what passed, and my attendant here shall give up his place to you.

Soc. To be sure; and I shall be grateful to you for listening.

Com. Thank you, too, for telling us.

Soc. That is thank you twice over. Listen then:—

Last night, or rather very early this morning, Hippocrates, the son of Apollodorus and the brother of Phason, gave a tremendous thump with his staff at my door; someone opened to him, and he came rushing in and bawled out: Socrates, are you awake or asleep?

I knew his voice, and said: Hippocrates, is that you? and do you bring any news?

Good news, he said; nothing but good.

Delightful, I said; but what is the news? and why have you come hither at this unearthly hour?

He drew nearer to me and said: Protagoras is come.

Yes, I replied; he came two days ago: have you only just heard of his arrival?

Yes, by the gods, he said; but not until yesterday evening.

At the same time he felt for the truckle-bed, and sat down at my feet, and then he said: Yesterday quite late in the evening, on my return from Oenoe whither I had gone in pursuit of my runaway slave Satyrus, as I meant to have told you, if some other matter had not come in the way;—on my return, when we had done supper and were about to retire to rest, my brother said to me: Protagoras is come. I was going to you at once, and then I thought that the night was far spent. But the moment sleep left me after my fatigue, I got up and came hither direct.

I, who knew the very courageous madness of the man, said: What is the matter? Has Protagoras robbed you of anything?

He replied, laughing: Yes, indeed he has, Socrates, of the wisdom which he keeps from me.

But, surely, I said, if you give him money, and make friends with him, he will make you as wise as he is himself.

Would to heaven, he replied, that this were the case! He might take all that I have, and all that my friends have, if he pleased. But that is why I have come to you now, in order that you may speak to him on my behalf; for I am young, and also I have never seen nor heard him; (when he visited Athens before I was but a child;) and all men praise him, Socrates; he is reputed to be the most accomplished of speakers. There is no reason why we should not go to him at once, and then we shall find him at home. He lodges, as I hear, with Callias the son of Hipponicus: let us start.

I replied: Not yet, my good friend; the hour is too early. But let us rise and take a turn in the court and wait about there until daybreak; when the day breaks, then we will go. For Protagoras is generally at home, and we shall be sure to find him; never fear.

Upon this we got up and walked about in the court, and I thought that I would make trial of the strength of his resolution. So I examined him and put questions to him. Tell me, Hippocrates, I said, as you are going to Protagoras, and will be paying your money to him, what is he to whom you are going? and what will he make of you? If, for example, you had thought of going to Hippocrates of Cos, the Asclepiad, and were about to give him your money, and someone had said to you: You are paying money to your namesake Hippocrates, O Hippocrates; tell me, what is he that you give him money? how would you have answered?

I should say, he replied, that I gave money to him as a physician.

And what will he make of you?

A physician, he said.

And if you were resolved to go to Polycleitus the Argive, or Pheidias the Athenian, and were intending to give them money, and someone had asked you: What are Polycleitus and Pheidias? and why do you give them this money?—how would you have answered?

I should have answered, that they were statuaries.

And what will they make of you?

A statuary, of course.

Well now, I said, you and I are going to Protagoras and we are ready to pay him money on your behalf. If our own means are sufficient, and we can gain him with these, we shall be only too glad; but if not, then we are to spend the money of your friends as well. Now suppose, that while we are thus enthusiastically pursuing our object someone were to say to us: Tell me, Socrates, and you Hippocrates, what is Protagoras, and why are you going to pay him money,—how should we answer? I know that Pheidias is a sculptor, and that Homer is a poet; but what appellation is given to Protagoras? how is he designated?

They call him a Sophist, Socrates, he replied.

Then we are going to pay our money to him in the character of a Sophist?

Certainly.

But suppose a person were to ask this further question: And how about yourself? What will Protagoras make of you, if you go to see him?

312

He answered, with a blush upon his face (for the day was just beginning to dawn, so that I could see him): Unless this differs in some way from the former instances, I suppose that he will make a Sophist of me.

By the gods, I said, and are you not ashamed at having to appear before the Hellenes in the character of a Sophist?

Indeed, Socrates, to confess the truth, I am.

But you should not assume, Hippocrates, that the

instruction of Protagoras is of this nature: may you not learn of him in the same way that you learned the arts of the grammarian, or musician, or trainer, not with the view of making any of them a profession, but only as a part of education, and because a private gentleman and freeman ought to know them?

Just so, he said; and that, in my opinion, is a far truer account of the teaching of Protagoras.

I said: I wonder whether you know what you are doing?

And what am I doing?

You are going to commit your soul to the care of a man whom you call a Sophist. And yet I hardly think that you know what a Sophist is; and if not, then you do not even know to whom you are committing your soul and whether the thing to which you commit yourself be good or evil.

I certainly think that I do know, he replied.

Then tell me, what do you imagine that he is?

I take him to be one who knows wise things, he replied, as his name implies.

And might you not, I said, affirm this of the painter and of the carpenter also: Do not they, too, know wise things? But suppose a person were to ask us: In what are the painters wise? We should answer: In what relates to the making of likenesses, and similarly of other things. And if he were further to ask: What is the wisdom of the Sophist, and what is the manufacture over which he presides?—how should we answer him?

How should we answer him, Socrates? What other answer could there be but that he presides over the art which makes men eloquent?

Yes, I replied, that is very likely true, but not enough; for in the answer a further question is involved: Of what does the Sophist make a man talk eloquently? The player on the lyre may be supposed to make a man talk eloquently about that which he makes him understand, that is about playing the lyre. Is not that true?

Yes.

Then about what does the Sophist make him eloquent? Must not he make him eloquent in that which he understands?

Yes, that may be assumed.

And what is that which the Sophist knows and makes his disciple know?

Indeed, he said, I cannot tell.

Then I proceeded to say: Well, but are you aware of the danger which you are incurring? If you were going to commit your body to someone, who might do good or harm to it, would you not carefully consider and ask the opinion of your friends and kindred, and deliberate many days as to whether you should give him the care of your body? But when the soul is in question, which you hold to be of far more value than the body, and upon the good or evil of which depends the well-being of your all—about this you never consulted either with your father or with your brother or with any one of us who are your companions. But no sooner does this foreigner appear, than you instantly commit your soul to his keeping. In the evening, as you say, you hear of him, and in the morning you go to him, never deliberating or taking the opinion of anyone as to whether you ought to intrust yourself to him or not;—you have quite made up your mind that you will at all hazards be a pupil of Protagoras, and are prepared to expend all the property of yourself and of your friends in carrying out at any price this determination, although, as you admit, you do not know him, and have never spoken with him: and you call him a Sophist, but are manifestly ignorant of what a Sophist is; and yet you are going to commit yourself to his keeping.

When he heard me say this, he replied: No other inference, Socrates, can be drawn from your words.

I proceeded: Is not a Sophist, Hippocrates, one who deals wholesale or retail in the food of the soul? To me that appears to be his nature.

And what, Socrates, is the food of the soul?

Surely, I said, knowledge is the food of the soul; and we must take care, my friend, that the Sophist does not deceive us when he praises what he sells, like the dealers wholesale or retail who sell the food of the body; for they praise indiscriminately all their goods, without knowing what are really beneficial or hurtful: neither do their customers know, with the exception of any trainer or physician who may

happen to buy of them. In like manner those who
carry about the wares of knowledge, and make the
round of the cities, and sell or retail them to any cus-
tomer who is in want of them, praise them all alike;
though I should not wonder, O my friend, if many
of them were really ignorant of their effect upon
the soul; and their customers equally ignorant, unless he who buys of them happens to be a physician
of the soul. If, therefore, you have understanding
of what is good and evil, you may safely buy knowledge of Protagoras or of anyone; but if not, then,   314
O my friend, pause, and do not hazard your dearest
interests at a game of chance. For there is far
greater peril in buying knowledge than in buying
meat and drink: the one you purchase of the wholesale or retailer, and carry them away in other vessels,
and before you receive them into the body as food,
you may deposit them at home and call in any experienced friend who knows what is good to be eaten
or drunken, and what not, and how much, and when;
and then the danger of purchasing them is not so
great. But you cannot buy the wares of knowledge
and carry them away in another vessel; when you
have paid for them you must receive them into the
soul and go your way, either greatly harmed or
greatly benefited; and therefore we should deliberate
and take counsel with our elders; for we are still
young—too young to determine such a matter. And
now let us go, as we were intending, and hear Protagoras; and when we have heard what he has to say,
we may take counsel of others; for not only is Protagoras at the house of Callias, but there is Hippias
of Elis, and, if I am not mistaken, Prodicus of Ceos,
and several other wise men.

To this we agreed, and proceeded on our way until
we reached the vestibule of the house; and there
we stopped in order to conclude a discussion which
had arisen between us as we were going along; and
we stood talking in the vestibule until we had finished
and come to an understanding. And I think that the
doorkeeper, who was a eunuch, and who was probably annoyed at the great inroad of the Sophists,
must have heard us talking. At any rate, when we
knocked at the door, and he opened and saw us, he

grumbled: They are Sophists—he is not at home; and instantly gave the door a hearty bang with both his hands. Again we knocked, and he answered without opening: Did you not hear me say that he is not at home, fellows? But, my friend, I said, you need not be alarmed; for we are not Sophists, and we are not come to see Callias, but we want to see Protagoras; and I must request you to announce us. At last, after a good deal of difficulty, the man was persuaded to open the door.

When we entered, we found Protagoras taking a walk in the cloister; and next to him, on one side, were walking Callias, the son of Hipponicus, and Paralus, the son of Pericles, who, by the mother's side, is his half-brother, and Charmides, the son of Glaucon. On the other side of him were Xanthippus, the other son of Pericles, Philippides, the son of Philomelus; also Antimoerus of Mende, who of all the disciples of Protagoras is the most famous, and intends to make sophistry his profession. A train of listeners followed him; the greater part of them appeared to be foreigners, whom Protagoras had brought with him out of the various cities visited by him in his journeys, he, like Orpheus, attracting them by his voice, and they following.[2] I should mention also that there were some Athenians in the company. Nothing delighted me more than the precision of their movements: they never got into his way at all; but when he and those who were with him turned back, then the band of listeners parted regularly on either side; he was always in front, and they wheeled round and took their places behind him in perfect order.

After him, as Homer says,[3] "I lifted up my eyes and saw" Hippias the Elean sitting in the opposite cloister on a chair of state, and around him were seated on benches Eryximachus, the son of Acumenus, and Phaedrus the Myrrhinusian, and Andron the son of Androtion, and there were strangers whom he had brought with him from his native city of Elis, and some others: they were putting to Hippias cer-

315

---

[2] Cp. Rep. x. 600 D.
[3] Od. xi. 601 foll.

tain physical and astronomical questions, and he, *ex cathedra,* was determining their several questions to them, and discoursing of them.

Also, "my eyes beheld Tantalus";[4] for Prodicus the Cean was at Athens: he had been lodged in a room which, in the days of Hipponicus, was a store-house; but, as the house was full, Callias had cleared this out and made the room into a guest-chamber. Now Prodicus was still in bed, wrapped up in sheep-skins and bedclothes, of which there seemed to be a great heap; and there was sitting by him on the couches near, Pausanias of the deme of Cerameis, and with Pausanias was a youth quite young, who is certainly remarkable for his good looks, and, if I am not mistaken, is also of a fair and gentle nature. I thought that I heard him called Agathon, and my suspicion is that he is the beloved of Pausanias. There was this youth, and also there were the two Adeiman-tuses, one the son of Cepis, and the other of Leu-colophides, and some others. I was very anxious to hear what Prodicus was saying, for he seems to me to be an all-wise and inspired man; but I was not   316 able to get into the inner circle, and his fine deep voice made an echo in the room which rendered his words inaudible.

No sooner had we entered than there followed us Alcibiades the beautiful, as you say, and I believe you; and also Critias the son of Callaeschrus.

On entering we stopped a little, in order to look about us, and then walked up to Protagoras, and I said: Protagoras, my friend Hippocrates and I have come to see you.

Do you wish, he said, to speak with me alone, or in the presence of the company?

Whichever you please, I said; you shall determine when you have heard the purpose of our visit.

And what is your purpose? he said.

I must explain, I said, that my friend Hippocrates is a native Athenian; he is the son of Apollodorus, and of a great and prosperous house, and he is him-self in natural ability quite a match for anybody of his own age. I believe that he aspires to political

4 Od. xi. 582.

eminence; and this he thinks that conversation with you is most likely to procure for him. And now you can determine whether you would wish to speak to him of your teaching alone or in the presence of the company.

Thank you, Socrates, for your consideration of me. For certainly a stranger finding his way into great cities, and persuading the flower of the youth in them to leave the company of their kinsmen or any other acquaintances, old or young, and live with him, under the idea that they will be improved by his conversation, ought to be very cautious; great jealousies are aroused by his proceedings, and he is the subject of many enmities and conspiracies. Now the art of the Sophist is, as I believe, of great antiquity; but in ancient times those who practiced it, fearing this odium, veiled and disguised themselves under various names, some under that of poets, as Homer, Hesiod, and Simonides, some, of hierophants and prophets, as Orpheus and Musaeus, and some, as I observe, even under the name of gymnastic masters, like Iccus of Tarentum, or the more recently celebrated Herodicus, now of Selymbria and formerly of Megara, who is a first-rate Sophist. Your own Agathocles pretended to be a musician, but was really an eminent Sophist; also Pythocleides the Cean; and there were many others; and all of them, as I was saying, adopted these arts as veils or disguises because they were afraid of the odium which they would incur. But that is not my way, for I do not 317 believe that they effected their purpose, which was to deceive the government, who were not blinded by them; and as to the people, they have no understanding, and only repeat what their rulers are pleased to tell them. Now to run away, and to be caught in running away, is the very height of folly, and also greatly increases the exasperation of mankind; for they regard him who runs away as a rogue, in addition to any other objections which they have to him; and therefore I take an entirely opposite course, and acknowledge myself to be a Sophist and instructor of mankind; such an open acknowledgment appears to me to be a better sort of caution than concealment. Nor do I neglect other precautions, and therefore I hope, as I may say, by the favor of heaven that no harm will come of the acknowledgment that I am a Sophist. And I have been now many years in the profession—for all my years when added up are many; there is no one here present of whom I might not be the father. Wherefore I should much prefer conversing with you, if you want to speak with me, in the presence of the company.

As I suspected that he would like to have a little display and glorification in the presence of Prodicus and Hippias, and would gladly show us to them in the light of his admirers, I said: But why should we not summon Prodicus and Hippias and their friends to hear us?

Very good, he said.

Suppose, said Callias, that we hold a council in which you may sit and discuss.—This was agreed upon, and great delight was felt at the prospect of hearing wise men talk; we ourselves took the chairs and benches, and arranged them by Hippias, where the other benches had been already placed. Meanwhile Callias and Alcibiades got Prodicus out of bed and brought in him and his companions.

When we were all seated, Protagoras said: Now that the company are assembled, Socrates, tell me about the young man of whom you were just now speaking.

318

I replied: I will begin again at the same point, Protagoras, and tell you once more the purport of my visit: this is my friend Hippocrates, who is desirous of making your acquaintance; he would like to know what will happen to him if he associates with you. I have no more to say.

Protagoras answered: Young man, if you associate with me, on the very first day you will return home a better man than you came, and better on the second day than on the first, and better every day than you were on the day before.

When I heard this, I said: Protagoras, I do not at all wonder at hearing you say this; even at your age, and with all your wisdom, if anyone were to teach you what you did not know before, you would become better no doubt: but please to answer in a different way—I will explain how by an example.

Let me suppose that Hippocrates, instead of desiring your acquaintance, wished to become acquainted with the young man Zeuxippus of Heraclea, who has lately been in Athens, and he had come to him as he has come to you, and had heard him say, as he has heard you say, that every day he would grow and become better if he associated with him: and then suppose that he were to ask him, "In what shall I become better, and in what shall I grow?"—Zeuxippus would answer, "In painting." And suppose that he went to Orthagoras the Theban, and heard him say the same thing, and asked him, "In what shall I become better day by day?" he would reply, "In flute playing." Now I want you to make the same sort of answer to this young man and to me, who am asking questions on his account. When you say that on the first day on which he associates with you he will return home a better man, and on every day will grow in like manner—in what, Protagoras, will he be better? and about what?

When Protagoras heard me say this, he replied: You ask questions fairly, and I like to answer a question which is fairly put. If Hippocrates comes to me he will not experience the sort of drudgery with which other Sophists are in the habit of insulting their pupils; who, when they have just escaped from the arts, are taken and driven back into them by these teachers, and made to learn calculation, and astronomy, and geometry, and music (he gave a look at Hippias as he said this); but if he comes to me, he will learn that which he comes to learn. And this is prudence in affairs private as well as public; he will learn to order his own house in the best manner, and he will be able to speak and act for the best in the affairs of the state.

Do I understand you, I said; and is your meaning 319 that you teach the art of politics, and that you promise to make men good citizens?

That, Socrates, is exactly the profession which I make.

Then, I said, you do indeed possess a noble art, if there is no mistake about this; for I will freely confess to you, Protagoras, that I have a doubt whether this art is capable of being taught, and yet I know

not how to disbelieve your assertion. And I ought
to tell you why I am of opinion that this art cannot
be taught or communicated by man to man. I say
that the Athenians are an understanding people, and
indeed they are esteemed to be such by the other
Hellenes. Now I observe that when we are met together in the assembly, and the matter in hand relates
to building, the builders are summoned as advisers;
when the question is one of shipbuilding, then the
shipwrights; and the like of other arts which they
think capable of being taught and learned. And if
some person offers to give them advice who is not
supposed by them to have any skill in the art, even
though he be good-looking, and rich, and noble,
they will not listen to him, but laugh and hoot at him,
until either he is clamored down and retires of himself; or if he persist, he is dragged away or put out
by the constables at the command of the prytanes.
This is their way of behaving about professors of the
arts. But when the question is an affair of state, then
everybody is free to have a say—carpenter, tinker,
cobbler, sailor, passenger; rich and poor, high and
low—anyone who likes gets up, and no one re-
proaches him, as in the former case, with not having
learned, and having no teacher, and yet giving advice;
evidently because they are under the impression that
this sort of knowledge cannot be taught. And not
only is this true of the state, but of individuals; the
best and wisest of our citizens are unable to impart   320
their political wisdom to others: as for example, Pericles, the father of these young men, who gave them
excellent instruction in all that could be learned from
masters, in his own department of politics neither
taught them, nor gave them teachers; but they were
allowed to wander at their own free will in a sort of
hope that they would light upon virtue of their own
accord. Or take another example: there was Cleinias
the younger brother of our friend Alcibiades, of
whom this very same Pericles was the guardian; and
he being in fact under the apprehension that Cleinias
would be corrupted by Alcibiades, took him away,
and placed him in the house of Ariphron to be educated; but before six months had elapsed, Ariphron
sent him back, not knowing what to do with him.

And I could mention numberless other instances of persons who were good themselves, and never yet made anyone else good, whether friend or stranger. Now I, Protagoras, having these examples before me, am inclined to think that virtue cannot be taught. But then again, when I listen to your words, I waver; and am disposed to think that there must be something in what you say, because I know that you have great experience, and learning, and invention. And I wish that you would, if possible, show me a little more clearly that virtue can be taught. Will you be so good?

That I will, Socrates, and gladly. But what would you like? Shall I, as an elder, speak to you as younger men in an apologue or myth, or shall I argue out the question?

To this several of the company answered that he should choose for himself.

Well, then, he said, I think that the myth will be more interesting.

Once upon a time there were gods only, and no mortal creatures. But when the time came that these also should be created, the gods fashioned them out of earth and fire and various mixtures of both elements in the interior of the earth; and when they were about to bring them into the light of day, they ordered Prometheus and Epimetheus to equip them, and to distribute to them severally their proper qualities. Epimetheus said to Prometheus: "Let me distribute, and do you inspect." This was agreed, and Epimetheus made the distribution. There were some to whom he gave strength without swiftness, while he equipped the weaker with swiftness; some he armed, and others he left unarmed; and devised for the latter some other means of preservation, making some large, and having their size as a protection, and others small, whose nature was to fly in the air or burrow in the ground; this was to be their way of escape. Thus did he compensate them with the view of preventing any race from becoming extinct. And when he had provided against their destruction by one another, he contrived also a means of protecting them against the seasons of heaven; clothing them with close hair and thick skins sufficient to defend

them against the winter cold and able to resist the
summer heat, so that they might have a natural bed
of their own when they wanted to rest; also he furnished them with the hoofs and hair and hard and
callous skins under their feet. Then he gave them
varieties of food,—herb of the soil to some, to others
fruits of trees, and to others roots, and to some again
he gave other animals as food. And some he made
to have few young ones, while those who were their
prey were very prolific; and in this manner the race
was preserved. Thus did Epimetheus, who, not being
very wise, forgot that he had distributed among the
brute animals all the qualities which he had to give—
and when he came to man, who was still unprovided,
he was terribly perplexed. Now while he was in this
perplexity, Prometheus came to inspect the distribution, and he found that the other animals were suitably furnished, but that man alone was naked and
shoeless, and had neither bed nor arms of defense.
The appointed hour was approaching when man in
his turn was to go forth into the light of day; and
Prometheus, not knowing how he could devise his salvation, stole the mechanical arts of Hephaestus and
Athene, and fire with them (they could neither have
been acquired nor used without fire), and gave them
to man. Thus man had the wisdom necessary to the
support of life, but political wisdom he had not; for
that was in the keeping of Zeus, and the power of
Prometheus did not extend to entering into the citadel
of heaven, were Zeus dwelt, who moreover had terrible sentinels; but he did enter by stealth into the
common workshop of Athene and Hephaestus, in
which they used to practice their favorite arts, and
carried off Hephaestus' art of working by fire, and
also the art of Athene, and gave them to man. And
in this way man was supplied with the means of life.
But Prometheus is said to have been afterwards
prosecuted for theft, owing to the blunder of Epimetheus.

Now man, having a share of the divine attributes, 322
was at first the only one of the animals who had any
gods, because he alone was of their kindred; and he
would raise altars and images of them. He was not
long inventing articulate speech and names; and he

also constructed houses and clothes and shoes and beds, and drew sustenance from the earth. Thus provided, mankind at first lived dispersed, and there were not cities. But the consequence was that they were destroyed by the wild beasts, for they were utterly weak in comparison of them, and their art was only sufficient to provide them with the means of life, and did not enable them to carry on war against the animals: food they had, but not as yet the art of government, of which the art of war is a part. After a while the desire of self-preservation gathered them into cities; but when they were gathered together, having no art of government, they evil intreated one another, and were again in process of dispersion and destruction. Zeus feared that the entire race would be exterminated, and so he sent Hermes to them, bearing reverence and justice to be the ordering principles of cities and the bonds of friendship and conciliation. Hermes asked Zeus how he should impart justice and reverence among men:— Should he distribute them as the arts are distributed; that is to say, to a favored few only, one skilled individual having enough of medicine or of any other art for many unskilled ones? "Shall this be the manner in which I am to distribute justice and reverence among men, or shall I give them to all?" "To all," said Zeus; "I should like them all to have a share, for cities cannot exist, if a few only share in the virtues, as in the arts. And further, make a law by my order, that he who has no part in reverence and justice shall be put to death, for he is a plague of the state."

And this is the reason, Socrates, why the Athenians and mankind in general, when the question relates to carpentering or any other mechanical art, allow but a few to share in their deliberations; and when anyone else interferes, then, as you say, they object, if he be not of the favored few; which, as I reply, is very natural. But when they meet to deliberate about political virtue, which proceeds only by way of justice and wisdom, they are patient enough of any man who speaks of them, as is also natural, because they think that every man ought to share in this sort of virtue, and that states could not exist if this were otherwise.

I have explained to you, Socrates, the reason of this phenomenon.

And that you may not suppose yourself to be deceived in thinking that all men regard every man as having a share of justice or honesty and of every other political virtue, let me give you a further proof, which is this. In other cases, as you are aware, if a man says that he is a good flute player, or skillful in any other art in which he has no skill, people either laugh at him or are angry with him, and his relations think that he is mad and go and admonish him; but when honesty is in question, or some other political virtue, even if they know that he is dishonest, yet, if the man comes publicly forward and tells the truth about his dishonesty, then, what in the other case was held by them to be good sense, they now deem to be madness. They say that all men ought to profess honesty whether they are honest or not, and that a man is out of his mind who says anything else. Their notion is, that a man must have some degree of honesty; and that if he has none at all he ought not to be in the world.

I have been showing that they are right in admitting every man as a counsellor about this sort of virtue, as they are of opinion that every man is a partaker of it. And I will now endeavor to show further that they do not conceive this virtue to be given by nature, or to grow spontaneously, but to be a thing which may be taught; and which comes to a man by taking pains. No one would instruct, no one would rebuke, or be angry with those whose calamities they suppose to be due to nature or chance; they do not try to punish or to prevent them from being what they are; they do but pity them. Who is so foolish as to chastise or instruct the ugly, or the diminutive, or the feeble? and for this reason. Because he knows that good and evil of this kind is the work of nature and of chance; whereas if a man is wanting in those good qualities which are attained by study and exercise and teaching, and has only the contrary evil qualities, other men are angry with him, and punish and reprove him——of these evil qualities one is impiety, another injustice, and they may be described generally as the very opposite of political virtue. In

324

such cases any man will be angry with another, and reprimand him—clearly because he thinks that by study and learning, the virtue in which the other is deficient may be acquired. If you will think, Socrates, of the nature of punishment, you will see at once that in the opinion of mankind virtue may be acquired; no one punishes the evil-doer under the notion, or for the reason, that he has done wrong— only the unreasonable fury of a beast acts in that manner. But he who desires to inflict rational punishment does not retaliate for a past wrong which cannot be undone; he has regard to the future, and is desirous that the man who is punished, and he who sees him punished, may be deterred from doing wrong again. He punishes for the sake of prevention, thereby clearly implying that virtue is capable of being taught. This is the notion of all who retaliate upon others either privately or publicly. And the Athenians, too, your own citizens, like other men, punish and take vengeance on all whom they regard as evil-doers; and hence, we may infer them to be of the number of those who think that virtue may be acquired and taught. Thus far, Socrates, I have shown you clearly enough, if I am not mistaken, that your countrymen are right in admitting the tinker and the cobbler to advise about politics, and also that they deem virtue to be capable of being taught and acquired

There yet remains one difficulty which has been raised by you about the sons of good men. What is the reason why good men teach their sons the knowledge which is gained from teachers, and make them wise in that, but do nothing toward improving them in the virtues which distinguish themselves? And here, Socrates, I will leave the apologue and resume the argument. Please to consider: Is there or is there not some one quality of which all the citizens must be partakers, if there is to be a city at all? In the answer to this question is contained the only solution of your difficulty; there is no other. For if there be any such quality, and this quality or unity is not the art of the carpenter, or the smith, or the potter, but justice and temperance and holiness and, in a word, manly virtue—if this is the quality of which

325

all men must be partakers, and which is the very
condition of their learning or doing anything else,
and if he who is wanting in this, whether he be a
child only or a grown-up man or woman, must be
taught and punished, until by punishment he becomes
better, and he who rebels against instruction and
punishment is either exiled or condemned to death
under the idea that he is incurable—if what I am
saying be true, good men have their sons taught other
things and not this, do consider how extraordinary
their conduct would appear to be. For we have
shown that they think virtue capable of being taught
and cultivated both in private and public; and, notwithstanding, they have their sons taught lesser
matters, ignorance of which does not involve the
punishment of death; but greater things, of which the
ignorance may cause death and exile to those who
have no training or knowledge of them—aye, and
confiscation as well as death, and, in a word, may be
the ruin of families—those things, I say, they are supposed not to teach them—not to take the utmost
care that they should learn. How improbable is this,
Socrates!

Education and admonition commence in the first
years of childhood, and last to the very end of life.
Mother and nurse and father and tutor are vying with
one another about the improvement of the child as
soon as ever he is able to understand what is being
said to him: he cannot say or do anything without
their setting forth to him that this is just and that is
unjust; this is honorable, that is dishonorable; this is
holy, that is unholy; do this and abstain from that.
And if he obeys, well and good; if not, he is straight-
ened by threats and blows, like a piece of bent or
warped wood. At a later stage they send him to
teachers, and enjoin them to see to his manners even
more than to his reading and music; and the teachers
do as they are desired. And when the boy has learned
his letters and is beginning to understand what is
written, as before he understood only what was spoken, they put into his hands the works of great poets,
which he reads sitting on a bench at school; in these
are contained many admonitions, and many tales, and
praises, and encomia of ancient famous men, which

326

he is required to learn by heart, in order that he may imitate or emulate them and desire to become like them. Then, again, the teachers of the lyre take similar care that their young disciple is temperate and gets into no mischief; and when they have taught him the use of the lyre, they introduce him to the poems of other excellent poets, who are the lyric poets; and these they set to music, and make their harmonies and rhythms quite familiar to the children's souls, in order that they may learn to be more gentle, and harmonious, and rhythmical, and so more fitted for speech and action; for the life of man in every part has need of harmony and rhythm. Then they send them to the master of gymnastic, in order that their bodies may better minister to the virtuous mind, and that they may not be compelled through bodily weakness to play the coward in war or on any other occasion. This is what is done by those who have the means, and those who have the means are the rich; their children begin to go to school soonest and leave off latest. When they have done with masters, the state again compels them to learn the laws, and live after the pattern which they furnish, and not after their own fancies; and just as in learning to write, the writing-master first draws lines with a style for the use of the young beginner, and gives him the tablet and makes him follow the lines, so the city draws the laws, which were the invention of good lawgivers living in the olden time; these are given to the young man, in order to guide him in his conduct whether he is commanding or obeying; and he who transgresses them is to be corrected, or, in other words, called to account, which is a term used not only in your country, but also in many others, seeing that justice calls men to account. Now when there is all this care about virtue private and public, why, Socrates, do you still wonder and doubt whether virtue can be taught? Cease to wonder, for the opposite would be far more surprising.

But why then do the sons of good fathers often turn out ill? There is nothing very wonderful in this; for, as I have been saying, the existence of a state implies that virtue is not any man's private possession. If so—and nothing can be truer—then I will further

ask you to imagine, as an illustration, some other
pursuit or branch of knowledge which may be assumed equally to be the condition of the existence of
a state. Suppose that there could be no state unless
we were all flute players, as far as each had the
capacity, and everybody was freely teaching everybody the art, both in private and public, and reprov-
ing the bad player as freely and openly as every man
now teaches justice and the laws, not concealing
them as he would conceal the other arts, but imparting them—for all of us have a mutual interest in the
justice and virtue of one another, and this is the
reason why everyone is so ready to teach justice and
the laws;—suppose, I say, that there were the same
readiness and liberality among us in teaching one
another flute playing, do you imagine, Socrates, that
the sons of good flute players would be more likely
to be good than the sons of bad ones? I think not.
Would not their sons grow up to be distinguished or
undistinguished according to their own natural capacities as flute players, and the son of a good player
would often turn out to be a bad one, and the son of
a bad player to be a good one, and all flute players
would be good enough in comparison of those who
were ignorant and unacquainted with the art of flute
playing? In like manner I would have you consider
that he who appears to you to be the worst of those
who have been brought up in laws and humanities,
would appear to be a just man and a master of justice
if he were to be compared with men who had no
education, or courts of justice, or laws, or any restraints upon them which compelled them to practice
virtue—with the savages, for example, whom the poet
Pherecrates exhibited on the stage at the last year's
Lenaean festival. If you were living among men such
as the man-haters in his Chorus, you would be only
too glad to meet with Eurybates and Phrynondas, and
you would sorrowfully long to revisit the rascality of
this part of the world. And you, Socrates, are dis-
contented, and why? Because all men are teachers of
virtue, each one according to his ability; and you say,
Where are the teachers? You might as well ask, Who   328
teaches Greek? For of that too there will not be any
teachers found. Or you might ask, Who is to teach

the sons of our artisans this same art which they have learned of their fathers? He and his fellow-workmen have taught them to the best of their ability—but who will carry them further in their arts? And you would certainly have a difficulty, Socrates, in finding a teacher of them; but there would be no difficulty in finding a teacher of those who are wholly ignorant. And this is true of virtue or of anything else; if a man is better able than we are to promote virtue ever so little, we must be content with the result. A teacher of this sort I believe myself to be, and above all other men to have the knowledge which makes a man noble and good; and I give my pupils their money's worth, and even more, as they themselves confess. And therefore I have introduced the following mode of payment:—When a man has been my pupil, if he likes he pays my price, but there is no compulsion; and if he does not like, he has only to go into a temple and take an oath of the value of the instructions, and he pays no more than he declares to be their value.

Such is my Apologue, Socrates, and such is the argument by which I endeavor to show that virtue may be taught, and that this is the opinion of the Athenians. And I have also attempted to show that you are not to wonder at good fathers having bad sons, or at good sons having bad fathers, of which the sons of Polycleitus afford an example, who are the companions of our friends here, Paralus and Xanthippus, but are nothing in comparison with their father; and this is true of the sons of many other artists. As yet I ought not to say the same of Paralus and Xanthippus themselves, for they are young and there is still hope of them.

Protagoras ended, and in my ear
"So charming left his voice, that I the while
Thought him still speaking; still stood fixed to hear."[5]
At length, when the truth dawned upon me, that he had really finished, not without difficulty I began to collect myself, and looking at Hippocrates, I said to him: O son of Apollodorus, how deeply grateful I am to you for having brought me hither; I would not

---

[5] Borrowed by Milton, *Paradise Lost*, viii. 2, 3.

have missed the speech of Protagoras for a great deal.
For I used to imagine that no human care could make
men good; but I know better now. Yet I have still one
very small difficulty which I am sure that Protagoras will easily explain, as he has already explained
so much. If a man were to go and consult Pericles or   329
any of our great speakers about these matters, he
might perhaps hear as fine a discourse; but then when
one has a question to ask of any of them, like books,
they can neither answer nor ask; and if anyone challenges the least particular of their speech, they go
ringing on in a long harangue, like brazen pots,
which when they are struck continue to sound unless
someone puts his hand upon them; whereas our
friend Protagoras can not only make a good speech,
as he has already shown, but when he is asked a
question he can answer briefly; and when he asks
he will wait and hear the answer; and this is a very
rare gift. Now I, Protagoras, want to ask of you a
little question, which if you will only answer, I shall
be quite satisfied. You were saying that virtue can
be taught;—that I will take upon your authority,
and there is no one to whom I am more ready to
trust. But I marvel at one thing about which I should
like to have my mind set at rest. You were speaking
of Zeus sending justice and reverence to men; and
several times while you were speaking, justice, and
temperance, and holiness, and all these qualities,
were described by you as if together they made up
virtue. Now I want you to tell me truly whether
virtue is one whole, of which justice and temperance
and holiness are parts; or whether all these are only
the names of one and the same thing: that is the
doubt which still lingers in my mind.

There is no difficulty, Socrates, in answering that
the qualities of which you are speaking are the parts
of virtue which is one.

And are they parts, I said, in the same sense in
which mouth, nose, and eyes, and ears, are the parts
of a face; or are they like the parts of gold, which
differ from the whole and from one another only in
being larger or smaller?

I should say that they differed, Socrates, in the

first way; they are related to one another as the parts of a face are related to the whole face.

And do men have some one part and some another part of virtue? Or if a man has one part, must he also have all the others?

By no means, he said; for many a man is brave and not just, or just and not wise.

You would not deny, then, that courage and wisdom are also parts of virtue?

Most undoubtedly they are, he answered; and   330
wisdom is the noblest of the parts.

And they are all different from one another? I said.
Yes.

And has each of them a distinct function like the parts of the face;—the eye, for example, is not like the ear, and has not the same functions; and the other parts are none of them like one another, either in their functions, or in any other way? I want to know whether the comparison holds concerning the parts of virtue. Do they also differ from one another in themselves and in their functions? For that is clearly what the simile would imply.

Yes, Socrates, you are right in supposing that they differ.

Then, I said, no other part of virtue is like knowledge, or like justice, or like courage, or like temperance, or like holiness?

No, he answered.

Well then, I said, suppose that you and I inquire into their natures. And first, you would agree with me that justice is of the nature of a thing, would you not? That is my opinion: would it not be yours also?

Mine also, he said.

And suppose that someone were to ask us, saying, "O Protagoras, and you, Socrates, what about this thing which you were calling justice, is it just or unjust?"—and I were to answer, just: would you vote with me or against me?

With you, he said.

Thereupon I should answer to him who asked me, that justice is of the nature of the just: would not you?

Yes, he said.

And suppose that he went on to say: "Well now, is there also such a thing as holiness?"—we should answer, "Yes," if I am not mistaken?

Yes, he said.

Which you would also acknowledge to be a thing—should we not say so?

He assented.

"And is this a sort of thing which is of the nature of the holy, or of the nature of the unholy?" I should be angry at his putting such a question, and should say, "Peace, man; nothing can be holy if holiness is not holy." What would you say? Would you not answer in the same way?

Certainly, he said.

And then after this suppose that he came and asked us, "What were you saying just now? Perhaps I may not have heard you rightly, but you seemed to me to be saying that the parts of virtue were not the same as one another." I should reply, "You certainly heard that said, but not, as you imagine, by me; for I only asked the question; Protagoras gave the answer." And suppose that he turned to you and said, "Is this true, Protagoras? and do you maintain that one part of virtue is unlike another, and is this your position?"—how would you answer him?

I could not help acknowledging the truth of what he said, Socrates.

Well then, Protagoras, we will assume this; and now supposing that he proceeded to say further, "Then holiness is not of the nature of justice, nor justice of the nature of holiness, but of the nature of unholiness; and holiness is of the nature of the not just, and therefore of the unjust, and the unjust is the unholy": how shall we answer him? I should certainly answer him on my own behalf that justice is holy, and that holiness is just; and I would say in like manner on your behalf also, if you would allow me, that justice is either the same with holiness, or very nearly the same; and above all I would assert that justice is like holiness and holiness is like justice; and I wish that you would tell me whether I may be permitted to give this answer on your behalf, and whether you would agree with me.

He replied, I cannot simply agree, Socrates, to the

proposition that justice is holy and that holiness is just, for there appears to me to be a difference between them. But what matter? if you please I please; and let us assume, if you will, that justice is holy, and that holiness is just.

Pardon me, I replied; I do not want this "if you wish" or "if you will" sort of conclusion to be proven, but I want you and me to be proven: I mean to say that the conclusion will be best proven if there be no "if."

Well, he said, I admit that justice bears a resemblance to holiness, for there is always some point of view in which everything is like every other thing; white is in a certain way like black, and hard is like soft, and the most extreme opposites have some qualities in common; even the parts of the face which, as we were saying before, are distinct and have different functions, are still in a certain point of view similar, and one of them is like another of them. And you may prove that they are like one another on the same principle that all things are like one another; and yet things which are like in some particular ought not to be called alike, nor things which are unlike in some particular, however slight, unlike.

And do you think, I said in a tone of surprise, that justice and holiness have but a small degree of likeness?

Certainly not; any more than I agree with what I understand to be your view.

Well, I said, as you appear to have a difficulty   332
about this, let us take another of the examples which you mentioned instead. Do you admit the existence of folly?

I do.

And is not wisdom the very opposite of folly?

That is true, he said.

And when men act rightly and advantageously they seem to you to be temperate?

Yes, he said.

And temperance makes them temperate?

Certainly.

And they who do not act rightly act foolishly, and in acting thus are not temperate?

I agree, he said.

Then to act foolishly is the opposite of acting temperately?

He assented.

And foolish actions are done by folly, and temperate actions by temperance?

He agreed.

And that is done strongly which is done by strength, and that which is weakly done, by weakness?

He assented.

And that which is done with swiftness is done swiftly, and that which is done with slowness, slowly?

He assented again.

And that which is done in the same manner, is done by the same; and that which is done in an opposite manner by the opposite?

He agreed.

Once more, I said, is there anything beautiful?

Yes.

To which the only opposite is the ugly?

There is no other.

And is there anything good?

There is.

To which the only opposite is the evil?

There is no other.

And there is the acute in sound?

True.

To which the only opposite is the grave?

There is no other, he said, but that.

Then every opposite has one opposite only and no more?

He assented.

Then now, I said, let us recapitulate our admissions. First of all we admitted that everything has one opposite and not more than one?

We did so.

And we admitted also that what was done in opposite ways was done by opposites?

Yes.

And that which was done foolishly, as we further admitted, was done in the opposite way to that which was done temperately?

Yes.

And that which was done temperately was done by temperance, and that which was done foolishly by folly?

He agreed.

And that which is done in opposite ways is done by opposites?

Yes.

And one thing is done by temperance, and quite another thing by folly?

Yes.

And in opposite ways?

Certainly.

And therefore by opposites:—then folly is the opposite of temperance?

Clearly.

And do you remember that folly has already been acknowledged by us to be the opposite of wisdom?

He assented.

And we said that everything has only one opposite?

Yes.

Then, Protagoras, which of the two assertions shall we renounce? One says that everything has but one opposite; the other that wisdom is distinct from temperance, and that both of them are parts of virtue; and that they are not only distinct, but dissimilar, both in themselves and in their functions, like the parts of a face. Which of these two assertions shall we renounce? For both of them together are certainly not in harmony; they do not accord or agree: for how can they be said to agree if everything is assumed to have only one opposite and not more than one, and yet folly, which is one, has clearly the two opposites—wisdom and temperance? Is not that true, Protagoras? What else would you say?

He assented, but with great reluctance.

Then temperance and wisdom are the same, as before justice and holiness appeared to us to be nearly the same. And now, Protagoras, I said, we must finish the inquiry, and not faint. Do you think that an unjust man can be temperate in his injustice?

I should be ashamed. Socrates, he said, to acknowledge this, which nevertheless many may be found to assert.

333

And shall I argue with them or with you? I replied.

I would rather, he said, that you should argue with the many first, if you will.

Whichever you please, if you will only answer me and say whether you are of their opinion or not. My object is to test the validity of the argument; and yet the result may be that I who ask and you who answer may both be put on our trial.

Protagoras at first made a show of refusing, as he said that the argument was not encouraging; at length, he consented to answer.

Now then, I said, begin at the beginning and answer me. You think that some men are temperate, and yet unjust?

Yes, he said; let that be admitted.

And temperance is good sense?

Yes.

And good sense is good counsel in doing injustice?

Granted.

If they succeed, I said, or if they do not succeed?

If they succeed.

And you would admit the existence of goods?

Yes.

And is the good that which is expedient for man?

Yes, indeed, he said: and there are some things which may be inexpedient, and yet I call them good.

I thought that Protagoras was getting ruffled and excited; he seemed to be setting himself in an attitude of war. Seeing this, I minded my business, and gently said:—

When you say, Protagoras, that things inexpedient 334 are good, do you mean inexpedient for man only, or inexpedient altogether? and do you call the latter good?

Certainly not the last, he replied; for I know of many things—meats, drinks, medicines, and ten thousand other things, which are inexpedient for man, and some which are expedient; and some which are neither expedient nor inexpedient for man, but only for horses; and some for oxen only, and some for dogs; and some for no animals, but only for trees; and some for the roots of trees and not for their branches, as for example, manure, which is a good thing when laid about the roots of a tree, but utterly destructive if thrown upon the shoots and young branches; or I may instance olive oil, which is mischievous to all plants, and generally most injurious to the hair of every animal with the exception of man, but beneficial to human hair and to the human body generally; and even in this application (so various and changeable is the nature of the benefit), that which is the greatest good to the outward parts of a man, is a very great evil to his inward parts: and for this reason physicians always forbid their patients the use of oil in their food, except in very small quantities, just enough to extinguish the disagreeable sensation of smell in meats and sauces.

When he had given this answer, the company cheered him. And I said: Protagoras, I have a wretched memory, and when anyone makes a long speech to me I never remember what he is talking about. As then, if I had been deaf, and you were going to converse with me, you would have had to raise your voice; so now, having such a bad memory, I will ask you to cut your answers shorter, if you would take me with you.

What do you mean? he said: how am I to shorten my answers? shall I make them too short?

Certainly not, I said.

But short enough?

Yes, I said.

Shall I answer what appears to me to be short enough, or what appears to you to be short enough?

I have heard, I said, that you can speak and teach others to speak about the same things at such length that words never seemed to fail, or with such brevity that no one could use fewer of them. Please therefore, if you talk with me, to adopt the latter or more compendious method.

Socrates, he replied, many a battle of words have I fought, and if I had followed the method of disputation which my adversaries desired, as you want me to do, I should have been no better than another, and the name of Protagoras would have been nowhere.

I saw that he was not satisfied with his previous answers, and that he would not play the part of answerer any more if he could help; and I considered that there was no call upon me to continue the con-

versation; so I said: Protagoras, I do not wish to
force the conversation upon you if you had rather
not, but when you are willing to argue with me in
such a way that I can follow you, then I will argue
with you. Now you, as is said of you by others and
as you say of yourself, are able to have discussions in
shorter forms of speech as well as in longer, for you
are a master of wisdom; but I cannot manage these
long speeches: I only wish that I could. You, on the
other hand, who are capable of either, ought to speak
shorter as I beg you, and then we might converse.
But I see that you are disinclined, and as I have an
engagement which will prevent my staying to hear
you at greater length (for I have to be in another
place), I will depart; although I should have liked
to have heard you.

Thus I spoke, and was rising from my seat, when
Callias seized me by the right hand, and in his left
hand caught hold of this old cloak of mine. He said:
We cannot let you go, Socrates, for if you leave us
there will be an end of our discussions: I must therefore beg you to remain, as there is nothing in the
world that I should like better than to hear you and
Protagoras discourse. Do not deny the company this
pleasure.

Now I had got up, and was in the act of departure.
Son of Hipponicus, I replied, I have always admired,
and do now heartily applaud and love your philosophical spirit, and I would gladly comply with your
request, if I could. But the truth is that I cannot.
And what you ask is as great an impossibility to me,
as if you bade me run a race with Crison of Himera, 336
when in his prime, or with some one of the long
or day course runners. To such a request I should
reply that I would fain ask the same of my own
legs; but they refuse to comply. And therefore if you
want to see Crison and me in the same stadium, you
must bid him slacken his speed to mine, for I cannot
run quickly, and he can run slowly. And in like manner if you want to hear me and Protagoras discoursing, you must ask him to shorten his answers,
and keep to the point, as he did at first; if not, how
can there be any discussion? For discussion is one

thing, and making an oration is quite another, in my humble opinion.

But you see, Socrates, said Callias, that Protagoras may fairly claim to speak in his own way, just as you claim to speak in yours.

Here Alcibiades interposed, and said: That Callias, is not a true statement of the case. For our friend Socrates admits that he cannot make a speech——in this he yields the palm to Protagoras: but I should be greatly surprised if he yielded to any living man in the power of holding and apprehending an argument. Now if Protagoras will make a similar admission, and confess that he is inferior to Socrates in argumentative skill, that is enough for Socrates; but if he claims a superiority in argument as well, let him ask and answer——not, when a question is asked, slipping away from the point, and instead of answering, making a speech at such length that most of his hearers forget the question at issue (not that Socrates is likely to forget——I will be bound for that, although he may pretend in fun that he has a bad memory). And Socrates appears to me to be more in the right than Protagoras; that is my view, and every man ought to say what he thinks.

When Alcibiades had done speaking, someone—— Critias, I believe——went on to say: O Prodicus and Hippias, Callias appears to me to be a partisan of Protagoras: and this led Alcibiades, who loves opposition, to take the other side. But we should not be partisans either of Socrates or of Protagoras; let us rather unite in entreating both of them not to break up the discussion.

Prodicus added: That, Critias, seems to me to be well said, for those who are present at such discussions ought to be impartial hearers of both the speakers; remembering, however, that impartiality is not the same as equality, for both sides should be impartially heard, and yet an equal meed should not be assigned to both of them; but to the wiser a higher meed should be given, and a lower to the less wise. And I as well as Critias would beg you, Protagoras and Socrates, to grant our request, which is, that you will argue with one another and not wrangle;

for friends argue with friends out of goodwill, but
only adversaries and enemies wrangle. And then our
meeting will be delightful; for in this way you, who
are the speakers, will be most likely to win esteem,
and not praise only, among us who are your audience; for esteem is a sincere conviction of the hearers'
souls, but praise is often an insincere expression of
men uttering falsehoods contrary to their conviction.
And thus we who are the hearers will be gratified and
not pleased; for gratification is of the mind when receiving wisdom and knowledge, but pleasure is of the
body when eating or experiencing some other bodily
delight. Thus spoke Prodicus, and many of the company applauded his words.

Hippias the sage spoke next. He said: All of you
who are here present I reckon to be kinsmen and
friends and fellow-citizens by nature and not by law;
for by nature like is akin to like, whereas law is the
tyrant of mankind, and othen compels us to do many
things which are against nature. How great would be
the disgrace then, if we, who know the nature of
things, and are the wisest of the Hellenes, and as such
are met together in this city, which is the metropolis
of wisdom, and in the greatest and most glorious
house of this city, should have nothing to show
worthy of this height of dignity, but should only
quarrel with one another like the meanest of mankind! I do pray and advise you, Protagoras, and
you, Socrates, to agree upon a compromise. Let us
be your peacemakers. And do not you, Socrates, aim
at this precise and extreme brevity in discourse, if
Protagoras objects, but loosen and let go the reins   338
of speech, that your words may be grander and more
becoming to you.[6] Neither do you, Protagoras, go
forth on the gale with every sail set out of sight of
land into an ocean of words, but let there be a mean
observed by both of you. Do as I say. And let me also
persuade you to choose an arbiter or overseer or
president; he will keep watch over your words and
will prescribe their proper length.

This proposal was received by the company with
universal approval; Callias said that he would not

6 Reading ὑμῖν.

let me off, and they begged me to choose an arbiter.
But I said that to choose an umpire of discourse
would be unseemly; for if the person chosen was
inferior, then the inferior or worse ought not to pre-
side over the better; or if he was equal, neither would
that be well; for he who is our equal will do as we do,
and what will be the use of choosing him? And if you
say, "Let us have a better then,"—to that I answer
that you cannot have anyone who is wiser than Protagoras. And if you choose another who is not
really better, and whom you only say is better, to put
another over him as though he were an inferior person would be an unworthy reflection on him; not
that, as far as I am concerned, any reflection is of
much consequence to me. Let me tell you then what
I will do in order that the conversation and discussion may go on as you desire. If Protagoras is not
disposed to answer, let him ask and I will answer;
and I will endeavor to show at the same time how,
as I maintain, he ought to answer: and when I have
answered as many questions as he likes to ask, let him
in like manner answer me; and if he seems to be not
very ready at answering the precise question asked of
him, you and I will unite in entreating him, as you
entreated me, not to spoil the discussion. And this
will require no special arbiter—all of you shall be
arbiters.

This was generally approved, and Protagoras,
though very much against his will, was obliged to
agree that he would ask questions; and when he had
put a sufficient number of them, that he would answer
in his turn those which he was asked in short replies.
He began to put his questions as follows:—

I am of opinion, Socrates, he said, that skill in
poetry is the principal part of education; and this
I conceive to be the power of knowing what compositions of the poets are correct, and what are not,
and how they are to be distinguished, and of explaining when asked the reason of the difference. And I
propose to transfer the question which you and I
have been discussing to the domain of poetry; we will
speak as before of virtue, but in reference to a passage of a poet. Now Simonides says to Scopas the
son of Creon the Thessalian:—

339

"Hardly on the one hand can a man become truly good, built four-square in hands and feet and mind, a work without a flaw." Do you know the poem? or shall I repeat the whole?

There is no need, I said; for I am perfectly well acquainted with the ode—I have made a careful study of it.

Very well, he said. And do you think that the ode is a good composition, and true?

Yes, I said, both good and true.

But if there is a contradiction, can the composition be good or true?

No, not in that case, I replied.

And is there not a contradiction? he asked. Reflect.

Well, my friend, I have reflected.

And does not the poet proceed to say, "I do not agree with the word of Pittacus, albeit the utterance of a wise man: Hardly can a man be good?" Now you will observe that this is said by the same poet.

I know it.

And do you think, he said, that the two sayings are consistent?

Yes, I said, I think so (at the same time I could not help fearing that there might be something in what he said). And you think otherwise?

Why, he said, how can he be consistent in both? First of all, premising as his own thought, "Hardly can a man become truly good"; and then a little further on in the poem, forgetting, and blaming Pittacus and refusing to agree with him, when he says, "Hardly can a man be good," which is the very same thing. And yet when he blames him who says the same with himself, he blames himself; so that he must be wrong either in his first or his second assertion.

Many of the audience cheered and applauded this. And I felt at first giddy and faint, as if I had received a blow from the hand of an expert boxer, when I heard his words and the sound of the cheering; and to confess the truth, I wanted to get time to think what the meaning of the poet really was. So I turned to Prodicus and called him. Prodicus, I said, Simonides is a countryman of yours, and you ought to come to his aid. I must appeal to you, like the river Scamander in Homer, who, when beleaguered by

Achilles, summons the Simoïs to aid him, saying:
"Brother dear, let us both together stay the force
of the hero."[7]

And I summon you, for I am afraid that Protagoras will make an end of Simonides. Now is the
time to rehabilitate Simonides, by the application of
your philosophy of synonyms which enables you to
distinguish "will" and "wish," and make other charming distinctions like those which you drew just now.
And I should like to know whether you would agree
with me; for I am of opinion that there is no contradiction in the words of Simonides. And first of all I
wish that you would say whether, in your opinion,
Prodicus, "being" is the same as "becoming."

Not the same, certainly, replied Prodicus.

Did not Simonides first set forth, as his own view,
that "Hardly can a man become truly good"?

Quite right, said Prodicus.

And then he blames Pittacus, not, as Protagoras
imagines, for repeating that which he says himself,
but for saying something different from himself. Pittacus does not say as Simonides says, that hardly can
a man become good, but hardly can a man be good:
and our friend Prodicus would maintain that being,
Protagoras, is not the same as becoming; and if they
are not the same, then Simonides is not inconsistent
with himself. I dare say that Prodicus and many
others would say, as Hesiod says,

"On the one hand, hardly can a man become good,
For the gods have made virtue the reward of toil;
But on the other hand, when you have climbed
    the height,
Then, to retain virtue, however difficult the
    acquisition, is easy."[8]

Prodicus heard and approved; but Protagoras said:
Your correction, Socrates, involves a greater error
than is contained in the sentence which you are correcting.

Alas! I said, Protagoras; then I am a sorry physician, and do but aggravate a disorder which I am
seeking to cure.

[7] Il. xxi. 308.
[8] Works and Days, 264 foll.

Such is the fact, he said.

How so? I ask d.

The poet, he replied, could never have made such a mist ke as to say that virtue, which in the opinion of ll men is the hardest of all things, can be easily retained.

Well, I said, and how fortunate are we in having Prodicus among us, at the right moment; for he has a wisdom, Protagoras, which, as I imagine, is more than human and of very ancient date, and may be as old as Simonides or even older. Learned as you are in many things, you appear to know nothing of this; but I know, for I am a disciple of his. And now, if I am not mistaken, you do not understand the word "hard" (χαλεπόν) in the sense which Simonides intended; and I must correct you, as Prodicus corrects me when I use the word "awful" (δεινόν) as a term of praise. If I say that Protagoras or anyone else is an "awfully" wise man, he asks me if I am not ashamed of calling that which is good "awful"; and then he explains to me that the term "awful" is always taken in a bad sense, and that no one speaks of being "awfully" healthy or wealthy, or "awful" peace, but of "awful" disease, "awful" war, "awful" poverty, meaning by the term "awful," evil. And I think that Simonides and his countrymen the Ceans, when they spoke of "hard" meant "evil," or something which you do not understand. Let us ask Prodicus, for he ought to be able to answer questions about the dialect of Simonides. What did he mean, Prodicus, by the term "hard"?

Evil, said Prodicus.

And therefore, I said, Prodicus, he blames Pittacus for saying, "Hard is the good," just as if that were equivalent to saying, Evil is the good.

Yes, he said, that was certainly his meaning; and he is twitting Pittacus with ignorance of the use of terms, which in a Lesbian, who has been accustomed to speak a barbarous language, is natural.

Do you hear, Protagoras, I asked, what our friend Prodicus is saying? And have you an answer for him?

You are entirely mistaken, Prodicus, said Protagoras; and I know very well that Simonides in using the word "hard" meant what all of us mean, not evil, but that which is not easy—that which takes a great deal of trouble: of this I am positive.

I said: I also incline to believe, Protagoras, that this was the meaning of Simonides, of which our friend Prodicus was very well aware, but he thought that he would make fun, and try if you could maintain your thesis; for that Simonides could never have meant the other is clearly proved by the context, in which he says that God only has this gift. Now he cannot surely mean to say that to be good is evil, when he afterwards proceeds to say that God only has this gift, and that this is the attribute of him and of no other. For if this be his meaning, Prodicus would impute to Simonides a character of recklessness which is very unlike his countrymen. And I should like to tell you, I said, what I imagine to be the real meaning of Simonides in this poem, if you will test what, in your way of speaking, would be called my skill in poetry; or if you would rather, I will be the listener.

To this proposal Protagoras replied: As you please; —and Hippias, Prodicus, and the others told me by all means to do as I proposed.

Then now, I said, I will endeavor to explain to you my opinion about this poem of Simonides. There is a very ancient philosophy which is more cultivated in Crete and Lacedaemon than in any other part of Hellas, and there are more philosophers in those countries than anywhere else in the world. This, however, is a secret which the Lacedaemonians deny; and they pretend to be ignorant, just because they do not wish to have it thought that they rule the world by wisdom, like the Sophists of whom Protagoras was speaking, and not by valor of arms; considering that if the reason of their superiority were disclosed, all men would be practicing their wisdom. And this secret of theirs has never been discovered by the imitators of Lacedaemonian fashions in other cities, who go about with their ears bruised in imitation of them, and have the caestus bound on their arms, and are always in training, and wear short cloaks; for they imagine that these are the practices which have enabled the Lacedaemonians to conquer the other Hellenes. Now when the Lacedaemonians want to unbend and hold free conversation with their wise men, and are no longer satisfied with mere secret intercourse, they drive out all these laconizers, and any other foreigners who may happen to be in their country, and they hold a philosophical *séance* unknown to strangers; and they themselves forbid their young men to go out into other cities—in this they are like the Cretans—in order that they may not unlearn the lessons which they have taught them. And in Lacedaemon and Crete not only men but also women have a pride in their high cultivation. And hereby you may know that I am right in attributing to the Lacedaemonians this excellence in philosophy and speculation: If a man converses with the most ordinary Lacedaemonian, he will find him seldom good for much in general conversation, but at any point in the discourse he will be darting out some notable saying, terse and full of meaning, with unerring aim; and the person with whom he is talking seems to be like a child in his hands. And many of our own age and of former ages have noted that the true Lacedaemonian type of character has the love of philosophy even stronger than the love of gymnastics; they are conscious that only a perfectly educated man is capable of uttering such expressions. Such were Thales of Miletus, and Pittacus of Mitylene, and Bias of Priene, and our own Solon, and Cleobulus the Lindian, and Myson the Chenian; and seventh in the catalogue of wise men was the Lacedaemonian Chilo. All these were lovers and emulators and disciples of the culture of the Lacedaemonians, and anyone may perceive that their wisdom was of this character; consisting of short memorable sentences, which they severally uttered. And they met together and dedicated in the temple of Apollo at Delphi, as the first-fruits of their wisdom, the far-famed inscriptions, which are in all men's mouths—"Know thyself," and "Nothing too much."

Why do I say all this? I am explaining that this Lacedaemonian brevity was the style of primitive philosophy. Now there was a saying of Pittacus which was privately circulated and received the approbation of the wise, "Hard is it to be good." And Simonides, who was ambitious of the fame of wis-

343

dom, was aware that if he could overthrow this saying, then, as if he had won a victory over some famous athlete, he would carry off the palm among his contemporaries. And if I am not mistaken, he composed the entire poem with the secret intention of damaging Pittacus and his saying.

Let us all unite in examining his words, and see whether I am speaking the truth. Simonides must have been a lunatic, if, in the very first words of the poem, wanting to say only that to become good is hard, he inserted μέν, "on the one hand" ["on the one hand to become good is hard"]; there would be no reason for the introduction of μέν, unless you suppose him to speak with a hostile reference to the words of Pittacus. Pittacus is saying "Hard is it to be good," and he, in refutation of this thesis, rejoins that the truly hard thing, Pittacus, is to become good, not joining "truly" with "good," but with "hard." Not, that the hard thing is to be truly good, as though there were some truly good men, and there were others who were good but not truly good (this would be a very simple observation, and quite unworthy of Simonides); but you must suppose him to make a trajection of the word "truly" (ἀληθέως), construing the saying of Pittacus thus (and let us imagine Pittacus to be speaking and Simonides answering him): "O my friends," says Pittacus, "hard is it to be good," and Simonides answers, "In that, Pittacus, you are mistaken; the difficulty is not to be good, but on the one hand, to become good, four-square in hands and feet and mind, without a flaw—that is hard truly." This way of reading the passage accounts for the insertion of μέν, "on the one hand," and for the position at the end of the clause of the word "truly," and all that follows shows this to be the meaning. A great deal might be said in praise of the details of the poem, which is a charming piece of workmanship, and very finished, but such minutiae would be tedious. I should like, however, to point out the general intention of the poem, which is certainly designed in every part to be a refutation of the saying of Pittacus. For he speaks in what follows a little further on as if he meant to argue that although there is a difficulty in becoming good, yet this is possible for a

344

time, and only for a time. But having become good,
to remain in a good state and be good, as you, Pittacus, affirm, is not possible, and is not granted to
man; God only has this blessing; "but man cannot
help being bad when the force of circumstances overpowers him." Now whom does the force of circumstance overpower in the command of a vessel?—not
the private individual, for he is always overpowered;
and as one who is already prostrate cannot be overthrown, and only he who is standing upright but not
he who is prostrate can be laid prostrate, so the
force of circumstances can only overpower him who,
at some time or other, has resources, and not him
who is at all times helpless. The descent of a great
storm may make the pilot helpless, or the severity
of the season the husbandman or the physician; for
the good may become bad, as another poet witnesses:
"The good are sometimes good and sometimes bad."
But the bad does not become bad; he is always bad.
So that when the force of circumstances overpowers
the man of resources and skill and virtue, then he
cannot help being bad. And you, Pittacus, are saying, "Hard is it to be good." Now there is a difficulty
in becoming good; and yet this is possible; but to be
good is an impossibility:

"For he who does well is the good man, and he who
does ill is the bad." But what sort of doing is good   345
in letters? and what sort of doing makes a man good
in letters? Clearly the knowing of them. And what
sort of well-doing makes a man a good physician?
Clearly the knowledge of the art of healing the sick.
"But he who does ill is the bad." Now who becomes a
bad physician? Clearly he who is in the first place a
physician, and in the second place a good physician;
for he may become a bad one also: but none of us
unskilled individuals can by any amount of doing ill
become physicians, any more than we can become
carpenters or anything of that sort; and he who by
doing ill cannot become a physician at all, clearly
cannot become a bad physician. In like manner the
good may become deteriorated by time, or toil, or
disease, or other accident (the only real doing ill is
to be deprived of knowledge), but the bad man will
never become bad, for he is always bad; and if he

were to become bad, he must previously have been
good. Thus the words of the poem tend to show that
on the one hand a man cannot be continuously good,
but that he may become good and may also become
bad; and again that

"They are the best for the longest time whom the
gods love."

All this relates to Pittacus, as is further proved by
the sequel. For he adds:

"Therefore I will not throw away my span of life
to no purpose in searching after the impossible, hop-
ing in vain to find a perfectly faultless man among
those who partake of the fruit of the broad-bosomed
earth; if I find him, I will send you word."

(This is the vehement way in which he pursues his
attack upon Pittacus throughout the whole poem):

"But him who does in evil, voluntarily I praise
and love; not even the gods war against necessity."

All this has a similar drift, for Simonides was not
so ignorant as to say that he praised those who did no
evil voluntarily, as though there were some who did
evil voluntarily. For no wise man, as I believe, will
allow that any human being errs voluntarily, or
voluntarily does evil and dishonorable actions; but
they are very well aware that all who do evil and dishonorable things do them against their will. And
Simonides never says that he praises him who does
no evil voluntarily; the word "voluntarily" applies to
himself. For he was under the impression that a good
man might often compel himself to love and praise
another,[9] and to be the friend and approver of another; and that there might be an involuntary love,
such as a man might feel to an unnatural father or
mother, or country, or the like. Now bad men, when
their parents or country have any defects, look on
them with malignant joy, and find fault with them
and expose and denounce them to others, under the
idea that the rest of mankind will be less likely to
take themselves to task and accuse them of neglect;
and they blame their defects far more than they deserve, in order that the odium which is necessarily incurred by them may be increased: but the good man

346

[9] Reading φιλεῖν καὶ ἐπαινεῖν καὶ φίλον τινὶ κ. τ. λ.

dissembles his feelings, and constrains himself to
praise them; and if they have wronged him and he is
angry, he pacifies his anger and is reconciled, and
compels himself to love and praise his own flesh and
blood. And Simonides, as is probable, considered
that he himself had often had to praise and magnify
a tyrant or the like, much against his will, and he also
wishes to imply to Pittacus that he does not censure
him because he is censorious.

"For I am satisfied [he says] when a man is neither
bad nor very stupid; and when he knows justice
(which is the health of states), and is of sound mind,
I will find no fault with him, for I am not given to
finding fault, and there are innumerable fools."

(Implying that if he delighted in censure he might
have abundant opportunity of finding fault).

"All things are good with which evil is unmingled."

In these latter words he does not mean to say that
all things are good which have no evil in them, as
you might say "All things are white which have no
black in them," for that would be ridiculous; but he
means to say that he accepts and finds no fault with
the moderate or intermediate state.

"I do not hope, [he says] to find a perfectly blame-
less man among those who partake of the fruits of
the broad-bosomed earth (if I find him, I will send
you word); in this sense I praise no man. But he who
is moderately good, and does no evil, is good enough
for me, who love and approve every one."

(And here observe that he uses a Lesbian word,
ἐπαίνημι (approve), because he is addressing Pittacus—

"Who love and *approve* every one *voluntarily*, who
does no evil: and that the stop should be put after
"voluntarily"); but there are some whom I involun-
tarily praise and love. And you, Pittacus, I would
never have blamed, if you had spoken what was
moderately good and true; but I do blame you because, putting on the appearance of truth, you are
speaking falsely about the highest matters." And this,
I said, Prodicus and Protagoras, I take to be the
meaning of Simonides in this poem.

Hippias said: I think, Socrates, that you have
given a very good explanation of the poem; but I

347

have also an excellent interpretation of my own which I will propound to you, if you will allow me.

Nay, Hippias, said Alcibiades; not now, but at some other time. At present we must abide by the compact which was made between Socrates and Protagoras, to the effect that as long as Protagoras is willing to ask, Socrates should answer; or that if he would rather answer, then that Socrates should ask.

I said: I wish Protagoras either to ask or answer as he is inclined; but I would rather have done with poems and odes, if he does not object, and come back to the question about which I was asking you at first, Protagoras, and by your help make an end of that. The talk about the poets seems to me like a commonplace entertainment to which a vulgar company have recourse; who, because they are not able to converse or amuse one another, while they are drinking, with the sound of their own voices and conversation, by reason of their stupidity, raise the prices of flute girls in the market, hiring for a great sum the voice of a flute instead of their own breath, to be the medium of intercourse among them: but where the company are real gentlemen and men of education, you will see no flute girls, nor dancing girls, nor harp girls; and they have no nonsense or games, but are contented with one another's conversation, of which their own voices are the medium, and which they carry on by turns and in an orderly manner, even though they are very liberal in their potations. And a company like this of ours, and men such as we profess to be, do not require the help of another's voice, or of the poets whom you cannot interrogate about the meaning of what they are saying; people who cite them declaring, some that the poet has one meaning, and others that he has another, and the point which is in dispute can never be decided. This sort of entertainment they decline, and prefer to talk with one another, and put one another to the proof in conversation. And these are the models 348 which I desire that you and I should imitate. Leaving the poets, and keeping to ourselves, let us try the mettle of one another and make proof of the truth in conversation. If you have a mind to ask, I am ready to answer; or if you would rather, do you answer, and give me the opportunity of resuming and completing our unfinished argument.

I made these and some similar observations; but Protagoras would not distinctly say which he would do. Thereupon Alcibiades turned to Callias, and said:—Do you think, Callias, that Protagoras is fair in refusing to say whether he will or will not answer? for I certainly think that he is unfair; he ought either to proceed with the argument, or distinctly to refuse to proceed, that we may know his intention; and then Socrates will be able to discourse with someone else, and the rest of the company will be free to talk with one another.

I think that Protagoras was really made ashamed by these words of Alcibiades, and when the prayers of Callias and the company were superadded, he was at last induced to argue, and said that I might ask and he would answer.

So I said: Do not imagine, Protagoras, that I have any other interest in asking questions of you but that of clearing up my own difficulties. For I think that Homer was very right in saying that "When two go together, one sees before the other,"[10] for all men who have a companion are readier in deed, word, or thought; but if a man "Sees a thing when he is alone," he goes about straightway seeking until he finds someone to whom he may show his discoveries, and who may confirm him in them. And I would rather hold discourse with you than with anyone, because I think that no man has a better understanding of most things which a good man may be expected to understand, and in particular of virtue. For who is there, but you?—who not only claim to be a good man and a gentleman, for many are this, and yet have not the power of making others good—whereas you are not only good yourself, but also the cause of goodness in others. Moreover such confidence have you in yourself, that although other Sophists conceal their profession, you proclaim in the face of Hellas that you are a Sophist or teacher of virtue and education, and are the first who demanded pay in

[10] Il. x. 224.

return. How then can I do otherwise than invite you
to the examination of these subjects, and ask questions and consult with you? I must, indeed. And I
should like once more to have my memory refreshed
by you about the questions which I was asking you at
first, and also to have your help in considering them.
If I am not mistaken the question was this: Are
wisdom and temperance and courage and justice and
holiness five names of the same thing? or has each of
the names a separate underlying essence and corresponding thing having a peculiar function, no one of
them being like any other of them? And you replied
that the five names were not the names of the same
thing, but that each of them had a separate object,
and that all these objects were parts of virtue,
not in the same way that the parts of gold are like
each other and the whole of which they are parts,
but as the parts of the face are unlike the whole of
which they are parts and one another, and have each
of them a distinct function. I should like to know
whether this is still your opinion, or if not, I will ask
you to define your meaning, and I shall not take you
to task if you now make a different statement. For
I dare say that you may have said what you did only
in order to make trial of me.

I answer, Socrates, he said, that all these qualities
are parts of virtue, and that four out of the five are
to some extent similar, and that the fifth of them,
which is courage, is very different from the other
four, as I prove in this way: You may observe that
many men are utterly unrighteous, unholy, intemperate, ignorant, who are nevertheless remarkable for
their courage.

Stop, I said; I should like to think about that.
When you speak of brave men, do you mean the confident, or another sort of nature?

Yes, he said; I mean the impetuous, ready to go
at that which others are afraid to approach.

In the next place, you would affirm virtue to be a
good thing, of which good thing you assert yourself
to be a teacher.

Yes, he said: I should say the best of all things, if
I am in my right mind.

And is it partly good and partly bad, I said, or wholly good?

Wholly good, and in the highest degree.

Tell me then; who are they who have confidence   350
when diving into a well?

I should say, the divers.

And the reason of this is that they have knowledge?

Yes, that is the reason.

And who have confidence when fighting on horse-back—the skilled horseman or the unskilled?

The skilled.

And who when fighting with light shields—the peltasts or the nonpeltasts?

The peltasts. And that is true of all other things, he said, if that is your point: those who have knowledge are more confident than those who have no knowledge, and they are more confident after they have learned than before.

And have you not seen persons utterly ignorant, I said, of these things, and yet confident about them?

Yes, he said, I have seen such persons far too confident.

And are not these confident persons also courageous?

In that case, he replied, courage would be a base thing, for the men of whom we are speaking are surely madmen.

Then who are the courageous? Are they not the confident?

Yes, he said; to that statement I adhere.

And those, I said, who are thus confident without knowledge are really not courageous, but mad; and in that case the wisest are also the most confident, and being the most confident are also the bravest, and upon that view again wisdom will be courage.

Nay, Socrates, he replied, you are mistaken in your remembrance of what was said by me. When you asked me, I certainly did say that the courageous are the confident; but I was never asked whether the confident are the courageous; if you had asked me, I should have answered "Not all of them": and what I did answer you have not proved to be false, although you proceeded to show that those who have knowledge are more courageous than they were before they had knowledge, and more courageous than others who have no knowledge, and were then led on to think that courage is the same as wisdom. But in this way of arguing you might come to imagine that strength is wisdom. You might begin by asking whether the strong are able, and I should say "Yes"; and then whether those who know how to wrestle are not more able to wrestle than those who do not know how to wrestle, and more able after than before they had learned, and I should assent. And when I had admitted this, you might use my admissions in such a way as to prove that upon my view wisdom is strength; whereas in that case I should not have admitted, any more than in the other, that the able are strong, although I have admitted that the strong are able. For there is a difference between ability and strength; the former is given by knowledge as well as by madness or rage, but strength comes from nature and a healthy state of the body. And in like manner I say of confidence and courage, that they are not the same; and I argue that the courageous are confident, but not all the confident courageous. For confidence may be given to men by art, and also, like ability, by madness and rage; but courage comes to them from nature and the healthy state of the soul.

351

I said: You would admit, Protagoras, that some men live well and others ill?

He assented.

And do you think that a man lives well who lives in pain and grief?

He does not.

But if he lives pleasantly to the end of his life, will he not in that case have lived well?

He will.

Then to live pleasantly is good, and to live unpleasantly an evil?

Yes, he said, if the pleasure be good and honorable.

And do you, Protagoras, like the rest of the world, call some pleasant things evil and some painful things good?——for I am rather disposed to say that things are good in as far as they are pleasant, if they have no consequences of another sort, and in as far as they are painful they are bad.

I do not know, Socrates, he said, whether I can

venture to assert in that unqualified manner that the pleasant is the good and the painful the evil. Having regard not only to my present answer, but also to the whole of my life, I shall be safer, if I am not mistaken, in saying that there are some pleasant things which are not good, and that there are some painful things which are good, and some which are not good, and that there are some which are neither good nor evil.

And you would call pleasant, I said, the things which participate in pleasure or create pleasure?

Certainly, he said.

Then my meaning is, that in as far as they are pleasant they are good; and my question would imply that pleasure is a good in itself.

According to your favorite mode of speech, Socrates, "let us reflect about this," he said; and if the reflection is to the point, and the result proves that pleasure and good are really the same, then we will agree; but if not, then we will argue.

And would you wish to begin the inquiry? I said; or shall I begin?

You ought to take the lead, he said; for you are the author of the discussion.

May I employ an illustration? I said. Suppose 352 someone who is inquiring into the health or some other bodily quality of another:—he looks at his face and at the tips of his fingers, and then he says, Uncover your chest and back to me that I may have a better view:—that is the sort of thing which I desire in this speculation. Having seen what your opinion is about good and pleasure, I am minded to say to you: Uncover your mind to me, Protagoras, and reveal your opinion about knowledge, that I may know whether you agree with the rest of the world. Now the rest of the world are of opinion that knowledge is a principle not of strength, or of rule, or of command: their notion is that a man may have knowledge, and yet that the knowledge which is in him may be overmastered by anger, or pleasure, or pain, or love, or perhaps by fear—just as if knowledge were a slave, and might be dragged about anyhow. Now is that your view? or do you think that knowledge is a noble and commanding thing, which cannot be overcome, and will not allow a man, if he only knows the difference of good and evil, to do anything which is contrary to knowledge, but that wisdom will have strength to help him?

I agree with you, Socrates, said Protagoras; and not only so, but I, above all other men, am bound to say that wisdom and knowledge are the highest of human things.

Good, I said, and true. But are you aware that the majority of the world are of another mind; and that men are commonly supposed to know the things which are best, and not to do them when they might? And most persons whom I have asked the reason of this have said that when men act contrary to knowledge they are overcome by pain, or pleasure, or some of those affections which I was just now mentioning.

Yes, Socrates, he replied; and that is not the only point about which mankind are in error.

Suppose, then, that you and I endeavor to instruct and inform them what is the nature of this affection which they call "being overcome by pleasure," and which they affirm to be the reason why they do not always do what is best. When we say to them: Friends, you are mistaken, and are saying what is not true, they would probably reply: Socrates and Protagoras, if this affection of the soul is not to be called "being overcome by pleasure," pray, what is it, and by what name would you describe it?

But why, Socrates, should we trouble ourselves about the opinion of the many, who just say anything that happens to occur to them?

I believe, I said, that they may be of use in helping us to discover how courage is related to the other parts of virtue. If you are disposed to abide by our agreement, that I should show the way in which, as I think, our recent difficulty is most likely to be cleared up, do you follow; but if not, never mind.

You are quite right, he said; and I would have you proceed as you have begun.

Well then, I said, let me suppose that they repeat their question, What account do you give of that which, in our way of speaking, is termed being overcome by pleasure? I should answer thus: Listen, and Protagoras and I will endeavor to show you. When men are overcome by eating and drinking and other sensual desires which are pleasant, and they, knowing them to be evil, nevertheless indulge in them, would you not say that they were overcome by pleasure? They will not deny this. And suppose that you and I were to go on and ask them again: "In what way do you say that they are evil—in that they are pleasant and give pleasure at the moment, or because they cause disease and poverty and other like evils in the future? Would they still be evil, if they had no attendant evil consequences, simply because they give the consciousness of pleasure of whatever nature?"— Would they not answer that they are not evil on account of the pleasure which is immediately given by them, but on account of the after consequences— diseases and the like?

I believe, said Protagoras, that the world in general would answer as you do.

And in causing diseases do they not cause pain? and in causing poverty do they not cause pain;— they would agree to that also, if I am not mistaken?

Protagoras assented.

Then I should say to them, in my name and yours: Do you think them evil for any other reason, except because they end in pain and rob us of other pleasures:—there again they would agree?

We both of us thought that they would.

And then I should take the question from the opposite point of view, and say: "Friends, when you speak of goods being painful, do you not mean remedial goods, such as gymnastic exercises, and military service, and the physician's use of burning, cutting, drugging, and starving? Are these the things which are good but painful?"—they would assent to me?

He agreed.

"And do you call them good because they occasion the greatest immediate suffering and pain; or because, afterwards, they bring health and improvement of the bodily conditions and the salvation of states and power over others and wealth?"—they would agree to the latter alternative, if I am not mistaken?

He assented.

"Are these things good for any other reason except

that they end in pleasure, and get rid of and avert pain? Are you looking to any other standard but pleasure and pain when you call them good?"—they would acknowledge that they were not?

I think so, said Protagoras.

"And do you not pursue after pleasure as a good, and avoid pain as an evil?"

He assented.

"Then you think that pain is an evil and pleasure is a good: and even pleasure you deem an evil, when it robs you of greater pleasures than it gives, or causes pains greater than the pleasure. If, however, you call pleasure an evil in relation to some other end or standard, you will be able to show us that standard. But you have none to show."

I do not think that they have, said Protagoras.

"And have you not a similar way of speaking about pain? You call pain a good when it takes away greater pains than those which it has, or gives pleasures greater than the pains: then if you have some standard other than pleasure and pain to which you refer when you call actual pain a good, you can show what that is. But you cannot."

True, said Protagoras.

Suppose again, I said, that the world says to me: "Why do you spend many words and speak in many ways on this subject?" Excuse me, friends, I should reply; but in the first place there is a difficulty in explaining the meaning of the expression "overcome by pleasure"; and the whole argument turns upon this. And even now, if you see any possible way in which evil can be explained as other than pain, or good as other than pleasure, you may still retract. Are you satisfied, then, at having a life of pleasure which is without pain? If you are, and if you are unable to show any good or evil which does not end in pleasure and pain, hear the consequences:—If what you say is true, then the argument is absurd which affirms that a man often does evil knowingly, when he might abstain, because he is seduced and overpowered by pleasure; or again, when you say that a man knowingly refuses to do what is good because he is overcome at the moment by pleasure. And that this is ridiculous will be evident if only we give up the use of various names, such as pleasant and painful, and good and evil. As there are two things, let us call them by two names—first, good and evil, and then pleasant and painful. Assuming this, let us go on to say that a man does evil knowing that he does evil. But someone will ask, Why? Because he is overcome, is the first answer. And by what is he overcome? the inquirer will proceed to ask. And we shall not be able to reply "By pleasure," for the name of pleasure has been exchanged for that of good. In our answer, then, we shall only say that he is overcome. "By what?" he will reiterate. By the good, we shall have to reply; indeed we shall. Nay, but our questioner will rejoin with a laugh, if he be one of the swaggering sort, "That is too ridiculous, that a man should do what he knows to be evil when he ought not, because he is overcome by good. Is that, he will ask, because the good was worthy or not worthy of conquering the evil?" And in answer to that we shall clearly reply, Because it was not worthy; for if it had been worthy, then he who, as we say, was overcome by pleasure, would not have been wrong. "But how," he will reply, "can the good be unworthy of the evil, or the evil of the good?" Is not the real explanation that they are out of proportion to one another, either as greater and smaller, or more and fewer? This we cannot deny. And when you speak of being overcome—"what do you mean," he will say, "but that you choose the greater evil in exchange for the lesser good?" Admitted. And now substitute the names of pleasure and pain for good and evil, and say, not as before, that a man does what is evil knowingly, but that he does what is painful knowingly, and because he is overcome by pleasure, which is unworthy to overcome. What measure is there of the relations of pleasure to pain other than excess and defect, which means that they become greater and smaller, and more and fewer, and differ in degree? For if anyone says: "Yes, Socrates, but immediate pleasure differs widely from future pleasure and pain"— To that I should reply: And do they differ in anything but in pleasure and pain? There can be no other measure of them. And do you, like a skillful weigher, put into the balance the pleasures and the

356

pains, and their nearness and distance, and weigh them, and then say which outweighs the other. If you weigh pleasures against pleasures, you of course take the more and greater; or if you weigh pains against pains, you take the fewer and the less; or if pleasures against pains, then you choose that course of action in which the painful is exceeded by the pleasant, whether the distant by the near or the near by the distant; and you avoid that course of action in which the pleasant is exceeded by the painful. Would you not admit, my friends, that this is true? I am confident that they cannot deny this.

He agreed with me.

Well then, I shall say, if you agree so far, be so good as to answer me a question: Do not the same magnitudes appear larger to your sight when near, and smaller when at a distance? They will acknowledge that. And the same holds of thickness and number, also sounds, which are in themselves equal, are greater, when near, and lesser when at a distance. They will grant that also. Now suppose happiness to consist in doing or choosing the greater, and in not doing or in avoiding the less, what would be the saving principle of human life? Would not the art of measuring be the saving principle; or would the power of appearance? Is not the latter that deceiving art which makes us wander up and down and take the things at one time of which we repent at another, both in our actions and in our choice of things great and small? But the art of measurement would do away with the effect of appearances, and, showing the truth, would fain teach the soul at last to find rest in the truth, and would thus save our life. Would not mankind generally acknowledge that the art which accomplishes this result is the art of measurement?

Yes, he said, the art of measurement.

Suppose, again, the salvation of human life to depend on the choice of odd and even, and on the knowledge of when a man ought to choose the greater or less, either in reference to themselves or to each other, and whether near or at a distance; what would be the saving principle of our lives? Would not knowledge?—a knowledge of measuring, when the question is one of excess and defect, and a

357

knowledge of number, when the question is of odd
and even? The world will assent, will they not?

Protagoras himself thought that they would.

Well then, my friends, I say to them; seeing that
the salvation of human life has been found to consist
in the right choice of pleasures and pains—in the
choice of the more and the fewer, and the greater
and the less, and the nearer and remoter, must not
this measuring be a consideration of their excess and
defect and equality in relation to each other?

This is undeniably true.

And this, as possessing measure, must undeniably
also be an art and science?

They will agree, he said.

The nature of that art or science will be a matter
of future consideration; but the existence of such a
science furnishes a demonstrative answer to the question which you asked of me and Protagoras. At the
time when you asked the question, if you remember,
both of us were agreeing that there was nothing
mightier than knowledge, and that knowledge, in
whatever existing, must have the advantage over
pleasure and all other things; and then you said that
pleasure often got the advantage even over a man
who has knowledge; and we refused to allow this, and
you rejoined: O Protagoras and Socrates, what is the
meaning of being overcome by pleasure if not this?—
tell us what you call such a state:—if we had immediately and at the time answered "Ignorance," you
would have laughed at us. But now, in laughing at us,
you will be laughing at yourselves: for you also admitted that men err in their choice of pleasures and
pains; that is, in their choice of good and evil, from
defect of knowledge; and you admitted, further, that
they err, not only from defect of knowledge in
general, but of that particular knowledge which is
called measuring. And you are also aware that the
erring act which is done without knowledge is done
in ignorance. This, therefore, is the meaning of being
overcome by pleasure;—ignorance, and that the
greatest. And our friends Protagoras and Prodicus
and Hippias declare that they are the physicians of
ignorance; but you, who are under the mistaken
impression that ignorance is not the cause, and that

the art of which I am speaking cannot be taught, neither go yourselves, nor send your children, to the Sophists, who are the teachers of these things—you take care of your money and give them none; and the result is, that you are the worse off both in public and private life:—Let us suppose this to be our answer to the world in general: And now I should like to ask you, Hippias, and you, Prodicus, as well as Protagoras (for the argument is to be yours as well as ours), whether you think that I am speaking the truth or not?

358

They all thought that what I said was entirely true.

Then you agree, I said, that the pleasant is the good, and the painful evil. And here I would beg my friend Prodicus not to introduce his distinction of names, whether he is disposed to say pleasurable, delightful, joyful. However, by whatever name he prefers to call them, I will ask you, most excellent Prodicus, to answer in my sense of the words.

Prodicus laughed and assented, as did the others.

Then, my friends, what do you say to this? Are not all actions honorable and useful, of which the tendency is to make life painless and pleasant? The honorable work is also useful and good?

This was admitted.

Then, I said, if the pleasant is the good, nobody does anything under the idea or conviction that some other thing would be better and is also attainable, when he might do the better. And this inferiority of a man to himself is merely ignorance, as the superiority of a man to himself is wisdom.

They all assented.

And is not ignorance the having a false opinion and being deceived about important matters?

To this also they unanimously assented.

Then, I said, no man voluntarily pursues evil, or that which he thinks to be evil. To prefer evil to good is not in human nature; and when a man is compelled to choose one of two evils, no one will choose the greater when he may have the less.

All of us agreed to every word of this.

Well, I said, there is a certain thing called fear or terror; and here, Prodicus, I should particularly like to know whether you would agree with me in defining this fear or terror as expectation of evil.

Protagoras and Hippias agreed, but Prodicus said that this was fear and not terror.

Never mind, Prodicus, I said; but let me ask whether, if our former assertions are true, a man will pursue that which he fears when he is not compelled? Would not this be in flat contradiction to the admission which has been already made, that he thinks the things which he fears to be evil; and no one will pursue or voluntarily accept that which he thinks to be evil?

That also was universally admitted.

Then, I said, these, Hippias and Prodicus, are our premises; and I would beg Protagoras to explain to us how he can be right in what he said at first. I do not mean in what he said quite at first, for his first statement, as you may remember, was that whereas there were five parts of virtue none of them was like any other of them; each of them had a separate function. To this, however, I am not referring, but to the assertion which he afterwards made that of the five virtues four were nearly akin to each other, but that the fifth, which was courage, differed greatly from the others. And of this he gave me the following proof. He said: You will find, Socrates, that some of the most impious, and unrighteous, and intemperate, and ignorant of men are among the most courageous; which proves that courage is very different from the other parts of virtue. I was surprised at his saying this at the time, and I am still more surprised now that I have discussed the matter with you. So I asked him whether by the brave he meant the confident. Yes, he replied, and the impetuous or goers. (You may remember, Protagoras, that this was your answer.)

He assented.

Well then, I said, tell us against what are the courageous ready to go—against the same dangers as the cowards?

No, he answered.

Then against something different?

Yes, he said.

359

Then the cowards go where there is safety, and the courageous where there is danger?

Yes, Socrates, so men say.

Very true, I said. But I want to know against what do you say that the courageous are ready to go—against dangers, believing them to be dangers, or not against dangers?

No, said he; the former case has been proved by you in the previous argument to be impossible.

That, again, I replied, is quite true. And if this has been rightly proven, then no one goes to meet what he thinks to be dangers, since the want of self-control, which makes men rush into dangers, has been shown to be ignorance.

He assented.

And yet the courageous man and the coward alike go to meet that about which they are confident; so that, in this point of view, the cowardly and the courageous go to meet the same things.

And yet, Socrates, said Protagoras, that to which the coward goes is the opposite of that to which the courageous goes; the one, for example, is ready to go to battle, and the other is not ready.

And is going to battle honorable or disgraceful? I said.

Honorable, he replied.

And if honorable, then already admitted by us to be good; for all honorable actions we have admitted to be good.

That is true; and to that opinion I shall always adhere.

True, I said. But which of the two are they who, as you say, are unwilling to go to war, which is a good and honorable thing?

The cowards, he replied.

And what is good and honorable, I said, is also pleasant?

It has certainly been acknowledged to be so, he replied.

And do the cowards knowingly refuse to go to the nobler, and pleasanter, and better?

The admission of that, he replied, would belie our former admissions.

But does not the courageous man also go to meet the better, and pleasanter, and nobler?

That must be admitted.

And the courageous man has no base fear or base confidence?

True, he replied.

And if not base, then honorable?

He admitted this.

And if honorable, then good?

Yes.

But the fear and confidence of the coward or foolhardy or madman, on the contrary, are base?

He assented.

And these base fears and confidences originate in ignorance and uninstructedness?

True, he said.

Then as to the motive from which the cowards act, do you call it cowardice or courage?

I should say cowardice, he replied.

And have they not been shown to be cowards through their ignorance of dangers?

Assuredly, he said.

And because of that ignorance they are cowards?

He assented.

And the reason why they are cowards is admitted by you to be cowardice?

He again assented.

Then the ignorance of what is and is not dangerous is cowardice?

He nodded assent.

But surely courage, I said, is opposed to cowardice?

Yes.

Then the wisdom which knows what are and are not dangers is opposed to the ignorance of them?

To that again he nodded assent.

And the ignorance of them is cowardice?

To that he very reluctantly nodded assent.

And the knowledge of that which is and is not dangerous is courage, and is opposed to the ignorance of these things?

At this point he would no longer nod assent, but was silent.

And why, I said, do you neither assent nor dissent, Protagoras?

Finish the argument by yourself, he said.

I only want to ask one more question, I said. I want to know whether you still think that there are men who are most ignorant and yet most courageous?

You seem to have a great ambition to make me answer, Socrates, and therefore I will gratify you, and say, that this appears to me to be impossible consistently with the argument.

My only object, I said, in continuing the discussion, has been the desire to ascertain the nature and relations of virtue; for if this were clear, I am very sure that the other controversy which has been carried on at great length by both of us—you affirming and I denying that virtue can be taught—would also become clear. The result of our discussion appears to me to be singular. For if the argument had a human voice, that voice would be heard laughing at us and saying: "Protagoras and Socrates, you are strange beings; there are you, Socrates, who were saying that virtue cannot be taught, contradicting yourself now by your attempt to prove that all things are knowledge, including justice, and temperance, and courage—which tends to show that virtue can certainly be taught; for if virtue were other than knowledge, as Protagoras attempted to prove, then clearly virtue cannot be taught; but if virtue is entirely knowledge, as you are seeking to show, then I cannot but suppose that virtue is capable of being taught. Protagoras, on the other hand, who started by saying that it might be taught, is now eager to prove it to be anything rather than knowledge; and if this is true, it must be quite incapable of being taught." Now I, Protagoras, perceiving this terrible confusion of our ideas, have a great desire that they should be cleared up. And I should like to carry on the discussion until we ascertain what virtue is, and whether capable of being taught or not, lest haply Epimetheus should trip us up and deceive us in the argument, as he forgot us in the story; I prefer your Prometheus to your Epimetheus, for of him I make use, whenever I am busy about these questions, in Promethean care of my own life. And if you have no objection, as I said at first, I should like to have your help in the inquiry.

Protagoras replied: Socrates, I am not of a base nature, and I am the last man in the world to be envious. I cannot but applaud your energy and your conduct of an argument. As I have often said, I admire you above all men whom I know, and far above all men of your age; and I believe that you will become very eminent in philosophy. Let us come back to the subject at some future time; at present we had better turn to something else.

By all means, I said, if that is your wish; for I too ought long since to have kept the engagement of which I spoke before, and only tarried because I could not refuse the request of the noble Callias. So the conversation ended, and we went our way.

Outline of the Symposium

I. Introduction (172a–177e)
  A. Frame 1: with Apollodorus (172a–174a)
    1. memory; the secondhand character of the narration (172a–173b)
      a. the tale has already been rehearsed to Glaucon (172b–c)
      b. the events took place long ago, when narrator and hearer were children (172d–173a)
      c. story originally came from Aristodemus, a lover of Socrates (173b)
    2. Apollodorus thinks everything but philosophy a waste of time, and this is his mania (173b–174a)
  B. Frame 2: beginning of narrative by Aristodemus, going to the dinner (174a–175e)
  C. Drinking and the making of speeches (175e–177e)
II. Phaedrus (178a–180c)
  A. Eros is among the oldest gods, and is without parents (178a–b)
  B. Eros the cause of the greatest goods for man (178b–180b)
    1. in life (178b–179b)
      a. in private—the greatest good in youth is to have an honorable lover
      b. in public—it is impossible for one to perform noble deeds without Eros
      c. in the military—army should be composed of lovers and beloveds, as shame will prevent cowardice
    2. in death (179b–180b)
      a. Alcestis—dying for her husband
      b. Orpheus—a cowardly musician, who died at the hands of women
  C. Conclusion—Eros the oldest and most honorable of the gods, who has the authority to provide virtue and happiness for men living or dead (180b)
  D. Other, forgotten speeches following that of Phaedrus (180c)
III. Pausanias (180c–185c)

A. Criticism of Phaedrus—Eros should not be considered one (180c)
B. Eros as twofold (180c–181a)
  1. no Aphrodite without Eros, but Aphrodite is twofold (180d–181a)
    a. the elder, daughter of heaven (the Heavenly or Ouranian)
    b. the younger, daughter of Zeus and Dione (the Popular or Pandemian)
  2. Eros is good only when done nobly (181a–182a)
    a. Eros of the Pandemian Aphrodite is popular and works by chance, on the meaner sort of men
    b. Eros of Ouranian Aphrodite
C. Customs of (Pandemian) Eros in various city-states (182a–d)
  1. Elis and Boeotia—no art (sophos) of speech, hence a simple ordinance to gratify lovers (182a–b)
  2. Ionia—gratification in Eros, together with philosophy and sports, a disgrace (182b–c)
  3. tyrannies—Aristogeiton and Harmodius (182c–d)
D. Customs of (Ouranian) Eros of Athens—complicated laws, which are better (182d–185c)
  1. explanation of the laws (182d–184c)
    a. Eros held to be fine, and encouraged
    b. Eros held to be shameful, and forbidden
    c. solution: Eros is neither noble nor base in itself, but only the way it is done: wicked is love of the body, which is temporary
  2. the right way to Ouranian Eros (in Athens) (184c–185b)
    a. it lies through virtue and love of wisdom
    b. gratification permissible only when one educates another
    c. dishonorable and honorable deceptions
  3. conclusion (185b–c)
IV. Interlude: hiccoughs of Aristophanes, and prescribed cure (185c–e)
V. Eryximachus (185e–188e)
  A. Criticism of Pausanias (185e–186a)
  B. The sciences as knowledge of Eros (186a–188d)
    1. medicine (186a–187a)
      a. Eros not merely an impulse of human souls toward beautiful men but an attraction of all creatures to a great variety of things

    b. sound desire different from unsound, and medicine encourages the sound, for medicine is knowledge of erotics; so in the body with respect to filling and evacuating

    c. the physician must be able to make friends of opponents in the body: hot-cold, bitter-sweet, dry-wet

  2. music (187a–188a)

    a. the art is made (interpreting Heraclitus) through bringing to agreement of grave and acute

    b. music a knowledge of erotics relating to harmony or rhythm

    c. in applying these to men, we now must have Ouranian Eros, sprung from the muse

    d. Pandemian Eros comes from various (unregulated) songs

  3. astronomy (188a–b)

    a. harmony in the order of seasons

    b. ill effects of wanton Eros in the stars

  4. mantic art (188b–d)

    a. this supervises the health of these loves

    b. so this art is purveyor of friendship between gods and men

C. Conclusion: love, as a single whole, exerts a complete power, but what is consummated for a good purpose, temperately and justly, is the strongest. I may have omitted points which Aristophanes must supply (188d–e)

VI. Interlude: hiccoughs of Aristophanes now over; he will try to say something laughable but not ridiculous. Banter between him and Eryximachus (189a–c)

VII. Aristophanes (189c–193e)

A. He intends to speak differently from Eryximachus and Pausanias, for human beings have not seen the power of Eros (189c–d)

  1. he is most friendly (189c–d)

  2. he heals man's ills (189d)

  3. this should be taught to mankind at large (189d)

B. We must discuss the nature of man and what it has undergone (189d–192e)

  1. nature of men (189c–190b)

    a. originally different, with three sexes, including androgyne

    b. form was round, with double sets of limbs, etc.

      c. male was offspring of sun, female of earth,
         androgyne of moon
    2. what men have undergone (190b–192e)
      a. their strength prompted conspiracy against gods,
         so Zeus, not wishing to kill them and lose sacri-
         fices, lessened their strength by slicing them in
         two. Apollo then turned their parts frontward,
         smoothed, and healed them. They then sought
         their counterparts and perished clinging to them
      b. Zeus tried a new device, so they could beget
         upon each other rather than the earth
  C. Conclusion: cause of erotic desire (192e–193e)
    1. the cause of love is now clear; and love is the
      desire and pursuit of the whole (192e–193a)
    2. we were formerly one, and are now many, and
      each of us may be split again, like bas-reliefs on
      tombstones; hence we should exhort to a pious ob-
      servance of the gods in all things. In this way, all,
      including Pausanias and Agathon, may find his
      own, by chance, and restore his ancient state
      (193a–d)
    3. aside to Eryximachus (193d–e)
VIII. Interlude: Eryximachus—Socrates—Agathon—Soc-
    rates—Phaedrus—Agathon (193e–194e)
IX. Agathon (194e–197e)
  A. Introductory: criticism of former speakers for speak-
    ing not of the god himself but of the goods he gives
    mankind (194e)
  B. We shall praise Eros for what sort he is and then for
    what he brings (195a–197e)
    1. What sort Eros is (195a–197c)
      a. Eros is most beautiful
        i. he is youngest of the gods
        ii. he is most delicate, hence requires a poet
          such as Homer to describe him. He lives in
          the characters and souls of gods and men
        iii. he is most pliant of form—grace
      b. Eros is most virtuous
        i. with respect to injuries—just
        ii. with respect to pleasures—temperate
        iii. brave
        iv. wise
    2. Eros the cause of good things for others (197c–e)
X. Interlude: Socrates—Eryximachus (198a–b)

the essence of beauty, and relinquishing the rest for this

δ. the man whose soul is in contact with real truth and virtue is immortal

D. Conclusion of Socrates' speech: (212b–c)
 1. this was what Diotima told me, and I try to tell others (212b)
 2. every man should honor love especially (212b–c)
 3. this is a eulogy of love (212c)

XII. Interlude (212c–215a)
 A. Applause for Socrates from everyone but Aristophanes (212c–d)
 B. Entry of Alcibiades, drunk (212d–213b)
 C. Encounter of Alcibiades and Socrates (213b–e)
 D. New plans (213e–215a)
  1. for drinking (213e–214b)
  2. for speaking about Socrates (214b–215a)

XIII. Alcibiades (215a–222b)
 A. Manner of praising Socrates to everyone: by likenesses (215a–217e)
  1. Socrates like the statuettes of Silenus and like the satyr Marsyas in figure (215a)
  2. Socrates like them in every other way: (215a–217e)
   a. a piper, but in prose, without an instrument—he overwhelms his hearers with his speech
   b. erotically inclined
   c. affects stupidity outwardly, but inwardly he despises the inclinations of his fellows—their ambitions and desires
    i. in lone meetings with Alcibiades
    ii. in training
    iii. at supper
 B. Digression: we would not tell what is to follow to everyone, except when we are drunk (217e–218b)
  1. in children and wine there is truth
  2. we would not speak to those who had not our same experience, but everyone in this audience does have
 C. Resumption (218b–219e)
  1. Socrates not really asleep, and not shy
  2. Socrates unwilling to exchange reputed for real beauties
  3. Socrates disdains the charms of Alcibiades, and is to be tried for this

SYMPOSIUM

APOLLODORUS	ARISTOPHANES
PHAEDRUS	AGATHON
PAUSANIAS	SOCRATES
ERYXIMACHUS	ALCIBIADES

A TROOP OF REVELLERS

CONCERNING the things about which you ask to be informed I believe that I am not ill-prepared with an answer. For the day before yesterday I was coming from my own home at Phalerum to the city, and one of my acquaintance, who had caught a sight of me from behind, calling out playfully in the distance, said: Apollodorus, O thou Phalerian[1] man, halt! So I did as I was bid; and then he said, I was looking for you, Apollodorus, only just now, that I might ask you about the speeches in praise of love, which were delivered by Socrates, Alcibiades, and others, at Agathon's supper. Phoenix, the son of Philip, told another person who told me of them; his narrative was very indistinct, but he said that you knew, and I wish that you would give me an account of them. Who, if not you, should be the reporter of the words of your friend? And first tell me, he said, were you present at this meeting?

Your informant, Glaucon, I said, must have been very indistinct indeed, if you imagine that the occasion was recent; or that I could have been of the party.

Why, yes, he replied, I thought so.

Impossible: I said. Are you ignorant that for many years Agathon has not resided at Athens; and not

---

[1] Probably a play of words on φαλαρòς, "bald-headed."

three have elapsed since I became acquainted with
Socrates, and have made it my daily business to
know all that he says and does. There was a time
when I was running about the world, fancying myself
to be well employed, but I was really a most wretched
being, no better than you are now. I thought that I
ought to do anything rather than be a philosopher.

Well, he said, jesting apart, tell me when the meeting occurred.

In our boyhood, I replied, when Agathon won the
prize with his first tragedy, on the day after that
on which he and his chorus offered the sacrifice of
victory.

Then it must have been a long while ago, he said;
and who told you—did Socrates?

No indeed, I replied, but the same person who told
Phoenix;—he was a little fellow, who never wore any
shoes, Aristodemus, of the deme of Cydathenaeum.
He had been at Agathon's feast; and I think that in
those days there was no one who was a more devoted
admirer of Socrates. Moreover, I have asked Socrates
about the truth of some parts of his narrative, and
he confirmed them. Then, said Glaucon, let us have
the tale over again; is not the road to Athens just
made for conversation? And so we walked, and
talked of the discourses on love; and therefore, as
I said at first, I am not ill-prepared to comply with
your request, and will have another rehearsal of them
if you like. For to speak or to hear others speak
of philosophy always gives me the greatest pleasure,
to say nothing of the profit. But when I hear another
strain, especially that of you rich men and traders,
such conversation displeases me; and I pity you who
are my companions, because you think that you
are doing something when in reality you are doing
nothing. And I dare say that you pity me in return,
whom you regard as an unhappy creature, and very
probably you are right. But I certainly know of you
what you only think of me—there is the difference.

Companion. I see, Apollodorus, that you are just
the same—always speaking evil of yourself, and of
others; and I do believe that you pity all mankind,
with the exception of Socrates, yourself first of all,
true in this to your old name, which, however, de-

served, I know not how you acquired, of Apollodorus the madman; for you are always raging against yourself and everybody but Socrates.

Apollodorus. Yes, friend, and the reason why I am said to be mad, and out of my wits, is just because I have these notions of myself and you: no other evidence is required.

Com. No more of that, Apollodorus; but let me renew my request that you would repeat the conversation.

Apoll. Well, the tale of love was on this wise:— But perhaps I had better begin at the beginning, and endeavor to give you the exact words of Aristodemus:

He said that he met Socrates fresh from the bath and sandalled; and the sight of the sandals was unusual, he asked him whither he was going that he had been converted into such a beau:—

To a banquet at Agathon's, he replied, whose invitation to his sacrifice of victory I refused yesterday, fearing a crowd, but promising that I would come today instead; and so I have put on my finery, because he is such a fine man. What say you to going with me unasked?

I will do as you bid me, I replied.

Follow then, he said, and let us demolish the proverb:—"To the feasts of inferior men the good unbidden go"; instead of which our proverb will run:—"To the feasts of the good the good unbidden go"; and this alteration may be supported by the authority of Homer himself, who not only demolishes but literally outrages the proverb. For, after picturing Agamemnon as the most valiant of men, he makes Menelaus, who is but a faint-hearted warrior, come unbidden[2] to the banquet of Agamemnon, who is feasting and offering sacrifices, not the better to the worse, but the worse to the better.

I rather fear, Socrates, said Aristodemus, lest this may still be my case; and that, like Menelaus in Homer, I shall be the inferior person, who "To the feasts of the wise unbidden goes."

But I shall say that I was bidden of you, and then you will have to make an excuse. "Two going to-

---

[2] *Iliad* ii. 408, and xvii. 588.

gether," he replied, in Homeric fashion, one or other of them may invent an excuse by the way.[3]

This was the style of their conversation as they went along, Socrates dropped behind in a fit of abstraction, and desired Aristodemus, who was waiting, to go on before him. When he reached the house of Agathon he found the doors wide open, and a comical thing happened. A servant coming out met him, and led him at once into the banqueting hall in which the guests were reclining, for the banquet was about to begin. Welcome, Aristodemus, said Agathon, as soon as he appeared—you are just in time to sup with us; if you come on any other matter put it off, and make one of us, as I was looking for you yesterday and meant to have asked you, if I could have found you. But what have you done with Socrates?

I turned round, but Socrates was nowhere to be seen; and I had to explain that he had been with me a moment before, and that I came by his invitation to the supper.

You were quite right in coming, said Agathon; but where is he himself?

He was behind me just now, as I entered, he said, and I cannot think what has become of him.   175

Go and look for him, boy, said Agathon, and bring him in; and do you, Aristodemus, meanwhile take the place by Eryximachus.

The servant then assisted him to wash, and he lay down, and presently another servant came in and reported that our friend Socrates had retired into the portico of the neighboring house. "There he is fixed," said he, "and when I call to him he will not stir."

How strange, said Agathon; then you must call him again, and keep calling him.

Let him alone, said my informant; he has a way of stopping anywhere and losing himself without any reason. I believe that he will soon appear; do not therefore disturb him.

Well, if you think so, I will leave him, said Agathon. And then, turning to the servants, he added,

[3] Iliad x. 224.

"Let us have supper without waiting for him. Serve up whatever you please, for there is no one to give you orders; hitherto I have never left you to yourselves. But on this occasion imagine that you are our hosts, and that I and the company are your guests; treat us well, and then we shall commend you." After this, supper was served, but still no Socrates; and during the meal Agathon several times expressed a wish to send for him, but Aristodemus objected; and at last when the feast was about half over—for the fit, as usual, was not of long duration—Socrates entered. Agathon, who was reclining alone at the end of the table, begged that he would take the place next to him; that "I may touch you," he said, "and have the benefit of that wise thought which came into your mind in the portico, and is now in your possession; for I am certain that you would not have come away until you had found what you sought."

How I wish, said Socrates, taking his place as he was desired, that wisdom could be infused by touch, out of the fuller into the emptier man, as water runs through wool out of a fuller cup into an emptier one; if that were so, how greatly should I value the privilege of reclining at your side! For you would have filled me full with a stream of wisdom plenteous and fair; whereas my own is of a very mean and questionable sort, no better than a dream. But yours is bright and full of promise, and was manifested forth in all the splendor of youth the day before yesterday, in the presence of more than thirty thousand Hellenes.

You are mocking, Socrates, said Agathon, and ere long you and I will have to determine who bears off the palm of wisdom—of this Dionysus shall be the judge; but at present you are better occupied with supper.

Socrates took his place on the couch, and supped with the rest; and then libations were offered, and after a hymn had been sung to the god, and there had been the usual ceremonies, they were about to commence drinking, when Pausanias said, And now, my friends, how can we drink with least injury to ourselves? I can assure you that I feel severely the effect of yesterday's potations, and must have time to recover; and I suspect that most of you are in the

176

same predicament, for you were of the party yesterday. Consider then: How can the drinking be made easiest?

I entirely agree, said Aristophanes, that we should, by all means, avoid hard drinking, for I was myself one of those who were yesterday drowned in drink.

I think that you are right, said Eryximachus, the son of Acumenus; but I should still like to hear one other person speak: Is Agathon able to drink hard?

I am not equal to it, said Agathon.

Then, said Eryximachus, the weak heads like myself, Aristodemus, Phaedrus, and others who never can drink, are fortunate in finding that the stronger ones are not in a drinking mood. (I do not include Socrates, who is able either to drink or to abstain, and will not mind, whichever we do.) Well, as none of the company seem disposed to drink much, I may be forgiven for saying, as a physician, that drinking deep is a bad practice, which I never follow, if I can help, and certainly do not recommend to another, least of all to anyone who still feels the effects of yesterday's carouse.

I always do what you advise, and especially what you prescribe as a physician, rejoined Phaedrus the Myrrhinusian, and the rest of the company, if they are wise, will do the same.

It was agreed that drinking was not to be the order of the day, but that they were all to drink only so much as they pleased.

Then, said Eryximachus, as you are all agreed that drinking is to be voluntary, and that there is to be no compulsion, I move, in the next place, that the flute girl, who has just made her appearance, be told to go away and play to herself, or, if she likes, to the women who are within.[4] Today let us have conversation instead; and, if you will allow me, I will tell you what sort of conversation. This proposal having been accepted, Eryximachus proceeded as follows:—

I will begin, he said, after the manner of Melanippe in Euripides, "Not mine the word" which I am about to speak, but that of Phaedrus. For often he says to me in an indignant tone:—"What a strange thing

₁₇₇

4 Cp. Prot. 347.

it is, Eryximachus, that, whereas other gods have poems and hymns made in their honor, the great and glorious god, Love, has no encomiast among all the poets who are so many. There are the worthy sophists too—the excellent Prodicus for example, who have descanted in prose on the virtues of Heracles and other heroes; and, what is still more extraordinary, I have met with a philosophical work in which the utility of salt has been made the theme of an eloquent discourse; and many other like things have had a like honor bestowed upon them. And only to think that there should have been an eager interest created about them, and yet that to this day no one has ever dared worthily to hymn Love's praises! So entirely has this great deity been neglected." Now in this Phaedrus seems to me to be quite right, and therefore I want to offer him a contribution; also I think that at the present moment we who are here assembled cannot do better than honor the god Love. If you agree with me, there will be no lack of conversation; for I mean to propose that each of us in turn, going from left to right, shall make a speech in honor of Love. Let him give us the best which he can; and Phaedrus, because he is sitting first on the left hand, and because he is the father of the thought, shall begin.

No one will vote against you, Eryximachus, said Socrates. How can I oppose your motion, who profess to understand nothing but matters of love; nor, I presume, will Agathon and Pausanias; and there can be no doubt of Aristophanes, whose whole concern is with Dionysus and Aphrodite; nor will anyone disagree of those whom I see around me. The proposal, as I am aware, may seem rather hard upon us whose place is last; but we shall be contented if we hear some good speeches first. Let Phaedrus begin the praise of Love, and good luck to him. All the company expressed their assent, and desired him to do as Socrates bade him.

Aristodemus did not recollect all that was said, nor do I recollect all that he related to me; but I will tell you what I thought most worthy of remembrance, and what the chief speakers said.

Phaedrus began by affirming that Love is a mighty

god, and wonderful among gods and men, but especially wonderful in his birth. For he is the eldest of the gods, which is an honor to him; and a proof of his claim to this honor is, that of his parents there is no memorial; neither poet nor prose-writer has ever affirmed that he had any. As Hesiod says: "First Chaos came, and then broad-bosomed Earth, The everlasting seat of all that is, And Love."

In other words, after Chaos, the Earth and Love, these two, came into being. Also Parmenides sings of Generation: "First in the train of gods, he fashioned Love."

And Acusilaus agrees with Hesiod. Thus numerous are the witnesses who acknowledge Love to be the eldest of the gods. And not only is he the eldest, he is also the source of the greatest benefits to us. For I know not any greater blessing to a young man who is beginning life than a virtuous lover, or to the lover than a beloved youth. For the principle which ought to be the guide of men who would nobly live— that principle, I say, neither kindred, nor honor, nor wealth, nor any other motive is able to implant so well as love. Of what am I speaking? Of the sense of honor and dishonor, without which neither states nor individuals ever do any good or great work. And I say that a lover who is detected in doing any dishonorable act, or submitting through cowardice when any dishonor is done to him by another, will be more pained at being detected by his beloved than at being seen by his father, or by his companions, or by anyone else. The beloved too, when he is found in any disgraceful situation, has the same feeling about his lover. And if there were only some way of contriving that a state or an army should be made up of lovers and their loves,[5] they would be the very best governors of their own city, abstaining from all dishonor, and emulating one another in honor; and when fighting at each other's side, although a mere handful, they would overcome the world. For what lover would not choose rather to be seen by all mankind than by his beloved, either when abandoning his post or throwing away his arms? He would be ready to die

179

[5] Cp. Rep. v. 468 D.

a thousand deaths rather than endure this. Or who would desert his beloved or fail him in the hour of danger? The veriest coward would become an inspired hero, equal to the bravest, at such a time; Love would inspire him. That courage which, as Homer says, the god breathes into the souls of some heroes, Love of his own nature infuses into the lover.

Love will make men dare to die for their beloved— love alone; and women as well as men. Of this, Alcestis, the daughter of Pelias, is a monument to all Hellas; for she was willing to lay down her life on behalf of her husband, when no one else would, although he had a father and mother; but the tenderness of her love so far exceeded theirs, that she made them seem to be strangers in blood to their own son, and in the name only related to him; and so noble did this action of hers appear to the gods, as well as to men, that among the many who have done virtuously she is one of the very few to whom, in admiration of her noble action, they have granted the privilege of returning alive to earth; such exceeding honor is paid by the gods to the devotion and virtue of love. But Orpheus, the son of Oeagrus, the harper, they sent empty away, and presented to him an apparition only of her whom he sought, but herself they would not give up, because he showed no spirit; he was only a harp player, and did not dare like Alcestis to die for love, but was contriving how he might enter Hades alive; moreover, they afterwards caused him to suffer death at the hands of women, as the punishment of his cowardliness. Very different was the reward of the true love of Achilles towards his lover Patroclus— his lover and not his love (the notion that Patroclus was the beloved one is a foolish error into which Aeschylus has fallen, for Achilles was surely the fairer of the two, fairer also than all the other heroes; and, as Homer informs us, he was still beardless, and younger far). And greatly as the gods honor the 180 virtue of love, still the return of love on the part of the beloved to the lover is more admired and valued and rewarded by them, for the lover is more divine; because he is inspired by God. Now Achilles was quite aware, for he had been told by his mother, that he might avoid death and return home, and live to

a good old age, if he abstained from slaying Hector.
Nevertheless he gave his life to revenge his friend,
and dared to die, not only in his defense, but after
he was dead. Wherefore the gods honored him even
above Alcestis, and sent him to the Islands of the
Blest. These are my reasons for affirming that Love
is the eldest and noblest and mightiest of the gods,
and the chicfcst author and giver of virtue in life, and
of happiness after death.

This, or something like this, was the speech of
Phaedrus; and some other speeches followed which
Aristodemus did not remember; the next which he
repeated was that of Pausanias. Phaedrus, he said, the
argument has not been set before us, I think, quite
in the right form;—we should not be called upon to
praise Love in such an indiscriminate manner. If
there were only one Love, then what you said would
be well enough; but since there are more Loves
than one, you should have begun by determining
which of them was to be the theme of our praises. I
will amend this defect; and first of all I will tell you
which Love is deserving of praise, and then try to
hymn the praiseworthy one in a manner worthy of
him. For we all know that Love is inseparable from
Aphrodite, and if there were only one Aphrodite
there would be only one Love; but as there are two
goddesses there must be two Loves. And am I not
right in asserting that there are two goddesses? The
elder one, having no mother, who is called the
heavenly Aphrodite—she is the daughter of Uranus;
the younger, who is the daughter of Zeus and Dione
—her we call common; and the Love who is her
fellow-worker is rightly named common, as the other
love is called heavenly. All the gods ought to have
praise given to them, but not without distinction of
their natures; and therefore I must try to distinguish
the characters of the two Loves. Now actions vary
according to the manner of their performance. Take,
for example, that which we are now doing, drinking,
singing and talking—these actions are not in themselves either good or evil, but they turn out in this or
that way according to the mode of performing them;
and when well done they are good, and when wrongly
done they are evil; and in like manner not every love,

181

but only that which has a noble purpose, is noble and worthy of praise. The Love who is the offspring of the common Aphrodite is essentially common, and has no discrimination, being such as the meaner sort of men feel, and is apt to be of women as well as of youths, and is of the body rather than of the soul— the most foolish beings are the objects of this love which desires only to gain an end, but never thinks of accomplishing the end nobly, and therefore does good and evil quite indiscriminately. The goddess who is his mother is far younger than the other, and she was born of the union of the male and female, and partakes of both. But the offspring of the heavenly Aphrodite is derived from a mother in whose birth the female has no part,—she is from the male only; this is that love which is of youths, and the goddess being older, there is nothing of wantonness in her. Those who are inspired by this love turn to the male, and delight in him who is the more valiant and intelligent nature; any one may recognize the pure enthusiasts in the very character of their attachments. For they love not boys, but intelligent beings whose reason is beginning to be developed, much about the time at which their beards begin to grow. And in choosing young men to be their companions, they mean to be faithful to them, and pass their whole life in company with them, not to take them in their inexperience, and deceive them, and play the fool with them, or run away from one to another of them. But the love of young boys should be forbidden by law, because their future is uncertain; they may turn out good or bad, either in body or soul, and much noble enthusiasm may be thrown away upon them; in this matter the good are a law to themselves, and the coarser sort of lovers ought to be restrained by force, as we restrain or attempt to restrain them from fixing their affections on women of free birth. These are the persons who bring a reproach on love; and some have been led to deny the lawfulness of such attachments because they see the impropriety and evil of them; for surely nothing that is decorously and lawfully done can justly be censured. Now here and in Lacedaemon the rules about love are perplexing, but in

182

most cities they are simple and easily intelligible; in Elis and Boeotia, and in countries having no gifts of eloquence, they are very straightforward; the law is simply in favor of these connections, and no one, whether young or old, has anything to say to their discredit; the reason being, as I suppose, that they are men of few words in those parts, and therefore the lovers do not like the trouble of pleading their suit. In Ionia and other places, and generally in countries which are subject to the barbarians, the custom is held to be dishonorable; loves of youths share the evil repute in which philosophy and gymnastics are held, because they are inimical to tyranny; for the interests of rulers require that their subjects should be poor in spirit[6] and that there should be no strong bond of friendship or society among them, which love, above all other motives, is likely to inspire, as our Athenian tyrants learned by experience; for the love of Aristogeiton and the constancy of Harmodius had a strength which undid their power. And, therefore, the ill-repute into which these attachments have fallen is to be ascribed to the evil condition of those who make them to be ill-reputed; that is to say, to the self-seeking of the governors and the cowardice of the governed; on the other hand, the indiscriminate honor which is given to them in some countries is attributable to the laziness of those who hold this opinion of them. In our own country a far better principle prevails, but, as I was saying, the explanation of it is rather perplexing. For, observe that open loves are held to be more honorable than secret ones, and that the love of the noblest and highest, even if their persons are less beautiful than others, is especially honorable. Consider, too, how great is the encouragement which all the world gives to the lover; neither is he supposed to be doing anything dishonorable; but if he succeeds he is praised, and if he fails he is blamed. And in the pursuit of his love the custom of mankind allows him to do many strange things, which philosophy would bitterly censure if they were done from any motive of interest, or wish for office or power. We may pray, and entreat, and

183

[6] Cp. Arist. Politics, v. 11. § 15.

supplicate, and swear, and lie on a mat at the door, and endure a slavery worse than that of any slave— in any other case friends and enemies would be equally ready to prevent him, but now there is no friend who will be ashamed of him and admonish him, and no enemy will charge him with meanness or flattery; the actions of a lover have a grace which ennobles them; and custom has decided that they are highly commendable and that there is no loss of character in them; and, what is strangest of all, he only may swear and forswear himself (so men say), and the gods will forgive his transgression, for there is no such thing as a lover's oath. Such is the entire liberty which gods and men have allowed the lover, according to the custom which prevails in our part of the world. From this point of view a man fairly argues that in Athens to love and to be loved is held to be a very honorable thing. But when parents forbid their sons to talk with their lovers, and place them under a tutor's care, who is appointed to see to these things, and their companions and equals cast in their teeth anything of the sort which they may observe, and their elders refuse to silence the reprovers and do not rebuke them—anyone who reflects on all this will, on the contrary, think that we hold these practices to be most disgraceful. But, as I was saying at first, the truth as I imagine is, that whether such practices are honorable or whether they are dishonorable is not a simple question; they are honorable to him who follows them honorably, dishonorable to him who follows them dishonorably. There is dishonor in yielding to the evil, or in an evil manner; but there is honor in yielding to the good, or in an honorable manner. Evil is the vulgar lover who loves the body rather than the soul, inasmuch as he is not even stable, because he loves a thing which is in itself unstable, and therefore when the bloom of youth which he was desiring is over, he takes wing and flies away, in spite of all his words and promises; whereas the love of the noble disposition is life-long, for it becomes one with the everlasting. The custom of our country would have both of them proven well and truly, and would have us yield to the one sort of lover and avoid the other, and therefore encourages some to pursue, and others to fly; testing both the lover and beloved in contests and trials, until they show to which of the two classes they respectively belong. And this is the reason why, in the first place, a hasty attachment is held to be dishonorable, because time is the true test of this as of most other things; and secondly there is a dishonor in being overcome by the love of money, or of wealth, or of political power, whether a man is frightened into surrender by the loss of them, or, having experienced the benefits of money and political corruption, is unable to rise above the seductions of them. For none of these things are of a permanent or lasting nature; not to mention that no generous friendship ever sprang from them. There remains, then, only one way of honorable attachment which custom allows in the beloved, and this is the way of virtue; for as we admitted that any service which the lover does to him is not to be accounted flattery or a dishonor to himself, so the beloved has one way only of voluntary service which is not dishonorable, and this is virtuous service.

For we have a custom, and according to our custom anyone who does service to another under the idea that he will be improved by him either in wisdom, or in some other particular of virtue—such a voluntary service, I say, is not to be regarded as a dishonor, and is not open to the charge of flattery. And these two customs, one the love of youth, and the other the practice of philosophy and virtue in general, ought to meet in one, and then the beloved may honorably indulge the lover. For when the lover and beloved come together, having each of them a law, and the lover thinks that he is right in doing any service which he can to his gracious loving one; and the other that he is right in showing any kindness which he can to him who is making him wise and good; the one capable of communicating wisdom and virtue, the other seeking to acquire them with a view to education and wisdom; when the two laws of love are fulfilled and meet in one— then, and then only, may the beloved yield with honor to the lover. Nor when love is of this disinterested sort is there any disgrace in being deceived, but in every other case there is equal disgrace in being or not being deceived. For he who is gracious to his lover under the impression that he is rich, and is disappointed on his gains because he turns out to be poor, is disgraced all the same: for he has done his best to show that he would give himself up to any one's "uses base" for the sake of money; but this is not honorable. And on the same principle he who gives himself to a lover because he is a good man, and in the hope that he will be improved by his company, shows himself to be virtuous, even though the object of his affection turn out to be a villain, and to have no virtue; and if he is deceived he has committed a noble error. For he has proved that for his part he will do anything for anybody with a view to virtue and improvement, than which there can be nothing nobler. Thus noble in every case is the acceptance of another for the sake of virtue. This is that love which is the love of the heavenly goddess, and is heavenly, and of great price to individuals and cities, making the lover and the beloved alike eager in the work of their own improvement. But all other loves are the offspring of the other, who is the common goddess. To you, Phaedrus, I offer this my contribution in praise of love, which is as good as I could make extempore.

Pāusănīãs cāme tŏ ă pāuse—this is the balanced way in which I have been taught by the wise to speak; and Aristodemus said that the turn of Aristophanes was next, but either he had eaten too much, or from some other cause he had the hiccough, and was obliged to change turns with Eryximachus the physician, who was reclining on the couch below him. Eryximachus, he said, you ought either to stop my hiccough, or to speak in my turn until I have left off.

I will do both, said Eryximachus: I will speak in your turn, and do you speak in mine; and while I am speaking let me recommend you to hold your breath, and if after you have done so for some time the hiccough is no better, then gargle with a little water; and if it still continues, tickle your nose with something

and sneeze; and if you sneeze once or twice, even the
most violent hiccough is sure to go. I will do as you
prescribe, said Aristophanes, and now get on.

Eryximachus spoke as follows: Seeing that Pau-   186
sanias made a fair beginning, and but a lame ending,
I must endeavor to supply his deficiency. I think that
he has rightly distinguished two kinds of love. But my
art further informs me that the double love is not
merely an affection of the soul of man towards the
fair, or towards anything, but is to be found in the
bodies of all animals and in productions of the earth,
and I may say in all that is; such is the conclusion
which I seem to have gathered from my own art of
medicine, whence I learn how great and wonderful
and universal is the deity of love, whose empire ex-
tends over all things, divine as well as human. And
from medicine I will begin that I may do honor to
my art. There are in the human body these two kinds
of love, which are confessedly different and unlike,
and being unlike, they have loves and desires which
are unlike; and the desire of the healthy is one, and
the desire of the diseased is another; and as Pausanias
was just now saying that to indulge good men is
honorable, and bad men dishonorable:—so too in
the body the good and healthy elements are to be
indulged, and the bad elements and the elements of
disease are not to be indulged, but discouraged. And
this is what the physician has to do, and in this the art
of medicine consists: for medicine may be regarded
generally as the knowledge of the loves and desires of
the body, and how to satisfy them or not; and the
best physician is he who is able to separate fair love
from foul, or to convert one into the other; and he
who knows how to eradicate and how to implant
love, whichever is required, and can reconcile the
most hostile elements in the constitution and make
them loving friends, is a skillful practitioner. Now
the most hostile are the most opposite, such as hot
and cold, bitter and sweet, moist and dry, and the
like. And my ancestor, Asclepius, knowing how to
implant friendship and accord in these elements, was
the creator of our art, as our friends the poets here
tell us, and I believe them; and not only medicine in
every branch, but the arts of gymnastic and hus-

bandry are under his dominion. Anyone who pays the least attention to the subject will also perceive that in music there is the same reconciliation of opposites; and I suppose that this must have been the meaning of Heracleitus, although his words are not accurate; for he says that The One is united by disunion, like the harmony of the bow and the lyre. Now there is an absurdity in saying that harmony is discord or is composed of elements which are still in a state of discord. But what he probably meant was, that harmony is composed of differing notes of higher or lower pitch which disagreed once, but are now reconciled by the art of music; for if the higher and lower notes still disagreed, there could be no harmony—clearly not. For harmony is a symphony, and symphony is an agreement; but an agreement of disagreements while they disagree there cannot be; you cannot harmonize that which disagrees. In like manner rhythm is compounded of elements short and long, once differing and now in accord; which accordance, as in the former instance, medicine, so in all these other cases, music implants, making love and unison to grow up among them; and thus music, too, is concerned with the principles of love in their application to harmony and rhythm. Again, in the essential nature of harmony and rhythm there is no difficulty in discerning love which has not yet become double. But when you want to use them in actual life, either in the composition of songs or in the correct performance of airs or meters composed already, which latter is called education, then the difficulty begins, and the good artist is needed. Then the old tale has to be repeated of fair and heavenly love—the love of Urania the fair and heavenly muse, and of the duty of accepting the temperate, and those who are as yet intemperate only that they may become temperate, and of preserving their love; and again, of the vulgar Polyhymnia, who must be used with circumspection that the pleasure may be enjoyed, but may not generate licentiousness; just as in my own art it is a great matter so to regulate the desires of the epicure that he may gratify his tastes without the attendant evil of disease. Whence I infer that in music, in medicine, in all other things human as well as divine, both loves ought to be noted as far as may be, for they are both present.

The course of the seasons is also full of both these principles; and when, as I was saying, the elements of hot and cold, moist and dry, attain the harmonious love of one another and blend in temperance and harmony, they bring to men, animals, and plants health and plenty, and do them no harm; whereas the wanton love, getting the upper hand and affecting the seasons of the year, is very destructive and injurious, being the source of pestilence, and bringing many other kinds of diseases on animals and plants; for hoar-frost and hail and blight spring from the excesses and disorders of these elements of love, which to know in relation to the revolutions of the heavenly bodies and the seasons of the year is termed astronomy. Furthermore all sacrifices and the whole province of divination, which is the art of communion between gods and men—these, I say, are concerned only with the preservation of the good and the cure of the evil love. For all manner of impiety is likely to ensue if, instead of accepting and honoring and reverencing the harmonious love in all his actions, a man honors the other love, whether in his feelings toward gods or parents, toward the living or the dead. Wherefore the business of divination is to see to these loves and to heal them, and divination is the peacemaker of gods and men, working by a knowledge of the religious or irreligious tendencies which exist in human loves. Such is the great and mighty, or rather omnipotent force of love in general. And the love, more especially, which is concerned with the good, and which is perfected in company with temperance and justice, whether among gods or men, has the greatest power, and is the source of all our happiness and harmony, and makes us friends with the gods who are above us, and with one another. I dare say that I too have omitted several things which might be said in praise of Love, but this was not intentional, and you, Aristophanes, may now supply the omission or take some other line of commendation; for I perceive that you are rid of the hiccough.

Yes, said Aristophanes, who followed, the hiccough

is gone; not, however, until I applied the sneezing; and I wonder whether the harmony of the body has a love of such noises and ticklings, for I no sooner applied the sneezing than I was cured.

Eryximachus said: Beware, friend Aristophanes, although you are going to speak, you are making fun of me; and I shall have to watch and see whether I cannot have a laugh at your expense, when you might speak in peace.

You are quite right, said Aristophanes, laughing. I will unsay my words; but do you please not to watch me, as I fear that in the speech which I am about to make, instead of others laughing with me, which is to the manner born of our muse and would be all the better, I shall only be laughed at by them.

Do you expect to shoot your bolt and escape, Aristophanes? Well, perhaps if you are very careful and bear in mind that you will be called to account, I may be induced to let you off.

Aristophanes professed to open another vein of discourse; he had a mind to praise Love in another way, unlike that either of Pausanias or Eryximachus. Mankind, he said, judging by their neglect of him, have never, as I think, at all understood the power of Love. For if they had understood him they would surely have built noble temples and altars, and offered solemn sacrifices in his honor; but this is not done, and most certainly ought to be done: since of all the gods he is the best friend of men, the helper and the healer of the ills which are the great impediment to the happiness of the race. I will try to describe his power to you, and you shall teach the rest of the world what I am teaching you. In the first place, let me treat of the nature of man and what has happened to it; for the original human nature was not like the present, but different. The sexes were not two as they are now, but originally three in number; there was man, woman, and the union of the two, having a name corresponding to this double nature, which had once a real existence, but is now lost, and the word "Androgynous" is only preserved as a term of reproach. In the second place, the primeval man was round, his back and sides forming a circle; and he had four hands and four feet, one head with two faces, looking opposite ways, set on a round neck and precisely alike; also four ears, two privy members, and the remainder to correspond. He could walk upright as men now do, backwards or forwards as he pleased, and he could also roll over and over at a great pace, turning on his four hands and four feet, eight in all, like tumblers going over and over with their legs in the air; this was when he wanted to run fast. Now the sexes were three, and such as I have described them; because the sun, moon, and earth are three; and the man was originally the child of the sun, the woman of the earth, and the man-woman of the moon, which is made up of sun and earth, and they were all round and moved round and round like their parents. Terrible was their might and strength, and the thoughts of their hearts were great, and they made an attack upon the gods; of them is told the tale of Otys and Ephialtes who, as Homer says, dared to scale heaven, and would have laid hands upon the gods. Doubt reigned in the celestial councils. Should they kill them and annihilate the race with thunderbolts, as they had done the giants, then there would be an end of the sacrifices and worship which men offered to them; but, on the other hand, the gods could not suffer their insolence to be unrestrained. At last, after a good deal of reflection, Zeus discovered a way. He said: "Methinks I have a plan which will humble their pride and improve their manners; men shall continue to exist, but I will cut them in two and then they will be diminished in strength and increased in numbers; this will have the advantage of making them more profitable to us. They shall walk upright on two legs, and if they continue insolent and will not be quiet, I will split them again and they shall hop about on a single leg." He spoke and cut men in two, like a sorb-apple which is halved for pickling, or as you might divide an egg with a hair; and as he cut them one after another, he bade Apollo give the face and the half of the neck a turn in order that the man might contemplate the section of himself: he would thus learn a lesson of humility. Apollo was also bidden to heal their wounds and compose their forms. So he gave a turn to the face and pulled the skin from the sides all

over that which in our language is called the belly,
like the purses which draw in, and he made
one mouth at the center, which he fastened in a knot
(the same which is called the navel); he also molded   191
the breast and took out most of the wrinkles, much
as a shoemaker might smooth leather upon a last; he
left a few, however, in the region of the belly and
navel, as a memorial of the primeval state. After the
division the two parts of man, each desiring his other
half, came together, and throwing their arms about
one another, entwined in mutual embraces, longing
to grow into one, they were on the point of dying
from hunger and self-neglect, because they did not
like to do any thing apart; and when one of the halves
died and the other survived, the survivor sought
another mate, man or woman as we call them—
being the sections of entire men or women,—and
clung to that. They were being destroyed, when Zeus
in pity of them invented a new plan: he turned the
parts of generation round to the front, for this had
not been always their position, and they sowed the
seed no longer as hitherto like grasshoppers in the
ground, but in one another; and after the transposi-
tion the male generated in the female in order that
by the mutual embraces of man and woman they
might breed, and the race might continue; or if man
came to man they might be satisfied, and rest, and go
their ways to the business of life: so ancient is the
desire of one another which is implanted in us, re-
uniting our original nature, making one of two, and
healing the state of man. Each of us when separated,
having one side only, like a flat fish, is but the in-
denture of a man, and he is always looking for his
other half. Men who are a section of that double
nature which was once called Androgynous are lovers
of women; adulterers are generally of this breed,
and also adulterous women who lust after men: the
women who are a section of the woman do not care
for men, but have female attachments; the female
companions are of this sort. But they who are a section of the male follow the male, and while they are
young, being slices of the original man, they hang   192
about men and embrace them, and they are themselves the best of boys and youths, because they have

the most manly nature. Some indeed assert that they
are shameless, but this is not true; for they do not
act thus from any want of shame, but because they
are valiant and manly, and have a manly counte-
nance, and they embrace that which is like them. And
these when they grow up become our statesmen, and
these only, which is a great proof of the truth of what
I am saying. When they reach manhood they are
lovers of youth, and are not naturally inclined to
marry or beget children—if at all, they do so only in
obedience to the law; but they are satisfied if they
may be allowed to live with one another unwedded;
and such a nature is prone to love and ready to
return love, always embracing that which is akin to
him. And when one of them meets with his other
half, the actual half of himself, whether he be a lover
of youth or a lover of another sort, the pair are lost
in an amazement of love and friendship and intimacy,
and will not be out of the other's sight, as I may say,
even for a moment: these are the people who pass
their whole lives together; yet they could not explain
what they desire of one another. For the intense
yearning which each of them has towards the other
does not appear to be the desire of lover's intercourse, but of something else which the soul of either
evidently desires and cannot tell, and of which she
has only a dark and doubtful presentiment. Suppose
Hephaestus, with his instruments, to come to the pair
who are lying side by side and to say to them, "What
do you people want of one another?" they would be
unable to explain. And suppose further, that when
he saw their perplexity he said: "Do you desire to be
wholly one; always day and night to be in one another's company? for it this is what you desire, I am
ready to melt you into one and let you grow together, so that being two you shall become one, and
while you live live a common life as if you were a
single man, and after your death in the world below
still be one departed soul instead of two—I ask
whether this is what you lovingly desire, and whether
you are satisfied to attain this?"—there is not a man
of them who when he heard the proposal would deny
or would not acknowledge that this meeting and
melting into one another, this becoming one instead

of two, was the very expression of his ancient need.[7] And the reason is that human nature was originally one and we were a whole, and the desire and pursuit of the whole is called love. There was a time, I say, when we were one, but now because of the wickedness of mankind God has dispersed us, as the Arcadians were dispersed into villages by the Lacedaemonians.[8] And if we are not obedient to the gods, there is a danger that we shall be split up again and go about in basso-relievo, like the profile figures having only half a nose which are sculptured on monuments, and that we shall be like tallies. Wherefore let us exhort all men to piety, that we may avoid evil, and obtain the good, of which Love is to us the lord and minister; and let no one oppose him—he is the enemy of the gods who oppose him. For if we are friends of the God and at peace with him we shall find our own true loves, which rarely happens in this world at present. I am serious, and therefore I must beg Eryximachus not to make fun or to find any allusion in what I am saying to Pausanias and Agathon, who, as I suspect, are both of the manly nature, and belong to the class which I have been describing. But my words have a wider application—they include men and women everywhere; and I believe that if our loves were perfectly accomplished, and each one returning to his primeval nature had his original true love, then our race would be happy. And if this would be best of all, the best in the next degree and under present circumstances must be the nearest approach to such an union; and that will be the attainment of a congenial love. Wherefore, if we would praise him who has given to us the benefit, we must praise the god Love, who is our greatest benefactor, both leading us in this life back to our own nature, and giving us high hopes for the future, for he promises that if we are pious, he will restore us to our original state, and heal us and make us happy and blessed. This, Eryximachus, is my discourse of love, which, although different to yours, I must beg you to leave unassailed by the shafts of your ridicule, in order that each may

193

[7] Cp. Arist. Pol. ii. 4, § 6.
[8] Cp. Arist. Pol. ii. 2, § 3.

have his turn; each, or rather either, for Agathon and Socrates are the only ones left.

Indeed, I am not going to attack you, said Eryximachus, for I thought your speech charming, and did I not know that Agathon and Socrates are masters in the art of love, I should be really afraid that they would have nothing to say, after the world of things which have been said already. But, for all that, I am not without hopes.

Socrates said: You played your part well, Eryximachus; but if you were as I am now, or rather as I shall be when Agathon has spoken, you would, indeed, be in a great strait.

You want to cast a spell over me, Socrates, said Agathon, in the hope that I may be disconcerted at the expectation raised among the audience that I shall speak well.

I should be strangely forgetful, Agathon, replied Socrates, of the courage and magnanimity which you showed when your own compositions were about to be exhibited, and you came upon the stage with the actors and faced the vast theater altogether undismayed, if I thought that your nerves could be fluttered at a small party of friends.

Do you think, Socrates, and Agathon, that my head is so full of the theater as not to know how much more formidable to a man of sense a few good judges are than many fools?

Nay, replied Socrates, I should be very wrong in attributing to you, Agathon, that or any other want of refinement. And I am quite aware that if you happened to meet with any whom you thought wise, you would care for their opinion much more than for that of the many. But then we, having been a part of the foolish many in the theater, cannot be regarded as the select wise; though I know that if you chanced to be in the presence, not of one of ourselves, but of some really wise man, you would be ashamed of disgracing yourself before him—would you not?

Yes, said Agathon.

But before the many you would not be ashamed, if you thought that you were doing something disgraceful in their presence?

Here Phaedrus interrupted them, saying: Do not

answer him, my dear Agathon; for if he can only get a partner with whom he can talk, especially a good-looking one, he will no longer care about the completion of our plan. Now I love to hear him talk; but just at present I must not forget the encomium on Love which I ought to receive from him and from everyone. When you and he have paid your tribute to the god, then you may talk.

Very good, Phaedrus, said Agathon; I see no reason why I should not proceed with my speech, as I shall have many other opportunities of conversing with Socrates. Let me say first how I ought to speak, and then speak:—

The previous speakers, instead of praising the god Love, or unfolding his nature, appear to have congratulated mankind on the benefits which he confers upon them. But I would rather praise the god first, and then speak of his gifts; this is always the right way of praising everything. May I say without impiety or offense, that of all the blessed gods he is the most blessed because he is the fairest and best? And he is the fairest: for, in the first place, he is the youngest, and of his youth he is himself the witness, fleeing out of the way of age, who is swift enough, swifter truly than most of us like:—Love hates him and will not come near him; but youth and love live and move together—like to like, as the proverb says. Many things were said by Phaedrus about Love in which I agree with him; but I cannot agree that he is older than Iapetus and Kronos:—not so; I maintain him to be the youngest of the gods, and youthful ever. The ancient doings among the gods of which Hesiod and Parmenides spoke, if the tradition of them be true, were done of Necessity and not of Love; had Love been in those days, there would have been no chaining or mutilation of the gods, or other violence, but peace and sweetness, as there is now in heaven, since the rule of Love began. Love is young and also tender; he ought to have a poet like Homer to describe his tenderness, as Homer says of Ate, that she is a goddess and tender:—

"Her feet are tender, for she sets her steps,
   Not on the ground but on the heads of men:"
herein is an excellent proof of her tenderness, that

195

she walks not upon the hard but upon the soft. Let us adduce a similar proof of the tenderness of Love; for he walks not upon the earth, nor yet upon the skulls of men, which are not so very soft, but in the hearts and souls of both gods and men, which are of all things the softest; in them he walks and dwells and makes his home. Not in every soul without exception, for where there is hardness he departs, where there is softness there he dwells; and nestling always with his feet and in all manner of ways in the softest of soft places, how can he be other than the softest of all things? Of a truth he is the tenderest as well as the youngest, and also he is of flexile form; for if he were hard and without flexure he could not enfold all things, or wind his way into and out of every soul of man undiscovered. And a proof of his flexibility and symmetry of form is his grace, which is universally admitted to be in an especial manner the attribute of Love; ungrace and love are always at war with one another. The fairness of his complexion is revealed by his habitation among the flowers; for he dwells not amid bloomless or fading beauties, whether of body or soul or aught else, but in the place of flowers and scents, there he sits and abides. Concerning the beauty of the god I have said enough; and yet there remains much more which I might say. Of his virtue I have now to speak: his greatest glory is that he can neither do nor suffer wrong to or from any god or any man; for he suffers not by force if he suffers; force comes not near him, neither when he acts does he act by force. For all men in all things serve him of their own free will, and where there is voluntary agreement, there, as the laws which are the lords of the city say, is justice. And not only is he just but exceedingly temperate, for Temperance is the acknowledged ruler of the pleasures and desires, and no pleasure ever masters Love; he is their master and they are his servants; and if he conquers them he must be temperate indeed. As to courage, even the God of War is no match for him; he is the captive and Love is the lord, for love, the love of Aphrodite, masters him, as the tale runs; and the master is stronger than the servant. And if he conquers the bravest of all others, he must be himself the bravest.

196

Of his courage and justice and temperance I have spoken, but I have yet to speak of his wisdom; and according to the measure of my ability I must try to do my best. In the first place he is a poet (and here, like Eryximachus, I magnify my art), and he is also the source of poesy in others, which he could not be if he were not himself a poet. And at the touch of him everyone becomes a poet,[9] even though he had no music in him before[9]; this also is a proof that Love is a good poet and accomplished in all the fine arts; for no one can give to another that which he has not himself, or teach that of which he has no knowledge. Who will deny that the creation of the animals is his doing? Are they not all the works of his wisdom, born and begotten of him? And as to the artists, do we not know that he only of them whom love inspires has the light of fame?—he whom Love touches not walks in darkness. The arts of medicine and archery and divination were discovered by Apollo, under the guidance of love and desire; so that he too is a disciple of Love. Also the melody of the Muses, the metallurgy of Hephaestus, the weaving of Athene, the empire of Zeus over gods and men, are all due to Love, who was the inventor of them. And so Love set in order the empire of the gods—the love of beauty, as is evident, for with deformity Love has no concern. In the days of old, as I began by saying, dreadful deeds were done among the gods, for they were ruled by Necessity; but now since the birth of Love, and from the Love of the beautiful, has sprung every good in heaven and earth. Therefore, Phaedrus, I say of Love that he is the fairest and best in himself, and the cause of what is fairest and best in all other things. And there comes into my mind a line of poetry in which he is said to be the god who

> "Gives peace on earth and calms the stormy deep,
> Who stills the winds and bids the sufferer sleep."

This is he who empties men of disaffection and fills them with affection, who makes them to meet together at banquets such as these; in sacrifices, feasts, dances, he is our lord—who sends courtesy and sends away discourtesy, who gives kindness ever and never gives

[9] A fragment of the Sthenoboea of Euripides.

unkindness; the friend of the good, the wonder of
the wise, the amazement of the gods; desired by those
who have no part in him, and precious to those who
have the better part in him; parent of delicacy, luxury,
desire, fondness, softness, grace; regardful of the
good, regardless of the evil: in every word, work,
wish, fear—savior, pilot, comrade, helper; glory of
gods and men, leader best and brightest: in whose
footsteps let every man follow, sweetly singing in his
honor and joining in that sweet strain with which
love charms the souls of gods and men. Such is the
speech, Phaedrus, half-playful, yet having a certain
measure of seriousness, which, according to my
ability, I dedicate to the god.

When Agathon had done speaking, Aristodemus   198
said that there was a general cheer; the young man
was thought to have spoken in a manner worthy of
himself, and of the god. And Socrates, looking at
Eryximachus, said: Tell me, son of Acumenus, was
there not reason in my fears? and was I not a true
prophet when I said that Agathon would make a
wonderful oration, and that I should be in a strait?

The part of the prophecy which concerns Agathon,
replied Eryximachus, appears to me to be true; but
not the other part—that you will be in a strait.

Why, my dear friend, said Socrates, must not I or
anyone be in a strait who has to speak after he has
heard such a rich and varied discourse? I am especially struck with the beauty of the concluding words
—who could listen to them without amazement?
When I reflected on the immeasurable inferiority of
my own powers, I was ready to run away for shame,
if there had been a possibility of escape. For I was
reminded of Gorgias, and at the end of his speech I
fancied that Agathon was shaking at me the Gorgi-
nian or Gorgonian head of the great master of rhetoric, which was simply to turn me and my speech
into stone, as Homer says,[10] and strike me dumb.
And then I perceived how foolish I had been in
consenting to take my turn with you in praising love,
and saying that I too was a master of the art, when I
really had no conception how anything ought to be

[10] Odyssey, λ. 632.

praised. For in my simplicity I imagined that the
topics of praise should be true, and that this being
presupposed, out of the true the speaker was to
choose the best and set them forth in the best manner. And I felt quite proud, thinking that I knew the
nature of true praise, and should speak well. Whereas
I now see that the intention was to attribute to Love
every species of greatness and glory, whether really
belonging to him or not, without regard to truth or
falsehood—that was no matter; for the original proposal seems to have been not that each of you should
really praise Love, but only that you should appear
to praise him. And so you attribute to Love every
imaginable form of praise which can be gathered
anywhere; and you say that "he is all this," and "the
cause of all that," making him appear the fairest and
best of all to those who know him not, for you cannot impose upon those who know him. And a noble
and solemn hymn of praise have you rehearsed. But
as I misunderstood the nature of the praise when
I said that I would take my turn, I must beg to be
absolved from the promise which I made in ignorance, and which (as Euripides would say[11]) was a
promise of the lips and not of the mind. Farewell
then to such a strain: for I do not praise in that
way; no, indeed, I cannot. But if you like to hear the
truth about love, I am ready to speak in my own
manner, though I will not make myself ridiculous by
entering into any rivalry with you. Say then, Phaedrus, whether you would like to have the truth
about love, spoken in any words and in any order
which may happen to come into my mind at the
time. Will that be agreeable to you?

Aristodemus said that Phaedrus and the company
bid him speak in any manner which he thought best.
Then, he added, let me have your permission first to
ask Agathon a few more questions, in order that I
may take his admissions as the premises of my
discourse.

I grant the permission, said Phaedrus: put your
questions. Socrates then proceeded as follows:—

In the magnificent oration which you have just

[11] Eurip. Hyppolytus, l. 612.

uttered, I think that you were right, my dear Agathon, in proposing to speak of the nature of Love first and afterwards of his works—that is a way of beginning which I very much approve. And as you have spoken so eloquently of his nature, may I ask you further, Whether love is the love of something or of nothing? And here I must explain myself: I do not want you to say that love is the love of a father or the love of a mother—that would be ridiculous; but to answer as you would, if I asked is a father a father of something? to which you would find no difficulty in replying, of a son or daughter: and the answer would be right.

Very true, said Agathon.

And you would say the same of a mother?

He assented.

Yet let me ask you one more question in order to illustrate my meaning: Is not a brother to be regarded essentially as a brother of something?

Certainly, he replied.

That is, of a brother or sister?

Yes, he said.

And now, said Socrates, I will ask about Love:—Is Love of something or of nothing?

Of something, surely, he replied.   200

Keep in mind what this is, and tell me what I want to know—Whether Love desires that of which love is.

Yes, surely.

And does he possess, or does he not possess, that which he loves and desires?

Probably not, I should say.

Nay, replied Socrates, I would have you consider whether "necessarily" is not rather the word. The inference that he who desires something is in want of something, and that he who desires nothing is in want of nothing, is in my judgment, Agathon, absolutely and necessarily true. What do you think?

I agree with you, said Agathon.

Very good. Would he who is great, desire to be great, or he who is strong, desire to be strong?

That would be inconsistent with our previous admissions.

True. For he who is anything cannot want to be
that which he is?

Very true.

And yet, added Socrates, if a man being strong desired to be strong, or being swift desired to be swift,
or being healthy desired to be healthy, in that case
he might be thought to desire something which he
already has or is. I give the example in order that
we may avoid misconception. For the possessors of
these qualities, Agathon, must be supposed to have
their respective advantages at the time, whether they
choose or not; and who can desire that which he
has? Therefore, when a person says, I am well and
wish to be well, or I am rich and wish to be rich,
and I desire simply to have what I have—to him
we shall reply: "You, my friend, having wealth and
health and strength, want to have the continuance of
them; for at this moment, whether you choose or no,
you have them. And when you say, I desire that
which I have and nothing else, is not your meaning
that you want to have what you now have in the
future?" He must agree with us—must he not?

He must, replied Agathon.

Then, said Socrates, he desires that what he has
at present may be preserved to him in the future,
which is equivalent to saying that he desires something which is nonexistent to him, and which as yet
he has not got.

Very true, he said.

Then he and everyone who desires, desires that
which he has not already, and which is future and
not present, and which he has not, and is not, and of
which he is in want;—these are the sort of things
which love and desire seek?

Very true, he said.

Then now, said Socrates, let us recapitulate the
argument. First, is not love of something, and of
something too which is wanting to a man?

Yes, he replied.

201

Remember further what you said in your speech,
or if you do not remember I will remind you: you
said that the love of the beautiful set in order the
empire of the gods, for that of deformed things

there is no love—did you not say something of that kind?

Yes, said Agathon.

Yes, my friend, and the remark was a just one. And if this is true, Love is the love of beauty and not of deformity?

He assented.

And the admission has been already made that Love is of something which a man wants and has not?

True, he said.

Then Love wants and has not beauty?

Certainly, he replied.

And would you call that beautiful which wants and does not possess beauty?

Certainly not.

Then would you still say that love is beautiful?

Agathon replied: I fear that I did not understand what I was saying.

You made a very good speech, Agathon, replied Socrates; but there is yet one small question which I would fain ask:—Is not the good also the beautiful?

Yes.

Then in wanting the beautiful, love wants also the good?

I cannot refute you, Socrates, said Agathon:— Let us assume that what you say is true.

Say rather, beloved Agathon, that you cannot refute the truth; for Socrates is easily refuted.

And now, taking my leave of you, I will rehearse a tale of love which I heard from Diotima of Mantineia,[12] a woman wise in this and in many other kinds of knowledge, who in the days of old, when the Athenians offered sacrifice before the coming of the plague, delayed the disease ten years. She was my instructress in the art of love, and I shall repeat to you what she said to me, beginning with the admissions made by Agathon, which are nearly if not quite the same which I made to the wise woman when she questioned me: I think that this will be the easiest way, and I shall take both parts myself

[12] Cp. I. Alcibiades.

as well as I can.[13] As you, Agathon, suggested,[14] I must speak first of the being and nature of Love, and then of his works. First I said to her in nearly the same words which he used to me, that Love was a mighty god, and likewise fair; and she proved to me as I proved to him that, by my own showing, Love was neither fair nor good. "What do you mean, Diotima," I said, "is love then evil and foul?" "Hush," she cried; "must that be foul which is not fair?" "Certainly," I said. "And is that which is not wise, ignorant? do you not see that there is a mean between wisdom and ignorance?" "And what may that be?" I said. "Right opinion," she replied; "which, as you know, being incapable of giving a reason, is not knowledge (for how can knowledge be devoid of reason? nor again, ignorance, for neither can ignorance attain the truth), but is clearly something which is a mean between ignorance and wisdom." "Quite true," I replied. "Do not then insist," she said, "that what is not fair is of necessity foul, or what is not good evil; or infer that because love is not fair and good he is therefore foul and evil; for he is in a mean between them." "Well," I said, "Love is surely admitted by all to be a great god." "By those who know or by those who do not know?" "By all." "And how, Socrates," she said with a smile, "can Love be acknowledged to be a great god by those who say that he is not a god at all?" "And who are they?" I said. "You and I are two of them," she replied. "How can that be?" I said. "It is quite intelligible," she replied; "for you yourself would acknowledge that the gods are happy and fair—of course you would—would you dare to say that any god was not?" "Certainly not," I replied. "And you mean by the happy, those who are the possessors of things good or fair?" "Yes." "And you admitted that Love, because he was in want, desires those good and fair things of which he is in want?" "Yes, I did." "But how can he be a god who has no portion in what is either good or fair?" "Impossible." "Then you see that you also deny the divinity of Love."

202

---

[13] Cp. Gorgias, 505 E.
[14] Supra, 195 A.

"What then is Love?" I asked. "Is he mortal?" "No." "What then?" "As in the former instance, he is neither mortal nor immortal, but in a mean between the two." "What is he, Diotima?" "He is a great spirit (δαίμων), and like all spirits he is intermediate between the divine and the mortal." "And what," I said, "is his power?" "He interprets," she replied, "between gods and men, conveying and taking across to the gods the prayers and sacrifices of men, and to men the commands and replies of the gods; he is the mediator who spans the chasm which divides them, and therefore in him all is bound together, and through him the arts of the prophet and the priest, their sacrifices and mysteries and charms, and all prophecy and incantation, find their way. For God mingles not with man; but through Love all the intercourse and converse of god with man, whether awake or asleep, is carried on. The wisdom which understands this is spiritual; all other wisdom, such as that of arts and handicrafts, is mean and vulgar. Now these spirits or intermediate powers are many and diverse, and one of them is Love." "And who," I said, "was his father, and who his mother?" "The tale," she said, "will take time; nevertheless I will tell you. On the birthday of Aphrodite there was a feast of the gods, at which the god Poros or Plenty, who is the son of Metis or Discretion, was one of the guests. When the feast was over, Penia or Poverty, as the manner is on such occasions, came about the doors to beg. Now Plenty, who was the worse for nectar (there was no wine in those days), went into the garden of Zeus and fell into a heavy sleep; and Poverty considering her own straitened circumstances, plotted to have a child by him, and accordingly she lay down at his side and conceived Love, who partly because he is naturally a lover of the beautiful, and because Aphrodite is herself beautiful, and also because he was born on her birthday, is her follower and attendant. And as his parentage is, so also are his fortunes. In the first place he is always poor, and anything but tender and fair, as the many imagine him; and he is rough and squalid, and has no shoes, nor a house to dwell in; on the bare earth exposed he lies under the open heaven, in

203

the streets, or at the doors of houses, taking his rest; and like his mother he is always in distress. Like his father too, whom he also partly resembles, he is always plotting against the fair and good; he is bold, enterprising, strong, a mighty hunter, always weaving some intrigue or other, keen in the pursuit of wisdom, fertile in resources; a philosopher at all times, terrible as an enchanter, sorcerer, sophist. He is by nature neither mortal nor immortal, but alive and flourishing at one moment when he is in plenty, and dead at another moment, and again alive by reason of his father's nature. But that which is always flowing in is always flowing out, and so he is never in want and never in wealth; and further, he is in a mean between ignorance and knowledge. The truth of the matter is this: No god is a philosopher or seeker after wisdom, for he is wise already; nor does any man who is wise seek after wisdom. Neither do the ignorant seek after wisdom. For herein is the evil of ignorance, that he who is neither good nor wise is nevertheless satisfied with himself: he has no desire for that of which he feels no want." "But who then, Diotima," I said, "are the lovers of wisdom, if they are neither the wise nor the foolish?" "A child may answer that question," she replied; "they are those who are in a mean between the two; Love is one of them. For wisdom is a most beautiful thing, and Love is of the beautiful; and therefore Love is also a philosopher or lover of wisdom, and being a lover of wisdom is in a mean between the wise and the ignorant. And of this to his birth is the cause; for his father is wealthy and wise, and his mother poor and foolish. Such, my dear Socrates, is the nature of the spirit Love. The error in your conception of him was very natural, and as I imagine from what you say, has arisen out of a confusion of love and the beloved, which made you think that love was all beautiful. For the beloved is the truly beautiful, and delicate, and perfect, and blessed; but the principle of love is of another nature, and is such as I have described."

I said: "O thou stranger woman, thou sayest well; but, assuming Love to be such as you say, what is the use of him to men?" "That, Socrates," she replied,

"I will attempt to unfold: of his nature and birth I have already spoken; and you acknowledge that love is of the beautiful. But someone will say: Of the beautiful in what, Socrates and Diotima?—or rather let me put the question more clearly, and ask: When a man loves the beautiful, what does he desire?" I answered her "That the beautiful may be his." "Still," she said, "the answer suggests a further question: What is given by the possession of beauty?" "To what you have asked," I replied, "I have no answer ready." "Then," she said, "let me put the word 'good' in the place of the beautiful, and repeat the question once more: If he who loves the good, what is it then that he loves?" "The possession of the good," I said. "And what does he gain who possesses the good?" "Happiness," I replied; "there is less difficulty in answering that question." "Yes," she said, "the happy are made happy by the acquisition of good things. Nor is there any need to ask why a man desires happiness; the answer is already final." "You are right," I said. "And is this wish and this desire common to all? and do all men always desire their own good, or only some men?—what say you?" "All men," I replied; "the desire is common to all." "Why, then," she rejoined, "are not all men, Socrates, said to love, but only some of them? whereas you say that all men are always loving the same things." "I myself wonder," I said, "why this is." "There is nothing to wonder at," she replied; "the reason is that one part of love is separated off and receives the name of the whole, but the other parts have other names." "Give an illustration," I said. She answered me as follows: "There is poetry, which, as you know, is complex and manifold. All creation or passage of nonbeing into being is poetry or making, and the processes of all art are creative; and the masters of arts are all poets or makers." "Very true." "Still," she said, "you know that they are not called poets, but have other names; only that portion of the art which is separated off from the rest, and is concerned with music and meter, is termed poetry, and they who possess poetry in this sense of the word are called poets." "Very true," I said. "And the same holds of love. For you may say generally that all de-

205

sire of good and happiness is only the great and subtle power of love; but they who are drawn towards him by any other path, whether the path of money-making or gymnastics or philosophy, are not called lovers—the name of the whole is appropriated to those whose affection takes one form only—they alone are said to love, or to be lovers." "I dare say," I replied, "that you are right." "Yes," she added, "and you hear people say that lovers are seeking for their other half; but I say that they are seeking neither for the half of themselves, nor for the whole, unless the half or the whole be also a good. And they will cut off their own hands and feet and cast them away, if they are evil; for they love not what is their own, unless perchance there be someone who calls what belongs to him the good, and what belongs to another the evil. For there is nothing which men love but the good. Is there anything?" "Certainly, I should say, that there is nothing." "Then," she said, "the simple truth is, that men love the good." "Yes," I said. "To which must be added that they love the possession of the good?" "Yes, that must be added." "And not only the possession, but the everlasting possession of the good?" "That must be added too." "Then love," she said, "may be described generally as the love of the everlasting possession of the good?" "That is most true."

"Then if this be the nature of love, can you tell me further," she said, "what is the manner of the pursuit? what are they doing who show all this eagerness and heat which is called love? and what is the object which they have in view? Answer me." "Nay, Diotima," I replied, "if I had known, I should not have wondered at your wisdom, neither should I have come to learn from you about this very matter." "Well," she said, "I will teach you:—The object which they have in view is birth in beauty, whether of body or soul." "I do not understand you," I said; "the oracle requires an explanation." "I will make my meaning clearer," she replied. "I mean to say, that all men are bringing to the birth in their bodies and in their souls. There is a certain age at which human nature is desirous of procreation—procreation which must be in beauty and not in deformity;

and this procreation is the union of man and woman, and is a divine thing; for conception and generation are an immortal principle in the mortal creature, and in the inharmonious they can never be. But the deformed is always inharmonious with the divine, and the beautiful harmonious. Beauty, then, is the destiny or goddess of parturition who presides at birth, and therefore, when approaching beauty, the conceiving power is propitious, and diffusive, and benign, and begets and bears fruit: at the sight of ugliness she frowns and contracts and has a sense of pain, and turns away, and shrivels up, and not without a pang refrains from conception. And this is the reason why, when the hour of conception arrives, and the teeming nature is full, there is such a flutter and ecstasy about beauty whose approach is the alleviation of the pain of travail. For love, Socrates, is not, as you imagine, the love of the beautiful only." "What then?" "The love of generation and of birth in beauty." "Yes," I said. "Yes, indeed," she replied. "But why of generation?" "Because to the mortal creature, generation is a sort of eternity and immortality," she replied; "and if, as has been already admitted, love is of the everlasting possession of the good, all men will necessarily desire immortality together with good: Wherefore love is of immortality."

207

All this she taught me at various times when she spoke of love. And I remember her once saying to me, "What is the cause, Socrates, of love, and the attendant desire? See you not how all animals, birds, as well as beasts, in their desire of procreation, are in agony when they take the infection of love, which begins with the desire of union; whereto is added the care of offspring, on whose behalf the weakest are ready to battle against the strongest even to the uttermost, and to die for them, and will let themselves be tormented with hunger or suffer anything in order to maintain their young. Man may be supposed to act thus from reason; but why should animals have these passionate feelings? Can you tell me why?" Again I replied that I did not know. She said to me: "And do you expect ever to become a master in the art of love, if you do not know this?" "But I have told you already, Diotima, that my ignorance is the reason why I come to you; for I am conscious that I want a teacher; tell me then the cause of this and of the other mysteries of love." "Marvel not," she said, "if you believe that love is of the immortal, as we have several times acknowledged; for here again, and on the same principle too, the mortal nature is seeking as far as is possible to be everlasting and immortal: and this is only to be attained by generation, because generation always leaves behind a new existence in the place of the old. Nay even in the life of the same individual there is succession and not absolute unity: a man is called the same, and yet in the short interval which elapses between youth and age, and in which every animal is said to have life and identity, he is undergoing a perpetual process of loss and reparation—hair, flesh, bones, blood, and the whole body are always changing. Which is true not only of the body, but also of the soul, whose habits, tempers, opinions, desires, pleasures, pains, fears, never remain the same in any one of us, but are always coming and going; and equally true of knowledge, and what is still more surprising to us mortals, not only do the sciences in general spring up and decay, so that in respect of them we are never the same; but each of them individually experiences a like change. For what is implied in the word 'recollection,' but the departure of knowledge, which is ever being forgotten, and is renewed and preserved by recollection, and appears to be the same although in reality new, according to that law of succession by which all mortal things are preserved, not absolutely the same, but by substitution, the old worn-out mortality leaving another new and similar existence behind—unlike the divine, which is always the same and not another? And in this way, Socrates, the mortal body, or mortal anything, partakes of immortality; but the immortal in another way. Marvel not then at the love which all men have of their offspring; for that universal love and interest is for the sake of immortality."

208

I was astonished at her words, and said: "Is this really true, O thou wise Diotima?" And she answered with all the authority of an accomplished sophist: "Of that, Socrates, you may be assured;—think only of the ambition of men, and you will wonder at the senselessness of their ways, unless you consider how they are stirred by the love of an immortality of fame. They are ready to run all risks greater far than they would have run for their children, and to spend money and undergo any sort of toil, and even to die, for the sake of leaving behind them a name which shall be eternal. Do you imagine that Alcestis would have died to save Admetus, or Achilles to avenge Patroclus, or your own Codrus in order to preserve the kingdom for his sons, if they had not imagined that the memory of their virtues, which still survives among us, would be immortal? Nay," she said, "I am persuaded that all men do all things, and the better they are the more they do them, in hope of the glorious fame of immortal virtue; for they desire the immortal.

"Those who are pregnant in the body only, betake themselves to women and beget children—this is the character of their love; their offspring, as they hope, will preserve their memory and give them the blessedness and immortality which they desire in the future. But souls which are pregnant—for there certainly are men who are more creative in their souls than in their bodies—conceive that which is proper for the soul to conceive or contain. And what are these conceptions?—wisdom and virtue in general. And such creators are poets and all artists who are deserving of the name inventor. But the greatest and fairest sort of wisdom by far is that which is concerned with the ordering of states and families, and which is called temperance and justice. And he who in youth has the seed of these implanted in him and is himself inspired, when he comes to maturity desires to beget and generate. He wanders about seeking beauty that he may beget offspring—for in deformity he will beget nothing—and naturally embraces the beautiful rather than the deformed body; above all when he finds a fair and noble and well-nurtured soul, he embraces the two in one person, and to such an one he is full of speech about virtue and the nature and pursuits of a good man; and he tries to educate him; and at the touch of the beautiful which is ever present to his memory, even when absent, he brings forth that

209

which he had conceived long before, and in company with him tends that which he brings forth; and they are married by a far nearer tie and have a closer friendship than those who beget mortal children, for the children who are their common offspring are fairer and more immortal. Who, when he thinks of Homer and Hesiod and other great poets, would not rather have their children than ordinary human ones? Who would not emulate them in the creation of children such as theirs, which have preserved their memory and given them everlasting glory? Or who would not have such children as Lycurgus left behind him to be the saviors, not only of Lacedaemon, but of Hellas, as one may say? There is Solon, too, who is the revered father of Athenian laws; and many others there are in many other places, both among Hellenes and barbarians, who have given to the world many noble works, and have been the parents of virtue of every kind; and many temples have been raised in their honor for the sake of children such as theirs; which were never raised in honor of anyone, for the sake of his mortal children.

"These are the lesser mysteries of love, into which even you, Socrates, may enter; to the greater and more hidden ones which are the crown of these, and to which, if you pursue them in a right spirit, they will lead, I know not whether you will be able to attain. But I will do my utmost to inform you, and do you follow if you can. For he who would proceed aright in this matter should begin in youth to visit beautiful forms; and first, if he be guided by his instructor aright, to love one such form only—out of that he should create fair thoughts; and soon he will of himself perceive that the beauty of one form is akin to the beauty of another; and then if beauty of form in general is his pursuit, how foolish would he be not to recognize that the beauty in every form is one and the same! And when he perceives this he will abate his violent love of the one, which he will despise and deem a small thing, and will become a lover of all beautiful forms; in the next stage he will consider that the beauty of the mind is more honorable than the beauty of the outward form. So that if a virtuous soul have but a little comeliness,

210

he will be content to love and tend him, and will search out and bring to the birth thoughts which may improve the young, until he is compelled to contemplate and see the beauty of institutions and laws, and to understand that the beauty of them all is of one family, and that personal beauty is a trifle; and after laws and institutions he will go on to the sciences, that he may see their beauty, being not like a servant in love with the beauty of one youth or man or institution, himself a slave mean and narrow-minded, but drawing towards and contemplating the vast sea of beauty, he will create many fair and noble thoughts and notions in boundless love of wisdom; until on that shore he grows and waxes strong, and at last the vision is revealed to him of a single science, which is the science of beauty everywhere. To this I will proceed; please to give me your very best attention:

"He who has been instructed thus far in the things of love, and who has learned to see the beautiful in due order and succession, when he comes toward the end will suddenly perceive a nature of wondrous beauty (and this, Socrates, is the final cause of all our former toils)—a nature which in the first place is everlasting, not growing and decaying, or waxing and waning; secondly, not fair in one point of view and foul in another, or at one time or in one relation or at one place fair, at another time or in another relation or at another place foul, as if fair to some and foul to others, or in the likeness of a face or hands or any other part of the bodily frame, or in any form of speech or knowledge, or existing in any other being, as for example, in an animal, or in heaven, or in earth, or in any other place; but beauty absolute, separate, simple, and everlasting, which without diminution and without increase, or any change, is imparted to the ever-growing and perishing beauties of all other things. He who from these ascending under the influence of true love, begins to perceive that beauty, is not far from the end. And the true order of going, or being led by another, to the things of love, is to begin from the beauties of earth and mount upwards for the sake of that other beauty, using these as steps only, and from one going

211

on to two, and from two to all fair forms, and from
fair forms to fair practices, and from fair practices
to fair notions, until from fair notions he arrives at
the notion of absolute beauty, and at last knows what
the essence of beauty is. This, my dear Socrates,"
said the stranger of Mantineia, "is that life above all
others which man should live, in the contemplation
of beauty absolute; a beauty which if you once beheld, you would see not to be after the measure of
gold, and garments, and fair boys and youths, whose
presence now entrances you; and you and many a
one would be content to live seeing them only and
conversing with them without meat or drink, if
that were possible—you only want to look at them
and to be with them. But what if man had eyes to
see the true beauty—the divine beauty, I mean, pure
and clear and unalloyed, not clogged with the pollu-
tions of mortality and all the colors and vanities of
human life—thither looking, and holding converse
with the true beauty simple and divine? Remember   212
how in that communion only, beholding beauty with
the eye of the mind, he will be enabled to bring
forth, not images of beauty, but realities (for he has
hold not of an image but of a reality), and bringing
forth and nourishing true virtue to become the friend
of God and be immortal, if mortal man may. Would
that be an ignoble life?"

Such, Phaedrus—and I speak not only to you, but
to all of you—were the words of Diotima; and I am
persuaded of their truth. And being persuaded of
them, I try to persuade others, that in the attainment
of this end human nature will not easily find a helper
better than love. And therefore, also, I say that every
man ought to honor him as I myself honor him, and
walk in his ways, and exhort others to do the same,
and praise the power and spirit of love according to
the measure of my ability now and ever.

The words which I have spoken, you, Phaedrus,
may call an encomium of love, or anything else
which you please.

When Socrates had done speaking, the company
applauded, and Aristophanes was beginning to say
something in answer to the allusion which Socrates

had made to his own speech,[15] when suddenly there
was a great knocking at the door of the house, as of
revellers, and the sound of a flute girl was heard.
Agathon told the attendants to go and see who were
the intruders. "If they are friends of ours," he said,
"invite them in, but if not, say that the drinking is
over." A little while afterwards they heard the voice
of Alcibiades resounding in the court; he was in a
great state of intoxication, and kept roaring and
shouting "Where is Agathon? Lead me to Agathon,"
and at length, supported by the flute girl and some of
his attendants, he found his way to them. "Hail,
friends," he said, appearing at the door crowned with
a massive garland of ivy and violets, his head flowing with ribands. "Will you have a very drunken man
as a companion of your revels? Or shall I crown
Agathon, which was my intention in coming, and go
away? For I was unable to come yesterday, and
therefore I am here today, carrying on my head these
ribands, that taking them from my own head, I may
crown the head of this fairest and wisest of men, as
I may be allowed to call him. Will you laugh at me
because I am drunk? Yet I know very well that I am   213
speaking the truth, although you may laugh. But first
tell me; if I come in shall we have the understanding
of which I spoke?[16] Will you drink with me or not?"

The company were vociferous in begging that he
would take his place among them, and Agathon
specially invited him. Thereupon he was led in by the
people who were with him; and as he was being
led, intending to crown Agathon, he took the ribands
from his own head and held them in front of his
eyes; he was thus prevented from seeing Socrates,
who made way for him, and Alcibiades took the
vacant place between Agathon and Socrates, and in
taking the place he embraced Agathon and crowned
him. Take off his sandals, said Agathon, and let him
make a third on the same couch.

By all means; but who makes the third partner in
our revels? said Alcibiades, turning round and starting up as he caught sight of Socrates. By Heracles,

[15] p. 205 E.
[16] Supra 212 D. Will you have a very drunken man? etc.

he said, what is this? here is Socrates always lying in wait for me, and always, as his way is, coming out at all sorts of unsuspected places: and now, what have you to say for yourself, and why are you lying here, where I perceive that you have contrived to find a place, not by a joker or lover of jokes, like Aristophanes, but by the fairest of the company?

Socrates turned to Agathon and said: I must ask you to protect me, Agathon; for the passion of this man has grown quite a serious matter to me. Since I became his admirer I have never been allowed to speak to any other fair one, or so much as to look at them. If I do, he goes wild with envy and jealously, and not only abuses me but can hardly keep his hands off me, and at this moment he may do me some harm. Please to see to this, and either reconcile me to him, or, if he attempts violence, protect me, as I am in bodily fear of his mad and passionate attempts.

There can never be reconciliation between you and me, said Alcibiades; but for the present I will defer your chastisement. And I must beg you, Agathon, to give me back some of the ribands that I may crown the marvelous head of this universal despot—I would not have him complain of me for crowning you, and neglecting him, who in conversation is the conqueror of all mankind; and this not only once, as you were the day before yesterday, but always. Whereupon, taking some of the ribands, he crowned Socrates, and again reclined.

Then he said: You seem, my friends, to be sober, which is a thing not to be endured; you must drink—for that was the agreement under which I was admitted—and I elect myself master of the feast until you are well drunk. Let us have a large goblet, Agathon, or rather, he said, addressing the attendant, bring me that wine-cooler. The wine-cooler which had caught his eye was a vessel holding more than two quarts—this he filled and emptied, and bade the attendant fill it again for Socrates. Observe, my friends, said Alcibiades, that this ingenious trick of mine will have no effect on Socrates, for he can drink any quantity of wine and not be at all nearer being drunk. Socrates drank the cup which the attendant filled for him.

Eryximachus said: What is this, Alcibiades? Are we

to have neither conversation nor singing over our cups; but simply to drink as if we were thirsty?

Alcibiades replied: Hail, worthy son of a most wise and worthy sire!

The same to you, said Eryximachus; but what shall we do?

That I leave to you, said Alcibiades.

"The wise physician skilled our wounds to heal"[17] shall prescribe and we will obey. What do you want?

Well, said Eryximachus, before you appeared we had passed a resolution that each one of us in turn should make a speech in praise of love, and as good a one as he could: the turn was passed round from left to right; and as all of us have spoken, and you have not spoken but have well drunken, you ought to speak, and then impose upon Socrates any task which you please, and he on his righthand neighbor, and so on.

That is good, Eryximachus, said Alcibiades; and yet the comparison of a drunken man's speech with those of sober men is hardly fair; and I should like to know, sweet friend, whether you really believe what Socrates was just now saying; for I can assure you that the very reverse is the fact, and that if I praise anyone but himself in his presence, whether God or man, he will hardly keep his hands off me.

For shame, said Socrates.

Hold your tongue, said Alcibiades, for by Poseidon, there is no one else whom I will praise when you are of the company.

Well then, said Eryximachus, if you like praise Socrates.

What do you think, Eryximachus? said Alcibiades: shall I attack him and inflict the punishment before you all?

What are you about? said Socrates; are you going to raise a laugh at my expense? Is that the meaning of your praise?

I am going to speak the truth, if you will permit me.

I not only permit, but exhort you to speak the truth.

[17] From Pope's Homer, Il. xi. 514.

Then I will begin at once, said Alcibiades, and if I say anything which is not true, you may interrupt me if you will, and say "that is a lie," though my intention is to speak the truth. But you must not wonder if I speak anyhow as things come into my mind; for the fluent and orderly enumeration of all your singularities is not a task which is easy to a man in my condition.

And now, my boys, I shall praise Socrates in a figure which will appear to him to be a caricature, and yet I speak, not to make fun of him, but only for the truth's sake. I say, that he is exactly like the busts of Silenus, which are set up in the statuaries' shops, holding pipes and flutes in their mouths; and they are made to open in the middle, and have images of gods inside them. I say also that he is like Marsyas the satyr. You yourself will not deny, Socrates, that your face is like that of a satyr. Aye, and there is a resemblance in other points too. For example, you are a bully, as I can prove by witnesses, if you will not confess. And are you not a flute player? That you are, and a performer far more wonderful than Marsyas. He indeed with instruments used to charm the souls of men by the powers of his breath, and the players of his music do so still: for the melodies of Olympus[18] are derived from Marsyas who taught them, and these, whether they are played by a great master or by a miserable flute girl, have a power which no others have; they alone possess the soul and reveal the wants of those who have need of gods and mysteries, because they are divine. But you produce the same effect with your words only, and do not require the flute; that is the difference between you and him. When we hear any other speaker, even a very good one, he produces absolutely no effect upon us, or not much, whereas the mere fragments of you and your words, even at secondhand, and however imperfectly repeated, amaze and possess the souls of every man, woman, and child who comes within hearing of them. And if I were not afraid that you would think me hopelessly drunk, I would have sworn as well as spoken to the influence which they

215

[18] Cp. Arist. Pol. viii. 5. 16.

have always had and still have over me. For my heart
leaps within me more than that of any Corybantian
reveller, and my eyes rain tears when I hear them.
And I observe that many others are affected in the
same manner. I have heard Pericles and other great
orators, and I thought that they spoke well, but I
never had any similar feeling; my soul was not
stirred by them, nor was I angry at the thought of my
own slavish state. But this Marsyas has often brought
me to such a pass, that I have felt as if I could hardly   216
endure the life which I am leading (this, Socrates,
you will admit); and I am conscious that if I did not
shut my ears against him, and fly as from the voice
of the siren, my fate would be like that of others—
he would transfix me, and I should grow old sitting at
his feet. For he makes me confess that I ought not to
live as I do, neglecting the wants of my own soul, and
busying myself with the concerns of the Athenians;
therefore I hold my ears and tear myself away from
him. And he is the only person who ever made me
ashamed, which you might think not to be in my
nature, and there is no one else who does the same.
For I know that I cannot answer him or say that I
ought not to do as he bids, but when I leave his
presence the love of popularity gets the better of me.
And therefore I run away and fly from him, and
when I see him I am ashamed of what I have con-
fessed to him. Many a time have I wished that he
were dead, and yet I know that I should be much
more sorry than glad, if he were to die: so that I
am at my wit's end.

And this is what I and many others have suffered
from the flute playing of this satyr. Yet hear me once
more while I show you how exact the image is, and
how marvelous his power. For let me tell you: none
of you know him; but I will reveal him to you; having
begun, I must go on. See you how fond he is of the
fair? He is always with them and is always being
smitten by them, and then again he knows nothing
and is ignorant of all things—such is the appearance
which he puts on. Is he not like a Silenus in this?
To be sure he is: his outer mask is the carved head of
the Silenus; but, O my companions in drink, when he
is opened, what temperance there is residing within!

Know you that beauty and wealth and honor, at which the many wonder, are of no account with him, and are utterly despised by him: he regards not at all the persons who are gifted with them; mankind are nothing to him; all his life is spent in mocking and flouting at them. But when I opened him, and looked within at his serious purpose, I saw in him divine and golden images of such fascinating beauty that I was ready to do in a moment whatever Socrates commanded: they may have escaped the observation of others, but I saw them. Now I fancied that he was seriously enamored of my beauty, and I thought that I should therefore have a grand opportunity of hearing him tell what he knew, for I had a wonderful opinion of the attractions of my youth. In the prosecution of this design, when I next went to him, I sent away the attendant who usually accompanied me (I will confess the whole truth, and beg you to listen; and if I speak falsely, do you, Socrates, expose the falsehood). Well, he and I were alone together, and I thought that when there was nobody with us, I should hear him speak the language which lovers use to their loves when they are by themselves, and I was delighted. Nothing of the sort; he conversed as usual, and spent the day with me and then went away. Afterwards I challenged him to the palaestra; and he wrestled and closed with me several times when there was no one present; I fancied that I might succeed in this manner. Not a bit; I made no way with him. Lastly, as I had failed hitherto, I thought that I must take stronger measures and attack him boldly, and, as I had begun, not give him up, but see how matters stood between him and me. So I invited him to sup with me, just as if he were a fair youth, and I a designing lover. He was not easily persuaded to come; he did, however, after a while accept the invitation, and when he came the first time, he wanted to go away at once as soon as supper was over, and I had not the face to detain him. The second time, still in pursuance of my design, after we had supped, I went on conversing far into the night, and when he wanted to go away, I pretended that the hour was late and that he had much better remain. So he lay down on the couch next to me, the

same on which he had supped, and there was no one
but ourselves sleeping in the apartment. All this may
be told without shame to anyone. But what follows I
could hardly tell you if I were sober. Yet as the
proverb says, "In vino veritas," whether with boys, or
without them;[19] and therefore I must speak. Nor,
again, should I be justified in concealing the lofty
actions of Socrates when I come to praise him. Moreover I have felt the serpent's sting; and he who has
suffered, as they say, is willing to tell his fellow-
sufferers only, as they alone will be likely to under-   218
stand him, and will not be extreme in judging of the
sayings or doings which have been wrung from his
agony. For I have been bitten by a more than viper's
tooth; I have known in my soul, or in my heart, or
in some other part, that worst of pangs, more violent
in ingenuous youth than any serpent's tooth, the pang
of philosophy, which will make a man say or do anything. And you whom I see around me, Phaedrus and
Agathon and Eryximachus and Pausanias and Aristodemus and Aristophanes, all of you, and I need
not say Socrates himself, have had experience of the
same madness and passion in your longing after wisdom. Therefore listen and excuse my doings then and
my sayings now. But let the attendants and other pro-
fane and unmannered persons close up the doors of
their ears.

When the lamp was put out and the servants had
gone away, I thought that I must be plain with him
and have no more ambiguity. So I gave him a shake,
and I said: "Socrates, are you asleep?" "No," he said.
"Do you know what I am meditating?" "What are
you meditating?" he said "I think," I replied, "that of
all the lovers whom I have ever had you are the only
one who is worthy of me, and you appear to be too
modest to speak. Now I feel that I should be a fool to
refuse you this or any other favor, and therefore I
come to lay at your feet all that I have and all that
my friends have, in the hope that you will assist me
in the way of virtue, which I desire above all things,
and in which I believe that you can help me better

---

[19] In allusion to the two proverbs, οἶνος καὶ παῖδες ἀληθεῖς, and
οἶνος καὶ ἀλήθεια.

than anyone else. And I should certainly have more reason to be ashamed of what wise men would say if I were to refuse a favor to such as you, than of what the world, who are mostly fools, would say of me if I granted it." To these words he replied in the ironical manner which is so characteristic of him: —"Alcibiades, my friend, you have indeed an elevated aim if what you say is true, and if there really is in me any power by which you may become better; truly you must see in me some rare beauty of a kind infinitely higher than any which I see in you. And therefore, if you mean to share with me and to ex- 219 change beauty for beauty, you will have greatly the advantage of me; you will gain true beauty in return for appearance—like Diomede, gold in exchange for brass. But look again, sweet friend, and see whether you are not deceived in me. The mind begins to grow critical when the bodily eye fails, and it will be a long time before you get old." Hearing this, I said: "I have told you my purpose, which is quite serious, and do you consider what you think best for you and me." "That is good," he said; "at some other time then we will consider and act as seems best about this and about other matters." Whereupon, I fancied that he was smitten, and that the words which I had uttered like arrows had wounded him, and so without waiting to hear more I got up, and throwing my coat about him crept under his thread-bare cloak, as the time of year was winter, and there I lay during the whole night having this wonderful monster in my arms. This thing, Socrates, will not be denied by you. And yet, notwithstanding all, he was so superior to my solicitations, so contemptuous and derisive and disdainful of my beauty—which really, as I fancied, had some attractions—hear, O judges; for judges you shall be of the haughty virtue of Socrates—nothing more happened, but in the morning when I awoke (let all the gods and goddesses be my witnesses) I arose as from the couch of a father or an elder brother.

What do you suppose must have been my feelings, after this rejection, at the thought of my own dishonor? And yet I could not help wondering at his natural temperance and self-restraint and manli-

ness. I never imagined that I could have met with
a man such as he is in wisdom and endurance. And
therefore I could not be angry with him or renounce
his company, any more than I could hope to win
him. For I well knew that if Ajax could not be
wounded by steel, much less he by money; and my
only chance of captivating him by my personal attractions had failed. So I was at my wit's end; no
one was ever more hopelessly enslaved by another.
All this happened before he and I went on the expedition to Potidaea; there we messed together, and
I had the opportunity of observing his extraordinary
power of sustaining fatigue. His endurance was
simply marvellous when, being cut off from our sup-   220
plies, we were compelled to go without food—on
such occasions, which often happen in time of war,
he was superior not only to me but to everybody;
there was no one to be compared to him. Yet at a
festival he was the only person who had any real
powers of enjoyment; though not willing to drink, he
could if compelled beat us all at that—wonderful
to relate! no human being had ever seen Socrates
drunk; and his powers, if I am not mistaken, will
be tested before long. His fortitude in enduring cold
was also surprising. There was a severe frost, for
the winter in that region is really tremendous, and
everybody else either remained indoors, or if they
went out had on an amazing quantity of clothes, and
were well shod, and had their feet swathed in felt
and fleeces: in the midst of this, Socrates with his
bare feet on the ice and in his ordinary dress marched
better than the other soldiers who had shoes, and
they looked daggers at him because he seemed to
despise them.

I have told you one tale, and now I must tell you
another, which is worth hearing, "Of the doings and
sufferings of the enduring man" while he was on
the expedition. One morning he was thinking about
something which he could not resolve; he would
not give it up, but continued thinking from early
dawn until noon—there he stood fixed in thought;
and at noon attention was drawn to him, and the
rumor ran through the wondering crowd that Socrates had been standing and thinking about some-

thing ever since the break of day. At last, in the
evening after supper, some Ionians out of curiosity
(I should explain that this was not in winter but in
summer), brought out their mats and slept in the
open air that they might watch him and see whether
he would stand all night. There he stood until the
following morning; and with the return of light he
offered up a prayer to the sun, and went his way.[20]
I will also tell, if you please—and indeed I am
bound to tell—of his courage in battle; for who but
he saved my life? Now this was the engagement in
which I received the prize of valor: for I was
wounded and he would not leave me, but he rescued
me and my arms; and he ought to have received the
prize of valor which the generals wanted to confer
on me partly on account of my rank, and I told
them so (this, again, Socrates will not impeach or
deny), but he was more eager than the generals that
I and not he should have the prize. There was another occasion on which his behavior was very   221
remarkable—in the flight of the army after the
battle of Delium, where he served among the heavy-
armed,—I had a better opportunity of seeing him
than at Potidaea, for I was myself on horseback, and
therefore comparatively out of danger. He and Laches
were retreating, for the troops were in flight, and I
met them and told them not to be discouraged, and
promised to remain with them; and there you might
see him, Aristophanes, as you describe,[21] just as he
is in the streets of Athens, stalking like a pelican, and
rolling his eyes, calmly contemplating enemies as well
as friends, and making very intelligible to anybody,
even from a distance, that whoever attacked him
would be likely to meet with a stout resistance; and
in this way he and his companion escaped—for this is
the sort of man who is never touched in war; those
only are pursued who are running away headlong.
I particularly observed how superior he was to Laches
in presence of mind. Many are the marvels which
I might narrate in praise of Socrates; most of his
ways might perhaps be paralleled in another man, but

[20] Cp. supra, 175 B.
[21] Aristoph. Clouds, 362.

his absolute unlikeness to any human being that is
or ever has been is perfectly astonishing. You may
imagine Brasidas and others to have been like
Achilles; or you may imagine Nestor and Antenor to
have been like Pericles; and the same may be said
of other famous men, but of this strange being you
will never be able to find any likeness, however remote, either among men who now are or who ever
have been—other than that which I have already
suggested of Silenus and the satyrs; and they represent
in a figure not only himself, but his words. For, although I forgot to mention this to you before, his
words are like the images of Silenus which open;
they are ridiculous when you first hear them; he
clothes himself in language that is like the skin of the
wanton satyr—for his talk is of pack-asses and smiths
and cobblers and curriers, and he is always repeating
the same things in the same words,[22] so that any ignorant or inexperienced person might feel disposed to
laugh at him; but he who opens the bust and sees   222
what is within will find that they are the only words
which have a meaning in them, and also the most divine, abounding in fair images of virtue, and of the
widest comprehension, or rather extending to the
whole duty of a good and honorable man.

This, friends, is my praise of Socrates. I have added
my blame of him for his ill-treatment of me; and
he has ill-treated not only me, but Charmides the
son of Glaucon, and Euthydemus the son of Diocles,
and many others in the same way—beginning as their
lover he has ended by making them pay their addresses to him. Wherefore I say to you, Agathon,
"Be not deceived by him; learn from me and take
warning, and do not be a fool and learn by experience, as the proverb says."

When Alcibiades had finished, there was a laugh at
his outspokenness; for he seemed to be still in love
with Socrates. You are sober, Alcibiades, said Socrates, or you would never have gone so far about to
hide the purpose of your satyr's praises, for all
this long story is only an ingenious circumlocution,
of which the point comes in by the way at the end;

[22] Cp. Gorg. 490, 491, 517.

you want to get up a quarrel between me and Agathon, and your notion is that I ought to love you and nobody else, and that you and you only ought to love Agathon. But the plot of this Satyric or Silenic drama has been detected, and you must not allow him, Agathon, to set us at variance.

I believe you are right, said Agathon, and I am disposed to think that his intention in placing himself between you and me was only to divide us; but he shall gain nothing by that move; for I will go and lie on the couch next to you.

Yes, yes, replied Socrates, by all means come here and lie on the couch below me.

Alas, said Alcibiades, how I am fooled by this man; he is determined to get the better of me at every turn. I do beseech you, allow Agathon to lie between us.

Certainly not, said Socrates, as you praised me, and I in turn ought to praise my neighbor on the right, he will be out of order in praising me again when he ought rather to be praised by me, and I must entreat you to consent to this, and not be jealous, for I have a great desire to praise the youth.   223

Hurrah! cried Agathon, I will rise instantly, that I may be praised by Socrates.

The usual way, said Alcibiades; where Socrates is, no one else has any chance with the fair; and now how readily has he invented a specious reason for attracting Agathon to himself.

Agathon arose in order that he might take his place on the couch by Socrates, when suddenly a band of revellers entered, and spoiled the order of the banquet. Someone who was going out having left the door open, they had found their way in, and made themselves at home; great confusion ensued, and everyone was compelled to drink large quantities of wine. Aristodemus said that Eryximachus, Phaedrus, and others went away—he himself fell asleep, and as the nights were long took a good rest; he was awakened towards daybreak by a crowing of cocks, and when he awoke, the others were either asleep, or had gone away; there remained only Socrates, Aristophanes, and Agathon, who were drinking out of a large goblet which they passed round, and Socrates was discoursing to them. Aristodemus was only half awake, and he did not hear the beginning of the discourse; the chief thing which he remembered was Socrates compelling the other two to acknowledge that the genius of comedy was the same with that of tragedy, and that the true artist in tragedy was an artist in comedy also. To this they were constrained to assent, being drowsy, and not quite following the argument. And first of all Aristophanes dropped off, then, when the day was already dawning, Agathon. Socrates, having laid them to sleep, rose to depart; Aristodemus, as his manner was, following him. At the Lyceum he took a bath, and passed the day as usual. In the evening he retired to rest at his own home.

**Outline of the Apology
(also called The Apology of Socrates or
Defense of Socrates)**

I. Defense proper—against Socrates' accusers (17a–35d)
  A. Introduction—manner and order of defense (17a–19a)
    1. falsehoods will be heard from accusers, truth from Socrates (17a–18a)
    2. defense must consider both old accusers and recent, in that order (18a–19a)
  B. Consideration of charges in context of Socrates' whole life (19a–34b)
    1. statement of charges, and their systematic refutation (19a–28a)
      a. charges of former accusers (19a–24b)
        i. Socrates pursues improper studies and makes the worse appear the better argument (19a–b)
        ii. obvious falsehood of these long-standing accusations (19c–20c)
        iii. Socrates has acquired bad reputation for a sort of wisdom (20c–22e)
        iv. but he will persist in this questioning, in spite of prejudice (22e–24b)
      b. charges of Meletus (24b–28a)
        i. statement: Socrates corrupts youth, does not believe in state divinities, and believes in new ones (24b)
        ii. questioning of Meletus (24c–28a)
    2. justification of Socrates' manner of life (28a–34b)
      a. in matters of duty a man should consider the chance of death from incurring ill-will (28a–28d)
      b. Socrates will continue to obey commands of God (28d–30c)
      c. the city must not put a benefactor to death (30c–31c)
      d. the divine sign has prevented Socrates from undertaking public life (31c–32e)

   33b)
f. even so, the youth appear to enjoy conversing
   with Socrates (33b–34b)
C. Conclusion of defense: no plea for pity will be
   offered (34b–35e)
II. After conviction—against unjust penalty (35e–38c)
   A. Closeness of the vote, 280–220 (35e–36b)
   B. Alternative proposals of punishment (36b–38c)
      1. death proposed by accusers (36b)
      2. free meals in the Prytaneum proposed by Socrates
         (36b–38b)
      3. 30 minas proposed by Socrates' friends (38b–c)
III. After condemnation to death (38c–42a)
   A. Address to condemning judges (38c–39e)
      1. nobility required to refrain from begging for
         acquittal (38c–39b)
      2. prophecy to condemning judges (39c–39e)
   B. Address to the real judges, those who voted for
      acquittal (39e–42a)
      1. the condemnation is doubtless a good thing (39e–
         40a)
         a. the divine sign allows Socrates to accept death
            (40a–40c)
         b. death is either of two possibilities, both good
            (40c–41c)
      2. no evil befalls a good man (41c–42a)
      3. whether better to die or to live is known to none
         but God (42a)

APOLOGY

SOCRATES   MELETUS

How you, O Athenians, have been affected by my accusers, I cannot tell; but I know that they almost made me forget who I was—so persuasively did they speak; and yet they have hardly uttered a word of truth. But of the many falsehoods told by them, there was one which quite amazed me;—I mean when they said that you should be upon your guard and not allow yourselves to be deceived by the force of my eloquence. To say this, when they were certain to be detected as soon as I opened my lips and proved myself to be anything but a great speaker, did indeed appear to me most shameless—unless by the force of eloquence they mean the force of truth; for if such is their meaning, I admit that I am eloquent. But in how different a way from theirs! Well, as I was saying, they have scarcely spoken the truth at all; but from me you shall hear the whole truth: not, however, delivered after their manner in a set oration duly ornamented with words and phrases. No, by heaven! but I shall use the words and arguments which occur to me at the moment; for I am confident in the justice of my cause[1]: at my time of life I ought not to be appearing before you, O men of Athens, in the character of a juvenile orator—let no one expect it of me. And I must beg of you to grant me a favor:—If I defend myself in my accustomed manner, and you hear me using the words which I have been in the habit of using in the agora, at the tables of the money-changers, or anywhere else, I would ask you not to be surprised, and not to interrupt me on this account. For I am more than

[1] Or, I am certain that I am right in taking this course.

seventy years of age, and appearing now for the
first time in a court of law, I am quite a stranger
to the language of the place; and therefore I would
have you regard me as if I were really a stranger,   18
whom you would excuse if he spoke in his native
tongue, and after the fashion of his country;—Am
I making an unfair request of you? Never mind the
manner, which may or may not be good; but think
only of the truth of my words, and give heed to
that: let the speaker speak truly and the judge decide justly.

And first, I have to reply to the older charges
and to my first accusers, and then I will go on to the
later ones. For of old I have had many accusers, who
have accused me falsely to you during many years;
and I am more afraid of them than of Anytus and his
associates, who are dangerous, too, in their own way.
But far more dangerous are the others, who began
when you were children, and took possession of your
minds with their falsehoods, telling of one Socrates,
a wise man, who speculated about the heaven above,
and searched into the earth beneath, and made the
worse appear the better cause. The disseminators
of this tale are the accusers whom I dread; for their
hearers are apt to fancy that such inquirers do not
believe in the existence of the gods. And they are
many, and their charges against me are of ancient
date, and they were made by them in the days when
you were more impressible than you are now—in
childhood, or it may have been in youth—and the
cause when heard went by default, for there was
none to answer. And hardest of all, I do not know
and cannot tell the names of my accusers; unless
in the chance case of a Comic poet. All who from
envy and malice have persuaded you—some of
them having first convinced themselves—all this
class of men are most difficult to deal with; for I
cannot have them up here, and cross-examine them,
and therefore I must simply fight with shadows in
my own defense and argue when there is no one
who answers. I will ask you then to assume with me,
as I was saying, that my opponents are of two kinds;
one recent, the other ancient: and I hope that you
will see the propriety of my answering the latter

first, for these accusations you heard long before the others, and much oftener.

Well, then, I must make my defense, and endeavor to clear away in a short time, a slander which has lasted a long time. May I succeed, if to succeed be for my good and yours, or likely to avail me in my cause! The task is not an easy one; I quite understand the nature of it. And so leaving the event with God, in obedience to the law I will now make my defense.

I will begin at the beginning, and ask what is the accusation which has given rise to the slander of me, and in fact has encouraged Meletus to prefer this charge against me. Well, what do the slanderers say? They shall be my prosecutors, and I will sum up their words in an affidavit: "Socrates is an evil-doer, and a curious person, who searches into things under the earth and in heaven, and he makes the worse appear the better cause; and he teaches the aforesaid doctrines to others." Such is the nature of the accusation: it is just what you have yourselves seen in the comedy of Aristophanes,[2] who has introduced a man whom he calls Socrates, going about and saying that he walks in air, and talking a deal of nonsense concerning matters of which I do not pretend to know either much or little—not that I mean to speak disparagingly of anyone who is a student of natural philosophy. I should be very sorry if Meletus could bring so grave a charge against me. But the simple truth is, O Athenians, that I have nothing to do with physical speculations. Very many of those here present are witnesses to the truth of this, and to them I appeal. Speak then, you who have heard me, and tell your neighbors whether any of you have ever known me hold forth in few words or in many upon such matters. . . . You hear their answer. And from what they say of this part of the charge you will be able to judge of the truth of the rest.

As little foundation is there for the report that I am a teacher, and take money; this accusation has no more truth in it than the other. Although, if

2 Aristoph., Clouds, 225 ff.

a man were really able to instruct mankind, to receive money for giving instruction would, in my
opinion, be an honor to him. There is Gorgias of
Leontium, and Prodicus of Ceos, and Hippias of
Elis, who go the round of the cities, and are able
to persuade the young men to leave their own citizens by whom they might be taught for nothing,   20
and come to them whom they not only pay, but are
thankful if they may be allowed to pay them. There
is at this time a Parian philosopher residing in
Athens, of whom I have heard; and I came to hear
of him in this way:—I came across a man who has
spent a world of money on the Sophists, Callias, the
son of Hipponicus, and knowing that he had sons,
I asked him: "Callias," I said, "if your two sons
were foals or calves, there would be no difficulty in
finding someone to put over them; we should hire a
trainer of horses, or a farmer probably, who would
improve and perfect them in their own proper virtue
and excellence; but as they are human beings, whom
are you thinking of placing over them? Is there anyone who understands human and political virtue? You
must have thought about the matter, for you have
sons; is there any one?" "There is," he said. "Who
is he?" said I; "and of what country? and what does
he charge?" "Evenus the Parian," he replied; "he
is the man, and his charge is five minae." Happy is
Evenus, I said to myself, if he really has this wisdom, and teaches at such a moderate charge. Had
I the same, I should have been very proud and conceited; but the truth is that I have no knowledge of
the kind.

I dare say, Athenians, that someone among you
will reply, "Yes, Socrates, but what is the origin
of these accusations which are brought against you;
there must have been something strange which you
have been doing? All these rumors and this talk
about you would never have arisen if you had been
like other men: tell us, then, what is the cause of
them, for we should be sorry to judge hastily of
you." Now I regard this as a fair challenge, and I
will endeavor to explain to you the reason why I am
called wise and have such an evil fame. Please to
attend then. And although some of you may think

that I am joking, I declare that I will tell you the entire truth. Men of Athens, this reputation of mine has come of a certain sort of wisdom which I possess. If you ask me what kind of wisdom, I reply, wisdom such as may perhaps be attained by man, for to that extent I am inclined to believe that I am wise; whereas the persons of whom I was speaking have a superhuman wisdom, which I may fail to describe, because I have it not myself; and he who says that I have, speaks falsely, and is taking away my character. And here, O men of Athens, I must beg you not to interrupt me, even if I seem to say something extravagant. For the word which I will speak is not mine. I will refer you to a witness who is worthy of credit; that witness shall be the God of Delphi—he will tell you about my wisdom, if I have any, and of what sort it is. You must have known Chaerephon; he was early a friend of mine, and also a friend of yours, for he shared in the recent exile of the people, and returned with you. Well, Chaerephon, as you know, was very impetuous in all his doings, and he went to Delphi and boldly asked the oracle to tell him whether—as I was saying, I must beg you not to interrupt—he asked the oracle to tell him whether any one was wiser than I was, and the Pythian prophetess answered, that there was no man wiser. Chaerephon is dead himself; but his brother, who is in court, will confirm the truth of what I am saying.

21

Why do I mention this? Because I am going to explain to you why I have such an evil name. When I heard the answer, I said to myself, What can the god mean? and what is the interpretation of his riddle? for I know that I have no wisdom, small or great. What then can he mean when he says that I am the wisest of men? And yet he is a god, and cannot lie; that would be against his nature. After long consideration, I thought of a method of trying the question. I reflected that if I could only find a man wiser than myself, then I might go to the god with a refutation in my hand. I should say to him, "Here is a man who is wiser than I am; but you said that I was the wisest." Accordingly I went to one who had the reputation of wisdom, and observed him—his name I need not mention; he was a politician whom I selected for examination—and the result was as follows: When I began to talk with him, I could not help thinking that he was not really wise, although he was thought wise by many, and still wise by himself; and thereupon I tried to explain to him that he thought himself wise, but was not really wise; and the consequence was that he hated me, and his enmity was shared by several who were present and heard me. So I left him, saying to myself, as I went away: Well, although I do not suppose that either of us knows anything really beautiful and good, I am better off than he is—for he knows nothing, and thinks that he knows; I neither know nor think that I know. In this latter particular, then, I seem to have slightly the advantage of him. Then I went to another who had still higher pretensions to wisdom, and my conclusion was exactly the same. Whereupon I made another enemy of him, and of many others besides him.

Then I went to one man after another, being not unconscious of the enmity which I provoked, and I lamented and feared this: but necessity was laid upon me—the word of God, I thought, ought to be considered first. And I said to myself, Go I must to all who appear to know, and find out the meaning of the oracle. And I swear to you, Athenians, by the dog I swear!—for I must tell you the truth—the result of my mission was just this: I found that the men most in repute were all but the most foolish; and that others less esteemed were really wiser and better. I will tell you the tale of my wanderings and of the "Herculean" labors, as I may call them, which I endured only to find at last the oracle irrefutable. After the politicians, I went to the poets; tragic, dithyrambic, and all sorts. And there, I said to myself, you will be instantly detected; now you will find out that you are more ignorant than they are. Accordingly, I took them some of the most elaborate passages in their own writings, and asked what was the meaning of them—thinking that they would teach me something. Will you believe me? I am almost ashamed to confess the truth, but I must say that there is hardly a person present who would not have talked better about their poetry than they did themselves. Then I knew that not by wisdom do poets write poetry, but by a sort of genius and inspiration; they are like diviners or soothsayers who also say many fine things, but do not understand the meaning of them. The poets appeared to me to be much in the same case; and I further observed that upon the strength of their poetry they believed themselves to be the wisest of men in other things in which they were not so wise. So I departed, conceiving myself to be superior to them for the same reason that I was superior to the politicians.

At last I went to the artisans, for I was conscious that I knew nothing at all, as I may say, and I was sure that they knew many fine things; and here I was not mistaken, for they did know many things of which I was ignorant, and in this they certainly were wiser than I was. But I observed that even the good artisans fell into the same error as the poets;— because they were good workmen they thought that they also knew all sorts of high matters, and this defect in them overshadowed their wisdom; and therefore I asked myself on behalf of the oracle, whether I would like to be as I was, neither having their knowledge nor their ignorance, or like them in both; and I made answer to myself and to the oracle that I was better off as I was.

This inquisition has led to my having many enemies of the worst and most dangerous kind, and has given occasion also to many calumnies. And I am called wise, for my hearers always imagine that I myself possess the wisdom which I find wanting in others: but the truth is, O men of Athens, that God only is wise; and by his answer he intends to show that the wisdom of men is worth little or nothing; he is not speaking of Socrates, he is only using my name by way of illustration, as if he said, He, O men, is the wisest, who, like Socrates, knows that his wisdom is in truth worth nothing. And so I go about the world, obedient to the god, and search and make inquiry into the wisdom of anyone, whether citizen or stranger, who appears to be wise; and if he is not wise, then in vindication of the oracle I show him that he is not wise; and my occu-

23

pation quite absorbs me, and I have no time to give either to any public matter of interest or to any concern of my own, but I am in utter poverty by reason of my devotion to the god.

There is another thing:—young men of the richer classes, who have not much to do, come about me of their own accord; they like to hear the pretenders examined, and they often imitate me, and proceed to examine others; there are plenty of persons, as they quickly discover, who think that they know something, but really know little or nothing; and then those who are examined by them instead of being angry with themselves are angry with me: This confounded Socrates, they say; this villainous misleader of youth!—and then if somebody asks them, Why, what evil does he practice or teach? they do not know, and cannot tell; but in order that they may not appear to be at a loss, they repeat the ready-made charges which are used against all philosophers about teaching things up in the clouds and under the earth, and having no gods, and making the worse appear the better cause; for they do not like to confess that their pretence of knowledge has been detected—which is the truth; and as they are numerous and ambitious and energetic, and are drawn up in battle array and have persuasive tongues, they have filled your ears with their loud and inveterate calumnies. And this is the reason why my three accusers, Meletus and Anytus and Lycon, have set upon me; Meletus, who has a quarrel with me on behalf of the poets; Anytus, on behalf of the craftsmen and politicians; Lycon, on behalf of the rhetoricians: and as I said at the beginning, I cannot expect to get rid of such a mass of calumny all in a moment. And this, O men of Athens, is the truth and the whole truth; I have concealed nothing, I have dissembled nothing. And yet, I know that my plainness of speech makes them hate me, and what is their hatred but a proof that I am speaking the truth?— Hence has arisen the prejudice against me; and this is the reason of it, as you will find out either in this or in any future inquiry.

I have said enough in my defense against the first class of my accusers; I turn to the second class.

24

They are headed by Meletus, that good man and true lover of his country, as he calls himself. Against these, too, I must try to make a defense:—Let their affidavit be read: it contains something of this kind: It says that Socrates is a doer of evil, who corrupts the youth; and who does not believe in the gods of the state, but has other new divinities of his own. Such is the charge; and now let us examine the particular counts. He says that I am a doer of evil, and corrupt the youth; but I say, O men of Athens, that Meletus is a doer of evil, in that he pretends to be in earnest when he is only in jest, and is so eager to bring men to trial from a pretended zeal and interest about matters in which he really never had the smallest interest. And the truth of this I will endeavor to prove to you.

Come hither, Meletus, and let me ask a question of you. You think a great deal about the improvement of youth?

Yes, I do.

Tell the judges, then, who is their improver; for you must know, as you have taken the pains to discover their corrupter; and are citing and accusing me before them. Speak, then, and tell the judges who their improver is.—Observe, Meletus, that you are silent, and have nothing to say. But is not this rather disgraceful, and a very considerable proof of what I was saying, that you have no interest in the matter? Speak up, friend, and tell us who their improver is.

The laws.

But that, my good sir, is not my meaning. I want to know who the person is, who, in the first place, knows the laws.

The judges, Socrates, who are present in court.

What, do you mean to say, Meletus, that they are able to instruct and improve youth?

Certainly they are.

What, all of them, or some only and not others?

All of them.

By the goddess Herè, that is good news! There are plenty of improvers, then. And what do you say of the audience—do they improve them?

Yes, they do.

And the senators?

Yes, the senators improve them.

But perhaps the members of the assembly corrupt them?—or do they too improve them?

They improve them.

Then every Athenian improves and elevates them; all with the exception of myself; and I alone am their corrupter? Is that what you affirm?

That is what I stoutly affirm.

I am very unfortunate if you are right. But suppose I ask you a question: How about horses? Does one man do them harm and all the world good? Is not the exact opposite the truth? One man is able to do them good, or at least not many;—the trainer of horses, that is to say, does them good, and others who have to do with them rather injure them? Is not that true, Meletus, of horses, or of any other animals? Most assuredly it is; whether you and Anytus say yes or no. Happy indeed would be the condition of youth if they had one corrupter only, and all the rest of the world were their improvers. But you, Meletus, have sufficiently shown that you never had a thought about the young: your carelessness is seen in your not caring about the very things which you bring against me.

And now, Meletus, I will ask you another question—by Zeus I will: Which is better, to live among bad citizens, or among good ones? Answer, friend, I say; the question is one which may be easily answered. Do not the good do their neighbors good, and the bad do them evil?

Certainly.

And is there anyone who would rather be injured than benefited by those who live with him? Answer, my good friend, the law requires you to answer—does anyone like to be injured?

Certainly not.

And when you accuse me of corrupting and deteriorating the youth, do you allege that I corrupt them intentionally or unintentionally?

Intentionally, I say.

But you have just admitted that the good do their neighbors good, and evil do them evil. Now, is that a truth which your superior wisdom has recog-

nized thus early in life, and am I, at my age, in such
darkness and ignorance as not to know that if a man
with whom I have to live is corrupted by me, I am
very likely to be harmed by him; and yet I corrupt him, and intentionally, too—so you say, although neither I nor any other human being is
ever likely to be convinced by you. But either I do
not corrupt them, or I corrupt them unintentionally;
and on either view of the case you lie. If my offense
is unintentional, the law has no cognizance of unintentional offenses: you ought to have taken me
privately, and warned and admonished me; for if I
had been better advised, I should have left off doing
what I only did unintentionally—no doubt I should;
but you would have nothing to say to me and
refused to teach me. And now you bring me up in
this court, which is a place not of instruction, but
of punishment.

It will be very clear to you, Athenians, as I was
saying, that Meletus has no care at all, great or
small, about the matter. But still I should like to
know, Meletus, in what I am affirmed to corrupt the
young. I suppose you mean, as I infer from your
indictment, that I teach them not to acknowledge
the gods which the state acknowledges, but some
other new divinities or spiritual agencies in their
stead. These are the lessons by which I corrupt the
youth, as you say.

Yes, that I say emphatically.

Then, by the gods, Meletus, of whom we are
speaking, tell me and the court, in somewhat plainer
terms, what you mean! for I do not as yet understand whether you affirm that I teach other men to
acknowledge some gods, and therefore that I do
believe in gods, and am not an entire atheist—this
you do not lay to my charge—but only you say that
they are not the same gods which the city recognizes
—the charge is that they are different gods. Or, do
you mean that I am an atheist simply, and a teacher
of atheism?

I mean the latter—that you are a complete atheist.

What an extraordinary statement! Why do you
think so, Meletus? Do you mean that I do not believe
in the godhead of the sun or moon, like other men?

26

I assure you, judges, that he does not: for he says that the sun is stone, and the moon earth.

Friend Meletus, you think that you are accusing Anaxagoras: and you have but a bad opinion of the judges, if you fancy them illiterate to such a degree as not to know that these doctrines are found in the books of Anaxagoras the Clazomenian, which are full of them. And so, forsooth, the youth are said to be taught them by Socrates, when there are not unfrequently exhibitions of them at the theater[3] (price of admission one drachma at the most); and they might pay their money, and laugh at Socrates if he pretends to father these extraordinary views. And so, Meletus, you really think that I do not believe in any god?

I swear by Zeus that you believe absolutely in none at all.

Nobody will believe you, Meletus, and I am pretty sure that you do not believe yourself. I cannot help thinking, men of Athens, that Meletus is reckless and impudent, and that he has written this indictment in a spirit of mere wantonness and youthful bravado. Has he not compounded a riddle, thinking to try me? He said to himself:—I shall see whether the wise Socrates will discover my facetious contradiction, or whether I shall be able to deceive him and the rest of them. For he certainly does appear to me to contradict himself in the indictment as much as if he said that Socrates is guilty of not believing in the gods, and yet of believing in them— but this is not like a person who is in earnest.

27

I should like you, O men of Athens, to join me in examining what I conceive to be his inconsistency; and do you, Meletus, answer. And I must remind the audience of my request that they would not make a disturbance if I speak in my accustomed manner:

Did ever man, Meletus, believe in the existence of human things, and not of human beings? . . . I wish, men of Athens, that he would answer, and not be

[3] Probably in allusion to Aristophanes who caricatured, and to Euripides who borrowed the notions of Anaxagoras, as well as to other dramatic poets.

always trying to get up an interruption. Did ever
any man believe in horsemanship, and not in horses?
or in flute playing, and not in flute players? No, my
friend; I will answer to you and to the court, as you
refuse to answer for yourself. There is no man who
ever did. But now please to answer the next question: Can a man believe in spiritual and divine
agencies, and not in spirits or demigods?

He cannot.

How lucky I am to have extracted that answer,
by the assistance of the court! But then you swear
in the indictment that I teach and believe in divine
or spiritual agencies (new or old, no matter for that);
at any rate, I believe in spiritual agencies—so you
say and swear in the affidavit; and yet if I believe in
divine beings, how can I help believing in spirits or
demigods;—must I not? To be sure I must; and
therefore I may assume that your silence gives consent. Now what are spirits or demigods? are they not
either gods or the sons of gods?

Certainly they are.

But this is what I call the facetious riddle invented
by you: the demigods or spirits are gods, and you
say first that I do not believe in gods, and then
again that I do believe in gods; that is, if I believe
in demigods. For if the demigods are the illegitimate
sons of gods, whether by the nymphs or by any other
mothers, of whom they are said to be the sons—
what human being will ever believe that there are no
gods if they are the sons of gods? You might as well
affirm the existence of mules, and deny that of
horses and asses. Such nonsense, Meletus, could only
have been intended by you to make trial of me. You
have put this into the indictment because you had
nothing real of which to accuse me. But no one who
has a particle of understanding will ever be convinced by you that the same men can believe in
divine and superhuman things, and yet not believe   28
that there are gods and demigods and heroes.

I have said enough in answer to the charge of
Meletus: any elaborate defense is unnecessary; but I
know only too well how many are the enmities
which I have incurred, and this is what will be my
destruction if I am destroyed;—not Meletus, nor yet

Anytus, but the envy and detraction of the world, which has been the death of many good men, and will probably be the death of many more; there is no danger of my being the last of them.

Someone will say: And are you not ashamed, Socrates, of a course of life which is likely to bring you to an untimely end? To him I may fairly answer: There you are mistaken: a man who is good for anything ought not to calculate the chance of living or dying; he ought only to consider whether in doing anything he is doing right or wrong—acting the part of a good man or of a bad. Whereas, upon your view, the heroes who fell at Troy were not good for much, and the son of Thetis above all, who altogether despised danger in comparison with disgrace; and when he was so eager to slay Hector, his goddess mother said to him, that if he avenged his companion Patroclus, and slew Hector, he would die himself—"Fate," she said, in these or the like words, "waits for you next after Hector"; he, receiving this warning, utterly despised danger and death, and instead of fearing them, feared rather to live in dishonor, and not to avenge his friend. "Let me die forthwith," he replies, "and be avenged of my enemy, rather than abide here by the beaked ships, a laughing-stock and a burden of the earth." Had Achilles any thought of death and danger? For wherever a man's place is, whether the place which he has chosen or that in which he has been placed by a commander, there he ought to remain in the hour of danger; he should not think of death or of anything but of disgrace. And this, O men of Athens, is a true saying.

Strange, indeed, would be my conduct, O men of Athens, if I who, when I was ordered by the generals whom you chose to command me at Potidaea and Amphipolis and Delium, remained where they placed me, like any other man, facing death—if now, when, as I conceive and imagine, God orders me to fulfil the philosopher's mission of searching into myself and other men, I were to desert my post through fear of death, or any other fear; that would indeed be strange, and I might justly be arraigned in court for denying the existence of the gods, if I disobeyed

29

the oracle because I was afraid of death, fancying that I was wise when I was not wise. For the fear of death is indeed the pretense of wisdom, and not real wisdom, being a pretense of knowing the unknown; and no one knows whether death, which men in their fear apprehend to be the greatest evil, may not be the greatest good. Is not this ignorance of a disgraceful sort, the ignorance which is the conceit that man knows what he does not know? And in this respect only I believe myself to differ from men in general, and may perhaps claim to be wiser than they are:—that whereas I know but little of the world below, I do not suppose that I know: but I do know that injustice and disobedience to a better, whether God or man, is evil and dishonorable, and I will never fear or avoid a possible good rather than a certain evil And therefore if you let me go now, and are not convinced by Anytus, who said that since I had been prosecuted I must be put to death (or if not that I ought never to have been prosecuted at all); and that if I escape now, your sons will all be utterly ruined by listening to my words—if you say to me, Socrates, this time we will not mind Anytus, and you shall be let off, but upon one condition, that you are not to inquire and speculate in this way any more, and that if you are caught doing so again you shall die;—if this was the condition on which you let me go, I should reply: Men of Athens, I honor and love you; but I shall obey God rather than you, and while I have life and strength I shall never cease from the practice and teaching of philosophy, exhorting anyone whom I meet and saying to him after my manner: You, my friend,—a citizen of the great and mighty and wise city of Athens,—are you not ashamed of heaping up the greatest amount of money and honor and reputation, and caring so little about wisdom and truth and the greatest improvement of the soul, which you never regard or heed at all? And if the person with whom I am arguing, says: Yes, but I do care; then I do not leave him or let him go at once; but I proceed to interrogate and examine and cross-examine him, and if I think that he has no virtue in him, but only says that he has, I reproach him

with undervaluing the greater, and overvaluing the
less. And I shall repeat the same words to everyone   30
whom I meet, young and old, citizen and alien, but
especially to the citizens, inasmuch as they are my
brethren. For know that this is the command of
God; and I believe that no greater good has ever
happened in the state than my service to the God.
For I do nothing but go about persuading you all,
old and young alike, not to take thought for your
persons or your properties, but first and chiefly to
care about the greatest improvement of the soul.
I tell you that virtue is not given by money, but
that from virtue comes money and every other good
of man, public as well as private. This is my teaching, and if this is the doctrine which corrupts the
youth, I am a mischievous person. But if anyone
says that this is not my teaching, he is speaking an
untruth. Wherefore, O men of Athens, I say to you,
do as Anytus bids or not as Anytus bids, and either
acquit me or not; but whichever you do, understand that I shall never alter my ways, not even if
I have to die many times.

Men of Athens, do not interrupt, but hear me;
there was an understanding between us that you
should hear me to the end: I have something more
to say, at which you may be inclined to cry out; but
I believe that to hear me will be good for you, and
therefore I beg that you will not cry out. I would
have you know, that if you kill such an one as I
am, you will injure yourselves more than you will
injure me. Nothing will injure me, not Meletus nor
yet Anytus—they cannot, for a bad man is not permitted to injure a better than himself. I do not deny
that Anytus may, perhaps, kill him, or drive him
into exile, or deprive him of civil rights; and he may
imagine, and others may imagine, that he is inflict-
ing a great injury upon him: but there I do not
agree. For the evil of doing as he is doing—the evil
of unjustly taking away the life of another—is
greater far.

And now, Athenians, I am not going to argue for
my own sake, as you may think, but for yours, that
you may not sin against the God by condemning me,
who am his gift to you. For if you kill me you will

not easily find a successor to me, who, if I may use such a ludicrous figure of speech, am a sort of gadfly, given to the state by God; and the state is a great and noble steed who is tardy in his motions owing to his very size, and requires to be stirred into life. I am that gadfly which God has attached to the state, and all day long and in all places am always fastening upon you, arousing and persuading and reproaching you. You will not easily find another like me, and therefore I would advise you to spare me. I dare say that you may feel out of temper (like a person who is suddenly awakened from sleep), and you think that you might easily strike me dead as Anytus advises, and then you would sleep on for the remainder of your lives, unless God in his care of you sent you another gadfly. When I say that I am given to you by God, the proof of my mission is this:—if I had been like other men, I should not have neglected all my own concerns or patiently seen the neglect of them during all these years, and have been doing yours, coming to you individually like a father or elder brother, exhorting you to regard virtue; such conduct, I say, would be unlike human nature. If I had gained anything, or if my exhortations had been paid, there would have been some sense in my doing so, but now, as you will perceive, not even the impudence of my accusers dares to say that I have ever exacted or sought pay of anyone; of that they have no witness. And I have a sufficient witness to the truth of what I say—my poverty.

Someone may wonder why I go about in private giving advice and busying myself with the concerns of others, but do not venture to come forward in public and advise the state. I will tell you why. You have heard me speak at sundry times and in divers places of an oracle or sign which comes to me, and is the divinity which Meletus ridicules in the indictment. This sign, which is a kind of voice, first began to come to me when I was a child; it always forbids but never commands me to do anything which I am going to do. This is what deters me from being a politician. And rightly, as I think. For I am certain, O men of Athens, that if I had engaged in politics, I should have perished long ago, and done no good either to you or to myself. And do not be offended at my telling you the truth: for the truth is, that no man who goes to war with you or any other multitude, honestly striving against the many lawless and unrightous deeds which are done in a state, will save his life; he who will fight for the right, if he would live even for a brief space, must have a private station and not a public one.

I can give you convincing evidence of what I say, not words only, but what you value far more— actions. Let me relate to you a passage of my own life which will prove to you that I should never have yielded to injustice from any fear of death, and that "as I should have refused to yield" I must have died at once. I will tell you a tale of the courts, not very interesting perhaps, but nevertheless true. The only office of state which I ever held, O men of Athens, was that of senator: the tribe Antiochis, which is my tribe, had the presidency at the trial of the generals who had not taken up the bodies of the slain after the battle of Arginusae; and you proposed to try them in a body, contrary to law, as you all thought afterwards; but at the time I was the only one of the Prytanes who was opposed to the illegality, and I gave my vote against you; and when the orators threatened to impeach and arrest me, and you called and shouted, I made up my mind that I would run the risk, having law and justice with me, rather than take part in your injustice because I feared imprisonment and death. This happened in the days of the democracy. But when the oligarchy of the Thirty was in power, they sent for me and four others into the rotunda, and bade us bring Leon the Salaminian from Salamis, as they wanted to put him to death. This was a specimen of the sort of commands which they were always giving with the view of implicating as many as possible in their crimes; and then I showed, not in word only but in deed, that, if I may be allowed to use such an expression, I cared not a straw for death, and that my great and only care was lest I should do an unrighteous or unholy thing. For the strong arm of that oppressive power did not frighten me into doing wrong; and when we came out of the rotunda the other four went to Salamis and fetched Leon, but I went quietly home. For which I might have lost my life, had not the power of the Thirty shortly afterwards come to an end. And many will witness to my words.

Now do you really imagine that I could have survived all these years, if I had led a public life, supposing that like a good man I had always maintained the right and had made justice, as I ought, the first thing? No indeed, men of Athens, neither I nor any other man. But I have been always the same in all my actions, public as well as private, and never have I yielded any base compliance to those who are slanderously termed my disciples, or to any other. Not that I have any regular disciples. But if anyone likes to come and hear me while I am pursuing my mission, whether he be young or old, he is not excluded. Nor do I converse only with those who pay; but anyone, whether he be rich or poor, may ask and answer me and listen to my words; and whether he turns out to be a bad man or a good one, neither result can be justly imputed to me; for I never taught or professed to teach him anything. And if anyone says that he has ever learned or heard anything from me in private which all the world has not heard, let me tell you that he is lying.

But I shall be asked, Why do people delight in continually conversing with you? I have told you already, Athenians, the whole truth about this matter: they like to hear the cross-examination of the pretenders to wisdom; there is amusement in it. Now this duty of cross-examining other men has been imposed upon me by God; and has been signified to me by oracles, visions, and in every way in which the will of divine power was ever intimated to anyone. This is true, O Athenians or, if not true, would be soon refuted. If I am or have been corrupting the youth, those of them who are now grown up and become sensible that I gave them bad advice in the days of their youth should come forward as accusers, and take their revenge; or if they do not like to come themselves, some of their relatives, fathers, brothers, or other kinsmen, should say what evil their families have suffered at my hands. Now is

33

their time. Many of them I see in the court. There
is Crito, who is of the same age and of the same
deme with myself, and there is Critobulus his son,
whom I also see. Then again there is Lysanias of
Sphettus, who is the father of Aeschines—he is
present; and also there is Antiphon of Cephisus, who
is the father of Epigenes; and there are the brothers
of several who have associated with me. There is
Nicostratus the son of Theodotides, and the brother
of Theodotus (now Theodotus himself is dead, and
therefore he, at any rate, will not seek to stop him);
and there is Paralus the son of Demodocus, who had
a brother Theages; and Adeimantus the son of Ariston, whose brother Plato is present; and Aeantod-   34
orus, who is the brother of Apollodorus, whom I
also see. I might mention a great many others, some
of whom Meletus should have produced as witnesses
in the course of his speech; and let him still produce
them, if he has forgotten—I will make way for him.
And let him say, if he has any testimony of the sort
which he can produce. Nay, Athenians, the very
opposite is the truth. For all these are ready to witness on behalf of the corrupter, of the injurer of
their kindred, as Meletus and Anytus call me; not
the corrupted youth only—there might have been a
motive for that—but their uncorrupted elder relatives. Why should they too support me with their
testimony? Why, indeed, except for the sake of truth
and justice, and because they know that I am speaking the truth, and that Meletus is a liar.

Well, Athenians, this and the like of this is all the
defense which I have to offer. Yet a word more. Perhaps there may be someone who is offended at me,
when he calls to mind how he himself on a similar,
or even a less serious occasion, prayed and entreated
the judges with many tears, and how he produced
his children in court, which was a moving spectacle,
together with a host of relations and friends; whereas I, who am probably in danger of my life, will do
none of these things. The contrast may occur to his
mind, and he may be set against me, and vote in
anger because he is displeased at me on this account. Now if there be such a person among you,
—mind, I do not say that there is,—to him I may

fairly reply: My friend, I am a man, and like other men, a creature of flesh and blood, and not "of wood or stone," as Homer says; and I have a family, yes, and sons, O Athenians, three in number, one almost a man, and two others who are still young; and yet I will not bring any of them hither in order to petition you for an acquittal. And why not? Not from any self-assertion or want of respect for you. Whether I am or am not afraid of death is another question, of which I will not now speak. But, having regard to public opinion, I feel that such conduct would be discreditable, to myself, and to you, and to the whole state. One who has reached my years, and who has a name for wisdom, ought not to demean himself. Whether this opinion of me be deserved or not, at any rate the world has decided that Socrates is in some way superior to other men. And if those among you who are said to be superior in wisdom and courage, and any other virtue, demean themselves in this way, how shameful is their conduct! I have seen men of reputation, when they have been condemned, behaving in the strangest manner: they seemed to fancy that they were going to suffer something dreadful if they died, and that they could be immortal if you only allowed them to live; and I think that such are a dishonor to the state, and that any stranger coming in would have said of them that the most eminent men of Athens, to whom the Athenians themselves give honor and command, are no better than women. And I say that these things ought not to be done by those of us who have a reputation; and if they are done, you ought not to permit them; you ought rather to show that you are far more disposed to condemn the man who gets up a doleful scene and makes the city ridiculous, than him who holds his peace.

35

But, setting aside the question of public opinion, there seems to be something wrong in asking a favor of a judge, and thus procuring an acquittal, instead of informing and convincing him. For his duty is, not to make a present of justice, but to give judgment; and he has sworn that he will judge according to the laws, and not according to his own good pleasure; and we ought not to encourage you, nor should you allow yourself to be encouraged, in this habit of perjury—there can be no piety in that. Do not then require me to do what I consider dishonorable and impious and wrong, especially now, when I am being tried for impiety on the indictment of Meletus. For if, O men of Athens, by force of persuasion and entreaty I could overpower your oaths, then I should be teaching you to believe that there are no gods, and in defending should simply convict myself of the charge of not believing in them. But that is not so—far otherwise. For I do believe that there are gods, and in a sense higher than that in which any of my accusers believe in them. And to you and to God I commit my cause, to be determined by you as is best for you and me.

There are many reasons why I am not grieved, O men of Athens, at the vote of condemnation. I expected it, and am only surprised that the votes are so nearly equal; for I had thought that the majority against me would have been far larger; but now, had thirty votes gone over to the other side, I should have been acquitted. And I may say, I think, that I have escaped Meletus. I may say more; for without the assistance of Anytus and Lycon, anyone may see that he would not have had a fifth part of the votes, as the law requires, in which case he would have incurred a fine of a thousand drachmae.

And so he proposes death as the penalty. And what shall I propose on my part, O men of Athens? Clearly that which is my due. And what is my due? What return shall be made to the man who has never had the wit to be idle during his whole life; but has been careless of what the many care for— wealth, and family interests, and military offices, and speaking in the assembly, and magistracies, and plots, and parties. Reflecting that I was really too honest a man to be a politician and live, I did not go where I could do no good to you or to myself; but where I could do the greatest good privately to every one of you, thither I went, and sought to persuade every man among you that he must look to himself, and seek virtue and wisdom before he looks to his private interests, and look to the state before he looks to the interests of the state; and that this should be the order which he observes in all his actions. What shall be done to such an one? Doubtless some good thing, O men of Athens, if he has his reward; and the good should be of a kind suitable to him. What would be a reward suitable to a poor man who is your benefactor, and who desires leisure that he may instruct you? There can be no reward so fitting as maintenance in the Prytaneum, O men of Athens, a reward which he deserves far more than the citizen who has won the prize at Olympia in the horse or chariot race, whether the chariots were drawn by two horses or by many. For I am in want, and he has enough; and he only gives you the appearance of happiness, and I give you the reality. And if I am to estimate the penalty fairly, I should say that maintenance in the Prytaneum is the just return.

37

Perhaps you think that I am braving you in what I am saying now, as in what I said before about the tears and prayers. But this is not so. I speak rather because I am convinced that I never intentionally wronged anyone, although I cannot convince you—the time has been too short; if there were a law at Athens, as there is in other cities, that a capital cause should not be decided in one day, then I believe that I should have convinced you. But I cannot in a moment refute great slanders; and, as I am convinced that I never wronged another, I will assuredly not wrong myself. I will not say of myself that I deserve any evil, or propose any penalty. Why should I? Because I am afraid of the penalty of death which Meletus proposes? When I do not know whether death is a good or an evil, why should I propose a penalty which would certainly be an evil? Shall I say imprisonment? And why should I live in prison, and be the slave of the magistrates of the year—of the Eleven? Or shall the penalty be a fine, and imprisonment until the fine is paid? There is the same objection. I should have to lie in prison, for money I have none, and cannot pay. And if I say exile (and this may possibly be the penalty which you will affix), I must indeed be blinded by the love of life, if I am so irrational as to expect that when you, who are my own citizens, cannot endure my discourses and words, and have found them so grievous and odious that you will have no more of them, others are likely to endure me. No indeed, men of Athens, that is not very likely. And what a life should I lead, at my age, wandering from city to city, ever changing my place of exile, and always being driven out! For I am quite sure that wherever I go, there, as here, the young men will flock to me; and if I drive them away, their elders will drive me out at their request; and if I let them come, their fathers and friends will drive me out for their sakes.

Someone will say: Yes, Socrates, but cannot you hold your tongue, and then you may go into a foreign city, and no one will interfere with you? Now I have great difficulty in making you understand my answer to this. For if I tell you that to do as you say would be a disobedience to the God, and therefore that I cannot hold my tongue, you will not believe that I am serious; and if I say again that daily to discourse about virtue, and of those other things about which you hear me examining myself and others, is the greatest good of man, and that the unexamined life is not worth living, you are still less likely to believe me. Yet I say what is true, although a thing of which it is hard for me to persuade you. Also, I have never been accustomed to think that I deserve to suffer any harm. Had I money I might have estimated the offense at what I was able to pay, and not have been much the worse. But I have none, and therefore I must ask you to proportion the fine to my means. Well, perhaps I could afford a mina, and therefore I propose that penalty: Plato, Crito, Critobulus, and Apollodorus, my friends here, bid me say thirty minae, and they will be the sureties. Let thirty minae be the penalty; for which sum they will be ample security to you.

———————

Not much time will be gained, O Athenians, in return for the evil name which you will get from the detractors of the city, who will say that you killed

38

Socrates, a wise man; for they will call me wise,
even although I am not wise, when they want to
reproach you. If you had waited a little while, your
desire would have been fulfilled in the course of
nature. For I am far advanced in years, as you may
perceive, and not far from death. I am speaking now
not to all of you, but only to those who have condemned me to death. And I have another thing to
say to them: You think that I was convicted because
I had no words of the sort which would have pro-
cured my acquittal I mean, if I had thought fit to
leave nothing undone or unsaid. Not so; the deficiency which led to my conviction was not of words
—certainly no. But I had not the boldness or impudence or inclination to address you as you would
have liked me to do, weeping and wailing and la-
menting, and saying and doing many things which
you have been accustomed to hear from others, and
which, as I maintain, are unworthy of me. I thought
at the time that I ought not to do anything common
or mean when in danger: nor do I now repent of the
style of my defense; I would rather die having
spoken after my manner, than speak in your manner
and live. For neither in war nor yet at law ought
I or any man to use every way of escaping death.
Often in battle there can be no doubt that if a man
will throw away his arms, and fall on his knees
before his pursuers, he may escape death; and in
other dangers there are other ways of escaping death,
if a man is willing to say and do anything. The difficulty, my friends, is not to avoid death, but to avoid
unrighteousness; for that runs faster than death. I
am old and move slowly, and the slower runner has
overtaken me, and my accusers are keen and quick,
and the faster runner, who is unrighteousness, has
overtaken them. And now I depart hence condemned
by you to suffer the penalty of death—they too go
their ways condemned by the truth to suffer the
penalty of villainy and wrong; and I must abide by
my award—let them abide by theirs. I suppose that
these things may be regarded as fated,—and I think
that they are well.

And now, O men who have condemned me, I
would fain prophesy to you; for I am about to die,

39

and in the hour of death men are gifted with prophetic power. And I prophesy to you who are my
murderers, that immediately after my departure
punishment far heavier than you have inflicted on
me will surely await you. Me you have killed because you wanted to escape the accuser, and not to
give an account of your lives. But that will not be
as you suppose: far otherwise. For I say that there
will be more accusers of you than there are now;
accusers whom hitherto I have restrained: and as
they are younger they will be more inconsiderate
with you, and you will be more offended at them. If
you think that by killing men you can prevent someone from censuring your evil lives, you are mistaken; that is not a way of escape which is either
possible or honorable; the easiest and the noblest
way is not to be disabling others, but to be improving yourselves. This is the prophecy which I utter
before my departure to the judges who have condemned me.

Friends, who would have acquitted me, I would
like also to talk with you about the thing which has
come to pass, while the magistrates are busy, and
before I go to the place at which I must die. Stay
then a little, for we may as well talk with one another
while there is time. You are my friends, and I
should like to show you the meaning of this event   40
which has happened to me. O my judges—for you I
may truly call judges—I should like to tell you of a
wonderful circumstance. Hitherto the divine faculty
of which the internal oracle is the source has constantly been in the habit of opposing me even about
trifles, if I was going to make a slip or error in any
matter; and now as you see there has come upon me
that which may be thought, and is generally believed
to be, the last and worst evil. But the oracle made
no sign of opposition, either when I was leaving my
house in the morning, or when I was on my way to
the court, or while I was speaking, at anything which
I was going to say; and yet I have often been stopped
in the middle of a speech, but now in nothing I
either said or did touching the matter in hand has
the oracle opposed me. What do I take to be the
explanation of this silence? I will tell you. It is an

intimation that what has happened to me is a good, and that those of us who think that death is an evil are in error. For the customary sign would surely have opposed me had I been going to evil and not to good.

Let us reflect in another way, and we shall see that there is great reason to hope that death is a good; for one of two things—either death is a state of nothingness and utter unconsciousness, or, as men say, there is a change and migration of the soul from this world to another. Now if you suppose that there is no consciousness, but a sleep like the sleep of him who is undisturbed even by dreams, death will be an unspeakable gain. For if a person were to select the night in which his sleep was undisturbed even by dreams, and were to compare with this the other days and nights of his life, and then were to tell us how many days and nights he had passed in the course of his life better and more pleasantly than this one, I think that any man, I will not say a private man, but even the great king will not find many such days or nights, when compared with the others. Now if death be of such a nature, I say that to die is gain; for eternity is then only a single night. But if death is the journey to another place, and there, as men say, all the dead abide, what good, O my friends and judges, can be greater than this? If indeed when the pilgrim arrives in the world below, he is delivered from the professors of justice in this world, and finds the true judges who are said to give judgment there, Minos and Rhadamanthus and Aeacus and Triptolemus, and other sons of God who were righteous in their own life, that pilgrimage will be worth making. What would not a man give if he might converse with Orpheus and Musaeus and Hesiod and Homer? Nay, if this be true, let me die again and again. I myself, too, shall have a wonderful interest in there meeting and conversing with Palamedes, and Ajax the son of Telamon, and any other ancient hero who has suffered death through an unjust judgment; and there will be no small pleasure, as I think, in comparing my own sufferings with theirs. Above all, I shall then be able to continue my search into true and false knowledge; as

41

in this world, so also in the next; and I shall find out who is wise, and who pretends to be wise, and is not. What would not a man give, O judges, to be able to examine the leader of the great Trojan expedition; or Odysseus or Sisyphus, or numberless others, men and women too! What infinite delight would there be in conversing with them and asking them questions! In another world they do not put a man to death for asking questions: assuredly not. For besides being happier than we are, they will be immortal, if what is said is true.

Wherefore, O judges, be of good cheer about death, and know of a certainty, that no evil can happen to a good man, either in life or after death. He and his are not neglected by the gods; nor has my own approaching end happened by mere chance. But I see clearly that the time had arrived when it was better for me to die and be released from trouble; wherefore the oracle gave no sign. For which reason, also, I am not angry with my condemners, or with my accusers; they have done me no harm, although they did not mean to do me any good; and for this I may gently blame them.

Still I have a favor to ask of them. When my sons are grown up, I would ask you, O my friends, to punish them; and I would have you trouble them, as I have troubled you, if they seem to care about riches, or anything, more than about virtue; or if they pretend to be something when they are really nothing—then reprove them, as I have reproved you, for not caring about that for which they ought to care, and thinking that they are something when they are really nothing. And if you do this, both I and my sons will have received justice at your hands.

The hour of departure has arrived, and we go our ways—I to die, and you to live. Which is better God only knows.

Outline of the Phaedo

I. Frame introduction: Phaedo and Echecrates (57a–59c)
  A. Echecrates has heard little (57a–58c)
    1. about the execution of Socrates, though he has heard about the trial (57a–58a)
    2. about the reason for the delay in the execution (58a–c)
  B. Echecrates wishes to know what happened, what was said and done, and who was present (58c–59c)
    1. feelings of those present (58c–59b)
    2. identity of those present (59b–c)
II. Preliminary conversations (59c–63b)
  A. Character of Socrates (59c–61c)
    1. Socrates in relation to his family (59c–60a)
    2. Socrates as suffering pain and pleasure (60b–c)
    3. Socrates as maker of poems and music (60c–61c)
  B. Why is suicide not permitted when the philosopher should follow after the dying? (61d–63b)
    1. introductory (61d–e)
    2. why is it always wrong to commit suicide. (62a–c)
    3. why should a philosopher wish to die (62c–63b)
III. Defense by Socrates (63b–70c)
  A. Provisional account (63b–d)
    1. Socrates: I expect to go among good men, though I cannot be sure, and the gods will be good masters, hence something good is in store for the dead (63b–c)
    2. Simmias: you must share your good with others (63c–d)
  B. Interior interlude: Crito says the jailer wants Socrates to talk as little as possible, to avoid becoming warm and thus requiring far more poison (63d–e)
  C. Defense proper: Socrates will explain why a philosopher is courageous when he is to die, and hopes that when dead he will attain greatest blessings in that other land (63e–69e)
    1. the philosopher and the many (64a–b)
    2. three arguments regarding death (64c–69d)
      a. how philosophers desire death (64c–67b)
      b. how philosophers deserve death (67b–e)

   c. what sort of death the philosopher suffers (67e–
      69d)
3. summary: this is my defense, which I hope will
   be more persuasive than was the defense before
   the Athenian judges (69d–e)
4. objection by Cebes: the other things seem well
   said, but about the soul there is disbelief (69e–
   70c)
   a. men fear that when soul leaves body it no longer
      exists anywhere, and when it leaves the body
      it scatters like breath or smoke (70a)
   b. if soul existed anywhere as one, there would
      be reason for hope, but we must prove that
      when a man is dead the soul exists and has
      any power and intelligence (70a–b)
   c. Socrates: we should discuss the probabilities of
      these matters, which concern me (70b–c)

IV. Provisional proofs for immortality (70c–95e)
   A. First proof: cyclic alteration (70c–72d)
      1. whether souls of dead men are in Hades or not;
         we remember an ancient tradition that they go
         there and are born from the dead (70d)
      2. two kinds of generation, forward and back (70d–
         71c)
      3. joint search for intermediate processes (71c–72a)
      4. another method to prove we were not wrong
         (72a–d)
   B. Second proof: argument from recollection (72e–
      78a)
      1. proof proper (72e–76c)
         a. Cebes: Socrates has been fond of saying that
            learning is recollection; this would be impos-
            sible if the soul did not exist somewhere be-
            fore being born a human form (72e–74a)
         b. equality itself is recollected (74a–75c)
         c. acquisition and recollection (75c–76a)
         d. knowledge at birth and knowledge before birth
            (76a–c)
      2. objections and replies (76c–78a)
         a. Simmias (76c–77a)
         b. Cebes (77a–d)
         c. resolution of childish fear (77d–78a)
   C. Third proof: argument from kinship of souls to
      forms (78b–84b)

1. proof proper: the soul is more akin to the eternal than is the body (78b–80b)
   a. program: we must ask what sort of thing fittingly suffers dispersion, and which not, and then in which class the soul belongs (78b)
   b. stages of the proof (78b–80b)
2. corollary to the proof: degrees of connection between soul and body as determining career of soul (80c–84b)
   a. when a man dies the body does not undergo dissolution at once, but slowly, especially if embalmed in Egypt (80c–d)
   b. contrasting careers of purged and unpurged souls (80d–81c)
   c. life of the unpurged soul in its return to earth (81c–82a)
   d. life of the ordinary good man and of the philosopher (82a–d)
   e. steps in rescue of soul by philosophy (82d–83e)
   f. the aim of the philosopher (83e–84b)
D. Interludes, objections (84b–91c)
   1. second interior interlude (84b–85b)
   2. objections (85b–88b)
      a. Simmias (85b–86e)
      b. Cebes (86e–88b)
   3. second frame interlude, and third interior interlude (88b–89c)
   4. prelude to resuming the argument: danger of misology, which is the worst evil (89c–91c)
      a. misanthropy (89c–90b)
      b. misology (90b–91c)
E. Replies to Simmias and Cebes (91c–95e)
   1. preliminaries to reply to Simmias (91c–92a)
   2. refutation of soul as harmony (92b–95a)
      a. harmony and soul in relation to demonstrability (92b–e)
      b. harmony and soul in relation to variation of degree (92e–93c)
      c. soul as a harmony containing a harmony (93c–94b)
      d. soul as ruler of body (94b–e)
      e. conclusion: soul is not a harmony. Harmonia, the Theban goddess, has been moderately kind to us (94e–95a)

PHAEDO

PHAEDO   SIMMIAS

SOCRATES   CEBES

ATTENDANT OF THE PRISON   CRITO

APOLLODORUS

Echecrates. WERE you yourself, Phaedo, in the prison with Socrates on the day when he drank the poison?

57

Phaedo. Yes, Echecrates, I was.

Ech. I should so like to hear about his death. What did he say in his last hours? We were informed that he died by taking poison, but no one knew anything more; for no Phliasian ever goes to Athens now, and it is a long time since any stranger from Athens has found his way hither; so that we had no clear account.

Phaed. Did you not hear of the proceedings at the trial?

58

Ech. Yes: someone told us about the trial, and we could not understand why, having been condemned, he should have been put to death, not at the time, but long afterwards. What was the reason of this?

Phaed. An accident, Echecrates: the stern of the ship which the Athenians send to Delos happened to have been crowned on the day before he was tried.

Ech. What is this ship?

Phaed. It is the ship in which, according to Athenian tradition, Theseus went to Crete when he took with him the fourteen youths, and was the savior of them and of himself. And they are said to have vowed to Apollo at the time, that if they were saved they would send a yearly mission to Delos. Now this custom still continues, and the whole period of the voyage to and from Delos, beginning when the priest of Apollo crowns the stern of the ship, is a holy season, during which the city is not allowed to be polluted by public executions; and when the vessel is detained by contrary winds, the time spent in going and returning is very considerable. As I was saying, the ship was crowned on the day before the trial, and this was the reason why Socrates lay in prison and was not put to death until long after he was condemned.

Ech. What was the manner of his death, Phaedo? What was said or done? And which of his friends were with him? Or did the authorities forbid them to be present—so that he had no friends near him when he died?

Phaed. No; there were several of them with him.

Ech. If you have nothing to do, I wish that you would tell me what passed, as exactly as you can.

Phaed. I have nothing at all to do, and will try to gratify your wish. To be reminded of Socrates is always the greatest delight to me, whether I speak myself or hear another speak of him.

Ech. You will have listeners who are of the same mind with you, and I hope that you will be as exact as you can.

Phaed. I had a singular feeling at being in his company. For I could hardly believe that I was present at the death of a friend, and therefore I did not pity him, Echecrates; he died so fearlessly, and his words and bearing were so noble and gracious, that to me he appeared blessed. I thought that in going to the other world he could not be without a divine call, and that he would be happy, if any man ever was, when he arrived there; and therefore I did not pity him as might have seemed natural at such an hour. But I had not the pleasure which I usually feel in philosophical discourse (for philosophy was the theme of which we spoke). I was pleased, but in the pleasure there was also a strange admixture of pain; for I reflected that he was soon to die, and this double feeling was shared by us all; we were laughing and weeping by turns, especially

59

the excitable Apollodorus—you know the sort of man?

Ech. Yes.

Phaed. He was quite beside himself; and I and all of us were greatly moved.

Ech. Who were present?

Phaed. Of native Athenians there were, besides Apollodorus, Critobulus and his father Crito, Hermogenes, Epigenes, Aeschines, Antisthenes; likewise Ctesippus of the deme of Paeania, Menexenus, and some others; Plato, if I am not mistaken, was ill.

Ech. Were there any strangers?

Phaed. Yes, there were; Simmias the Theban, and Cebes, and Phaedondes; Euclid and Terpsion, who came from Megara.

Ech. And was Aristippus there, and Cleombrotus?

Phaed. No, they were said to be in Aegina.

Ech. Anyone else?

Phaed. I think that these were nearly all.

Ech. Well, and what did you talk about?

Phaed. I will begin at the beginning, and endeavor to repeat the entire conversation. On the previous days we had been in the habit of assembling early in the morning at the court in which the trial took place, and which is not far from the prison. There we used to wait talking with one another until the opening of the doors (for they were not opened very early); then we went in and generally passed the day with Socrates. On the last morning we assembled sooner than usual, having heard on the day before when we quitted the prison in the evening that the sacred ship had come from Delos; and so we arranged to meet very early at the accustomed place. On our arrival the jailer who answered the door, instead of admitting us, came out and told us to stay until he called us. "For the Eleven," he said, "are now with Socrates; they are taking off his chains, and giving orders that he is to die today." He soon returned and said that we might come in. On entering we found Socrates just released from chains, and Xanthippe, whom you know, sitting by him, and holding his child in her arms. When she saw us she uttered a cry and said, as women will: "O Socrates, this is the last time that either you will

60

converse with your friends, or they with you."
Socrates turned to Crito and said: "Crito, let someone take her home." Some of Crito's people accordingly led her away, crying out and beating herself.
And when she was gone, Socrates, sitting up on the
couch, bent and rubbed his leg, saying, as he was
rubbing: How singular is the thing called pleasure,
and how curiously related to pain, which might be
thought to be the opposite of it; for they are never
present to a man at the same instant, and yet he
who pursues either is generally compelled to take the
other; their bodies are two, but they are joined by a
single head. And I cannot help thinking that if
Aesop had remembered them, he would have made
a fable about God trying to reconcile their strife,
and how, when he could not, he fastened their heads
together; and this is the reason why when one comes
the other follows: as I know by my own experience
now, when after the pain in my leg which was caused
by the chain pleasure appears to succeed.

Upon this Cebes said: I am glad, Socrates, that
you have mentioned the name of Aesop. For it reminds me of a question which has been asked by
many, and was asked of me only the day before
yesterday by Evenus the poet—he will be sure to
ask it again, and therefore if you would like me to
have an answer ready for him, you may as well tell
me what I should say to him:—he wanted to know
why you, who never before wrote a line of poetry,
now that you are in prison are turning Aesop's
fables into verse, and also composing that hymn in
honor of Apollo.

Tell him, Cebes, he replied, what is the truth—
that I had no idea of rivalling him or his poems; to
do so, as I knew, would be no easy task. But I
wanted to see whether I could purge away a scruple
which I felt about the meaning of certain dreams.
In the course of my life I have often had intimations in dreams "that I should compose music."
The same dream came to me sometimes in one form,
and sometimes in another, but always saying the
same or nearly the same words: "Cultivate and
make music," said the dream. And hitherto I had
imagined that this was only intended to exhort and

encourage me in the study of philosophy, which has been the pursuit of my life, and is the noblest and best of music. The dream was bidding me do what I was already doing, in the same way that the competitor in a race is bidden by the spectators to run when he is already running. But I was not certain of this; for the dream might have meant music in the popular sense of the word, and being under sentence of death, and the festival giving me a respite, I thought that it would be safer for me to satisfy the scruple, and, in obedience to the dream, to compose a few verses before I departed. And first I made a hymn in honor of the god of the festival, and then considering that a poet, if he is really to be a poet, should not only put together words, but should invent stories, and that I have no invention, I took some fables of Aesop, which I had ready at hand and which I knew—they were the first I came upon —and turned them into verse. Tell this to Evenus, Cebes, and bid him be of good cheer; say that I would have him come after me if he be a wise man, and not tarry; and that today I am likely to be going, for the Athenians say that I must.

Simmias said: What a message for such a man! having been a frequent companion of his I should say that, as far as I know him, he will never take your advice unless he is obliged.

Why, said Socrates—is not Evenus a philosopher?

I think that he is, said Simmias.

Then he, or any man who has the spirit of philosophy, will be willing to die; but he will not take his own life, for that is held to be unlawful.

Here he changed his position, and put his legs off the couch on to the ground, and during the rest of the conversation he remained sitting.

Why do you say, inquired Cebes, that a man ought not to take his own life, but that the philosopher will be ready to follow the dying?

Socrates replied: And have you, Cebes and Simmias, who are the disciples of Philolaus, never heard him speak of this?

Yes, but his language was obscure, Socrates.

My words, too, are only an echo; but there is no reason why I should not repeat what I have heard:

and indeed, as I am going to another place, it is very meet for me to be thinking and talking of the nature of the pilgrimage which I am about to make. What can I do better in the interval between this and the setting of the sun?

Then tell me, Socrates, why is suicide held to be unlawful? as I have certainly heard Philolaus, about whom you were just now asking, affirm when he was staying with us at Thebes; and there are others who say the same, although I have never understood what was meant by any of them.

Do not lose heart, replied Socrates, and the day 62 may come when you will understand. I suppose that you wonder why, when other things which are evil may be good at certain times and to certain persons, death is to be the only exception, and why, when a man is better dead, he is not permitted to be his own benefactor, but must wait for the hand of another.

Very true, said Cebes, laughing gently and speaking in his native Boeotian.

I admit the appearance of inconsistency in what I am saying; but there may not be any real inconsistency after all. There is a doctrine whispered in secret that man is a prisoner who has no right to open the door and run away; this is a great mystery which I do not quite understand. Yet I too believe that the gods are our guardians, and that we men are a possession of theirs. Do you not agree?

Yes, I quite agree, said Cebes.

And if one of your own possessions, an ox or an ass, for example, took the liberty of putting himself out of the way when you had given no intimation of your wish that he should die, would you not be angry with him, and would you not punish him if you could?

Certainly, replied Cebes.

Then, if we look at the matter thus, there may be reason in saying that a man should wait, and not take his own life until God summons him, as he is now summoning me.

Yes, Socrates, said Cebes, there seems to be truth in what you say. And yet how can you reconcile this seemingly true belief that God is our guardian and we his possessions, with the willingness to die which you were just now attributing to the philosopher? That the wisest of men should be willing to leave a service in which they are ruled by the gods who are the best of rulers, is not reasonable; for surely no wise man thinks that when set at liberty he can take better care of himself than the gods take of him. A fool may perhaps think so—he may argue that he had better run away from his master, not considering that his duty is to remain to the end, and not to run away from the good, and that there would be no sense in his running away. The wise man will want to be ever with him who is better than himself. Now this, Socrates, is the reverse of what was just now said; for upon this view the wise man should sorrow and the fool rejoice at passing out of life.

The earnestness of Cebes seemed to please Socrates. Here, said he, turning to us, is a man who is always inquiring, and is not so easily convinced by the first thing which he hears.

And certainly, added Simmias, the objection which he is now making does appear to me to have some force. For what can be the meaning of a truly wise man wanting to fly away and lightly leave a master who is better than himself? And I rather imagine that Cebes is referring to you; he thinks that you are too ready to leave us, and too ready to leave the gods whom you acknowledge to be our good masters.

Yes, replied Socrates; there is reason in what you say. And so you think that I ought to answer your indictment as if I were in a court?

We should like you to do so, said Simmias.

Then I must try to make a more successful defense before you than I did before the judges. For I am quite ready to admit, Simmias and Cebes, that I ought to be grieved at death, if I were not persuaded in the first place that I am going to other gods who are wise and good (of which I am as certain as I can be of any such matters), and secondly (though I am not so sure of this last) to men departed, better than those whom I leave behind; and therefore I do not grieve as I might have done, for I have good hope that there is yet something remaining for the dead, and as has been said of old, some far better thing for the good than for the evil.

But do you mean to take away your thoughts with you, Socrates? said Simmias. Will you not impart them to us?—for they are a benefit in which we too are entitled to share. Moreover, if you succeed in convincing us, that will be an answer to the charge against yourself.

I will do my best, replied Socrates. But you must first let me hear what Crito wants; he has long been wishing to say something to me.

Only this, Socrates, replied Crito:—the attendant who is to give you the poison has been telling me, and he wants me to tell you, that you are not to talk much; talking, he says, increases heat, and this is apt to interfere with the action of the poison; persons who excite themselves are sometimes obliged to take a second or even a third dose.

Then, said Socrates, let him mind his business and be prepared to give the poison twice or even thrice if necessary; that is all.

I knew quite well what you would say, replied Crito; but I was obliged to satisfy him.

Never mind him, he said.

And now, O my judges, I desire to prove to you that the real philosopher has reason to be of good cheer when he is about to die, and that after death he may hope to obtain the greatest good in the other world. And how this may be, Simmias and Cebes, I will endeavor to explain. For I deem that the true votary of philosophy is likely to be misunderstood by other men; they do not perceive that he is always pursuing death and dying; and if this be so, and he has had the desire of death all his life long, why when his time comes should he repine at that which he has been always pursuing and desiring?

Simmias said laughingly: Though not in a laughing humor, you have made me laugh, Socrates; for I cannot help thinking that the many when they hear your words will say how truly you have described philosophers, and our people at home will likewise say that the life which philosophers desire is in reality death, and that they have found them out to be deserving of the death which they desire.

64

And they are right, Simmias, in thinking so, with the exception of the words "they have found them out"; for they have not found out either what is the nature of that death which the true philosopher deserves, or how he deserves or desires death. But enough of them:—let us discuss the matter among ourselves. Do we believe that there is such a thing as death?

To be sure, replied Simmias.

It is not the separation of soul and body? And to be dead is the completion of this; when the soul exists in herself, and is released from the body and the body is released from the soul, what is this but death?

Just so, he replied.

There is another question, which will probably throw light on our present inquiry if you and I can agree about it:—Ought the philosopher to care about the pleasures—if they are to be called pleasures—of eating and drinking?

Certainly not, answered Simmias.

And what about the pleasures of love—should he care for them?

By no means.

And will he think much of the other ways of indulging the body, for example, the acquisition of costly raiment, or sandals, or other adornments of the body? Instead of caring about them, does he not rather despise anything more than nature needs? What do you say?

I should say that the true philosopher would despise them.

Would you not say that he is entirely concerned with the soul and not with the body? He would like, as far as he can, to get away from the body and to turn to the soul.

Quite true.

In matters of this sort philosophers, above all other men, may be observed in every sort of way to dissever the soul from the communion of the body.

65

Very true.

Whereas, Simmias, the rest of the world are of opinion that to him who has no sense of pleasure and no part in bodily pleasure, life is not worth having; and that he who is indifferent about them is as good as dead.

That is also true.

What again shall we say of the actual acquirement of knowledge?—is the body, if invited to share in the inquiry, a hinderer or a helper? I mean to say, have sight and hearing any truth in them? Are they not, as the poets are always telling us, inaccurate witnesses? and yet, if even they are inaccurate and indistinct, what is to be said of the other senses?—for you will allow that they are the best of them?

Certainly, he replied.

Then when does the soul attain truth?—for in attempting to consider anything in company with the body she is obviously deceived.

True.

Then must not true existence be revealed to her in thought, if at all?

Yes.

And thought is best when the mind is gathered into herself and none of these things trouble her—neither sounds nor sights nor pain nor any pleasure,—when she takes leave of the body, and has as little as possible to do with it, when she has no bodily sense or desire, but is aspiring after true being?

Certainly.

And in this the philosopher dishonors the body; his soul runs away from his body and desires to be alone and by herself?

That is true.

Well, but there is another thing, Simmias: Is there or is there not an absolute justice?

Assuredly there is.

And an absolute beauty and absolute good?

Of course.

But did you ever behold any of them with your eyes?

Certainly not.

Or did you ever reach them with any other bodily sense?—and I speak not of these alone, but of absolute greatness, and health, and strength, and of the essence or true nature of everything. Has the reality of them ever been perceived by you through the bodily organs? or rather, is not the nearest ap-

proach to the knowledge of their several natures
made by him who so orders his intellectual vision as
to have the most exact conception of the essence
of each thing which he considers?

Certainly.

And he attains to the purest knowledge of them
who goes to each with the mind alone, not introducing or intruding in the act of thought sight or any
other sense together with reason, but with the very
light of the mind in her own clearness searches into   66
the very truth of each; he who has got rid, as far as
he can, of eyes and ears and, so to speak, of the
whole body, these being in his opinion distracting
elements which when they infect the soul hinder her
from acquiring truth and knowledge—who, if not he,
is likely to attain to the knowledge of true being?

What you say has a wonderful truth in it, Socrates, replied Simmias.

And when real philosophers consider all these
things, will they not be led to make a reflection which
they will express in words something like the following? "Have we not found," they will say, "a path
of thought which seems to bring us and our argument to the conclusion, that while we are in the
body, and while the soul is infected with the evils
of the body, our desire will not be satisfied? and
our desire is of the truth. For the body is a source
of endless trouble to us by reason of the mere re-
quirement of food; and is liable also to diseases
which overtake and impede us in the search after
true being: it fills us full of loves, and lusts, and
fears, and fancies of all kinds, and endless foolery,
and in fact, as men say, takes away from us the
power of thinking at all. Whence come wars, and
fightings, and factions? whence but from the body
and the lusts of the body? Wars are occasioned by
the love of money, and money has to be acquired
for the sake and in the service of the body; and
by reason of all these impediments we have no time
to give to philosophy; and last and worst of all,
even if we are at leisure and betake ourselves to
some speculation, the body is always breaking in
upon us, causing turmoil and confusion in our in-

quiries, and so amazing us that we are prevented
from seeing the truth. It has been proved to us by
experience that if we would have pure knowledge
of anything we must be quit of the body—the soul
in herself must behold things in themselves: and
then we shall attain the wisdom which we desire,
and of which we say that we are lovers; not while
we live, but after death; for if while in company
with the body, the soul cannot have pure knowledge, one of two things follows—either knowledge is
not to be attained at all, or, if at all, after death.
For then, and not till then, the soul will be parted
from the body and exist in herself alone. In this
present life, I reckon that we make the nearest approach to knowledge when we have the least possible intercourse or communion with the body, and
are not surfeited with the bodily nature, but keep
ourselves pure until the hour when God himself
is pleased to release us. And thus having got rid of
the foolishness of the body we shall be pure and
hold converse with the pure, and know of ourselves
the clear light everywhere, which is no other than
the light of truth." For the impure are not permitted
to approach the pure. These are the sort of words,
Simmias, which the true lovers of knowledge cannot
help saying to one another, and thinking. You would
agree; would you not?

Undoubtedly, Socrates.

But, O my friend, if this be true, there is great
reason to hope that, going whither I go, when I have
come to the end of my journey, I shall attain that
which has been the pursuit of my life. And therefore
I go on my way rejoicing, and not I only, but every
other man who believes that his mind has been made
ready and that he is in a manner purified.

Certainly, replied Simmias.

And what is purification but the separation of the
soul from the body, as I was saying before; the habit
of the soul gathering and collecting herself into
herself from all sides out of the body; the dwelling
in her own place alone, as in another life, so also
in this, as far as she can;—the release of the soul
from the chains of the body?

67

Very true, he said.

And this separation and release of the soul from the body is termed death?

To be sure, he said.

And the true philosophers, and they only, are ever seeking to release the soul. Is not the separation and release of the soul from the body their especial study?

That is true.

And, as I was saying at first, there would be a ridiculous contradiction in men studying to live as nearly as they can in a state of death, and yet repining when it comes upon them.

Clearly.

And the true philosophers, Simmias, are always occupied in the practice of dying, wherefore also to them least of all men is death terrible. Look at the matter thus:—if they have been in every way the enemies of the body, and are wanting to be alone with the soul, when this desire of theirs is granted, how inconsistent would they be if they trembled and repined, instead of rejoicing at their departure to that place where, when they arrive, they hope to gain that which in life they desired—and this was wisdom—and at the same time to be rid of the company of their enemy. Many a man has been willing to go to the world below animated by the hope of seeing there an earthly love, or wife, or son, and conversing with them. And will he who is a true lover of wisdom, and is strongly persuaded in like manner that only in the world below he can worthily enjoy her, still repine at death? Will he not depart with joy? Surely he will, O friend, if he be a true philosopher. For he will have a firm conviction that there, and there only, he can find wisdom in her purity. And if this be true, he would be very absurd, as I was saying, if he were afraid of death.

He would indeed, replied Simmias.

And when you see a man who is repining at the approach of death, is not his reluctance a sufficient proof that he is not a lover of wisdom, but a lover of the body, and probably at the same time a lover of either money or power, or both?

Quite so, he replied.

68

And is not courage, Simmias, a quality which is specially characteristic of the philosopher?

Certainly.

There is temperance again, which even by the vulgar is supposed to consist in the control and regulation of the passions, and in the sense of superiority to them—is not temperance a virtue belonging to those only who despise the body, and who pass their lives in philosophy?

Most assuredly.

For the courage and temperance of other men, if you will consider them, are really a contradiction.

How so?

Well, he said, you are aware that death is regarded by men in general as a great evil.

Very true, he said.

And do not courageous men face death because they are afraid of yet greater evils?

That is quite true.

Then all but the philosophers are courageous only from fear, and because they are afraid; and yet that a man should be courageous from fear, and because he is a coward, is surely a strange thing.

Very true.

And are not the temperate exactly in the same case? They are temperate because they are intemperate—which might seem to be a contradiction, but is nevertheless the sort of thing which happens with this foolish temperance. For there are pleasures which they are afraid of losing; and in their desire to keep them, they abstain from some pleasures, because they are overcome by others; and although to be conquered by pleasure is called by men intemperance, to them the conquest of pleasure consists in being conquered by pleasure. And that is what I mean by saying that, in a sense, they are made temperate through intemperance.

Such appears to be the case.

Yet the exchange of one fear or pleasure or pain for another fear or pleasure or pain, and of the greater for the less, as if they were coins, is not the exchange of virtue. O my blessed Simmias, is there not one true coin for which all things ought to be exchanged?—and that is wisdom; and only in exchange for this, and in company with this, is anything truly bought or sold, whether courage or temperance or justice. And is not all true virtue the companion of wisdom, no matter what fears or pleasures or other similar goods or evils may or may not attend her? But the virtue which is made up of these goods, when they are severed from wisdom and exchanged with one another, is a shadow of virtue only, nor is there any freedom or health or truth in her; but in the true exchange there is a purging away of all these things, and temperance, and justice, and courage, and wisdom herself are the purgation of them. The founders of the mysteries would appear to have had a real meaning, and were not talking nonsense when they intimated in a figure long ago that he who passes unsanctified and unitiated into the world below will lie in a slough, but that he who arrives there after initiation and purification will dwell with the gods. For "many," as they say in the mysteries, "are the thyrsus-bearers, but few are the mystics,"—meaning, as I interpret the words, "the true philosophers." In the number of whom, during my whole life, I have been seeking, according to my ability, to find a place;—whether I have sought in a right way or not, and whether I have succeeded or not, I shall truly know in a little while, if God will, when I myself arrive in the other world—such is my belief. And therefore I maintain that I am right, Simmias and Cebes, in not grieving or repining at parting from you and my masters in this world, for I believe that I shall equally find good masters and friends in another world. But most men do not believe this saying; if then I succeed in convincing you by my defense better than I did the Athenian judges, it will be well.

Cebes answered: I agree, Socrates, in the greater part of what you say. But in what concerns the soul, men are apt to be incredulous; they fear that when she has left the body her place may be nowhere, and that on the very day of death she may perish and come to an end—immediately on her release from the body, issuing forth dispersed like smoke or air and in her flight vanishing away into nothingness. If she could only be collected into herself after she

70

has obtained release from the evils of which you were speaking, there would be good reason to hope, Socrates, that what you say is true. But surely it requires a great deal of argument and many proofs to show that when the man is dead his soul yet exists, and has any force or intelligence.

True, Cebes, said Socrates; and shall I suggest that we converse a little of the probabilities of these things?

I am sure, said Cebes, that I should greatly like to know your opinion about them.

I reckon, said Socrates, that no one who heard me now, not even if he were one of my old enemies, the Comic poets, could accuse me of idle talking about matters in which I have no concern: If you please, then, we will proceed with the inquiry.

Suppose we consider the question whether the souls of men after death are or are not in the world below. There comes into my mind an ancient doctrine which affirms that they go from hence into the other world, and returning hither, are born again from the dead. Now if it be true that the living come from the dead, then our souls must exist in the other world, for if not, how could they have been born again? And this would be conclusive, if there were any real evidence that the living are only born from the dead; but if this is not so, then other arguments will have to be adduced.

Very true, replied Cebes.

Then let us consider the whole question, not in relation to man only, but in relation to animals generally, and to plants, and to everything of which there is generation, and the proof will be easier. Are not all things which have opposites generated out of their opposites? I mean such things as good and evil, just and unjust—and there are innumerable other opposites which are generated out of opposites. And I want to show that in all opposites there is of necessity a similar alternation; I mean to say, for example, that anything which becomes greater must become greater after being less.

True.

And that which becomes less must have been once greater and then have become less.

71

Yes.

And the weaker is generated from the stronger, and the swifter from the slower.

Very true.

And the worse is from the better, and the more just is from the more unjust.

Of course.

And is this true of all opposites? and are we convinced that all of them are generated out of opposites?

Yes.

And in this universal opposition of all things, are there not also two intermediate processes which are ever going on, from one to the other opposite, and back again; where there is a greater and a less there is also an intermediate process of increase and diminution, and that which grows is said to wax, and that which decays to wane?

Yes, he said.

And there are many other processes, such as division and composition, cooling and heating, which equally involve a passage into and out of one another. And this necessarily holds of all opposites, even though not always expressed in words—they are really generated out of one another, and there is a passing or process from one to the other of them?

Very true, he replied.

Well, and is there not an opposite of life, as sleep is the opposite of waking?

True, he said.

And what is it?

Death, he answered.

And these, if they are opposites, are generated the one from the other, and have their two intermediate processes also?

Of course.

Now, said Socrates, I will analyze one of the two pairs of opposites which I have mentioned to you, and also its intermediate processes, and you shall analyze the other to me. One of them I term sleep, the other waking. The state of sleep is opposed to the state of waking, and out of sleeping waking is generated, and out of waking, sleeping; and the

process of generation is in the one case falling
asleep, and in the other waking up. Do you agree?

I entirely agree.

Then, suppose that you analyze life and death to
me in the same manner. Is not death opposed to life?

Yes.

And they are generated one from the other?

Yes.

What is generated from the living?

The dead.

And what from the dead?

I can only say in answer—the living.

Then the living, whether things or persons, Cebes,
are generated from the dead?

This is clear, he replied.

Then the inference is that our souls exist in the
world below?

That is true.

And one of the two processes or generations is
visible—for surely the act of dying is visible?

Surely, he said.

What then is to be the result? Shall we exclude the
opposite process? and shall we suppose nature to
walk on one leg only? Must we not rather assign
to death some corresponding process of generation?

Certainly, he replied.

And what is that process?

Return to life.

And return to life, if there be such a thing, is the
birth of the dead into the world of the living?   72

Quite true.

Then here is a new way by which we arrive at the
conclusion that the living come from the dead, just
as the dead come from the living; and this, if true,
affords a most certain proof that the souls of the
dead exist in some place out of which they come
again.

Yes, Socrates, he said; the conclusion seems to
flow necessarily out of our previous admissions.

And that these admissions were not unfair, Cebes,
he said, may be shown, I think, as follows: If generation were in a straight line only, and there were
no compensation or circle in nature, no turn or
return of elements into their opposites, then you

know that all things would at last have the same form and pass into the same state, and there would be no more generation of them.

What do you mean? he said.

A simple thing enough, which I will illustrate by the case of sleep, he replied. You know that if there were no alternation of sleeping and waking, the tale of the sleeping Endymion would in the end have no meaning, because all other things would be asleep too, and he would not be distinguishable from the rest. Or if there were composition only, and no division of substances, then the chaos of Anaxagoras would come again. And in like manner, my dear Cebes, if all things which partook of life were to die, and after they were dead remained in the form of death, and did not come to life again, all would at last die, and nothing would be alive—what other result could there be? For if the living spring from any other things, and they too die, must not all things at last be swallowed up in death?[1]

There is no escape, Socrates, said Cebes; and to me your argument seems to be absolutely true.

Yes, he said, Cebes, it is and must be so, in my opinion; and we have not been deluded in making these admissions; but I am confident that there truly is such a thing as living again, and that the living spring from the dead, and that the souls of the dead are in existence, and that the good souls have a better portion than the evil.

Cebes added: Your favorite doctrine, Socrates, that knowledge is simply recollection, if true, also necessarily implies a previous time in which we have learned that which we now recollect. But this would be impossible unless our soul had been in some place before existing in the form of man; here then is another proof of the soul's immortality.

73

But tell me, Cebes, said Simmias, interposing, what arguments are urged in favor of this doctrine of recollection. I am not very sure at the moment that I remember them.

One excellent proof, said Cebes, is afforded by

[1] But cp. Rep. x. 611 A.

questions. If you put a question to a person in a right way, he will give a true answer of himself, but how could he do this unless there were knowledge and right reason already in him? And this is most clearly shown when he is taken to a diagram or to anything of that sort.[2]

But if, said Socrates, you are still incredulous, Simmias, I would ask you whether you may not agree with me when you look at the matter in another way;—I mean, if you are still incredulous as to whether knowledge is recollection?

Incredulous I am not, said Simmias; but I want to have this doctrine of recollection brought to my own recollection, and, from what Cebes has said, I am beginning to recollect and be convinced: but I should still like to hear what you were going to say.

This is what I would say, he replied:—We should agree, if I am not mistaken, that what a man recollects he must have known at some previous time.

Very true.

And what is the nature of this knowledge or recollection? I mean to ask, Whether a person who, having seen or heard or in any way perceived anything, knows not only that, but has a conception of something else which it the subject, not of the same but of some other kind of knowledge, may not be fairly said to recollect that of which he has the conception?

What do you mean?

I mean what I may illustrate by the following instance:—The knowledge of a lyre is not the same as the knowledge of a man?

True.

And yet what is the feeling of lovers when they recognize a lyre, or a garment, or anything else which the beloved has been in the habit of using? Do not they, from knowing the lyre, form in the mind's eye an image of the youth to whom the lyre belongs? And this is recollection. In like manner anyone who sees Simmias may remember Cebes; and there are endless examples of the same thing.

Endless, indeed, replied Simmias.

[2] Cp. Meno 83 ff.

And recollection is most commonly a process of recovering that which has been already forgotten through time and inattention.

Very true, he said.

Well; and may you not also from seeing the picture of a house or a lyre remember a man? and from the picture of Simmias, you may be led to remember Cebes?

True.

Or you may also be led to the recollection of Simmias himself?

Quite so.

And in all these cases, the recollection may be derived from things either like or unlike?

74

It may be.

And when the recollection is derived from like things, then another consideration is sure to arise, which is—whether the likeness in any degree falls short or not of that which is recollected?

Very true, he said.

And shall we proceed a step further, and affirm that there is such a thing as equality, not of one piece of wood or stone with another, but that, over and above this, there is absolute equality? Shall we say so?

Say so, yes, replied Simmias, and swear to it, with all the confidence in life.

And do we know the nature of this absolute essence?

To be sure, he said.

And whence did we obtain our knowledge? Did we not see equalities of material things, such as pieces of wood and stones, and gather from them the idea of an equality which is different from them? For you will acknowledge that there is a difference. Or look at the matter in another way:—Do not the same pieces of wood or stone appear at one time equal, and at another time unequal?

That is certain.

But are real equals ever equal? or is the idea of equality the same as of inequality?

Impossible, Socrates.

Then these (so-called) equals are not the same with the idea of equality?

I should say, clearly not, Socrates.

And yet from these equals, although differing from the idea of equality, you conceived and attained that idea?

Very true, he said.

Which might be like, or might be unlike them?

Yes.

But that makes no difference: whenever from seeing one thing you conceived another, whether alike or unlike, there must surely have been an act of recollection?

Very true.

But what would you say of equal portions of wood and stone, or other material equals? and what is the impression produced by them? Are they equals in the same sense in which absolute equality is equal? or do they fall short of this perfect equality in a measure?

Yes, he said, in a very great measure too.

And must we not allow, that when I or anyone, looking at any object, observes that the thing which he sees aims at being some other thing, but falls short of, and cannot be, that other thing, but is inferior, he who makes this observation must have had a previous knowledge of that to which the other, although similar, was inferior.

Certainly.

And has not this been our own case in the matter of equals and of absolute equality?

Precisely.

Then we must have known equality previously to the time when we first saw the material equals, and reflected that all these apparent equals strive to attain absolute equality, but fall short of it?

Very true.

And we recognize also that this absolute equality has only been known, and can only be known, through the medium of sight or touch, or of some other of the senses, which are all alike in this respect?

Yes, Socrates, as far as the argument is concerned, one of them is the same as the other.

From the senses then is derived the knowledge

that all sensible things aim at an absolute equality of which they fall short?

Yes.

Then before we began to see or hear or perceive in any way, we must have had a knowledge of absolute equality, or we could not have referred to that standard the equals which are derived from the senses?—for to that they all aspire, and of that they fall short.

No other inference can be drawn from the previous statements.

And did we not see and hear and have the use of our other senses as soon as we were born?

Certainly.

Then we must have acquired the knowledge of equality at some previous time?

Yes.

That is to say, before we were born, I suppose?

True.

And if we acquired this knowledge before we were born, and were born having the use of it, then we also knew before we were born and at the instant of birth not only the equal or the greater or the less, but all other ideas; for we are not speaking only of equality, but of beauty, goodness, justice, holiness, and of all which we stamp with the name of essence in the dialectical process, both when we ask and when we answer questions. Of all this we may certainly affirm that we acquired the knowledge before birth?

We may.

But if, after having acquired, we have not forgotten what in each case we acquired, then we must always have come into life having knowledge, and shall always continue to know as long as life lasts— for knowing is the acquiring and retaining knowledge and not forgetting. Is not forgetting, Simmias, just the losing of knowledge?

Quite true, Socrates.

But if the knowledge which we acquired before birth was lost by us at birth, and if afterwards by the use of the senses we recovered what we previously knew, will not the process which we call learning be a recovering of the knowledge which is natural to us, and may not this be rightly termed recollection?

Very true.

So much is clear—that when we perceive some- 76
thing, either by the help of sight, or hearing, or some other sense, from that perception we are able to obtain a notion of some other thing like or unlike which is associated with it but has been forgotten. Whence, as I was saying, one of two alternatives follows:—either we had this knowledge at birth, and continued to know through life; or, after birth, those who are said to learn only remember, and learning is simply recollection.

Yes, that is quite true, Socrates.

And which alternative, Simmias, do you prefer? Had we the knowledge at our birth, or did we recollect the things which we knew previously to our birth?

I cannot decide at the moment.

At any rate you can decide whether he who has knowledge will or will not be able to render an account of his knowledge? What do you say?

Certainly, he will.

But do you think that every man is able to give an account of these very matters about which we are speaking?

Would that they could, Socrates, but I rather fear that tomorrow, at this time, there will no longer be anyone alive who is able to give an account of them such as ought to be given.

Then you are not of opinion, Simmias, that all men know these things?

Certainly not.

They are in process of recollecting that which they learned before?

Certainly.

But when did our souls acquire this knowledge?—not since we were born as men?

Certainly not.

And therefore, previously?

Yes.

Then, Simmias, our souls must have existed without bodies before they were in the form of man, and must have had intelligence.

Unless indeed you suppose, Socrates, that these notions are given us at the very moment of birth; for this is the only time which remains.

Yes, my friend, but if so, when do we lose them? for they are not in us when we are born—what is admitted. Do we lose them at the moment of receiving them, or if not at what other time?

No, Socrates, I perceive that I was unconsciously talking nonsense.

Then may we not say, Simmias, that if, as we are always repeating, there is an absolute beauty, and goodness, and an absolute essence of all things; and if to this, which is now discovered to have existed in our former state, we refer all our sensations, and with this compare them, finding these ideas to be pre-existent and our inborn possession—then our souls must have had a prior existence, but if not, there would be no force in the argument? There is the same proof that these ideas must have existed before we were born, as that our souls existed before we were born; and if not the ideas, then not the souls.

Yes, Socrates; I am convinced that there is precisely the same necessity for the one as for the other; and the argument retreats successfully to the position that the existence of the soul before birth cannot be separated from the existence of the essence of which you speak. For there is nothing which to my mind is so patent as that beauty, goodness, and the other notions of which you were just now speaking, have a most real and absolute existence; and I am satisfied with the proof.

Well, but is Cebes equally satisfied? for I must convince him too.

I think, said Simmias, that Cebes is satisfied: although he is the most incredulous of mortals, yet I believe that he is sufficiently convinced of the existence of the soul before birth. But that after death the soul will continue to exist is not yet proven even to my own satisfaction. I cannot get rid of the feeling of the many to which Cebes was referring—the feeling that when the man dies the soul will be dispersed, and that this may be the extinction of her. For admitting that she may have been born elsewhere, and framed out of other elements, and was in existence before entering the human body, why after having entered in and gone out again may she not herself be destroyed and come to an end?

Very true, Simmias, said Cebes; about half of what was required has been proven; to wit, that our souls existed before we were born:—that the soul will exist after death as well as before birth is the other half of which the proof is still wanting, and has to be supplied; when that is given the demonstration will be complete.

But that proof, Simmias and Cebes, has been already given, said Socrates, if you put the two arguments together—I mean this and the former one, in which we admitted that everything living is born of the dead. For if the soul exists before birth, and in coming to life and being born can be born only from death and dying, must she not after death continue to exist, since she has to be born again?—Surely the proof which you desire has been already furnished. Still I suspect that you and Simmias would be glad to probe the argument further. Like children, you are haunted with a fear that when the soul leaves the body, the wind may really blow her away and scatter her; especially if a man should happen to die in a great storm and not when the sky is calm.

Cebes answered with a smile: Then, Socrates, you must argue us out of our fears—and yet, strictly speaking, they are not our fears, but there is a child within us to whom death is a sort of hobgoblin: him too we must persuade not to be afraid when he is alone in the dark.

Socrates said: Let the voice of the charmer be applied daily until you have charmed away the fear.

And where shall we find a good charmer of our fears, Socrates, when you are gone?

Hellas, he replied, is a large place, Cebes, and has many good men, and there are barbarous races not a few: seek for him among them all, far and wide, sparing neither pains nor money; for there is no better way of spending your money. And you must seek among yourselves too; for you will not find others better able to make the search.

The search, replied Cebes, shall certainly be made. And now, if you please, let us return to the point of the argument at which we digressed.

By all means, replied Socrates; what else should I please?

Very good.

Must we not, said Socrates, ask ourselves what that is which, as we imagine, is liable to be scattered, and about which we fear? and what again is that about which we have no fear? And then we may proceed further to inquire whether that which suffers dispersion is or is not of the nature of soul—our hopes and fears as to our own souls will turn upon the answers to these questions.

Very true, he said.

Now the compound or composite may be supposed to be naturally capable, as of being compounded, so also of being dissolved; but that which is uncompounded, and that only, must be, if anything is, indissoluble.

Yes; I should imagine so, said Cebes.

And the uncompounded may be assumed to be the same and unchanging, whereas the compound is always changing and never the same.

I agree, he said.

Then now let us return to the previous discussion. Is that idea or essence, which in the dialectical process we define as essence or true existence—whether essence of equality, beauty, or anything else—are these essences, I say, liable at times to some degree of change? or are they each of them always what they are, having the same simple self-existent and unchanging forms, not admitting of variation at all, or in any way, or at any time?

They must be always the same, Socrates, replied Cebes.

And what would you say of the many beautiful—whether men or horses or garments or any other things which are named by the same names and may be called equal or beautiful—are they all unchanging and the same always, or quite the reverse? May they not rather be described as almost always changing and hardly ever the same, either with themselves or with one another?

The latter, replied Cebes; they are always in a state of change.

And these you can touch and see and perceive with the senses, but the unchanging things you can only perceive with the mind—they are invisible and are not seen?

That is very true, he said.

Well then, added Socrates, let us suppose that there are two sorts of existences—one seen, the other unseen.

Let us suppose them.

The seen is the changing, and the unseen is the unchanging?

That may be also supposed.

And, further, is not one part of us body, another part soul?

To be sure.

And to which class is the body more alike and akin?

Clearly to the seen—no one can doubt that.

And is the soul seen or not seen?

Not by man, Socrates.

And what we mean by "seen" and "not seen" is that which is or is not visible to the eye of man?

Yes, to the eye of man.

And is the soul seen or not seen?

Not seen.

Unseen then?

Yes.

Then the soul is more like to the unseen, and the body to the seen?

That follows necessarily, Socrates.

And were we not saying long ago that the soul when using the body as an instrument of perception, that is to say, when using the sense of sight or hearing or some other sense (for the meaning of perceiving through the body is perceiving through the senses)— were we not saying that the soul too is then dragged by the body into the region of the changeable, and wanders and is confused; the world spins round her, and she is like a drunkard, when she touches change?

Very true.

But when returning into herself she reflects, then she passes into the other world, the region of purity,

and eternity, and immortality, and unchangeables,
which are her kindred, and with them she ever lives,
when she is by herself and is not let or hindered;
then she ceases from her erring ways, and being in
communion with the unchanging is unchanging.
And this state of the soul is called wisdom?

That is well and truly said, Socrates, he replied.

And to which class is the soul more nearly alike
and akin, as far as may be inferred from this argument, as well as from the preceding one?

I think, Socrates, that, in the opinion of everyone
who follows the argument, the soul will be infinitely
more like the unchangeable—even the most stupid
person will not deny that.

And the body is more like the changing?

Yes.

Yet once more consider the matter in another
light: When the soul and the body are united, then
nature orders the soul to rule and govern, and the
body to obey and serve. Now which of these two
functions is akin to the divine? and which to the
mortal? Does not the divine appear to you to be
that which naturally orders and rules, and the mortal
to be that which is subject and servant?

True.

And which does the soul resemble?

The soul resembles the divine, and the body the
mortal—there can be no doubt of that, Socrates.

Then reflect, Cebes: of all which has been said is
not this the conclusion?—that the soul is in the very
likeness of the divine, and immortal, and intellectual,
and uniform, and indissoluble, and unchangeable;
and that the body is in the very likeness of the human,
and mortal, and unintellectual, and multiform, and
dissoluble, and changeable. Can this, my dear Cebes,
be denied?

It cannot.

But if it be true, then is not the body liable to
speedy dissolution? and is not the soul almost or altogether indissoluble?

Certainly.

And do you further observe, that after a man is
dead, the body, or visible part of him, which is lying
in the visible world, and is called a corpse, and would

80

naturally be dissolved and decomposed and dissipated, is not dissolved or decomposed at once, but may remain for some time, nay even for a long time, if the constitution be sound at the time of death, and the season of the year favorable? For the body when shrunk and embalmed, as the manner is in Egypt, may remain almost entire through infinite ages; and even in decay, there are still some portions, such as the bones and ligaments, which are practically indestructible:—Do you agree?

Yes.

And is it likely that the soul, which is invisible, in passing to the place of the true Hades, which like her is invisible, and pure, and noble, and on her way to the good and wise God, whither, if God will, my soul is also soon to go—that the soul, I repeat, if this be her nature and origin, will be blown away and destroyed immediately on quitting the body, as the many say? That can never be, my dear Simmias and Cebes. The truth rather is, that the soul which is pure at departing and draws after her no bodily taint, having never voluntarily during life had connection with the body, which she is ever avoiding, herself gathered into herself;—and making such abstraction her perpetual study—which means that she has been a true disciple of philosophy; and therefore has in fact been always engaged in the practice of dying? For is not philosophy the study of death?—

Certainly—

That soul, I say, herself invisible, departs to the invisible world—to the divine and immortal and rational; thither arriving, she is secure of bliss and is released from the error and folly of men, their fears and wild passions and all other human ills, and for ever dwells, as they say of the initiated, in company with the gods.[3] Is not this true, Cebes?

Yes, said Cebes, beyond a doubt.

But the soul which has been polluted, and is impure at the time of her departure, and is the companion and servant of the body always, and is in love with and fascinated by the body and by the desires and pleasures of the body, until she is led to believe

81

[3] Cp. Apol. 40 E.

that the truth only exists in a bodily form, which a
man may touch and see and taste, and use for the
purposes of his lusts—the soul, I mean, accustomed
to hate and fear and avoid the intellectual principle,
which to the bodily eye is dark and invisible, and can
be attained only by philosophy;—do you suppose that
such a soul will depart pure and unalloyed?

Impossible, he replied.

She is held fast by the corporeal, which the continual association and constant care of the body have
wrought into her nature.

Very true.

And this corporeal element, my friend, is heavy and
weighty and earthy, and is that element of sight by
which a soul is depressed and dragged down again
into the visible world, because she is afraid of the
invisible and of the world below—prowling about
tombs and sepulchers, near which, as they tell us, are
seen certain ghostly apparitions of souls which have
not departed pure, but are cloyed with sight and
therefore visible.[4]

That is very likely, Socrates.

Yes, that is very likely, Cebes; and these must be
the souls, not of the good, but of the evil, which are
compelled to wander about such places in payment of
the penalty of their former evil way of life; and
they continue to wander until through the craving
after the corporeal which never leaves them, they are
imprisoned finally in another body. And they may be
supposed to find their prisons in the same natures
which they have had in their former lives.

[4] Compare Milton, Comus, 463 foll.:—

> But when lust,
> By unchaste looks, loose gestures, and foul talk,
> But most by lewd and lavish act of sin,
> Lets in defilement to the inward parts,
> The soul grows clotted by contagion,
> Imbodies, and imbrutes, till she quite lose,
> The divine property of her first being.
> Such are those thick and gloomy shadows damp
> Oft seen in charnel vaults and sepulchres.
> Lingering, and sitting by a new made grave,
> As loath to leave the body that it lov'd,
> And linked itself by carnal sensuality
> To a degenerate and degraded state.

What natures do you mean, Socrates?

What I mean is that men who have followed after gluttony, and wantonness, and drunkenness, and have had no thought of avoiding them, would pass into asses and animals of that sort. What do you think?

82

I think such an opinion to be exceedingly probable.

And those who have chosen the portion of injustice, and tyranny, and violence, will pass into wolves, or into hawks and kites;—whither else can we suppose them to go?

Yes, said Cebes; with such natures, beyond question.

And there is no difficulty, he said, in assigning to all of them places answering to their several natures and propensities?

There is not, he said.

Some are happier than others; and the happiest both in themselves and in the place to which they go are those who have practiced the civil and social virtues which are called temperance and justice, and are acquired by habit and attention without philosophy and mind.[5]

Why are they the happiest?

Because they may be expected to pass into some gentle and social kind which is like their own, such as bees or wasps or ants, or back again into the form of man, and just and moderate men may be supposed to spring from them.

Very likely.

No one who has not studied philosophy and who is not entirely pure at the time of his departure is allowed to enter the company of the gods, but the lover of knowledge only. And this is the reason, Simmias and Cebes, why the true votaries of philosophy abstain from all fleshly lusts, and hold out against them and refuse to give themselves up to them— not because they fear poverty or the ruin of their families, like the lovers of money, and the world in general; nor like the lover of power and honor, because they dread the dishonor or disgrace of evil deeds.

[5] Cp. Rep. x. 619 C.

No, Socrates, that would not become them, said
Cebes.

No indeed, he replied; and therefore they who
have any care of their own souls, and do not merely
live molding and fashioning the body, say farewell
to all this; they will not walk in the ways of the
blind: and when philosophy offers them purification
and release from evil, they feel that they ought not
to resist her influence, and whither she leads they
turn and follow.

What do you mean, Socrates?

I will tell you, he said. The lovers of knowledge are
conscious that the soul was simply fastened and glued
to the body—until philosophy received her, she could
only view real existence through the bars of a prison,
not in and through herself; she was wallowing in the
mire of every sort of ignorance, and by reason of lust
had become the principal accomplice in her own
capitivity. This was her original state; and then, as
I was saying, and as the lovers of knowledge are well
aware, philosophy, seeing how terrible was her con-
finement, of which she was to herself the cause, received and gently comforted her and sought to release
her, pointing out that the eye and the ear and the
other senses are full of deception, and persuading
her to retire from them, and abstain from all but the
necessary use of them, and be gathered up and collected into herself, bidding her trust in herself and
her own pure apprehension of pure existence, and to
mistrust whatever comes to her through other channels and is subject to variation; for such things are
visible and tangible, but what she sees in her own
nature is intelligible and invisible. And the soul of
the true philosopher thinks that she ought not to resist this deliverance, and therefore abstains from
pleasures and desires and pains and fears, as far as
she is able; reflecting that when a man has great joys
or sorrows or fears or desires, he suffers from them,
not merely the sort of evil which might be anticipated
—as for example, the loss of his health or property
which he has sacrificed to his lusts—but an evil
greater far, which is the greatest and worst of all
evils, and one of which he never thinks.

What is it, Socrates? said Cebes.

83

The evil is that when the feeling of pleasure or pain is most intense, every soul of man imagines the objects of this intense feeling to be then plainest and truest: but this is not so, they are really the things of sight.

Very true.

And is not this the state in which the soul is most enthralled by the body?

How so?

Why, because each pleasure and pain is a sort of nail which nails and rivets the soul to the body, until she becomes like the body, and believes that to be true which the body affirms to be true; and from agreeing with the body and having the same delights she is obliged to have the same habits and haunts, and is not likely ever to be pure at her departure to the world below, but is always infected by the body; and so she sinks into another body and there germinates and grows, and has therefore no part in the communion of the divine and pure and simple.

Most true, Socrates, answered Cebes.

And this, Cebes, is the reason why the true lovers of knowledge are temperate and brave; and not for the reason which the world gives.

Certainly not.

Certainly not! The soul of a philosopher will reason in quite another way; she will not ask philosophy to release her in order that when released she may deliver herself up again to the thraldom of pleasures and pains, doing a work only to be undone again, weaving instead of unweaving her Penelope's web. But she will calm passion, and follow reason, and dwell in the contemplation of her, beholding the true and divine (which is not matter of opinion), and thence deriving nourishment. Thus she seeks to live while she lives, and after death she hopes to go to her own kindered and to that which is like her, and to be freed from human ills. Never fear, Simmias and Cebes, that a soul which has been thus nurtured and has had these pursuits, will at her departure from the body be scattered and blown away by the winds and be nowhere and nothing.

When Socrates had done speaking, for a considerable time there was silence; he himself appeared to

84

be meditating, as most of us were, on what had been
said; only Cebes and Simmias spoke a few words to
one another. And Socrates observing them asked
what they thought of the argument, and whether there
was anything wanting? For, said he, there are many
points still open to suspicion and attack, if anyone
were disposed to sift the matter thoroughly. Should
you be considering some other matter I say no more,
but if you are still in doubt do not hesitate to say
exactly what you think, and let us have anything
better which you can suggest; and if you think that
I can be of any use, allow me to help you.

Simmias said: I must confess, Socrates, that doubts
did arise in our minds, and each of us was urging
and inciting the other to put the question which we
wanted to have answered but which neither of us
liked to ask, fearing that our importunity might be
troublesome at such a time.

Socrates replied with a smile: O Simmias, what are
you saying? I am not very likely to persuade other
men that I do not regard my present situation as a
misfortune, if I cannot even persuade you that I am
no worse off now than at any other time in my life.
Will you not allow that I have as much of the spirit
of prophecy in me as the swans? For they, when
they perceive that they must die, having sung all their
life long, do then sing more lustily than ever, rejoicing in the thought that they are about to go   85
away to the god whose ministers they are. But men,
because they are themselves afraid of death, slanderously affirm of the swans that they sing a lament at
the last, not considering that no bird sings when
cold, or hungry, or in pain, not even the nightingale,
nor the swallow, nor yet the hoopoe; which are
said indeed to tune a lay of sorrow, although I do not
believe this to be true of them any more than of
the swans. But because they are sacred to Apollo, they
have the gift of prophecy, and anticipate the good
things of another world; wherefore they sing and
rejoice in that day more than ever they did before.
And I too, believing myself to be the consecrated
servant of the same God, and the fellow-servant of
the swans, and thinking that I have received from
my master gifts of prophecy which are not inferior

to theirs, would not go out of life less merrily than
the swans. Never mind then, if this be your only
objection, but speak and ask anything which you like,
while the eleven magistrates of Athens allow.

Very good, Socrates, said Simmias; then I will
tell you my difficulty, and Cebes will tell you his. I
feel myself (and I dare say that you have the same
feeling), how hard or rather impossible is the attainment of any certainty about questions such as
these in the present life. And yet I should deem him
a coward who did not prove what is said about them
to the uttermost, or whose heart failed him before
he had examined them on every side. For he should
persevere until he has achieved one of two things:
either he should discover, or be taught the truth
about them; or, if this be impossible, I would have
him take the best and most irrefragable of human
theories, and let this be the raft upon which he sails
through life—not without risk, as I admit, if he cannot find some word of God which will more surely
and safely carry him. And now, as you bid me, I
will venture to question you, and then I shall not
have to reproach myself hereafter with not having
said at the time what I think. For when I consider the
matter, either alone or with Cebes, the argument does
certainly appear to me, Socrates, to be not sufficient.

Socrates answered: I dare say, my friend, that you
may be right, but I should like to know in what
respect the argument is insufficient.

In this respect, replied Simmias:—Suppose a person to use the same argument about harmony and
the lyre—might he not say that harmony is a thing
invisible, incorporeal, perfect, divine, existing in the   86
lyre which is harmonized, but that the lyre and the
strings are matter and material, composite, earthy,
and akin to mortality? And when someone breaks
the lyre, or cuts and rends the strings, then he who
takes this view would argue as you do, and on the
same analogy, that the harmony survives and has
not perished—you cannot imagine, he would say,
that the lyre without the strings, and the broken
strings themselves which are mortal remain, and yet
that the harmony, which is of heavenly and immortal nature and kindred, has perished—perished

before the mortal. The harmony must still be somewhere, and the wood and strings will decay before
anything can happen to that. The thought, Socrates,
must have occurred to your own mind that such is
our conception of the soul; and that when the body
is in a manner strung and held together by the elements of hot and cold, wet and dry, then the soul
is the harmony or due proportionate admixture of
them. But if so, whenever the strings of the body
are unduly loosened or overstrained through disease or other injury, then the soul, though most
divine, like other harmonies of music or of works of
art, of course perishes at once; although the material remains of the body may last for a considerable time, until they are either decayed or burnt.
And if anyone maintains that the soul, being the
harmony of the elements of the body, is first to perish in that which is called death, how shall we answer him?

Socrates looked fixedly at us as his manner was,
and said with a smile: Simmias has reason on his
side; and why does not some one of you who is
better able than myself answer him? for there is
force in his attack upon me. But perhaps, before we
answer him, we had better also hear what Cebes has
to say that we may gain time for reflection, and
when they have both spoken, we may either assent
to them, if there is truth in what they say, or if not,
we will maintain our position. Please to tell me then,
Cebes, he said, what was the difficulty which
troubled you?

Cebes said: I will tell you. My feeling is that the
argument is where it was, and open to the same objections which were urged before; for I am ready to
admit that the existence of the soul before entering   87
into the bodily form has been very ingeniously, and,
if I may say so, quite sufficiently proven; but the
existence of the soul after death is still, in my judgment, unproven. Now my objection is not the same as
that of Simmias; for I am not disposed to deny that
the soul is stronger and more lasting than the body,
being of opinion that in all such respects the soul very
far excels the body. Well then, says the argument
to me, why do you remain unconvinced?—When you

see that the weaker continues in existence after the man is dead, will you not admit that the more lasting must also survive during the same period of time? Now I will ask you to consider whether the objection, which, like Simmias, I will express in a figure, is of any weight. The analogy which I will adduce is that of an old weaver, who dies, and after his death somebody says:—He is not dead, he must be alive;—see, there is the coat which he himself wove and wore, and which remains whole and undecayed. And then he proceeds to ask of someone who is incredulous, whether a man lasts longer, or the coat which is in use and wear; and when he is answered that a man lasts far longer, thinks that he has thus certainly demonstrated the survival of the man, who is the more lasting, because the less lasting remains. But that, Simmias, as I would beg you to remark, is a mistake; anyone can see that he who talks thus is talking nonsense. For the truth is, that the weaver aforesaid, having woven and worn many such coats, outlived several of them; and was outlived by the last; but a man is not therefore proved to be slighter and weaker than a coat. Now the relation of the body to the soul may be expressed in a similar figure; and anyone may very fairly say in like manner that the soul is lasting, and the body weak and shortlived in comparison. He may argue in like manner that every soul wears out many bodies, especially if a man live many years. While he is alive the body deliquesces and decays, and the soul always weaves another garment and repairs the waste. But of course, whenever the soul perishes, she must have on her last garment, and this will survive her; and then at length, when the soul is dead, the body will show its native weakness, and quickly decompose and pass away. I would therefore rather not rely on the argument from superior strength to prove the continued existence of the soul after death. For granting even more than you affirm to be possible, and acknowledging not only that the soul existed before birth, but also that the souls of some exist, and will continue to exist after death, and will be born and die again, and that there is a natural strength in the soul which will hold out and be born many times—

88

nevertheless, we may be still inclined to think that she
will weary in the labors of successive births, and may
at last succumb in one of her deaths and utterly
perish; and this death and dissolution of the body
which brings destruction to the soul may be unknown to any of us, for no one of us can have had
any experience of it: and if so, then I maintain that
he who is confident about death has but a foolish
confidence, unless he is able to prove that the soul
is altogether immortal and imperishable. But if he
cannot prove the soul's immortality, he who is
about to die will always have reason to fear that
when the body is disunited, the soul also may utterly
perish.

All of us, as we afterwards remarked to one another, had an unpleasant feeling at hearing what they
said. When we had been so firmly convinced before,
now to have our faith shaken seemed to introduce
a confusion and uncertainty, not only into the previous argument, but into any future one; either we
were incapable of forming a judgment, or there
were no grounds of belief.

Ech. There I feel with you—by heaven I do,
Phaedo, and when you were speaking, I was beginning to ask myself the same question: What argument can I ever trust again? For what could be
more convincing than the argument of Socrates,
which has now fallen into discredit? That the soul
is a harmony is a doctrine which has always had
a wonderful attraction for me, and, when mentioned, came back to me at once, as my own original
conviction. And now I must begin again and find
another argument which will assure me that when
the man is dead the soul survives. Tell me, I implore
you, how did Socrates proceed? Did he appear to
share the unpleasant feeling which you mention?
or did he calmly meet the attack? And did he answer
forcibly or feebly? Narrate what passed as exactly
as you can.

Phaed. Often, Echecrates, I have wondered at Socrates, but never more than on that occasion. That he
should be able to answer was nothing, but what
astonished me was, first, the gentle and pleasant and
approving manner in which he received the words

89

of the young men, and then his quick sense of the wound which had been inflicted by the argument, and the readiness with which he healed it. He might be compared to a general rallying his defeated and broken army, urging them to accompany him and return to the field of argument.

Ech. What followed?

Phaed. You shall hear, for I was close to him on his right hand, seated on a sort of stool, and he on a couch which was a good deal higher. He stroked my head, and pressed the hair upon my neck— he had a way of playing with my hair; and then he said: Tomorrow, Phaedo, I suppose that these fair locks of yours will be severed.

Yes, Socrates, I suppose that they will, I replied.

Not so, if you will take my advice.

What shall I do with them? I said.

Today, he replied, and not tomorrow, if this argument dies and we cannot bring it to life again, you and I will both shave our locks: and if I were you, and the argument got away from me, and I could not hold my ground against Simmias and Cebes, I would myself take an oath, like the Argives, not to wear hair any more until I had renewed the conflict and defeated them.

Yes, I said; but Heracles himself is said not to be a match for two.

Summon me then, he said, and I will be your Iolaus until the sun goes down.

I summon you rather, I rejoined, not as Heracles summoning Iolaus, but as Iolaus might summon Heracles.

That will do as well, he said. But first let us take care that we avoid a danger.

Of what nature? I said.

Lest we become misologists, he replied: no worse thing can happen to a man than this. For as there are misanthropists or haters of men, there are also misologists or haters of ideas, and both spring from the same cause, which is ignorance of the world. Misanthropy arises out of the too great confidence of inexperience;—you trust a man and think him altogether true and sound and faithful, and then in a little while he turns out to be false and knavish;

and then another and another, and when this has
happened several times to a man, especially when it
happens among those whom he deems to be his
own most trusted and familiar friends, and he has
often quarrelled with them, he at last hates all men,
and believes that no one has any good in him at all.
You must have observed this trait of character?

I have.

And is not the feeling discreditable? Is it not obvious that such an one having to deal with other men,
was clearly without any experience of human nature;
for experience would have taught him the true state
of the case, that few are the good and few the evil, 90
and that the great majority are in the interval between them.

What do you mean? I said.

I mean, he replied, as you might say of the very
large and very small—that nothing is more uncom-
mon than a very large or very small man; and this
applies generally to all extremes, whether of great
and small, or swift and slow, or fair and foul, or
black and white: and whether the instances you
select be men or dogs or anything else, few are the
extremes, but many are in the mean between them.
Did you never observe this?

Yes, I said, I have.

And do you not imagine, he said, that if there
were a competition in evil, the worst would be found
to be very few?

Yes, that is very likely, I said.

Yes, that is very likely, he replied; although in this
respect arguments are unlike men—there I was led
on by you to say more than I had intended; but the
point of comparison was, that when a simple man
who has no skill in dialectics believes an argument
to be true which he afterwards imagines to be false,
whether really false or not, and then another and
another, he has no longer any faith left, and great
disputers, as you know, come to think at last that
they have grown to be the wisest of mankind; for
they alone perceive the utter unsoundness and in-
stability of all arguments, or indeed, of all things,
which, like the currents in the Euripus, are going up
and down in never-ceasing ebb and flow.

That is quite true, I said.

Yes, Phaedo, he replied, and how melancholy, if there be such a thing as truth or certainty or possibility of knowledge—that a man should have lighted upon some argument or other which at first seemed true and then turned out to be false, and instead of blaming himself and his own want of wit, because he is annoyed, should at last be too glad to transfer the blame from himself to arguments in general: and for ever afterwards should hate and revile them, and lose truth and the knowledge of realities.

Yes, indeed, I said; that is very melancholy.

Let us then, in the first place, he said, be careful of allowing or of admitting into our souls the notion that there is no health or soundness in any arguments at all. Rather say that we have not yet attained to soundness in ourselves, and that we must struggle manfully and do our best to gain health of mind— you and all other men having regard to the whole of your future life, and I myself in the prospect of death. For at this moment I am sensible that I have not the temper of a philosopher; like the vulgar, I am only a partisan. Now the partisan, when he is engaged in a dispute, cares nothing about the rights of the question, but is anxious only to convince his hearers of his own assertions. And the difference between him and me at the present moment is merely this—that whereas he seeks to convince his hearers that what he says is true, I am rather seeking to convince myself; to convince my hearers is a secondary matter with me. And do but see much I gain by the argument. For if what I say is true, then I do well to be persuaded of the truth; but if there be nothing after death, still, during the short time that remains, I shall not distress my friends with lamentations, and my ignorance will not last, but will die with me, and therefore no harm will be done. This is the state of mind, Simmias and Cebes, in which I approach the argument. And I would ask you to be thinking of the truth and not of Socrates: agree with me, if I seem to you to be speaking the truth; or if not, withstand me might and main, that I may not deceive you as well as myself in my enthusiasm, and like the bee, leave my sting in you before I die.

And now let us proceed, he said. And first of all let me be sure that I have in my mind what you were saying. Simmias, if I remember rightly, has fears and misgivings whether the soul, although a fairer and diviner thing than the body, being as she is in the form of harmony, may not perish first. On the other hand, Cebes appeared to grant that the soul was more lasting than the body, but he said that no one could know whether the soul, after having worn out many bodies, might not perish herself and leave her last body behind her; and that this is death, which is the destruction not of the body but of the soul, for in the body the work of destruction is ever going on. Are not these, Simmias and Cebes, the points which we have to consider?

They both agreed to this statement of them.

He proceeded: And did you deny the force of the whole preceding argument, or of a part only?

Of a part only, they replied.

And what did you think, he said, of that part of the argument in which we said that knowledge was recollection, and hence inferred that the soul must have previously existed somewhere else before she was enclosed in the body?

Cebes said that he had been wonderfully impressed by that part of the argument, and that his conviction remained absolutely unshaken. Simmias agreed, and added that he himself could hardly imagine the possibility of his ever thinking differently.

But, rejoined Socrates, you will have to think differently, my Theban friend, if you still maintain that harmony is a compound, and that the soul is a harmony which is made out of strings set in the frame of the body; for you will surely never allow yourself to say that a harmony is prior to the elements which compose it.

Never, Socrates.

But do you not see that this is what you imply when you say that the soul existed before she took the form and body of man, and was made up of elements which as yet had no existence? For harmony is not like the soul, as you suppose; but first the lyre, and the strings, and the sounds exist in a state of discord, and then harmony is made last of all, and perishes first. And how can such a notion of the soul as this agree with the other?

Not at all, replied Simmias.

And yet, he said, there surely ought to be harmony in a discourse of which harmony is the theme?

There ought, replied Simmias.

But there is no harmony, he said, in the two propositions that knowledge is recollection, and that the soul is a harmony. Which of them will you retain?

I think, he replied, that I have a much stronger faith, Socrates, in the first of the two, which has been fully demonstrated to me, than in the latter, which has not been demonstrated at all, but rests only on probable and plausible grounds; and is therefore believed by the many. I know too well that these arguments from probabilities are impostors, and unless great caution is observed in the use of them, they are apt to be deceptive—in geometry, and in other things too. But the doctrine of knowledge and recollection has been proven to me on trustworthy grounds: and the proof was that the soul must have existed before she came into the body, because to her belongs the essence of which the very name implies existence. Having, as I am convinced, rightly accepted this conclusion, and on sufficient grounds, I must, as I suppose, cease to argue or allow others to argue that the soul is a harmony.

Let me put the matter, Simmias, he said, in another point of view: Do you imagine that a harmony   93
or any other composition can be in a state other than that of the elements, out of which it is compounded?

Certainly not.

Or do or suffer anything other than they do or suffer?

He agreed.

Then a harmony does not, properly speaking, lead the parts or elements which make up the harmony, but only follows them.

He assented.

For harmony cannot possibly have any motion, or sound, or other quality which is opposed to its parts.

That would be impossible, he replied.

And does not the nature of every harmony depend upon the manner in which the elements are harmonized?

I do not understand you, he said.

I mean to say that a harmony admits of degrees, and is more of a harmony, and more completely a harmony, when more truly and fully harmonized, to any extent which is possible; and less of a harmony, and less completely a harmony, when less truly and fully harmonized.

True.

But does the soul admit of degrees? or is one soul in the very least degree more or less, or more or less completely, a soul than another?

Not in the least.

Yet surely of two souls, one is said to have intelligence and virtue, and to be good, and the other to have folly and vice, and to be an evil soul: and this is said truly?

Yes, truly.

But what will those who maintain the soul to be a harmony say of this presence of virtue and vice in the soul?—will they say that here is another harmony, and another discord, and that the virtuous soul is harmonized, and herself being a harmony has another harmony within her, and that the vicious soul is inharmonical and has no harmony within her?

I cannot tell, replied Simmias; but I suppose that something of the sort would be asserted by those who say that the soul is a harmony.

And we have already admitted that no soul is more a soul than another; which is equivalent to admitting that harmony is not more or less harmony, or more or less completely a harmony?

Quite true.

And that which is not more or less a harmony is not more or less harmonized?

True.

And that which is not more or less harmonized cannot have more or less of harmony, but only an equal harmony?

Yes, an equal harmony.

Then one soul not being more or less absolutely a soul than another, is not more or less harmonized?

Exactly.

And therefore has neither more nor less of discord, nor yet of harmony?

She has not.

And having neither more nor less of harmony or of discord, one soul has no more vice or virtue than another, if vice be discord and virtue harmony?

Not at all more.

Or speaking more correctly, Simmias, the soul, if she is a harmony, will never have any vice; because a harmony, being absolutely a harmony, has no part in the inharmonical.

94

No.

And therefore a soul which is absolutely a soul has no vice?

How can she have, if the previous argument holds?

Then, if all souls are equally by their nature souls, all souls of all living creatures will be equally good?

I agree with you, Socrates, he said.

And can all this be true, think you? he said; for these are the consequences which seem to follow from the assumption that the soul is a harmony?

It cannot be true.

Once more, he said, what ruler is there of the elements of human nature other than the soul, and especially the wise soul? Do you know of any?

Indeed, I do not.

And is the soul in agreement with the affections of the body? or is she at variance with them? For example, when the body is hot and thirsty, does not the soul incline us against drinking? and when the body is hungry, against eating? And this is only one instance out of ten thousand of the opposition of the soul to the things of the body.

Very true.

But we have already acknowledged that the soul, being a harmony, can never utter a note at variance with the tensions and relaxations and vibrations and other affections of the strings out of which she is composed; she can only follow, she cannot lead them?

It must be so, he replied.

And yet do we not now discover the soul to be doing the exact opposite—leading the elements of which she is believed to be composed; almost always opposing and coercing them in all sorts of ways throughout life, sometimes more violently with the pains of medicine and gymnastic; then again more gently; now threatening, now admonishing the desires, passions, fears, as if talking to a thing which is not herself, as Homer in the Odyssey represents Odysseus doing in the words—

"He beat his breast, and thus reproached his heart;
Endure, my heart; far worse hast thou endured!"
Do you think that Homer wrote this under the idea that the soul is a harmony capable of being led by the affections of the body, and not rather of a nature which should lead and master them—herself a far diviner thing than any harmony?

Yes, Socrates, I quite think so.

Then, my friend, we can never be right in saying that the soul is a harmony, for we should contradict   95
the divine Homer, and contradict ourselves.

True, he said.

Thus much, said Socrates, of Harmonia, your Theban goddess, who has graciously yielded to us; but what shall I say, Cebes, to her husband Cadmus, and how shall I make peace with him?

I think that you will discover a way of propitiating him, said Cebes; I am sure that you have put the argument with Harmonia in a manner that I could never have expected. For when Simmias was mentioning his difficulty, I quite imagined that no answer could be given to him, and therefore I was surprised at finding that his argument could not sustain the first onset of yours, and not impossibly the other, whom you call Cadmus, may share a similar fate.

Nay, my good friend, said Socrates, let us not boast, lest some evil eye should put to flight the word which I am about to speak. That, however, may be left in the hands of those above; while I draw near in Homeric fashion, and try the mettle of your words. Here lies the point:—You want to have it proven to you that the soul is imperishable and immortal, and the philosopher who is confident

in death appears to you to have but a vain and foolish confidence, if he believes that he will fare better
in the world below than one who has led another
sort of life, unless he can prove this: and you say
that the demonstration of the strength and divinity
of the soul, and of her existence prior to our becoming men, does not necessarily imply her immortality. Admitting the soul to be long-lived, and to
have known and done much in a former state, still
she is not on that account immortal; and her entrance into the human form may be a sort of disease
which is the beginning of dissolution, and may at
last, after the toils of life are over, end in that which
is called death. And whether the soul enters into the
body once only or many times, does not, as you say,
make any difference in the fears of individuals.
For any man, who is not devoid of sense, must fear,
if he has no knowledge and can give no account of
the soul's immortality. This, or something like this,
I suspect to be your notion, Cebes; and I designedly
recur to it in order that nothing may escape us, and
that you may, if you wish, add or subtract anything.

But, said Cebes, as far as I see at present, I have
nothing to add or subtract: I mean what you say
that I mean.

Socrates paused awhile, and seemed to be absorbed in reflection. At length he said: You are
raising a tremendous question, Cebes, involving the
whole nature of generation and corruption, about
which, if you like, I will give you my own experience; and if anything which I say is likely to avail
towards the solution of your difficulty you may
make use of it.

I should very much like, said Cebes, to hear
what you have to say.

Then I will tell you, said Socrates. When I was
young, Cebes, I had a prodigious desire to know
that department of philosophy which is called the
investigation of nature; to know the causes of things,
and why a thing is and is created or destroyed appeared to me to be a lofty profession; and I was
always agitating myself with the consideration of
questions such as these:—Is the growth of animals

the result of some decay which the hot and cold principle contracts, as some have said? Is the blood the element with which we think, or the air, or the fire? or perhaps nothing of the kind—but the brain may be the originating power of the perceptions of hearing and sight and smell, and memory and opinion may come from them, and science may be based on memory and opinion when they have attained fixity. And then I went on to examine the corruption of them, and then to the things of heaven and earth, and at last I concluded myself to be utterly and absolutely incapable of these inquiries, as I will satisfactorily prove to you. For I was fascinated by them to such a degree that my eyes grew blind to things which I had seemed to myself, and also to others, to know quite well; I forgot what I had before thought self-evident truths; e.g., such a fact as that the growth of man is the result of eating and drinking; for when by the digestion of food flesh is added to flesh and bone to bone, and whenever there is an aggregation of congenial elements, the lesser bulk becomes larger and the small man great. Was not that a reasonable notion?

Yes, said Cebes, I think so.

Well; but let me tell you something more. There was a time when I thought that I understood the meaning of greater and less pretty well; and when I saw a great man standing by a little one, I fancied that one was taller than the other by a head; or one horse would appear to be greater than another horse: and still more clearly did I seem to perceive that ten is two more than eight, and that two cubits are more than one, because two is the double of one.

And what is now your notion of such matters? said Cebes.

I should be far enough from imagining, he replied, that I knew the cause of any of them, by heaven I should; for I cannot satisfy myself that, when one is added to one, the one to which the addition is made becomes two, or that the two units added together make two by reason of the addition. I cannot understand how, when separated from the other, each of them was one and not two, and now, when they are brought together, the mere juxtaposi-

97

tion or meeting of them should be the cause of their becoming two: neither can I understand how the division of one is the way to make two; for then a different cause would produce the same effect—as in the former instance the addition and juxtaposition of one to one was the cause of two, in this the separation and subtraction of one from the other would be the cause. Nor am I any longer satisfied that I understand the reason why one or anything else is either generated or destroyed or is at all, but I have in my mind some confused notion of a new method, and can never admit the other.

Then I heard someone reading, as he said, from a book of Anaxagoras, that mind was the disposer and cause of all, and I was delighted at this notion, which appeared quite admirable, and I said to myself: If mind is the disposer, mind will dispose all for the best, and put each particular in the best place; and I argued that if anyone desired to find out the cause of the generation or destruction or existence of anything, he must find out what state of being or doing or suffering was best for that thing, and therefore a man had only to consider the best for himself and others, and then he would also know the worse, since the same science comprehended both. And I rejoiced to think that I had found in Anaxagoras a teacher of the causes of existence such as I desired, and I imagined that he would tell me first whether the earth is flat or round; and whichever was true, he would proceed to explain the cause and the necessity of this being so, and then he would teach me the nature of the best and show that this was best; and if he said that the earth was in the center, he would further explain that this position was the best, and I should be satisfied with the explanation given, and not want any other sort of cause. And I thought that I would then go on and ask him about the sun and moon and stars, and that he would explain to me their comparative swiftness, and their returnings and various states, active and passive, and how all of them were for the best. For I could not imagine that when he spoke of mind as the disposer of them, he would give any other account of their being as they are, except that this was best; and I thought that when he had explained to me in detail the cause of each and the cause of all, he would go on to explain to me what was best for each and what was good for all. These hopes I would not have sold for a large sum of money, and I seized the books and read them as fast as I could in my eagerness to know the better and the worse.

What expectations I had formed, and how grievously was I disappointed! As I proceeded, I found my philosopher altogether forsaking mind or any other principle of order, but having recourse to air, and ether, and water, and other eccentricities. I might compare him to a person who began by maintaining generally that mind is the cause of the actions of Socrates, but who, when he endeavored to explain the causes of my several actions in detail, went on to show that I sit here because my body is made up of bones and muscles; and the bones, as he would say, are hard and have joints which divide them, and the muscles are elastic, and they cover the bones, which have also a covering or environment of flesh and skin which contains them; and as the bones are lifted at their joints by the contraction or relaxation of the muscles, I am able to bend my limbs, and this is why I am sitting here in a curved posture—that is what he would say; and he would have a similar explanation of my talking to you, which he would attribute to sound, and air, and hearing, and he would assign ten thousand other causes of the same sort, forgetting to mention the true cause, which is, that the Athenians have thought fit to condemn me, and accordingly I have thought it better and more right to remain here and undergo my sentence; for I am inclined to think that these muscles and bones of mine would have gone off long ago to Megara or Boeotia—by the dog, they would, if they had been moved only by their own idea of what was best, and if I had not chosen the better and nobler part, instead of playing truant and running away, of enduring any punishment which the state inflicts. There is surely a strange confusion of causes and conditions in all this. It may be said, indeed, that without bones and muscles and the

99

other parts of the body I cannot execute my purposes. But to say that I do as I do because of them, and that this is the way in which mind acts, and not from the choice of the best, is a very careless and idle mode of speaking. I wonder that they cannot distinguish the cause from the condition, which the many, feeling about in the dark, are always mistaking and misnaming. And thus one man makes a vortex all round and steadies the earth by the heaven; another gives the air as a support to the earth, which is a sort of broad trough. Any power which in arranging them as they are arranges them for the best never enters into their minds; and instead of finding any superior strength in it, they rather expect to discover another Atlas of the world who is stronger and more everlasting and more containing than the good;—of the obligatory and containing power of the good they think nothing; and yet this is the principle which I would fain learn if anyone would teach me. But as I have failed either to discover myself, or to learn of anyone else, the nature of the best, I will exhibit to you, if you like, what I have found to be the second best mode of inquiring into the cause.

I should very much like to hear, he replied.

Socrates proceeded: I thought that as I had failed in the contemplation of true existence, I ought to be careful that I did not lose the eye of my soul; as people may injure their bodily eye by observing and gazing on the sun during an eclipse, unless they take the precaution of only looking at the image reflected in the water, or in some similar medium. So in my own case, I was afraid that my soul might be blinded altogether if I looked at things with my eyes or tried to apprehend them by the help of the senses. And I thought that I had better have recourse to the world of mind and seek there the truth of existence. I dare say that the simile is not perfect— for I am very far from admitting that he who contemplates existences through the medium of thought, sees them only "through a glass darkly," any more than he who considers them in action and operation. However, this was the method which I adopted: I first assumed some principle which I judged to be

100

the strongest, and then I affirmed as true whatever seemed to agree with this, whether relating to the cause or to anything else; and that which disagreed I regarded as untrue. But I should like to explain my meaning more clearly, as I do not think that you as yet understand me.

No indeed, replied Cebes, not very well.

There is nothing new, he said, in what I am about to tell you; but only what I have been always and everywhere repeating in the previous discussion and on other occasions: I want to show you the nature of that cause which has occupied my thoughts. I shall have to go back to those familiar words which are in the mouth of everyone, and first of all assume that there is an absolute beauty and goodness and greatness, and the like; grant me this, and I hope to be able to show you the nature of the cause, and to prove the immortality of the soul.

Cebes said: You may proceed at once with the proof, for I grant you this.

Well, he said, then I should like to know whether you agree with me in the next step; for I cannot help thinking, if there be anything beautiful other than absolute beauty should there be such, that it can be beautiful only in so far as it partakes of absolute beauty—and I should say the same of everything. Do you agree in this notion of the cause?

Yes, he said, I agree.

He proceeded: I know nothing and can understand nothing of any other of those wise causes which are alleged; and if a person says to me that the bloom of color, or form, or any such thing is a source of beauty, I leave all that, which is only confusing to me, and simply and singly, and perhaps foolishly, hold and am assured in my own mind that nothing makes a thing beautiful but the presence and participation of beauty in whatever way or manner obtained; for as to the manner I am uncertain, but I stoutly contend that by beauty all beautiful things become beautiful. This appears to me to be the safest answer which I can give, either to myself or to another, and to this I cling, in the persuasion that this principle will never be overthrown, and that to myself or to anyone who asks the question, I

may safely reply, That by beauty beautiful things
become beautiful. Do you not agree with me?

I do.

And that by greatness only great things become
great and greater greater, and by smallness the less
becomes less?

True.

Then if a person were to remark that A is taller
by a head than B, and B less by a head than A, you
would refuse to admit his statement, and would
stoutly contend what you mean is only that the
greater is greater by, and by reason of, greatness,
and the less is less only by, and by reason of, smallness; and thus you would avoid the danger of saying
that the greater is greater and the less less by the
measure of the head, which is the same in both,
and would also avoid the monstrous absurdity of
supposing that the greater man is greater by reason
of the head, which is small. You would be afraid
to draw such an inference, would you not?

Indeed, I should, said Cebes, laughing.

In like manner you would be afraid to say that
ten exceeded eight by, and by reason of, two; but
would say by, and by reason of, number; or you
would say that two cubits exceed one cubit not by
a half, but by magnitude?—for there is the same
liability to error in all these cases.

Very true, he said.

Again, would you not be cautious of affirming
that the addition of one to one, or the division of
one, is the cause of two? And you would loudly
asseverate that you know of no way in which anything comes into existence except by participation
in its own proper essence, and consequently, as far
as you know, the only cause of two is the participation in duality—this is the way to make two, and
the participation in one is the way to make one. You
would say: I will let alone puzzles of division and
addition—wiser heads than mine may answer them;
inexperienced as I am, and ready to start, as the
proverb says, at my own shadow, I cannot afford to
give up the sure ground of a principle. And if anyone assails you there, you would not mind him, or
answer him until you had seen whether the conse-

101

quences which follow agree with one another or
not, and when you are further required to give an
explanation of this principle, you would go on to
assume a higher principle, and a higher, until you
found a resting-place in the best of the higher; but
you would not confuse the principle and the consequences in your reasoning, like the Eristics—at least
if you wanted to discover real existence. Not that
this confusion signifies to them, who never care or
think about the matter at all, for they have the wit
to be well pleased with themselves however great
may be the turmoil of their ideas. But you, if you are
a philosopher, will certainly do as I say.

102

What you say is most true, said Simmias and
Cebes, both speaking at once.

Ech. Yes, Phaedo; and I do not wonder at their
assenting. Anyone who has the least sense will acknowledge the wonderful clearness of Socrates'
reasoning.

Phaed. Certainly, Echecrates; and such was the
feeling of the whole company at the time.

Ech. Yes, and equally of ourselves, who were
not of the company, and are now listening to your
recital. But what followed?

Phaed. After all this had been admitted, and they
had agreed that ideas exist, and that other things
participate in them and derive their names from
them, Socrates, if I remember rightly, said:—

This is your way of speaking; and yet when you
say that Simmias is greater than Socrates and less
than Phaedo, do you not predicate of Simmias both
greatness and smallness?

Yes, I do.

But still you allow that Simmias does not really
exceed Socrates, as the words may seem to imply,
because he is Simmias, but by reason of the size
which he has; just as Simmias does not exceed Socrates because he is Simmias, any more than because
Socrates is Socrates, but because he has smallness
when compared with the greatness of Simmias?

True.

And if Phaedo exceeds him in size, this is not because Phaedo is Phaedo, but because Phaedo has

greatness relatively to Simmias, who is comparatively smaller?

That is true.

And therefore Simmias is said to be great, and is also said to be small, because he is in a mean between them, exceeding the smallness of the one by his greatness, and allowing the greatness of the other to exceed his smallness. He added, laughing, I am speaking like a book, but I believe that what I am saying is true.

Simmias assented.

I speak as I do because I want you to agree with me in thinking, not only that absolute greatness will never be great and also small, but that greatness in us or in the concrete will never admit the small or admit of being exceeded: instead of this, one of two things will happen, either the greater will fly or retire before the opposite, which is the less, or at the approach of the less has already ceased to exist; but will not, if allowing or admitting of smallness, be changed by that; even as I, having received and admitted smallness when compared with Simmias, remain just as I was, and am the same small person. And as the idea of greatness cannot condescend ever to be or become small, in like manner the smallness in us cannot be or become great; nor can any other opposite which remains the same ever be or become its own opposite, but either passes away or perishes in the change.

That, replied Cebes, is quite my notion.

Hereupon one of the company, though I do not exactly remember which of them, said: In heaven's name, is not this the direct contrary of what was admitted before—that out of the greater came the less and out of the less the greater, and that opposites were simply generated from opposites; but now this principle seems to be utterly denied.

Socrates inclined his head to the speaker and listened. I like your courage, he said, in reminding us of this. But you do not observe that there is a difference in the two cases. For then we were speaking of opposites in the concrete, and now of the essential opposite which, as is affirmed, neither

103

in us nor in nature can ever be at variance with itself: then, my friend, we were speaking of things in
which opposites are inherent and which are called
after them, but now about the opposites which are
inherent in them and which give their name to them;
and these essential opposites will never, as we maintain, admit of generation into or out of one another.
At the same time, turning to Cebes, he said: Are you
at all disconcerted, Cebes, at our friend's objections?

No, I do not feel so, that Cebes; and yet I cannot
deny that I am often disturbed by objections.

Then we are agreed after all, said Socrates, that
the opposite will never in any case be opposed to
itself?

To that we are quite agreed, he replied.

Yet once more let me ask you to consider the
question from another point of view, and see
whether you agree with me:—There is a thing which
you term heat, and another thing which you term
cold?

Certainly.

But are they the same as fire and snow?

Most assuredly not.

Heat is a thing different from fire, and cold is
not the same with snow?

Yes.

And yet you will surely admit, that when snow, as
was before said, is under the influence of heat, they
will not remain snow and heat; but at the advance
of the heat, the snow will either retire or perish?

Very true, he replied.

And the fire too at the advance of the cold will
either retire or perish; and when the fire is under
the influence of the cold, they will not remain as
before, fire and cold.

That is true, he said.

And in some cases the name of the idea is not
only attached to the idea in an eternal connection,
but anything else which, not being the idea, exists
only in the form of the idea, may also lay claim to
it. I will try to make this clearer by an example:—
The odd number is always called by the name of
odd?

Very true.

But is this the only thing which is called odd? 104
Are there not other things which have their own
name, and yet are called odd, because, although
not the same as oddness, they are never without
oddness?—that is what I mean to ask—whether
numbers such as the number three are not of the
class of odd. And there are many other examples:
would you not say, for example, that three may be
called by its proper name, and also be called odd,
which is not the same with three? and this may be
said not only of three but also of five, and of every
alternate number—each of them without being
oddness is odd; and in the same way two and four,
and the other series of alternate numbers, has every
number even, without being evenness. Do you agree?

Of course.

Then now mark the point at which I am aiming:
—not only do essential opposites exclude one another, but also concrete things, which, although not
in themselves opposed, contain opposites: these, I
say, likewise reject the idea which is opposed to
that which is contained in them, and when it approaches them they either perish or withdraw. For
example; Will not the number three endure annihila-
tion or anything sooner than be converted into an
even number, while remaining three?

Very true, said Cebes.

And yet, he said, the number two is certainly not
opposed to the number three?

It is not.

Then not only do opposite ideas repel the advance
of one another, but also there are other natures
which repel the approach of opposites.

Very true, he said.

Suppose, he said, that we endeavor, if possible, to
determine what these are.

By all means.

Are they not, Cebes, such as compel the things
of which they have possession, not only to take their
own form, but also the form of some opposite?

What do you mean?

I mean, as I was just now saying, and as I am

sure that you know, that those things which are possessed by the number three must not only be three
in number, but must also be odd.

Quite true.

And on this oddness, of which the number three
has the impress, the opposite idea will never intrude?

No.

And this impress was given by the odd principle?

Yes.

And to the odd is opposed the even?

True.

Then the idea of the even number will never arrive
at three?

No.

Then three has no part in the even?

None.

Then the triad or number three is uneven?

Very true.

To return then to my distinction of natures which
are not opposed, and yet do not admit opposites—
as, in the instance given, three, although not opposed to the even, does not any the more admit
of the even, but always brings the opposite into play
on the other side; or as two does not receive the   105
odd, or fire the cold—from these examples (and
there are many more of them) perhaps you may
be able to arrive at the general conclusion, that not
only opposites will not receive opposites, but also
that nothing which brings the opposite will admit
the opposite of that which it brings, in that to
which it is brought. And here let me recapitulate—
for there is no harm in repetition. The number five
will not admit the nature of the even, any more than
ten, which is the double of five, will admit the
nature of the odd. The double has another opposite,
and is not strictly opposed to the odd, but nevertheless rejects the odd altogether. Nor again will
parts in the ratio 3:2, nor any fraction in which
there is a half, nor again in which there is a third,
admit the notion of the whole, although they are
not opposed to the whole: You will agree?

Yes, he said, I entirely agree and go along with
you in that.

And now, he said, let us begin again; and do not

you answer my question in the words in which I ask it: let me have not the old safe answer of which I spoke at first, but another equally safe, of which the truth will be inferred by you from what has been just said. I mean that if anyone asks you "what that is, of which the inherence makes the body hot," you will reply not heat (this is what I call the safe and stupid answer), but fire, a far superior answer, which we are now in a condition to give. Or if anyone asks you "why a body is diseased," you will not say from disease, but from fever; and instead of saying that oddness is the cause of odd numbers, you will say that the monad is the cause of them: and so of things in general, as I dare say that you will understand sufficiently without my adducing any further examples.

Yes, he said, I quite understand you.

Tell me, then, what is that of which the inherence will render the body alive?

The soul, he replied.

And is this always the case?

Yes, he said, of course.

Then whatever the soul possesses, to that she comes bearing life?

Yes, certainly.

And is there any opposite to life?

There is, he said.

And what is that?

Death.

Then the soul, as has been acknowledged, will never receive the opposite of what she brings.

Impossible, replied Cebes.

And now, he said, what did we just now call that principle which repels the even?

The odd.

And that principle which repels the musical or the just?

The unmusical, he said, and the unjust.

And what do we call that principle which does not admit of death?

The immortal, he said.

And does the soul admit of death?

No.

Then the soul is immortal?

Yes, he said.

And may we say that this has been proven?

Yes, abundantly proven, Socrates, he replied.

Supposing that the odd were imperishable, must   106
not three be imperishable?

Of course.

And if that which is cold were imperishable,
when the warm principle came attacking the snow,
must not the snow have retired whole and unmelted
—for it could never have perished, nor could it have
remained and admitted the heat?

True, he said.

Again, if the uncooling or warm principle were
imperishable, the fire when assailed by cold would
not have perished or have been extinguished, but
would have gone away unaffected?

Certainly, he said.

And the same may be said of the immortal: if
the immortal is also imperishable, the soul when
attacked by death cannot perish; for the preceding
argument shows that the soul will not admit of
death, or ever be dead, any more than three or the
odd number will admit of the even, or fire, or the
heat in the fire, of the cold. Yet a person may say:
"But although the odd will not become even at the
approach of the even, why may not the odd perish
and the even take the place of the odd?" Now
to him who makes this objection, we cannot answer
that the odd principle is imperishable; for this has
not been acknowledged, but if this had been acknowledged, there would have been no difficulty in
contending that at the approach of the even the
odd principle and the number three took their departure; and the same argument would have held
good of fire and heat and any other thing.

Very true.

And the same may be said of the immortal: if the
immortal is also imperishable, then the soul will be
imperishable as well as immortal; but if not, some
other proof of her imperishableness will have to be
given.

No other proof is needed, he said; for if the immortal, being eternal, is liable to perish, then nothing is imperishable.

Yes, replied Socrates, and yet all men will agree that God, and the essential form of life, and the immortal in general, will never perish.

Yes, all men, he said—that is true; and what is more, gods, if I am not mistaken, as well as men.

Seeing then that the immortal is indestructible, must not the soul, if she is immortal, be also imperishable?

Most certainly.

Then when death attacks a man, the mortal portion of him may be supposed to die, but the immortal retires at the approach of death and is preserved safe and sound?

True.

Then, Cebes, beyond question, the soul is immortal and imperishable, and our souls will truly exist in another world! 107

I am convinced, Socrates, said Cebes, and have nothing more to object; but if my friend Simmias, or anyone else, has any further objection to make, he had better speak out, and not keep silence, since I do not know to what other season he can defer the discussion, if there is anything which he wants to say or to have said.

But I have nothing more to say, replied Simmias; nor can I see any reason for doubt after what has been said. But I still feel and cannot help feeling uncertain in my own mind, when I think of the greatness of the subject and the feebleness of man.

Yes, Simmias, replied Socrates, that is well said: and I may add that first principles, even if they appear certain, should be carefully considered; and when they are satisfactorily ascertained, then, with a sort of hesitating confidence in human reason, you may, I think, follow the course of the argument; and if that be plain and clear, there will be no need for any further inquiry.

Very true.

But then, O my friends, he said, if the soul is really immortal, what care should be taken of her, not only in respect of the portion of time which is called life, but of eternity! And the danger of neglecting her from this point of view does indeed appear to be awful. If death had only been the end of all, the wicked would have had a good bargain in dying, for they would have been happily quit not only of their body, but of their own evil together with their souls. But now, inasmuch as the soul is manifestly immortal, there is no release or salvation from evil except the attainment of the highest virtue and wisdom. For the soul when on her progress to the world below takes nothing with her but nurture and education; and these are said greatly to benefit or greatly to injure the departed, at the very beginning of his journey thither.

For after death, as they say, the genius of each individual, to whom he belonged in life, leads him to a certain place in which the dead are gathered together, whence after judgment has been given they pass into the world below, following the guide, who is appointed to conduct them from this world to the other: and when they have there received their due and remained their time, another guide brings them back again after many revolutions of ages. Now this way to the other world is not, as Aeschylus says in the Telephus, a single and straight path—if that were so no guide would be needed, for no one could miss it; but there are many partings of the road, and windings, as I infer from the rites and sacrifices which are offered to the gods below in places where three ways meet on earth. The wise and orderly soul follows in the straight path and is conscious of her surroundings; but the soul which desires the body, and which, as I was relating before, has long been fluttering about the lifeless frame and the world of sight, is after many struggles and many sufferings hardly and with violence carried away by her attendant genius; and when she arrives at the place where the other souls are gathered, if she be impure and have done impure deeds, whether foul murders or other crimes which are the brothers of these, and the works of brothers in crime—from that soul everyone flees and turns away; no one will be her companion, no one her guide, but alone she wanders in extremity of evil until certain times are fulfilled, and when they are fulfilled, she is borne irresistibly to her own fitting habitation; as every pure and just soul which has passed through life in the company and under the guidance of the gods has also her own proper home.

Now the earth has divers wonderful regions, and is indeed in nature and extent very unlike the notions of geographers, as I believe on the authority of one who shall be nameless.

What do you mean, Socrates? said Simmias. I have myself heard many descriptions of the earth, but I do not know, and I should very much like to know, in which of these you put faith.

And I, Simmias, replied Socrates, if I had the art of Glaucus would tell you; although I know not that the art of Glaucus could prove the truth of my tale, which I myself should never be able to prove, and even if I could, I fear, Simmias, that my life would come to an end before the argument was completed. I may describe to you, however, the form and regions of the earth according to my conception of them.

That, said Simmias, will be enough.

Well, then, he said, my conviction is, that the earth is a round body in the center of the heavens, and therefore has no need of air or of any similar force to be a support, but is kept there and hindered from falling or inclining any way by the equability of the surrounding heaven and by her own equipoise. For that which, being in equipoise, is in the center of that which is equably diffused, will not incline any way in any degree, but will always remain in the same state and not deviate. And this is my first notion.

Which is surely a correct one, said Simmias.

Also I believe that the earth is very vast, and that we who dwell in the region extending from the river Phasis to the Pillars of Heracles inhabit a small portion only about the sea, like ants or frogs about a marsh, and that there are other inhabitants of many other like places; for everywhere on the face of the earth there are hollows of various forms and sizes, into which the water and the mist and the lower air collect. But the true earth is pure and situated in the pure heaven—there are the stars also; and it is the heaven which is commonly spoken of

109

by us as the ether, and of which our own earth is
the sediment gathering in the hollows beneath. But
we who live in these hollows are deceived into the
notion that we are dwelling above on the surface
of the earth; which is just as if a creature who was
at the bottom of the sea were to fancy that he was
on the surface of the water, and that the sea was the
heaven through which he saw the sun and the other
stars, he having never come to the surface by reason
of his feebleness and sluggishness, and having never
lifted up his head and seen, nor ever heard from one
who had seen, how much purer and fairer the world
above is than his own. And such is exactly our case:
for we are dwelling in a hollow of the earth, and
fancy that we are on the surface; and the air we call
heaven, in which we imagine that the stars move.
But the fact is, that owing to our feebleness and
sluggishness we are prevented from reaching the
surface of the air: for if any man could arrive at
the exterior limit, or take the wings of a bird and
come to the top, then like a fish who puts his head
out of the water and sees this world, he would see
a world beyond; and, if the nature of man could
sustain the sight, he would acknowledge that this
other world was the place of the true heaven and the
true light and the true earth. For our earth, and the
stones, and the entire region which surrounds us, are
spoilt and corroded, as in the sea all things are
corroded by the brine, neither is there any noble or
perfect growth, but caverns only, and sand, and an
endless slough of mud; and even the shore is not
to be compared to the fairer sights of this world.
And still less is this our world to be compared with
the other. Of that upper earth which is under the
heaven, I can tell you a charming tale, Simmias,
which is well worth hearing.

And we, Socrates, replied Simmias, shall be
charmed to listen to you.

The tale, my friend, he said, is as follows:—In
the first place, the earth, when looked at from above,
is in appearance streaked like one of those balls
which have leather coverings in twelve pieces, and
is decked with various colors, of which the colors
used by painters on earth are in a manner samples.

110

But there the whole earth is made up of them, and they are brighter far and clearer than ours; there is a purple of wonderful luster, also the radiance of gold, and the white which is in the earth is whiter than any chalk or snow. Of these and other colors the earth is made up, and they are more in number and fairer than the eye of man has ever seen; the very hollows (of which I was speaking) filled with air and water have a color of their own, and are seen like light gleaming amid the diversity of the other colors, so that the whole presents a single and continuous appearance of variety in unity. And in this fair region everything that grows—trees, and flowers, and fruits—are in a like degree fairer than any here; and there are hills, having stones in them in a like degree smoother, and more transparent, and fairer in color than our highly valued emeralds and sardonyxes and jaspers, and other gems, which are but minute fragments of them: for there all the stones are like our precious stones, and fairer still.[6] The reason is, that they are pure, and not, like our precious stones, infected or corroded by the corrupt briny elements which coagulate among us, and which breed foulness and disease both in earth and stones, as well as in animals and plants. They are the jewels of the upper earth, which also shines with gold and silver and the like, and they are set in the light of day and are large and abundant and in all places, making the earth a sight to gladden the beholder's eye. And there are animals and men, some in a middle region, others dwelling about the air as we dwell about the sea; others in islands which the air flows round, near the continent; and in a word, the air is used by them as the water and the sea are by us, and the ether is to them what the air is to us. Moreover, the temperament of their seasons is such that they have no disease, and live much longer than we do, and have sight and hearing and smell, and all the other senses, in far greater perfection, in the same proportion that air is purer than water or the ether than air. Also they have temples and sacred places in which the gods really dwell, and they hear

III

---

[6] Cp. Rev., esp. c. xxi. v. 18 ff.

their voices and receive their answers, and are conscious of them and hold converse with them; and they see the sun, moon, and stars as they truly are, and their other blessedness is of a piece with this.

Such is the nature of the whole earth, and of the things which are around the earth; and there are divers regions in the hollows on the face of the globe everywhere, some of them deeper and more extended than that which we inhabit, others deeper but with a narrower opening than ours, and some are shallower and also wider. All have numerous perforations, and there are passages broad and narrow in the interior of the earth, connecting them with one another; and there flows out of and into them, as into basins, a vast tide of water, and huge subterranean streams of perennial rivers, and springs hot and cold, and a great fire, and great rivers of fire, and streams of liquid mud, thin or thick (like the rivers of mud in Sicily, and the lava streams which follow them), and the regions about which they happen to flow are filled up with them. And there is a swinging or seesaw in the interior of the earth which moves all this up and down, and is due to the following cause:— There is a chasm which is the vastest of them all, and pierces right through the whole earth; this is that chasm which Homer describes in the words.— "Far off, where is the inmost depth beneath the earth," and which he in other places, and many other poets, have called Tartarus. And the seesaw is caused by the streams flowing into and out of this chasm, and they each have the nature of the soil through which they flow. And the reason why the streams are always flowing in and out, is that the watery element has no bed or bottom, but is swinging and surging up and down, and the surrounding wind and air do the same; they follow the water up and down, hither and thither, over the earth—just as in the act of respiration the air is always in process of inhalation and exhalation;—and the wind swinging with the water in and out produces fearful and irresistible blasts; when the waters retire with a rush into the lower parts of the earth, as they are called, they flow through the earth in those regions, and fill them up like water raised by a pump, and then when

112

they leave those regions and rush back hither, they again fill the hollows here, and when these are filled, flow through subterranean channels and find their way to their several places, forming seas, and lakes, and rivers, and springs. Thence they again enter the earth, some of them making a long circuit into many lands, others going to a few places and not so distant; and again fall into Tartarus, some at a point a good deal lower than that at which they rose, and others not much lower, but all in some degree lower than the point from which they came. And some burst forth again on the opposite side, and some on the same side, and some wind round the earth with one or many folds like the coils of a serpent, and descend as far as they can, but always return and fall into the chasm. The rivers flowing in either direction can descend only to the center and no further, for opposite to the rivers is a precipice.

Now these rivers are many, and mighty, and diverse, and there are four principal ones, of which the greatest and outermost is that called Oceanus, which flows round the earth in a circle; and in the opposite direction flows Acheron, which passes under the earth through desert places into the Acherusian lake: this is the lake to the shores of which the souls of the many go when they are dead, and after waiting an appointed time, which is to some a longer and to some a shorter time, they are sent back to be born again as animals. The third river passes out between the two, and near the place of outlet pours into a vast region of fire, and forms a lake larger than the Mediterranean Sea, boiling with water and mud; and proceeding muddy and turbid, and winding about the earth, comes, among other places, to the extremities of the Acherusian lake, but mingles not with the waters of the lake, and after making many coils about the earth plunges into Tartarus at a deeper level. This is that Pyriphlegethon, as the stream is called, which throws up jets of fire in different parts of the earth. The fourth river goes out on the opposite side, and falls first of all into a wild and savage region, which is all of a dark blue color, like lapis lazuli; and this is that river which is called

113

the Stygian river, and falls into and forms the Lake Styx, and after falling into the lake and receiving strange powers in the waters, passes under the earth, winding round in the opposite direction, and comes near the Acherusian lake from the opposite side to Pyriphlegethon. And the water of this river too mingles with no other, but flows round in a circle and falls into Tartarus over against Pyriphlegethon; and the name of the river, as the poets say, is Cocytus.

Such is the nature of the other world; and when the dead arrive at the place to which the genius of each severally guides them, first of all, they have sentence passed upon them, as they have lived well and piously or not. And those who appear to have lived neither well nor ill, go to the river Acheron, and embarking in any vessels which they may find, are carried in them to the lake, and there they dwell and are purified of their evil deeds, and having suffered the penalty of the wrongs which they have done to others, they are absolved, and receive the rewards of their good deeds, each of them according to his deserts. But those who appear to be incurable by reason of the greatness of their crimes—who have committed many and terrible deeds of sacrilege, murders foul and violent, or the like—such are hurled into Tartarus which is their suitable destiny, and they never come out. Those again who have committed crimes, which, although great, are not irremediable—who in a moment of anger, for example, have done some violence to a father or a mother, and have repented for the remainder of their lives, or, who have taken the life of another under the like extenuating circumstances—these are plunged into Tartarus, the pains of which they are compelled to undergo for a year, but at the end of the year the wave casts them forth—mere homicides by way of Cocytus, parricides and matricides by Pyriphlegethon—and they are borne to the Acherusian lake, and where they lift up their voices and call upon the victims whom they have slain or wronged, to have pity on them, and to be kind to them, and let them come out into the lake. And if they prevail, then they come forth and cease from their troubles; but if not, they are carried back again into Tartarus and from thence into the rivers unceasingly, until they obtain mercy from those whom they have wronged: for that is the sentence inflicted upon them by their judges. Those too who have been preeminent for holiness of life are released from this earthly prison, and go to their pure home which is above, and dwell in the purer earth; and of these, such as have duly purified themselves with philosophy live henceforth altogether without the body, in mansions fairer still, which may not be described, and of which the time would fail me to tell.

Wherefore, Simmias, seeing all these things, what ought not we to do that we may obtain virtue and wisdom in this life? Fair is the prize, and the hope great!

A man of sense ought not to say, nor will I be very confident, that the description which I have given of the soul and her mansions is exactly true. But I do say that, inasmuch as the soul is shown to be immortal, he may venture to think, not improperly or unworthily, that something of the kind is true. The venture is a glorious one, and he ought to comfort himself with words like these, which is the reason why I lengthen out the tale. Wherefore, I say, let a man be of good cheer about his soul, who having cast away the pleasures and ornaments of the body as alien to him and working harm rather than good, has sought after the pleasures of knowledge; and has arrayed the soul, not in some foreign attire, but in her own proper jewels, temperance, and justice, and courage, and nobility, and truth—in these adorned she is ready to go on her journey to the world below, when her hour comes. You, Simmias and Cebes, and all other men, will depart at some time or other. Me already, as a tragic poet would say, the voice of fate calls. Soon I must drink the poison; and I think that I had better repair to the bath first, in order that the women may not have the trouble of washing my body after I am dead.

When he had done speaking, Crito said: And have you any commands for us, Socrates—anything to say about your children, or any other matter in which we can serve you?

115

Nothing particular, Crito, he replied: only, as I have always told you, take care of yourselves; that is a service which you may be ever rendering to me and mine and to all of us, whether you promise to do so or not. But if you have no thought for yourselves, and care not to walk according to the rule which I have prescribed for you, not now for the first time, however much you may profess or promise at the moment, it will be of no avail.

We will do our best, said Crito: And in what way shall we bury you?

In any way that you like; but you must get hold of me, and take care that I do not run away from you. Then he turned to us, and added with a smile: —I cannot make Crito believe that I am the same Socrates who has been talking and conducting the argument; he fancies that I am the other Socrates whom he will soon see, a dead body—and he asks, How shall he bury me? And though I have spoken many words in the endeavor to show that when I have drunk the poison I shall leave you and go to the joys of the blessed—these words of mine, with which I was comforting you and myself, have had, as I perceive, no effect upon Crito. And therefore I want you to be surety for me to him now, as at the trial he was surety to the judges for me: but let the promise be of another sort; for he was surety for me to the judges that I would remain, and you must be my surety to him that I shall not remain, but go away and depart; and then he will suffer less at my death, and not be grieved when he sees my body being burned or buried. I would not have him sorrow at my hard lot, or say at the burial, Thus we lay out Socrates, or, Thus we follow him to the grave or bury him; for false words are not only evil in themselves, but they infect the soul with evil. Be of good cheer then, my dear Crito, and say that you are burying my body only, and do with that whatever is usual, and what you think best.

When he had spoken these words, he arose and went into a chamber to bathe; Crito followed him and told us to wait. So we remained behind, talking and thinking of the subject of discourse, and also of the greatness of our sorrow; he was like a father

116

of whom we were being bereaved, and we were about to pass the rest of our lives as orphans. When he had taken the bath his children were brought to him—(he had two young sons and an elder one); and the women of his family also came, and he talked to them and gave them a few directions in the presence of Crito; then he dismissed them and returned to us.

Now the hour of sunset was near, for a good deal of time had passed while he was within. When he came out, he sat down with us again after his bath, but not much was said. Soon the jailer, who was the servant of the Eleven, entered and stood by him, saying:—To you, Socrates, whom I know to be the noblest and gentlest and best of all who ever came to this place, I will not impute the angry feelings of other men, who rage and swear at me, when, in obedience to the authorities, I bid them drink the poison—indeed, I am sure that you will not be angry with me; for others, as you are aware, and not I, are to blame. And so fare you well, and try to bear lightly what must needs be—you know my errand. Then bursting into tears he turned away and went out.

Socrates looked at him and said: I return your good wishes, and will do as you bid. Then turning to us, he said, How charming the man is: since I have been in prison he has always been coming to see me, and at times he would talk to me, and was as good to me as could be, and now see how generously he sorrows on my account. We must do as he says, Crito; and therefore let the cup be brought, if the poison is prepared: if not, let the attendant prepare some.

Yet, said Crito, the sun is still upon the hilltops, and I know that many a one has taken the draught later, and after the announcement has been made to him, he has eaten and drunk, and enjoyed the society of his beloved; do not hurry—there is time enough.

Socrates said: Yes, Crito, and they of whom you speak are right in so acting, for they think that they will be gainers by the delay; but I am right in not following their example, for I do not think that I should gain anything by drinking the poison a little later; I should only be ridiculous in my own eyes for sparing and saving a life which is already forfeit. Please then to do as I say, and not to refuse me.

Crito made a sign to the servant, who was standing by; and he went out, and having been absent for some time, returned with the jailer carrying the cup of poison. Socrates said: You, my good friend, who are experienced in these matters, shall give me directions how I am to proceed. The man answered: You have only to walk about until your legs are heavy, and then to lie down, and the poison will act. At the same time he handed the cup to Socrates, who in the easiest and gentlest manner, without the least fear or change of color or feature, looking at the man with all his eyes, Echecrates, as his manner was, took the cup and said: What do you say about making a libation out of this cup to any god? May I, or not? The man answered: We only prepare, Socrates, just so much as we deem enough. I understand, he said: but I may and must ask the gods to prosper my journey from this to the other world—even so—and so be it according to my prayer. Then raising the cup to his lips, quite readily and cheerfully he drank off the poison. And hitherto most of us had been able to control our sorrow; but now when we saw him drinking, and saw too that he had finished the draught, we could no longer forbear, and in spite of myself my own tears were flowing fast; so that I covered my face and wept, not for him, but at the thought of my own calamity in having to part from such a friend. Nor was I the first; for Crito, when he found himself unable to restrain his tears, had got up, and I followed; and at that moment, Apollodorus, who had been weeping all the time, broke out in a loud and passionate cry which made cowards of us all. Socrates alone retained his calmness: What is this strange outcry? he said: I sent away the women mainly in order that they might not misbehave in this way, for I have been told that a man should die in peace. Be quiet then, and have patience. When we heard his words we were ashamed, and refrained our tears; and he walked about until, as he said, his legs began to fail, and then he lay on his back, according to the directions, and the man who gave him the poison now and then looked at his feet and legs; and after a while he pressed his foot hard, and asked him if he could feel; and he said, No; and then his leg, and so up- wards and upwards; and showed us that he was cold and stiff. And he felt them himself, and said: When the poison reaches the heart, that will be the end. He was beginning to grow cold about the groin, when he uncovered his face, for he had covered himself up, and said—they were his last words—he said: Crito, I owe a cock to Asclepius; will you re- member to pay the debt? The debt shall be paid, said Crito; is there anything else? There was no answer to this question; but in a minute or two a move- ment was heard, and the attendants uncovered him; his eyes were set, and Crito closed his eyes and mouth.

Such was the end, Echecrates, of our friend; con- cerning whom I may truly say, that of all the men of his time whom I have known, he was the wisest and justest and best.

Outline of the Republic (in Part)

REPUBLIC

SOCRATES   GLAUCON

ADEIMANTUS   LISTENERS

Book VI (in Part)

Still, I must implore you, Socrates, said Glaucon,
not to turn away just as you are reaching the goal; if
you will only give such an explanation of the good
as you have already given of justice and temperance
and the other virtues, we shall be satisfied.

Yes, my friend, and I shall be at least equally
satisfied, but I cannot help fearing that I shall fail,
and that my indiscreet zeal will bring ridicule upon
me. No, sweet sirs, let us not at present ask what is
the actual nature of the good, for to reach what is
now in my thoughts would be an effort too great for
me. But of the child of the good who is likest him, I
would fain speak, if I could be sure that you wished
to hear—otherwise, not.

By all means, he said, tell us about the child, and
you shall remain in our debt for the account of the
parent.

I do indeed wish, I replied, that I could pay, and
you receive, the account of the parent, and not, as
now, of the offspring only; take, however, this latter
by way of interest,[1] and at the same time have a
care that I do not render a false account, although
I have no intention of deceiving you.

Yes, we will take all the care that we can; proceed.

Yes, I said, but I must first come to an understanding with you, and remind you of what I have
mentioned in the course of this discussion, and at
many other times.

507

---

[1] A play upon τόκος, which means both "offspring" and
"interest."

What?

The old story, that there is a many beautiful and a many good, and so of other things which we describe and define; to all of them "many" is applied.

True, he said.

And there is an absolute beauty and an absolute good, and of other things to which the term "many" is applied there is an absolute; for they may be brought under a single idea, which is called the essence of each.

Very true.

The many, as we say, are seen but not known, and the ideas are known but not seen.

Exactly.

And what is the organ with which we see the visible things?

The sight, he said.

And with the hearing, I said, we hear, and with the other senses perceive the other objects of sense?

True.

But have you remarked that sight is by far the most costly and complex piece of workmanship which the artificer of the senses ever contrived?

No, I never have, he said.

Then reflect: has the ear or voice need of any third or additional nature in order that the one may be able to hear and the other to be heard?

Nothing of the sort.

No, indeed, I replied; and the same is true of most, if not all, the other senses—you would not say that any of them requires such an addition?

Certainly not.

But you see that without the addition of some other nature there is no seeing or being seen?

How do you mean?

Sight being, as I conceive, in the eyes, and he who has eyes wanting to see; color being also present in them, still unless there be a third nature specially adapted to the purpose, the owner of the eyes will see nothing and the colors will be invisible.

Of what nature are you speaking?

Of that which you term light, I replied.

True, he said.

Noble, then, is the body which links together sight

and visibility, and great beyond other bonds by no small difference of nature; for light is their bond, and light is no ignoble thing?

Nay, he said, the reverse of ignoble.

And which, I said, of the gods in heaven would you say was the lord of this element? Whose is that light which makes the eye to see perfectly and the visible to appear?

You mean the sun, as you and all mankind say.

May not the relation of sight to this deity be described as follows?

How?

Neither sight nor the eye in which sight resides is the sun?

No.

Yet of all the organs of sense the eye is the most like the sun?

By far the most like.

And the power which the eye possesses is a sort of effluence which is dispensed from the sun?

Exactly.

Then the sun is not sight, but the author of sight who is recognized by sight.

True, he said.

And this is he whom I call the child of the good, whom the good begat in his own likeness, to be in the visible world, in relation to sight and the things of sight, what the good is in the intellectual world in relation to mind and the things of mind.

Will you be a little more explicit? he said

Why, you know, I said, that the eyes, when a person directs them towards objects on which the light of day is no longer shining, but the moon and stars only, see dimly, and are nearly blind; they seem to have no clearness of vision in them?

Very true.

But when they are directed towards objects on which the sun shines, they see clearly and there is sight in them?

Certainly.

And the soul is like the eye: when resting upon that on which truth and being shine, the soul perceives and understands and is radiant with intelligence; but when turned towards the twilight of becoming and perishing, then she has opinion only, and goes blinking about, and is first of one opinion and then of another, and seems to have no intelligence?

Just so.

Now, that which imparts truth to the known and the power of knowing to the knower is what I would have you term the idea of good, and this you will deem to be the cause of science,[2] and of truth in so far as the latter becomes the subject of knowledge; beautiful too, as are both truth and knowledge, you will be right in esteeming this other nature as more beautiful than either; and, as in the previous instance, light and sight may be truly said to be like the sun, and yet not to be the sun, so in this other sphere, science and truth may be deemed to be like the good, but not the good; the good has a place of honor yet higher.

What a wonder of beauty that must be, he said, which is the author of science and truth, and yet surpasses them in beauty; for you surely cannot mean to say that pleasure is the good?

God forbid, I replied; but may I ask you to consider the image in another point of view?

In what point of view?

You would say, would you not, that the sun is not only the author of visibility in all visible things, but of generation and nourishment and growth, though he himself is not generation?

Certainly.

In like manner the good may be said to be not only the author of knowledge to all things known, but of their being and essence, and yet the good is not essence, but far exceeds essence in dignity and power.

Glaucon said, with a ludicrous earnestness: By the light of heaven, how amazing!

Yes, I said, and the exaggeration may be set down to you; for you made me utter my fancies.

And pray continue to utter them; at any rate let us hear if there is anything more to be said about the similitude of the sun.

---

[2] Reading διανοοῦ.

Yes, I said, there is a great deal more.

Then omit nothing, however slight.

I will do my best, I said; but I should think that a great deal will have to be omitted.

You have to imagine, then, that there are two ruling powers, and that one of them is set over the intellectual world, the other over the visible. I do not say heaven, lest you should fancy that I am playing upon the name (οὐρανός, ὁρατός). May I suppose that you have this distinction of the visible and intelligible fixed in your mind?

I have.

Now take a line which has been cut into two unequal[3] parts, and divide each of them again in the same proportion, and suppose the two main divisions to answer, one to the visible and the other to the intelligible, and then compare the subdivisions in respect of their clearness and want of clearness, and you will find that the first section in the sphere of the visible consists of images. And by images I 510 mean, in the first place, shadows, and in the second place, reflections in water and in solid, smooth and polished bodies and the like: Do you understand?

Yes, I understand.

Imagine, now, the other section, of which this is only the resemblance, to include the animals which we see, and everything that grows or is made.

Very good.

Would you not admit that both the sections of this division have different degrees of truth, and that the copy is to the original as the sphere of opinion is to the sphere of knowledge?

Most undoubtedly.

Next proceed to consider the manner in which the sphere of the intellectual is to be divided.

In what manner?

Thus:—There are two subdivisions, in the lower of which the soul uses the figures given by the former division as images; the inquiry can only be hypothetical, and instead of going upwards to a principle descends to the other end; in the higher of the two, the soul passes out of hypotheses, and goes up to a

[3] Reading ἄνισα.

principle which is above hypotheses, making no use
of images[4] as in the former case, but proceeding
only in and through the ideas themselves.

I do not quite understand your meaning, he said.

Then I will try again; you will understand me
better when I have made some preliminary remarks.
You are aware that students of geometry, arithmetic,
and the kindred sciences assume the odd and the
even and the figures and three kinds of angles and
the like in their several branches of science; these
are their hypotheses, which they and everybody are
supposed to know, and therefore they do not deign
to give any account of them either to themselves or
others; but they begin with them, and go on until
they arrive at last, and in a consistent manner, at
their conclusion?

Yes, he said, I know.

And do you not know also that although they
make use of the visible forms and reason about
them, they are thinking not of these, but of the
ideals which they resemble; not of the figures which
they draw, but of the absolute square and the absolute diameter, and so on—the forms which they
draw or make, and which have shadows and reflections in water of their own, are converted by them
into images, but they are really seeking to behold
the things themselves, which can only be seen with
the eye of the mind?

That is true.

And of this kind I spoke as the intelligible, although in the search after it the soul is compelled
to use hypotheses; not ascending to a first principle,
because she is unable to rise above the region of
hypothesis, but employing the objects of which the
shadows below are resemblances in their turn as
images, they having in relation to the shadows and
reflections of them a greater distinctness, and therefore a higher value.

I understand, he said, that you are speaking of
the province of geometry and the sister arts.

And when I speak of the other division of the
intelligible, you will understand me to speak of that

511

---

[4] Reading ὧνπερ ἐκεῖνο εἰκόνων.

other sort of knowledge which reason herself attains
by the power of dialectic, using the hypotheses not
as first principles, only as hypotheses—that is to
say, as steps and points of departure into a world
which is above hypotheses, in order that she may
soar beyond them to the first principle of the whole;
and clinging to this and then to that which depends on this, by successive steps she descends again
without the aid of any sensible object, from ideas,
through ideas, and in ideas she ends.

I understand you, he replied; not perfectly, for
you seem to me to be describing a task which is
really tremendous; but, at any rate, I understand you
to say that knowledge and being, which the science
of dialectic contemplates, are clearer than the notions of the arts, as they are termed, which proceed
from hypotheses only: these are also contemplated
by the understanding, and not by the senses: yet,
because they start from hypotheses and do not
ascend to a principle, those who contemplate them
appear to you not to exercise the higher reason upon
them, although when a first principle is added to
them they are cognizable by the higher reason.
And the habit which is concerned with geometry and
the cognate sciences I suppose that you would term
understanding and not reason, as being intermediate
between opinion and reason.

You have quite conceived my meaning, I said;
and now, corresponding to these four divisions, let
there be four faculties in the soul—reason answering to the highest, understanding to the second, faith
(or conviction) to the third, and perception of
shadows to the last—and let there be a scale of
them, and let us suppose that the several faculties
have clearness in the same degree that their objects
have truth.

I understand, he replied, and give my assent, and
accept your arrangement.

Book VII

And now, I said, let me show in a figure how far 514
our nature is enlightened or unenlightened:—Behold! human beings living in an underground den,
which has a mouth open towards the light and
reaching all along the den; here they have been
from their childhood, and have their legs and necks
chained so that they cannot move, and can only
see before them, being prevented by the chains
from turning round their heads. Above and behind
them a fire is blazing at a distance, and between the
fire and the prisoners there is a raised way; and
you will see, if you look, a low wall built along the
way, like the screen which marionette players have
in front of them, over which they show the puppets.

I see.

And do you see, I said, men passing along the
wall carrying all sorts of vessels, and statues and
figures of animals made of wood and stone and
various materials, which appear over the wall? Some
of them are talking, others silent,

You have shown me a strange image, and they are
strange prisoners.

Like ourselves, I replied; and they see only their
own shadows, or the shadows of one another, which
the fire throws on the opposite wall of the cave?

True, he said; how could they see anything but the
shadows if they were never allowed to move their
heads?

And of the objects which are being carried in like
manner they would only see the shadows?

Yes, he said.

And if they were able to converse with one another, would they not suppose that they were nam-
ing what was actually before them?[5]

Very true.

And suppose further that the prison had an echo
which came from the other side, would they not be

[5] Reading παρόντα.

sure to fancy when one of the passersby spoke that the voice which they heard came from the passing shadow?

No question, he replied.

To them, I said, the truth would be literally nothing but the shadows of the images.

That is certain.

And now look again, and see what will naturally follow if the prisoners are released and disabused of their error. At first, when any of them is liberated and compelled suddenly to stand up and turn his neck round and walk and look towards the light, he will suffer sharp pains; the glare will distress him, and he will be unable to see the realities of which in his former state he had seen the shadows: and then conceive someone saying to him, that what he saw before was an illusion, but that now, when he is approaching nearer to being and his eye is turned towards more real existence, he has a clearer vision —what will be his reply? And you may further imagine that his instructor is pointing to the objects as they pass and requiring him to name them—will he not be perplexed? Will he not fancy that the shadows which he formerly saw are truer than the objects which are now shown to him?

Far truer.

And if he is compelled to look straight at the light, will he not have a pain in his eyes which will make him turn away to take refuge in the objects of vision which he can see, and which he will conceive to be in reality clearer than the things which are now being shown to him?

True, he said.

And suppose once more, that he is reluctantly dragged up a steep and rugged ascent, and held fast until he is forced into the presence of the sun himself, is he not likely to be pained and irritated? When he approaches the light his eyes will be dazzled, and he will not be able to see anything at all of what are now called realities.

Not all in a moment, he said.

He will require to grow accustomed to the sight of the upper world. And first he will see the shadows best, next the reflections of men and other objects

516

in the water, and then the objects themselves; then he will gaze upon the light of the moon and the stars and the spangled heaven; and he will see the sky and the stars by night better than the sun or the light of the sun by day?

Certainly.

Last of all he will be able to see the sun, and not mere reflections of him in the water, but he will see him in his own proper place, and not in another; and he will contemplate him as he is.

Certainly.

He will then proceed to argue that this is he who gives the season and the years, and is the guardian of all that is in the visible world, and in a certain way the cause of all things which he and his fellows have been accustomed to behold?

Clearly, he said, he would first see the sun and then reason about him.

And when he remembered his old habitation, and the wisdom of the den and his fellow-prisoners, do you not suppose that he would felicitate himself on the change, and pity them?

Certainly, he would.

And if they were in the habit of conferring honors among themselves on those who were quickest to observe the passing shadows and to remark which of them went before, and which followed after, and which were together; and who were therefore best able to draw conclusions as to the future, do you think that he would care for such honors and glories, or envy the possessors of them? Would he not say with Homer, "Better to be the poor servant of a poor master," and to endure anything, rather than think as they do and live after their manner?

Yes, he said, I think that he would rather suffer anything than entertain these false notions and live in this miserable manner.

Imagine once more, I said, such an one coming suddenly out of the sun to be replaced in his old situation; would he not be certain to have his eyes full of darkness?

To be sure, he said.

And if there were a contest, and he had to compete in measuring the shadows with the prisoners who had never moved out of the den, while his sight was still weak, and before his eyes had become steady (and the time which would be needed to acquire this new habit of sight might be very considerable), would he not be ridiculous? Men would say of him that up he went and down he came without his eyes; and that it was better not even to think of ascending: and if anyone tried to loose another and lead him up to the light, let them only catch the offender, and they would put him to death.

No question, he said.

This entire allegory, I said, you may now append, dear Glaucon, to the previous argument; the prison-house is the world of sight, the light of the fire is the sun, and you will not misapprehend me if you interpret the journeys to be the ascent of the soul into the intellectual world according to my poor belief, which, at your desire, I have expressed—whether rightly or wrongly God knows. But, whether true or false, my opinion is that in the world of knowledge the idea of good appears last of all, and is seen only with an effort; and, when seen, is also inferred to be the universal author of all things beautiful and right, parent of light and of the lord of light in this visible world, and the immediate source of reason and truth in the intellectual; and that this is the power upon which he who would act rationally either in public or private life must have his eye fixed.

I agree, he said, as far as I am able to understand you.

Moreover, I said, you must not wonder that those who attain to this beatific vision are unwilling to descend to human affairs; for their souls are ever hastening into the upper world where they desire to dwell; which desire of theirs is very natural, if our allegory may be trusted.

Yes, very natural.

And is there anything surprising in one who passes from divine contemplations to the evil state of man, misbehaving himself in a ridiculous manner; if, while his eyes are blinking and before he has become accustomed to the surrounding darkness, he is compelled to fight in courts of law, or in other places, about the images or the shadows of images of justice, and is endeavoring to meet the conceptions of those who have never yet seen absolute justice?

Anything but surprising, he replied.

Anyone who has common sense will remember that the bewilderments of the eyes are of two kinds, and arise from two causes, either from coming out of the light or from going into the light, which is true of the mind's eye, quite as much as of the bodily eye; and he who remembers this when he sees anyone whose vision is perplexed and weak, will not be too ready to laugh; he will first ask whether that soul of man has come out of the brighter life, and is unable to see because unaccustomed to the dark, or having turned from darkness to the day is dazzled by excess light. And he will count the one happy in his condition and state of being, and he will pity the other; or, if he have a mind to laugh at the soul which comes from below into the light, there will be more reason in this than in the laugh which greets him who returns from above out of the light into the den.

That, he said, is a very just distinction.

But then, if I am right, certain professors of education must be wrong when they say that they can put a knowledge into the soul which was not there before, like sight into blind eyes.

They undoubtedly say this, he replied.

Whereas, our argument shows that the power and capacity of learning exists in the soul already; and that just as the eye was unable to turn from darkness to light without the whole body, so too the instrument of knowledge can only by the movement of the whole soul be turned from the world of becoming into that of being, and learn by degrees to endure the sight of being, and of the brightest and best of being, or in other words, of the good.

Very true.

And must there not be some art which will effect conversion in the easiest and quickest manner; not implanting the faculty of sight, for that exists already, but has been turned in the wrong direction, and is looking away from the truth?

Yes, he said, such an art may be presumed.

And whereas the other so-called virtues of the soul seem to be akin to bodily qualities, for even when they are not originally innate they can be implanted later by habit and exercise, the virtue of wisdom more than anything else contains a divine element which always remains, and by this conversion is rendered useful and profitable; or, on the other hand, hurtful and useless. Did you never observe the narrow intelligence flashing from the keen eye of a clever rogue—how eager he is, how clearly his paltry soul sees the way to his end; he is the reverse of blind, but his keen eyesight is forced into the service of evil, and he is mischievous in proportion to his cleverness?

519

Very true, he said.

But what if there had been a circumcision of such natures in the days of their youth; and they had been severed from those sensual pleasures, such as eating and drinking, which, like leaden weights, were attached to them at their birth, and which drag they down and turn the vision of their souls upon the things that are below—if, I say, they had been released from these impediments and turned in the opposite direction, the very same faculty in them would have seen the truth as keenly as they see what their eyes are turned to now.

Very likely.

Yes, I said; and there is another thing which is likely, or rather a necessary inference from what has preceded, that neither the uneducated and uninformed of the truth, nor yet those who never make an end of their education, will be able ministers of State; not the former, because they have no single aim of duty which is the rule of all their actions, private as well as public; nor the latter, because they will not act at all except upon compulsion, fancying that they are already dwelling apart in the islands of the blest.

Very true, he replied.

Then, I said, the business of us who are the founders of the State will be to compel the best minds to attain that knowledge which we have already shown to be the greatest of all—they must

continue to ascend until they arrive at the good;
but when they have ascended and seen enough we
must not allow them to do as they do now.

What do you mean?

I mean that they remain in the upper world: but
this must not be allowed; they must be made to
descend again among the prisoners in the den, and
partake of their labors and honors, whether they are
worth having or not.

But is not this unjust? he said; ought we to give
them a worse life, when they might have a better?

You have again forgotten, my friend, I said, the
intention of the legislator, who did not aim at making any one class in the State happy above the rest;
the happiness was to be in the whole State, and he
held the citizens together by persuasion and necessity, making them benefactors of the State, and there- 520
fore benefactors of one another; to this end he
created them, not to please themselves, but to be
his instruments in binding up the State.

True, he said, I had forgotten.

Observe, Glaucon, that there will be no injustice
in compelling our philosophers to have a care and
providence of others; we shall explain to them that
in other States, men of their class are not obliged
to share in the toils of politics: and this is reasonable, for they grow up at their own sweet will, and
the government would rather not have them. Being
self-taught, they cannot be expected to show any
gratitude for a culture which they have never received. But we have brought you into the world to
be rulers of the hive, kings of yourselves and of the
other citizens, and have educated you far better and
more perfectly than they have been educated, and
you are better able to share in the double duty.
Wherefore each of you, when his turn comes, must
go down to the general underground abode, and get
the habit of seeing in the dark. When you have
acquired the habit, you will see ten thousand times
better than the inhabitants of the den, and you will
know what the several images are, and what they
represent, because you have seen the beautiful and
just and good in their truth. And thus our State
which is also yours will be a reality, and not a

dream only, and will be administered in a spirit unlike that of other States, in which men fight with one another about shadows only and are distracted in the struggle for power, which in their eyes is a great good. Whereas the truth is that the State in which the rulers are most reluctant to govern is always the best and most quietly governed, and the State in which they are most eager, the worst.

Quite true, he replied.

And will our pupils, when they hear this, refuse to take their turn at the toils of State, when they are allowed to spend the greater part of their time with one another in the heavenly light?

Impossible, he answered; for they are just men, and the commands which we impose upon them are just; there can be no doubt that every one of them will take office as a stern necessity, and not after the fashion of our present rulers of State.

Yes, my friend, I said; and there lies the point. You must contrive for your future rulers another and a better life than that of a ruler, and then you may have a well-ordered State; for only in the State which offers this, will they rule who are truly rich, not in silver and gold, but in virtue and wisdom, which are the true blessings of life. Whereas if they go to the administration of public affairs, poor and hungering after their own private advantage, thinking that hence they are to snatch the chief good, order there can never be; for they will be fighting about office, and the civil and domestic broils which thus arise will be the ruin of the rulers themselves and of the whole State.

Most true, he replied.

And the only life which looks down upon the life of political ambition is that of true philosophy. Do you know of any other?

Indeed, I do not, he said.

And those who govern ought not to be lovers of the task? For, if they are, there will be rival lovers, and they will fight.

No question.

Who then are those whom we shall compel to be guardians? Surely they will be the men who are wisest about affairs of State, and by whom the

State is best administered, and who at the same time have other honors and another and a better life than that of politics?

They are the men, and I will choose them, he replied.

And now shall we consider in what way such guardians will be produced, and how they are to be brought from darkness to light—as some are said to have ascended from the world below to the gods?

By all means, he replied.

The process, I said, is not the turning over of an oyster-shell,[6] but the turning round of a soul passing from a day which is little better than night to the true day of being, that is, the ascent from below,[7] which we affirm to be true philosophy?

Quite so.

And should we not inquire what sort of knowledge has the power of effecting such a change?

Certainly.

What sort of knowledge is there which would draw the soul from becoming to being? And another consideration has just occurred to me: You will remember that our young men are to be warrior athletes?

Yes, that was said.

Then this new kind of knowledge must have an additional quality?

What quality?

Usefulness in war.

Yes, if possible.

There were two parts in our former scheme of education, were there not?

Just so.

There was gymnastic which presided over the growth and decay of the body, and may therefore be regarded as having to do with generation and corruption?

True.

[6] In allusion to a game in which two parties fled or pursued according as an oyster-shell which was thrown into the air fell with the dark or light side uppermost.
[7] Reading οὖσαν ἐπάνοδον.

Then that is not the knowledge which we are seeking to discover?

No.

But what do you say of music, what also entered to a certain extent into our former scheme?

Music, he said, as you will remember, was the counterpart of gymnastic, and trained the guardians by the influences of habit, by harmony making them harmonious, by rhythm rhythmical, but not giving them science; and the words whether fabulous or possibly true, had kindred elements of rhythm and harmony in them. But in music there was nothing which tended to that good which you are now seeking.

You are most accurate, I said, in your recollection; in music there certainly was nothing of the kind. But what branch of knowledge is there, my dear Glaucon, which is of the desired nature; since all the useful arts were reckoned mean by us?

Undoubtedly; and yet if music and gymnastic are excluded, and the arts are also excluded, what remains?

Well, I said, there may be nothing left of our special subjects; and then we shall have to take something which is not special, but of universal application.

What may that be?

A something which all arts and sciences and intelligences use in common, and which everyone first has to learn among the elements of education.

What is that?

The little matter of distinguishing one, two, and three—in a word, number and calculation:—do not all arts and sciences necessarily partake of them?

Yes.

Then the art of war partakes of them?

To be sure.

Then Palamedes, whenever he appears in tragedy, proves Agamemnon ridiculously unfit to be a general. Did you never remark how he declares that he had invented number, and had numbered the ships and set in array the ranks of the army at Troy; which implies that they had never been numbered before, and Agamemnon must be supposed literally to have been incapable of counting his own feet—how could he if he was ignorant of number? And if that is true, what sort of general must he have been?

I should say a very strange one, if this was as you say.

Can we deny that a warrior should have a knowledge of arithmetic?

Certainly he should, if he is to have the smallest understanding of military tactics, or indeed, I should rather say, if he is to be a man at all.

I should like to know whether you have the same notion which I have of this study?

What is your notion?

It appears to me to be a study of the kind which we are seeking, and which leads naturally to reflection, but never to have been rightly used; for the true use of it is simply to draw the soul towards being.

523

Will you explain your meaning? he said.

I will try, I said; and I wish you would share the inquiry with me, and say "yes" or "no" when I attempt to distinguish in my own mind what branches of knowledge have this attracting power, in order that we may have clearer proof that arithmetic is, as I suspect, one of them.

Explain, he said.

I mean to say that objects of sense are of two kinds; some of them do not invite thought because the sense is an adequate judge of them; while in the case of other objects sense is so untrustworthy that further inquiry is imperatively demanded.

You are clearly referring, he said, to the manner in which the senses are imposed upon by distance, and by painting in light and shade.

No, I said, that is not at all my meaning.

Then what is your meaning?

When speaking of uninviting objects, I mean those which do not pass from one sensation to the opposite; inviting objects are those which do; in this latter case the sense coming upon the object, whether at a distance or near, gives no more vivid idea of anything in particular than of its opposite.

An illustration will make my meaning clearer:—
here are three fingers—a little finger, a second finger,
and a middle finger.

Very good.

You may suppose that they are seen quite close:
And here comes the point.

What is it?

Each of them equally appears a finger, whether
seen in the middle or at the extremity, whether white
or black, or thick or thin—it makes no difference;
a finger is a finger all the same. In these cases a
man is not compelled to ask of thought the question
what is a finger? for the sight never intimates to
the mind that a finger is other than a finger.

True.

And therefore, I said, as we might expect, there
is nothing here which invites or excites intelligence.

There is not, he said.

But is this equally true of the greatness and smallness of the fingers? Can sight adequately perceive
them? and is no difference made by the circumstance
that one of the fingers is in the middle and another
at the extremity? And in like manner does the touch
adequately perceive the qualities of thickness or thin-
ness, of softness or hardness? And so of the other
senses; do they give perfect intimations of such matters? Is not their mode of operation on this wise—   524
the sense which is concerned with the quality of
hardness is necessarily concerned also with the
quality of softness, and only intimates to the soul
that the same thing is felt to be both hard and soft?

You are quite right, he said.

And must not the soul be perplexed at this intimation which the sense gives of a hard which is also
soft? What, again, is the meaning of light and heavy,
if that which is light is also heavy, and that which is
heavy, light?

Yes, he said, these intimations which the soul
receives are very curious and require to be explained.

Yes, I said, and in these perplexities the soul
naturally summons to her aid calculation and intelligence, that she may see whether the several objects
announced to her are one or two.

True.

And if they turn out to be two, is not each of them one and different?

Certainly.

And if each is one, and both are two, she will conceive the two as in a state of division, for if they were undivided they could only be conceived of as one?

True.

The eye certainly did see both small and great, but only in a confused manner; they were not distinguished.

Yes.

Whereas the thinking mind, intending to light up the chaos, was compelled to reverse the process, and look at small and great as separate and not confused.

Very true.

Was not this the beginning of the inquiry "What is great?" and "What is small?"

Exactly so.

And thus arose the distinction of the visible and the intelligible.

Most true.

This was what I meant when I spoke of impressions which invited the intellect, or the reverse—those which are simultaneous with opposite impressions, invite thought; those which are not simultaneous do not.

I understand, he said, and agree with you.

And to which class do unity and number belong?

I do not know, he replied.

Think a little and you will see that what has preceded will supply the answer; for if simple unity could be adequately perceived by the sight or by any other sense, then, as we were saying in the case of the finger, there would be nothing to attract towards being; but when there is some contradiction always present, and one is the reverse of one and involves the conception of plurality, then thought begins to be aroused within us, and the soul perplexed and wanting to arrive at a decision asks "What is absolute unity?" This is the way in which

the study of the one has a power of drawing and
converting the mind to the contemplation of true
being.

And surely, he said, this occurs notably in the
case of one; for we see the same thing to be both
one and infinite in multitude?

Yes, I said; and this being true of one must be
equally true of all number?

Certainly.

And all arithmetic and calculation have to do with
number?

Yes.

And they appear to lead the mind towards truth?

Yes, in a very remarkable manner.

Then this is knowledge of the kind for which
we are seeking, having a double use, military and
philosophical; for the man of war must learn the art
of number or he will not know how to array his
troops; and the philosopher also, because he has to
rise out of the sea of change and lay hold of true
being, and therefore he must be an arithmetician.

That is true.

And our guardian is both warrior and philosopher?

Certainly.

Then this is a kind of knowledge which legislation
may fitly prescribe; and we must endeavor to persuade those who are to be the principal men of our
State to go and learn arithmetic, not as amateurs,
but they must carry on the study until they see the
nature of numbers with the mind only; nor again,
like merchants or retail-traders, with a view to
buying or selling, but for the sake of their military
use, and of the soul herself; and because this will
be the easiest way for her to pass from becoming
to truth and being.

That is excellent, he said.

Yes, I said, and now having spoken of it, I must
add how charming the science is! and in how many
ways it conduces to our desired end, if pursued in
the spirit of a philosopher, and not of a shopkeeper!

How do you mean?

I mean, as I was saying, that arithmetic has a very
great and elevating effect, compelling the soul to
reason about abstract number, and rebelling against

the introduction of visible or tangible objects into the argument. You know how steadily the masters of the art repel and ridicule anyone who attempts to divide absolute unity when he is calculating, and if you divide, they multiply,[8] taking care that one shall continue one and not become lost in fractions.

That is very true.

Now, suppose a person were to say to them: O my friends, what are these wonderful numbers about which you are reasoning, in which, as you say, there is a unity such as you demand, and each unit is equal, invariable, indivisible—what would they answer?

They would answer, as I should conceive, that they were speaking of those numbers which can only be realized in thought.

Then you see that this knowledge may be truly called necessary, necessitating as it clearly does the use of the pure intelligence in the attainment of pure truth?

Yes; that is a marked characteristic of it.

And have you further observed, that those who have a natural talent for calculation are generally quick at every other kind of knowledge; and even the dull, if they have had an arithmetical training, although they may derive no other advantage from it, always becomes much quicker than they would otherwise have been.

Very true, he said.

And indeed, you will not easily find a more difficult study, and not many as difficult.

You will not.

And, for all these reasons, arithmetic is a kind of knowledge in which the best natures should be trained, and which must not be given up.

I agree.

Let this then be made one of our subjects of education. And next, shall we inquire whether the kindred science also concerns us?

---

[8] Meaning either (1) that they integrate the number because they deny the possibility of fractions; or (2) that division is regarded by them as a process of multiplication, for the fractions of one continue to be units.

You mean geometry?

Exactly so.

Clearly, he said, we are concerned with that part of geometry which relates to war; for in pitching a camp, or taking up a position, or closing or extending the lines of an army, or any other military maneuver, whether in actual battle or on a march, it will make all the difference whether a general is or is not a geometrician.

Yes, I said, but for that purpose a very little of either geometry or calculation will be enough; the question relates rather to the greater and more advanced part of geometry—whether that tends in any degree to make more easy the vision of the idea of good; and thither, as I was saying, all things tend which compel the soul to turn her gaze towards that place, where is the full perfection of being, which she ought, by all means, to behold.

True, he said.

Then if geometry compels us to view being, it concerns us; if becoming only, it does not concern us?

Yes, that is what we assert.

527

Yet anybody who has the least acquaintance with geometry will not deny that such a conception of the science is in flat contradiction to the ordinary language of geometricians.

How so?

They have in view practice only, and are always speaking, in a narrow and ridiculous manner, of squaring and extending and applying and the like— they confuse the necessities of geometry with those of daily life; whereas knowledge is the real object of the whole science.

Certainly, he said.

Then must not a further admission be made?

What admission?

That the knowledge at which geometry aims is knowledge of the eternal, and not of aught perishing and transient.

That, he replied, may be readily allowed, and is true.

Then, my noble friend, geometry will draw the soul towards truth, and create the spirit of philosophy, and raise up that which is now unhappily allowed to fall down.

Nothing will be more likely to have such an effect.

Then nothing should be more sternly laid down than that the inhabitants of your fair city should by all means learn geometry. Moreover the science has indirect effects, which are not small.

Of what kind? he said.

There are the military advantages of which you spoke, I said; and in all departments of knowledge, as experience proves, anyone who has studied geometry is infinitely quicker of apprehension than one who has not.

Yes indeed, he said, there is an infinite difference between them.

Then shall we propose this as a second branch of knowledge which our youth will study?

Let us do so, he replied.

And suppose we make astronomy the third—what do you say?

I am strongly inclined to it, he said; the observation of the seasons and of months and years is as essential to the general as it is to the farmer or sailor.

I am amused, I said, at your fear of the world, which makes you guard against the appearance of insisting upon useless studies; and I quite admit the difficulty of believing that in every man there is an eye of the soul which, when by other pursuits lost and dimmed, is by these purified and re-illumined; and is more precious far than ten thousand bodily eyes, for by it alone is truth seen. Now there are two classes of persons: one class of those who will agree with you and will take your words as a revelation; another class to whom they will be utterly unmeaning, and who will naturally deem them to be idle tales, for they see no sort of profit which is to be obtained from them. And therefore you had better decide at once with which of the two you are proposing to argue. You will very likely say with neither, and that your chief aim in carrying on the argument is your own improvement; at the same time you do not grudge to others any benefit which they may receive.

528

I think that I should prefer to carry on the argument mainly on my own behalf.

Then take a step backward, for we have gone wrong in the order of the sciences.

What was the mistake? he said.

After plane geometry, I said, we proceeded at once to solids in revolution, instead of taking solids in themselves; whereas after the second dimension the third, which is concerned with cubes and dimensions of depth, ought to have followed.

That is true, Socrates; but so little seems to be known as yet about these subjects.

Why, yes, I said, and for two reasons:—in the first place, no government patronizes them; this leads to a want of energy in the pursuit of them, and they are difficult; in the second place, students cannot learn them unless they have a director. But then a director can hardly be found, and even if he could, as matters now stand, the students, who are very conceited, would not attend to him. That, however, would be otherwise if the whole State became the director of these studies and gave honor to them; then disciples would want to come, and there would be continuous and earnest search, and discoveries would be made; since even now, disregarded as they are by the world, and maimed of their fair proportions, and although none of their votaries can tell the use of them, still these studies force their way by their natural charm, and very likely, if they had the help of the State, they would some day emerge into light.

Yes, he said, there is a remarkable charm in them. But I do not clearly understand the change in the order. First you began with a geometry of plane surfaces?

Yes, I said.

And you placed astronomy next, and then you made a step backward?

Yes, and I have delayed you by my hurry; the ludicrous state of solid geometry, which, in natural order, should have followed, made me pass over this branch and go on to astronomy, or motion of solids.

True, he said.

Then assuming that the science now omitted would

come into existence if encouraged by the State, let us go on to astronomy, which will be fourth.

The right order, he replied. And now Socrates, as you rebuked the vulgar manner in which I praised astronomy before, my praise shall be given in your own spirit. For everyone, as I think, must see that astronomy compels the soul to look upwards and leads us from this world to another.

Everyone but myself, I said; to everyone else this may be clear, but not to me.

And what then would you say?

I should rather say that those who elevate astronomy into philosophy appear to me to make us look downwards and not upwards.

What do you mean? he asked.

You, I replied, have in your mind a truly sublime conception of our knowledge of the things above. And I dare say that if a person were to throw his head back and study the fretted ceiling, you would still think that his mind was the percipient, and not his eyes. And you are very likely right, and I may be a simpleton: but, in my opinion, that knowledge only which is of being and of the unseen can make the soul look upwards, and whether a man gapes at the heavens or blinks on the ground, seeking to learn some particular of sense, I would deny that he can learn, for nothing of that sort is matter of science; his soul is looking downwards, not upwards, whether his way to knowledge is by water or by land, whether he floats, or only lies on his back.

I acknowledge, he said, the justice of your rebuke. Still I should like to ascertain how astronomy can be learned in any manner more conducive to that knowledge of which we are speaking?

I will tell you, I said: The starry heaven which we behold is wrought upon a visible ground, and therefore, although the fairest and most perfect of visible things, must necessarily be deemed inferior far to the true motions of absolute swiftness and absolute slowness, which are relative to each other, and carry with them that which is contained in them, in the true number and in every true figure. Now, these are to be apprehended by reason and intelligence, but not by sight.

529

True, he replied.

The spangled heavens should be used as a pattern and with a view to that higher knowledge; their beauty is like the beauty of figures or pictures excellently wrought by the hand of Daedalus, or some other great artist, which we may chance to behold; any geometrician who saw them would appreciate the exquisiteness of their workmanship, but he would never dream of thinking that in them he could find the true equal or the true double, or the truth of any other proportion.

530

No, he replied, such an idea would be ridiculous.

And will not a true astronomer have the same feeling when he looks at the movements of the stars? Will he not think that heaven and the things in heaven are framed by the Creator of them in the most perfect manner? But he will never imagine that the proportions of night and day, or of both to the month, or of the month to the year, or of the stars to these and to one another, and any other things that are material and visible can also be eternal and subject to no deviation—that would be absurd; and it is equally absurd to take so much pains in investigating their exact truth.

I quite agree, though I never thought of this before.

Then, I said, in astronomy, as in geometry, we should employ problems, and let the heavens alone if we would approach the subject in the right way and so make the natural gift of reason to be of any real use.

That, he said, is a work infinitely beyond our present astronomers.

Yes, I said; and there are many other things which must also have a similar extension given to them, if our legislation is to be of any value. But can you tell me of any other suitable study?

No, he said, not without thinking.

Motion, I said, has many forms, and not one only; two of them are obvious enough even to wits no better than ours; and there are others, as I imagine, which may be left to wiser persons.

But where are the two?

There is a second, I said, which is the counterpart of the one already named.

And what may that be?

The second, I said, would seem relatively to the ears to be what the first is to the eyes; for I conceive that as the eyes are designed to look up at the stars, so are the ears to hear harmonious motions; and these are sister sciences—as the Pythagoreans say, and we, Glaucon, agree with them?

Yes, he replied.

But this, I said, is a laborious study, and therefore we had better go and learn of them; and they will tell us whether there are any other applications of these sciences. At the same time, we must not lose sight of our own higher object.

What is that?

There is a perfection which all knowledge ought to reach, and which our pupils ought also to attain, and not to fall short of, as I was saying that they did in astronomy. For in the science of harmony, as you probably know, the same thing happens. The teachers of harmony compare the sounds and consonances which are heard only, and their labor, like that of the astronomers, is in vain.

531

Yes, by heaven! he said; and 'tis as good as a play to hear them talking about their condensed notes, as they call them; they put their ears close alongside of the strings like persons catching a sound from their neighbor's wall[9]——one set of them declaring that they distinguish an intermediate note and have found the least interval which should be the unit of measurement; the others insisting that the two sounds have passed into the same—either party setting their ears before their understanding.

You mean, I said, those gentlemen who tease and torture the strings and rack them on the pegs of the instrument: I might carry on the metaphor and speak after their manner of the blows which the plectrum gives, and make accusations against the strings, both of backwardness and forwardness to

[9] Or, "close alongside of their neighbour's instruments, as if to catch a sound from them."

sound; but this would be tedious, and therefore I will only say that these are not the men, and that I am referring to the Pythagoreans, of whom I was just now proposing to inquire about harmony. For they too are in error, like the astronomers; they investigate the numbers of the harmonies which are heard, but they never attain to problems—that is to say, they never reach the natural harmonies of number, or reflect why some numbers are harmonious and others not.

That, he said, is a thing of more than mortal knowledge.

A thing, I replied, which I would rather call useful; that is, if sought after with a view to the beautiful and good; but if pursued in any other spirit, useless.

Very true, he said.

Now, when all these studies reach the point of intercommunion and connection with one another, and come to be considered in their mutual affinities, then, I think, but not till then, will the pursuit of them have a value for our objects; otherwise there is no profit in them.

I suspect so; but you are speaking, Socrates, of a vast work.

What do you mean? I said; the prelude or what? Do you not know that all this is but the prelude to the actual strain which we have to learn? For you surely would not regard the skilled mathematician as a dialectician?

Assuredly not, he said; I have hardly ever known a mathematician who was capable of reasoning.

But do you imagine that men who are unable to give and take a reason will have the knowledge which we require of them?

Neither can this be supposed.

And so, Glaucon, I said, we have at last arrived at the hymn of dialectic. This is that strain which is of the intellect only, but which the faculty of sight will nevertheless be found to imitate; for sight, as you may remember, was imagined by us after a while to behold the real animals and stars, and last of all the sun himself. And so with dialectic; when a person starts on the discovery of the absolute by the light of reason only, and without any assistance of sense, and perseveres until by pure intelligence he arrives at the perception of the absolute good, he at last finds himself at the end of the intellectual world, as in the case of sight at the end of the visible.

Exactly, he said.

Then this is the progress which you call dialectic?

True.

But the release of the prisoners from chains, and their translation from the shadows to the images and to the light, and the ascent from the underground den to the sun, while in his presence they are vainly trying to look on animals and plants and the light of the sun, but are able to perceive even with their weak eyes the images[10] in the water [which are divine], and are the shadows of true existence (not shadows of images cast by a light of fire, which compared with the sun is only an image)—this power of elevating the highest principle in the soul to the contemplation of that which is best in existence, with which we may compare the raising of that faculty which is the very light of the body to the sight of that which is brightest in the material and visible world—this power is given, as I was saying, by all that study and pursuit of the arts which has been described.

I agree in what you are saying, he replied, which may be hard to believe, yet, from another point of view, is harder still to deny. This however is not a theme to be treated of in passing only, but will have to be discussed again and again. And so, whether our conclusion be true or false, let us assume all this, and proceed at once from the prelude or preamble to the chief strain,[11] and describe that in like manner. Say, then, what is the nature and what are the divisions of dialectic, and what are the paths which lead thither; for these paths will also lead to our final rest.

[10] Omitting ἐνταῦθα δὲ πρὸς φαντάσματα. The word θεῖα is bracketed by Stallbaum.

[11] A play upon the word νόμος, which means both "law" and "strain."

Dear Glaucon, I said, you will not be able to follow me here, though I would do my best, and you should behold not an image only but the absolute truth, according to my notion. Whether what I told you would or would not have been a reality I cannot venture to say; but you would have seen something like reality; of that I am confident.

Doubtless, he replied.

But I must also remind you, that the power of dialectic alone can reveal this, and only to one who is a disciple of the previous sciences.

Of that assertion you may be as confident as of the last.

And assuredly no one will argue that there is any other method of comprehending by any regular process all true existence or of ascertaining that each thing is in its own nature; for the arts in general are concerned with the desires or opinions of men, or are cultivated with a view to production and construction, or for the preservation of such productions and constructions; and as to the mathematical sciences which, as we were saying, have some apprehension of true being—geometry and the like—they only dream about being, but never can they behold the waking reality so long as they leave the hypotheses which they use unexamined, and are unable to give an account of them. For when a man knows not his own first principle, and when the conclusion and intermediate steps are also constructed out of he knows not what, how can he imagine that such a fabric of convention can ever become science?

Impossible, he said.

Then dialectic, and dialectic alone, goes directly to the first principle and is the only science which does away with hypotheses in order to make her ground secure; the eye of the soul, which is literally buried in an outlandish slough, is by her gentle aid lifted upwards; and she uses as handmaids and helpers in the work of conversion, the sciences which we have been discussing. Custom terms them sciences, but they ought to have some other name, implying greater clearness than opinion and less clearness than science: and this, in our previous sketch, was called understanding. But why should we dispute about names when we have realities of such importance to consider?

Why indeed, he said, when any name will do which expresses the thought of the mind with clearness?

At any rate, we are satisfied, as before, to have four divisions; two for intellect and two for opinion, and to call the first division science, the second understanding, the third belief, and the fourth perception of shadows, opinion being concerned with becoming, and intellect with being; and so to make a proportion: As being is to becoming, so is pure intellect to opinion. And as intellect is to opinion, so is science to belief, and understanding to the perception of shadows. But let us defer the further correlation and subdivision of the subjects of opinion and of intellect, for it will be a long inquiry, many times longer than this has been.

534

As far as I understand, he said, I agree.

And do you also agree, I said, in describing the dialectician as one who attains a conception of the essence of each thing? And he who does not possess and is therefore unable to impart this conception, in whatever degree he fails, may in that degree also be said to fail in intelligence? Will you admit so much?

Yes, he said; how can I deny it?

And you would say the same of the conception of the good? Until the person is able to abstract and define rationally the idea of good, and unless he can run the gauntlet of all objections, and is ready to disprove them, not by appeals to opinion, but to absolute truth, never faltering at any step of the argument—unless he can do all this, you would say that he knows neither the idea of good nor any other good; he apprehends only a shadow, if anything at all, which is given by opinion and not by science;—dreaming and slumbering in this life, before he is well awake here, he arrives at the world below, and has his final quietus.

In all that I should most certainly agree with you.

And surely you would not have the children of your ideal State, whom you are nurturing and educating—if the ideal ever becomes a reality—you would not allow the future rulers to be like posts,[12] having no reason in them, and yet to be set in authority over the highest matters?

Certainly not.

Then you will make a law that they shall have such an education as will enable them to attain the greatest skill in asking and answering questions?

Yes, he said, you and I together will make it.

Dialectic, then, as you will agree, is the coping-stone of the sciences, and is set over them; no other science can be placed higher—the nature of knowledge can no further go?

I agree, he said.

But to whom we are to assign these studies, and   535 in what way they are to be assigned, are questions which remain to be considered.

Yes, clearly.

You remember, I said, how the rulers were chosen before?

Certainly, he said.

The same natures must still be chosen, and the preference again given to the surest and the bravest, and, if possible, to the fairest; and, having noble and generous tempers, they should also have the natural gifts which will facilitate their education.

And what are these?

Such gifts as keenness and ready powers of acquisition; for the mind more often faints from the severity of study than from the severity of gymnastics: the toil is more entirely the mind's own, and is not shared with the body.

Very true, he replied.

Further, he of whom we are in search should have a good memory, and be an unwearied solid man who is a lover of labor in any line; or he will never be able to endure the great amount of bodily exercise and to go through all the intellectual discipline and study which we require of him.

Certainly, he said; he must have natural gifts.

The mistake at present is, that those who study philosophy have no vocation, and this, as I was

_____

[12] γραμμάς, literally "lines," probably the starting-point of a race-course.

before saying, is the reason why she has fallen into disrepute: her true sons should take her by the hand and not bastards.

What do you mean?

In the first place, her votary should not have a lame or halting industry—I mean, that he should not be half industrious and half idle: as, for example, when a man is a lover of gymnastic and hunting, and all other bodily exercises, but a hater rather than a lover of the labor of learning or listening or inquiring. Or the occupation to which he devotes himself may be of an opposite kind, and he may have the other sort of lameness.

Certainly, he said.

And as to truth, I said, is not a soul equally to be deemed halt and lame which hates voluntary falsehood and is extremely indignant at herself and others when they tell lies, but is patient of involuntary falsehood, and does not mind wallowing like a swinish beast in the mire of ignorance, and has no shame at being detected?

To be sure.

And, again, in respect of temperance, courage, magnificence, and every other virtue, should we not carefully distinguish between the true son and the bastard? for where there is no discernment of such qualities states and individuals unconsciously err; and the state makes a ruler, and the individual a friend, of one who, being defective in some part of virtue, is in a figure lame or a bastard.

That is very true, he said.

All these things, then, will have to be carefully considered by us; and if only those whom we introduce to this vast system of education and training are sound in body and mind, justice herself will have nothing to say against us, and we shall be the saviors of the constitution and of the State; but, if our pupils are men of another stamp, the reverse will happen, and we shall pour a still greater flood of ridicule on philosophy than she has to endure at present.

That would not be creditable.

Certainly not, I said; and yet perhaps, in thus turning jest into earnest I am equally ridiculous.

536

In what respect?

I had forgotten, I said, that we were not serious, and spoke with too much excitement. For when I saw philosophy so undeservedly trampled under foot of men I could not help feeling a sort of indignation at the authors of her disgrace: and my anger made me too vehement.

Indeed! I was listening, and did not think so.

But I, who am the speaker, felt that I was. And now let me remind you that, although in our former selection we chose old men, we must not do so in this. Solon was under a delusion when he said that a man when he grows old may learn many things—for he can no more learn much than he can run much; youth is the time for any extraordinary toil.

Of course.

And, therefore, calculation and geometry and all the other elements of instruction, which are a preparation for dialectic, should be presented to the mind in childhood; not, however, under any notion of forcing our system of education.

Why not?

Because a freeman ought not to be a slave in the acquisition of knowledge of any kind. Bodily exercise, when compulsory, does no harm to the body; but knowledge which is acquired under compulsion obtains no hold on the mind.

Very true.

Then, my good friend, I said, do not use compulsion, but let early education be a sort of amusement; you will then be better able to find out the natural bent.

537

That is a very rational notion, he said.

Do you remember that the children, too, were to be taken to see the battle on horseback; and that if there were no danger they were to be brought close up and, like young hounds, have a taste of blood given them?

Yes, I remember.

The same practice may be followed, I said, in all these things—labors, lessons, dangers—and he who is most at home in all of them ought to be enrolled in a select number.

At what age?

At the age when the necessary gymnastics are over: the period whether of two or three years which passes in this sort of training is useless for any other purpose; for sleep and exercise are unpropitious to learning; and the trial of who is first in gymnastic exercises is one of the most important tests to which our youth are subjected.

Certainly, he replied.

After that time those who are selected from the class of twenty years old will be promoted to higher honor, and the sciences which they learned without any order in their early education will now be brought together, and they will be able to see the natural relationship of them to one another and to true being.

Yes, he said, that is the only kind of knowledge which takes lasting root.

Yes, I said; and the capacity for such knowledge is the great criterion of dialectical talent: the comprehensive mind is always the dialectical.

I agree with you, he said.

These, I said, are the points which you must consider; and those who have most of this comprehension, and who are more steadfast in their learning, and in their military and other appointed duties, when they have arrived at the age of thirty will have to be chosen by you out of the select class, and elevated to higher honor; and you will have to prove them by the help of dialectic, in order to learn which of them is able to give up the use of sight and the other senses, and in company with truth to attain absolute being: And here, my friend, great caution is required.

Why great caution?

Do you not remark, I said, how great is the evil which dialectic has introduced?

What evil? he said.

The students of the art are filled with lawlessness.

Quite true, he said.

Do you think that there is anything so very unnatural or inexcusable in their case? or will you make allowance for them?

In what way make allowance?

I want you, I said, by way of parallel, to imagine

a supposititious son who is brought up in great
wealth; he is one of a great and numerous family,
and has many flatterers. When he grows up to manhood, he learns that his alleged are not his real
parents; but who the real are he is unable to discover. Can you guess how he will be likely to behave
towards his flatterers and his supposed parents, first
of all during the period when he is ignorant of the
false relation, and then again when he knows? Or
shall I guess for you?

If you please.

Then I should say, that while he is ignorant of
the truth he will be likely to honor his father and his
mother and his supposed relations more than the
flatterers; he will be less inclined to neglect them
when in need, or to do or say anything against
them; and he will be less willing to disobey them
in any important matter.

He will.

But when he has made the discovery, I should
imagine that he would diminish his honor and regard
for them, and would become more devoted to the
flatterers; their influence over him would greatly
increase; he would now live after their ways, and
openly associate with them, and, unless he were of
an unusually good disposition, he would trouble
himself no more about his supposed parents or other
relations.

Well, all that is very probable. But how is the
image applicable to the disciples of philosophy?

In this way: you know that there are certain
principles about justice and honor, which were
taught us in childhood, and under their parental
authority we have been brought up, obeying and
honoring them.

That is true.

There are also opposite maxims and habits of
pleasure which flatter and attract the soul, but do
not influence those of us who have any sense of
right, and they continue to obey and honor the
maxims of their fathers.

True.

Now, when a man is in this state, and the questioning spirit asks what is fair or honorable, and he

answers as the legislator has taught him, and then arguments many and diverse refute his words, until he is driven into believing that nothing is honorable any more than dishonorable, or just and good any more than the reverse, and so of all the notions which he most valued, do you think that he will still honor and obey them as before?

Impossible.

And when he ceases to think them honorable and natural as heretofore, and he fails to discover the true, can he be expected to pursue any life other than that which flatters his desires?

He cannot.

And from being a keeper of the law he is converted into a breaker of it?

Unquestionably.

Now all this is very natural in students of philosophy such as I have described, and also, as I was just now saying, most excusable.

Yes, he said; and, I may add, pitiable.

Therefore, that your feelings may not be moved to pity about our citizens who are now thirty years of age, every care must be taken in introducing them to dialectic.

Certainly.

There is a danger lest they should taste the dear delight too early; for youngsters, as you may have observed, when they first get the taste in their mouths, argue for amusement, and are always contradicting and refuting others in imitation of those who refute them; like puppy-dogs, they rejoice in pulling and tearing at all who come near them.

Yes, he said, there is nothing which they like better.

And when they have made conquests and received defeats at the hands of many, they violently and speedily get into a way of not believing anything which they believed before, and hence, not only they, but philosophy and all that relates to it is apt to have a bad name with the rest of the world.

Too true, he said.

But when a man begins to get older, he will no longer be guilty of such insanity; he will imitate the dialectician who is seeking for truth, and not the

eristic, who is contradicting for the sake of amusement; and the greater moderation of his character
will increase instead of diminishing the honor of the
pursuit.

Very true, he said.

And did we not make special provision for this,
when we said that the disciples of philosophy were
to be orderly and steadfast, not, as now, any chance
aspirant or intruder?

Very true.

Suppose, I said, the study of philosophy to take
the place of gymnastics and to be continued dili-
gently and earnestly and exclusively for twice the
number of years which were passed in bodily exercise—will that be enough?

Would you say six or four years? he asked.

Say five years, I replied; at the end of the time
they must be sent down again into the den and
compelled to hold any military or other office which
young men are qualified to hold: in this way they
will get their experience of life, and there will be
an opportunity of trying whether, when they are
drawn all manner of ways by temptation, they will
stand firm or flinch.

And how long is this stage of their lives to last? 540

Fifteen years, I answered; and when they have
reached fifty years of age, then let those who still
survive and have distinguished themselves in every
action of their lives and in every branch of knowledge come at last to their consummation; the time
has now arrived at which they must raise the eye of
the soul to the universal light which lightens all
things, and behold the absolute good; for that is the
pattern according to which they are to order the
State and the lives of individuals, and the remainder
of their own lives also; making philosophy their
chief pursuit, but, when their turn comes, toiling
also at politics and ruling for the public good, not as
though they were performing some heroic action, but
simply as a matter of duty; and when they have
brought up in each generation others like themselves and left them in their place to be governors of
the State, then they will depart to the Islands of the
Blest and dwell there; and the city will give them

public memorials and sacrifices and honor them, if the Pythian oracle consent, as demigods, but if not, as in any case blessed and divine.

You are a sculptor, Socrates, and have made statues of our governors faultless in beauty.

Yes, I said, Glaucon, and of our governesses too; for you must not suppose that what I have been saying applies to men only and not to women as far as their natures can go.

There you are right, he said, since we have made them to share in all things like the men.

Well, I said, and you would agree (would you not?) that what has been said about the State and the government is not a mere dream, and although difficult not impossible, but only possible in the way which has been supposed; that is to say, when the true philosopher kings are born in a State, one or more of them, despising the honors of this present world which they deem mean and worthless, esteeming above all things right and the honor that springs from right, and regarding justice as the greatest and most necessary of all things, whose ministers they are, and whose principles will be exalted by them when they set in order their own city?

How will they proceed?

They will begin by sending out into the country all the inhabitants of the city who are more than ten years old, and will take possession of their children, who will be unaffected by the habits of their parents; these they will train in their own habits and laws, I mean in the laws which we have given them: and in this way the State and constitution of which we were speaking will soonest and most easily attain happiness, and the nation which has such a constitution will gain most.

Yes, that will be the best way. And I think, Socrates, that you have very well described how, if ever, such a constitution might come into being.

Enough then of the perfect State, and of the man who bears its image—there is no difficulty in seeing how we shall describe him.

There is no difficulty, he replied; and I agree with you in thinking that nothing more need be said.

Book VIII

And so, Glaucon, we have arrived at the conclusion
that in the perfect State wives and children are to be   543
in common; and that all education and the pursuits
of war and peace are also to be common, and the
best philosophers and the bravest warriors are to be
their kings?

That, replied Glaucon, has been acknowledged.

Yes, I said; and we have further acknowledged
that the governors, when appointed themselves, will
take their soldiers and place them in houses such
as we were describing, which are common to all, and
contain nothing private, or individual; and about
their property, you remember what we agreed?

Yes, I remember that no one was to have any of
the ordinary possessions of mankind; they were
to be warrior athletes and guardians, receiving from
the other citizens, in lieu of annual payment, only
their maintenance, and they were to take care of
themselves and of the whole State.

True, I said; and now that this division of our
task is concluded, let us find the point at which we
digressed, that we may return into the old path.

There is no difficulty in returning; you implied,
then as now, that you had finished the description of
the State: you said that such a State was good, and
that the man was good who answered to it, although, as now appears, you had more excellent   544
things to relate both of State and man. And you said
further, that if this was the true form, then the
others were false; and of the false forms, you said,
as I remember, that there were four principal ones,
and that their defects, and the defects of the individuals corresponding to them, were worth examining. When we had seen all the individuals, and
finally agreed as to who was the best and who was
the worst of them, we were to consider whether the
best was not also the happiest, and the worst the
most miserable. I asked you what were the four
forms of government of which you spoke, and then

Polemarchus and Adeimantus put in their word; and you began again, and have found your way to the point at which we have now arrived.

Your recollection, I said, is most exact.

Then, like a wrestler, he replied, you must put yourself again in the same position; and let me ask the same questions, and do you give me the same answer which you were about to give me then.

Yes, if I can, I will, I said.

I shall particularly wish to hear what were the four constitutions of which you were speaking.

That question, I said, is easily answered: the four governments of which I spoke, so far as they have distinct names, are, first, those of Crete and Sparta, which are generally applauded; what is termed oligarchy comes next; this is not equally approved, and is a form of government which teems with evils: thirdly, democracy, which naturally follows oligarchy, although very different: and lastly comes tyranny, great and famous, which differs from them all, and is the fourth and worst disorder of a State. I do not know, do you? of any other constitution which can be said to have a distinct character. There are lordships and principalities which are bought and sold, and some other intermediate forms of government. But these are nondescripts and may be found equally among Hellenes and among barbarians.

Yes, he replied, we certainly hear of many curious forms of government which exist among them.

Do you know, I said, that governments vary as the dispositions of men vary, and that there must be as many of the one as there are of the other? For we cannot suppose that States are made of "oak and rock," and not out of the human natures which are in them, and which in a figure turn the scale and draw other things after them?

Yes, he said, the States are as the men are; they grow out of human characters.

Then if the constitutions of States are five, the dispositions of individual minds will also be five?

Certainly.

Him who answers to aristocracy, and whom we rightly call just and good, we have already described. 545

We have.

Then let us now proceed to describe the inferior sort of natures, being the contentious and ambitious, who answer to the Spartan polity; also the oligarchical, democratical, and tyrannical. Let us place the most just by the side of the most unjust, and when we see them we shall be able to compare the relative happiness or unhappiness of him who leads a life of pure justice or pure injustice. The inquiry will then be completed. And we shall know whether we ought to pursue injustice, as Thrasymachus advises, or in accordance with the conclusions of the argument to prefer justice.

Certainly, he replied, we must do as you say.

Shall we follow our old plan, which we adopted with a view to clearness, of taking the State first and then proceeding to the individual, and begin with the government of honor?—I know of no name for such a government other than timocracy, or perhaps timarchy. We will compare with this the like character in the individual; and, after that, consider oligarchical man; and then again we will turn our attention to democracy and the democratical man; and lastly, we will go and view the city of tyranny, and once more take a look into the tyrant's soul, and try to arrive at a satisfactory decision.

That way of viewing and judging of the matter will be very suitable.

First, then, I said, let us inquire how timocracy (the government of honor) arises out of aristocracy (the government of the best). Clearly, all political changes originate in divisions of the actual governing power; a government which is united, however small, cannot be moved.

Very true, he said.

In what way, then, will our city be moved, and in what manner will the two classes of auxiliaries and rulers disagree among themselves or with one another? Shall we, after the manner of Homer, pray the Muses to tell us "how discord first arose"? Shall we imagine them in solemn mockery, to play and jest with us as if we were children, and to address us in a lofty tragic vein, making believe to be in earnest?

How would they address us?

After this manner:—A city which is thus constituted can hardly be shaken; but, seeing that everything which has a beginning has also an end, even a
constitution such as yours will not last for ever, but
will in time be dissolved. And this is the dissolution:—In plants that grow in the earth, as well as in
animals that move on the earth's surface, fertility
and sterility of soul and body occur when the cir-
cumferences of the circles of each are completed,
which in short-lived existences pass over a short
space, and in long-lived ones over a long space. But
to the knowledge of human fecundity and sterility
all the wisdom and education of your rulers will not
attain; the laws which regulate them will not be
discovered by an intelligence which is alloyed with
sense, but will escape them, and they will bring
children into the world when they ought not. Now
that which is of divine birth has a period which is
contained in a perfect number,[13] but the period of
human birth is comprehended in a number in which
first increments by involution and evolution [*or*
squared and cubed] obtaining three intervals and
four terms of like and unlike, waxing and waning
numbers, make all the terms commensurable and
agreeable to one another.[14] The base of these (3)
with a third added (4) when combined with five
(20) and raised to the third power furnishes two
harmonies; the first a square which is a hundred
times as great ($400=4\times100$),[15] and the other a
figure having one side equal to the former, but oblong,[16] consisting of a hundred numbers squared
upon rational diameters of a square (i.e., omitting
fractions), the side of which is five ($7\times7=49\times$

[13] i.e., a cyclical number, such as 6, which is equal to the
sum of its divisors 1, 2, 3, so that when the circle or time
represented by 6 is completed, the lesser times or rotations
represented by 1, 2, 3, are also completed.
[14] Probably the numbers 3, 4, 5, 6 of which the three first=the
sides of the Pythagorean triangle. The terms will then be 3^3, 4^3,
5^3, which together$=6^3=216$.
[15] Or the first a square which is $100\times100=10,000$. The whole
number will then be $17,500=$a square of 100, and an oblong
of 100 by 75.
[16] Reading προμήκη δέ.

100=4900), each of them being less by one (than the perfect square which includes the fractions, sc. 50) or less by[17] two perfect squares of irrational diameters (of a square the side of which is 5= 50+50=100); and a hundred cubes of three (27 ×100=2700+4900+400=8000). Now this number represents a geometrical figure which has control over the good and evil of births. For when your guardians are ignorant of the law of births, and unite bride and bridegroom out of season, the children will not be goodly or fortunate. And though only the best of them will be appointed by their predecessors, still they will be unworthy to hold their fathers' places, and when they come into power as guardians, they will soon be found to fail in taking care of us, the Muses, first by undervaluing music; which neglect will soon extend to gymnastic; and hence the young men of your State will be less cultivated. In the succeeding generation rulers will be appointed who have lost the guardian power of testing the metal of your different races, which, like Hesiod's, are of gold and silver and brass and iron. And so iron will be mingled with silver, and brass with gold, and hence there will arise dissimilarity and inequality and irregularity, which always and in all places are causes of hatred and war. This the Muses affirm to be the stock from which discord has sprung, wherever arising; and this is their answer to us.

547

Yes, and we may assume that they answer truly.

Why, yes, I said, of course they answer truly; how can the Muses speak falsely?

And what do the Muses say next?

When discord arose, then the two races were drawn different ways: the iron and brass fell to acquiring money and land and houses and gold and silver; but the gold and silver races, not wanting money but having the true riches in their own nature, inclined towards virtue and the ancient order of things. There was a battle between them, and at last they agreed to distribute their land and houses

[17] Or, "consisting of two numbers squared upon irrational diameters," etc.=100.

among individual owners; and they enslaved their friends and maintainers, whom they had formerly protected in the condition of freemen, and made of them subjects and servants; and they themselves were engaged in war and in keeping a watch against them.

I believe that you have rightly conceived the origin of the change.

And the new government which thus arises will be of a form intermediate between oligarchy and aristocracy?

Very true.

Such will be the change, and after the change has been made, how will they proceed? Clearly, the new State, being in a mean between oligarchy and the perfect State, will partly follow one and partly the other, and will also have some peculiarities.

True, he said.

In the honor given to rulers, in the abstinence of the warrior class from agriculture, handicrafts, and trade in general, in the institution of common meals, and in the attention paid to gymnastics and military training—in all these respects this State will resemble the former.

True.

But in the fear of admitting philosophers to power, because they are no longer to be had simple and earnest, but are made up of mixed elements; and in turning from them to passionate and less complex characters, who are by nature fitted for war rather than peace; and in the value set by them upon military stratagems and contrivances, and in the waging of everlasting wars—this State will be for the most part peculiar.

548

Yes.

Yes, I said; and men of this stamp will be covetous of money, like those who live in oligarchies; they will have a fierce secret longing after gold and silver, which they will hoard in dark places, having magazines and treasuries of their own for the deposit and concealment of them; also castles which are just nests for their eggs, and in which they will spend large sums on their wives, or on any others whom they please.

That is most true, he said.

And they are miserly because they have no means of openly acquiring the money which they prize; they will spend that which is another man's on the gratification of their desires, stealing their pleasures and running away like children from the law, their father: they have been schooled not by gentle influences but by force, for they have neglected her who is the true Muse, the companion of reason and philosophy, and have honored gymnastic more than music.

Undoubtedly, he said, the form of government which you describe is a mixture of good and evil.

Why, there is a mixture, I said; but one thing, and one thing only, is predominantly seen—the spirit of contention and ambition; and these are due to the prevalence of the passionate or spirited element.

Assuredly, he said.

Such is the origin and such the character of this State, which has been described in outline only; the more perfect execution was not required, for a sketch is enough to show the type of the most perfectly just and most perfectly unjust; and to go through all the States and all the characters of men, omitting none of them, would be an interminable labor.

Very true, he replied.

Now what man answers to this form of government—how did he come into being, and what is he like?

I think, said Adeimantus, that in the spirit of contention which characterizes him, he is not unlike our friend Glaucon.

Perhaps, I said, he may be like him in that one point; but there are other respects in which he is very different.

In what respects?

He should have more of self-assertion and be less cultivated, and yet a friend of culture; and he should be a good listener, but no speaker. Such a person is apt to be rough with slaves, unlike the educated man, who is too proud for that; and he will also be courteous to freemen, and remarkably obedient to authority; he is a lover of power and a lover of

549

honor; claiming to be a ruler, not because he is eloquent, or on any ground of that sort, but because
he is a soldier and has performed feats of arms; he
is also a lover of gymnastic exercises and of the
chase.

Yes, that is the type of character which answers to
timocracy.

Such an one will despise riches only when he is
young; but as he gets older he will be more and more
attracted to them, because he has a piece of the avaricious nature in him, and is not singleminded
towards virtue, having lost his best guardian.

Who was that? said Adeimantus.

Philosophy, I said, tempered with music, who
comes and takes her abode in a man, and is the only
savior of his virtue throughout life.

Good, he said.

Such, I said, is the timocratical youth, and he is
like the timocratical State.

Exactly.

His origin is as follows:—He is often the young
son of a brave father, who dwells in an ill-governed
city, of which he declines the honors and offices,
and will not go to law, or exert himself in any way,
but is ready to waive his rights in order that he may
escape trouble.

And how does the son come into being?

The character of the son begins to develop when
he hears his mother complaining that her husband
has no place in the government, of which the consequence is that she has no precedence among other
women. Further, when she sees her husband not
very eager about money, and instead of battling
and railing in the law courts or assembly, taking
whatever happens to him quietly; and when she
observes that his thoughts always center in himself,
while he treats her with very considerable indif-
ference, she is annoyed, and says to her son that his
father is only half a man and far too easy-going:
adding all the other complaints about her own ill-
treatment which women are so fond of rehearsing.

Yes, said Adeimantus, they give us plenty of
them, and their complaints are so like themselves.

And you know, I said, that the old servants also,

who are supposesd to be attached to the family,
from time to time talk privately in the same strain
to the son; and if they see anyone who owes money
to his father, or is wronging him in any way, and
he fails to prosecute them, they tell the youth that   550
when he grows up he must retaliate upon people of
this sort, and be more of a man than his father. He
has only to walk abroad and he hears and sees the
same sort of thing: those who do their own business
in the city are called simpletons, and held in no
esteem, while the busybodies are honored and applauded. The result is that the young man, hearing
and seeing all these things—hearing, too, the words
of his father, and having a nearer view of his way
of life, and making comparisons of him and others—
is drawn opposite ways: while his father is watering
and nourishing the rational principle in his soul, the
others are encouraging the passionate and appetitive;
and he being not originally of a bad nature, but
having kept bad company, is at last brought by their
joint influence to a middle point, and gives up the
kingdom which is within him to the middle principle of contentiousness and passion, and becomes
arrogant and ambitious.

You seem to me to have described his origin
perfectly.

Then we have now, I said, the second form of
government and the second type of character?

We have.

Next, let us look at another man who, as Aeschylus says, "Is set over against another State"; or
rather, as our plan requires, begin with the State.

By all means.

I believe that oligarchy follows next in order.

And what manner of government do you term
oligarchy?

A government resting on a valuation of property,
in which the rich have power and the poor man is
deprived of it.

I understand, he replied.

Ought I not to begin by describing how the
change from timocracy to oligarchy arises?

Yes.

Well, I said, no eyes are required in order to see how the one passes into the other.

How?

The accumulation of gold in the treasury of private individuals is the ruin of timocracy; they invent illegal modes of expenditure; for what do they or their wives care about the law?

Yes, indeed.

And then one, seeing another grow rich, seeks to rival him, and thus the great mass of the citizens become lovers of money.

Likely enough.

And so they grow richer and richer, and the more they think of making a fortune the less they think of virtue; for when riches and virtue are placed together in the scales of the balance, the one always rises as the other falls.

True.

And in proportion as riches and rich men are honored in the State, virtue and the virtuous are dishonored.

551

Clearly.

And what is honored is cultivated, and that which has no honor is neglected.

That is obvious.

And so at last, instead of loving contention and glory, men become lovers of trade and money; they honor and look up to the rich man, and make a ruler of him, and dishonor the poor man.

They do so.

They next proceed to make a law which fixes a sum of money as the qualification of citizenship; the sum is higher in one place and lower in another, as the oligarchy is more or less exclusive; and they allow no one whose property falls below the amount fixed to have any share in the government. These changes in the constitution they effect by force of arms. If intimidation has not already done their work.

Very true.

And this, speaking generally, is the way in which oligarchy is established.

Yes, he said; but what are the characteristics of

this form of government, and what are the defects of which we were speaking?[18]

First of all, I said, consider the nature of the qualification. Just think what would happen if pilots were to be chosen according to their property, and a poor man were refused permission to steer, even though he were a better pilot?

You mean that they would shipwreck?

Yes; and is not this true of the government of anything?[19]

I should imagine so.

Except a city?—or would you include a city?

Nay, he said, the case of a city is the strongest of all, inasmuch as the rule of a city is the greatest and most difficult of all.

This, then, will be the first great defect of oligarchy?

Clearly.

And here is another defect which is quite as bad.

What defect?

The inevitable division: such a State is not one, but two States, the one of poor, the other of rich men; and they are living on the same spot and always conspiring against one another.

That, surely, is at least as bad.

Another discreditable feature is, that, for a like reason, they are incapable of carrying on any war. Either they arm the multitude, and then they are more afraid of them than of the enemy; or, if they do not call them out in the hour of battle, they are oligarchs indeed, few to fight as they are few to rule. And at the same time their fondness for money makes them unwilling to pay taxes.

552

How discreditable!

And, as we said before, under such a constitution the same persons have too many callings—they are husbandmen, tradesmen, warriors, all in one. Does that look well?

Anything but well.

There is another evil which is, perhaps, the greatest of all, and to which this State first begins to be liable.

What evil?

A man may sell all that he has, and another may acquire his property; yet after the sale he may dwell in the city of which he is no longer a part, being neither trader, nor artisan, nor horseman, nor hoplite, but only a poor, helpless creature.

Yes, that is an evil which also first begins in this State.

The evil is certainly not prevented there; for oligarchies have both the extremes of great wealth and utter poverty.

True.

But think again: In his wealthy days, while he was spending his money, was a man of this sort a whit more good to the State for the purposes of citizenship? Or did he only seem to be a member of the ruling body, although in truth he was neither ruler nor subject, but just a spendthrift?

As you say, he seemed to be a ruler, but was only a spendthrift.

May we not say that this is the drone in the house who is like the drone in the honeycomb, and that the one is the plague of the city as the other is of the hive?

Just so, Socrates.

And God has made the flying drones, Adeimantus, all without stings, whereas of the walking drones he has made some without stings but others have dreadful stings; of the stingless class are those who in their old age end as paupers; of the stingers come all the criminal class, as they are termed.

Most true, he said.

Clearly then, whenever you see paupers in a State, somewhere in that neighborhood there are hidden away thieves, and cut-purses and robbers of temples, and all sorts of malefactors.

Clearly.

Well, I said, and in oligarchical States do you not find paupers?

Yes, he said; nearly everybody is a pauper who is not a ruler.

And may we be so bold as to affirm that there are also many criminals to be found in them, rogues who have stings, and whom the authorities are careful to restrain by force?

Certainly, we may be so bold.

The existence of such persons is to be attributed to want of education, ill-training, and an evil constitution of the State?

True.

Such, then, is the form and such are the evils of oligarchy; and there may be many other evils.

Very likely.

Then oligarchy, or the form of government in which the rulers are elected for their wealth, may now be dismissed. Let us next proceed to consider the nature and origin of the individual who answers to this State.

553

By all means.

Does not the timocratical man change into the oligarchical on this wise?

How?

A time arrives when the representative of timocracy has a son: at first he begins by emulating his father and walking in his footsteps, but presently he sees him of a sudden foundering against the State as upon a sunken reef, and he and all that he has is lost; he may have been a general or some other high officer who is brought to trial under a prejudice raised by informers, and either put to death, or exiled, or deprived of the privileges of a citizen, and all his property taken from him.

Nothing more likely.

And the son has seen and known all this—he is a ruined man, and his fear has taught him to knock ambition and passion head-foremost from his bosom's throne; humbled by poverty he takes to moneymaking and by mean and miserly savings and hard work gets a fortune together. Is not such an one likely to seat the concupiscent and covetous element on the vacant throne and to suffer it to play the great king within him, girt with tiara and chain and scimitar?

Most true, he replied.

And when he has made reason and spirit sit down

on the ground obediently on either side of their
sovereign, and taught them to know their place, he
compels the one to think only of how lesser sums
may be turned into larger ones, and will not allow
the other to worship and admire anything but riches
and rich men, or to be ambitious of anything so
much as the acquisition of wealth and the means of
acquiring it.

Of all changes, he said, there is none so speedy
or so sure as the conversion of the ambitious youth
into the avaricious one.

And the avaricious, I said, is the oligarchical
youth?

Yes, he said; at any rate the individual out of
whom he came is like the State out of which oligarchy came.

Let us then consider whether there is any likeness
between them.

Very good.

First, then, they resemble one another in the
value which they set upon wealth?

Certainly.

Also in their penurious, laborious character; the
individual only satisfies his necessary appetites, and
confines his expenditure to them; his other desires
he subdues, under the idea that they are un-
profitable.

True.

· He is a shabby fellow, who saves something out
of everything and makes a purse for himself; and
this is the sort of man whom the vulgar applaud.
Is he not a true image of the State which he represents?

He appears to me to be so; at any rate money is
highly valued by him as well as by the State.

You see that he is not a man of cultivation, I said.

I imagine not, he said; had he been educated he
would never have made a blind god director of his
chorus, or given him chief honor.[20]

Excellent! I said. Yet consider: Must we not
further admit that owing to this want of cultivation

[20] Reading καὶ ἐτίμα μάλιστα, Εὖ ἦν δ' ἐγώ, according to
Schneider's excellent emendation.

there will be found in him drone-like desires as of pauper and rogue, which are forcibly kept down by his general habit of life?

True.

Do you know where you will have to look if you want to discover his rogueries?

Where must I look?

You should see him where he has some great opportunity of acting dishonestly, as in the guardianship of an orphan.

Aye.

It will be clear enough then that in his ordinary dealings which give him a reputation for honesty he coerces his bad passions by an enforced virtue; not making them see that they are wrong, or taming them by reason, but by necessity and fear constraining them, and because he trembles for his possessions.

To be sure.

Yes, indeed, my dear friend, but you will find that the natural desires of the drone commonly exist in him all the same whenever he has to spend what is not his own.

Yes, and they will be strong in him too.

The man, then, will be at war with himself; he will be two men, and not one; but, in general, his better desires will be found to prevail over his inferior ones.

True.

For these reasons such an one will be more respectable than most people; yet the true virtue of a unanimous and harmonious soul will flee far away and never come near him.

I should expect so.

And surely, the miser individually will be an ignoble competitor in a State for any prize of victory, or other object of honorable ambition; he will not spend his money in the contest for glory; so afraid is he of awakening his expensive appetites and inviting them to help and join in the struggle; in true oligarchical fashion he fights with a small part only of his resources, and the result commonly is that he loses the prize and saves his money.

555

Very true.

Can we any longer doubt, then, that the miser and money-maker answers to the oligarchical State?

There can be no doubt.

Next comes democracy; of this the origin and nature have still to be considered by us; and then we will inquire into the ways of the democratic man, and bring him up for judgment.

That, he said, is our method.

Well, I said, and how does the change from oligarchy into democracy arise? Is it not on this wise?— The good at which such a state aims is to become as rich as possible, a desire which is insatiable?

What then?

The rulers, being aware that their power rests upon their wealth, refuse to curtail by law the extravagance of the spendthrift youth because they gain by their ruin; they take interest from them and buy up their estates and thus increase their own wealth and importance?

To be sure.

There can be no doubt that the love of wealth and the spirit of moderation cannot exist together in citizens of the same State to any considerable extent; one or the other will be disregarded.

That is tolerably clear.

And in oligarchical States, from the general spread of carelessness and extravagance, men of good family have often been reduced to beggary?

Yes, often.

And still they remain in the city; there they are, ready to sting and fully armed, and some of them owe money, some have forfeited their citizenship; a third class are in both predicaments; and they hate and conspire against those who have got their property, and against everybody else, and are eager for revolution.

That is true.

On the other hand, the men of business, stooping as they walk, and pretending not even to see those whom they have already ruined, insert their sting— that is, their money—into someone else who is not on his guard against them, and recover the parent sum many times over multiplied into a family of children: and so they make drone and pauper to abound in State.

Yes, he said, there are plenty of them—that is 556 certain.

The evil blazes up like a fire; and they will not extinguish it, either by restricting a man's use of his own property, or by another remedy:

What other?

One which is the next best, and has the advantage of compelling the citizens to look to their characters:—Let there be a general rule that everyone shall enter into voluntary contracts at his own risk, and there will be less of this scandalous money-making, and the evils of which we were speaking will be greatly lessened in the State.

Yes, they will be greatly lessened.

At present the governors, induced by the motives which I have named, treat their subjects badly; while they and their adherents, especially the young men of the governing class, are habituated to lead a life of luxury and idleness both of body and mind; they do nothing, and are incapable of resisting either pleasure or pain.

Very true.

They themselves care only for making money, and are as indifferent as the pauper to the cultivation of virtue.

Yes, quite as indifferent.

Such is the state of affairs which prevails among them. And often rulers and their subjects may come in one another's way, whether on a pilgrimage or a march, as fellow-soldiers or fellow-sailors; aye and they may observe the behavior of each other in the very moment of danger—for where danger is, there is no fear that the poor will be despised by the rich —and very likely the wiry sunburnt poor man may be placed in battle at the side of a wealthy one who has never spoilt his complexion and has plenty of superfluous flesh—when he sees such an one puffing and at his wits' end, how can he avoid drawing the conclusion that men like him are only rich because no one has the courage to despoil them? And when they meet in private will not people be saying to one another "Our warriors are not good for much"?

Yes, he said, I am quite aware that this is their way of talking.

And, as in a body which is diseased the addition of a touch from without may bring on illness, and sometimes even when there is no external provocation a commotion may arise within—in the same way wherever there is weakness in the State there is also likely to be illness, of which the occasions may be very slight, the one party introducing from without their oligarchical, the other their democratical allies, and then the State falls sick, and is at war with herself; and may be at times distracted, even when there is no external cause.

Yes, surely.

And then democracy comes into being after the poor have conquered their opponents, slaughtering some and banishing some, while to the remainder they give an equal share of freedom and power; and this is the form of government in which the magistrates are commonly elected by lot.

Yes, he said, that is the nature of democracy, whether the revolution has been effected by arms, or whether fear has caused the opposite party to withdraw.

And now what is their manner of life, and what sort of government have they? for as the government is, such will be the man.

Clearly, he said.

In the first place, are they not free; and is not the city full of freedom and frankness—a man may say and do what he likes?

'Tis said so, he replied.

And where freedom is, the individual is clearly able to order for himself his own life as he pleases?

Clearly.

Then in this kind of State there will be the greatest variety of human natures?

There will.

This, then, seems likely to be the fairest of States, being like an embroidered robe which is spangled with every sort of flower.[21] And just as women and children think a variety of colors to be of all things

557

---

[21] Omitting τί μήν; ἔφη.

most charming, so there are many men to whom this State, which is spangled with the manners and characters of mankind, will appear to be the fairest of States.

Yes.

Yes, my good Sir, and there will be no better in which to look for a government.

Why?

Because of the liberty which reigns there—they have a complete assortment of constitutions; and he who has a mind to establish a State, as we have been doing, must go to a democracy as he would to a bazaar at which they sell them, and pick out the one that suits him; then, when he has made his choice, he may found his State.

He will be sure to have patterns enough.

And there being no necessity, I said, for you to govern in this State, even if you have the capacity, or to be governed, unless you like, or go to war when the rest go to war, or to be at peace when others are at peace, unless you are so disposed— there being no necessity also, because some law forbids you to hold office or be a dicast, that you should not hold office or be a dicast, if you have a fancy—is not this a way of life which for the moment is supremely delightful?

558

For the moment, yes.

And is not their humanity to the condemned[22] in some cases quite charming? Have you not observed how, in a democracy, many persons, although they have been sentenced to death or exile, just stay where they are and walk about the world—the gentleman parades like a hero, and nobody sees or cares?

Yes, he replied, many and many a one.

See too, I said, the forgiving spirit of democracy, and the "don't care" about trifles, and the disregard which she shows of all the fine principles which we solemnly laid down at the foundation of the city— as when we said that, except in the case of some rarely gifted nature, there never will be a good man who has not from his childhood been used to play

[22] Or, "the philosophical temper of the condemned."

amid things of beauty and make of them a joy and a study—how grandly does she trample all these fine notions of ours under her feet, never giving a thought to the pursuits which make a statesman, and promoting to honor anyone who professes to be the people's friend.

Yes, she is of a noble spirit.

These and other kindred characteristics are proper to democracy, which is a charming form of government, full of variety and disorder, and dispensing a sort of equality to equals and unequals alike.

We know her well.

Consider now, I said, what manner of man the individual is, or rather consider, as in the case of the State, how he comes into being.

Very good, he said.

Is not this the way—he is the son of the miserly and oligarchical father who has trained him in his own habits?

Exactly.

And, like his father, he keeps under by force the pleasures which are of the spending and not of the getting sort, being those which are called unnecessary?

Obviously.

Would you like, for the sake of clearness, to distinguish which are the necessary and which are the unnecessary pleasures?

I should.

Are not necessary pleasures those of which we cannot get rid, and of which the satisfaction is a benefit to us? And they are rightly so, because we are framed by nature to desire both what is beneficial and what is necessary, and cannot help it.

True.

559

We are not wrong therefore in calling them necessary?

We are not.

And the desires of which a man may get rid, if he takes pains from his youth upwards—of which the presence, moreover, does no good, and in some cases the reverse of good—shall we not be right in saying that all these are unnecessary?

Yes, certainly.

Suppose we select an example of either kind, in order that we may have a general notion of them?

Very good.

Will not the desire of eating, that is, of simple food and condiments, in so far as they are required for health and strength, be of the necessary class?

That is what I should suppose.

The pleasure of eating is necessary in two ways; it does us good and it is essential to the continuance of life?

Yes.

But the condiments are only necessary in so far as they are good for health?

Certainly.

And the desire which goes beyond this, of more delicate food, or other luxuries, which might generally be got rid of, if controlled and trained in youth, and is hurtful to the body, and hurtful to the soul in the pursuit of wisdom and virtue, may be rightly called unnecessary?

Very true.

May we not say that these desires spend, and that the others make money because they conduce to production?

Certainly.

And of the pleasures of love, and all other pleasures, the same holds good?

True.

And the drone of whom we spoke was he who has surfeited in pleasures and desires of this sort, and was the slave of the unnecessary desires, whereas he who was subject to the necessary only was miserly and oligarchical?

Very true.

Again, let us see how the democratical man grows out of the oligarchical: the following, as I suspect, is commonly the process.

What is the process?

When a young man who has been brought up as we were just now describing, in a vulgar and miserly way, has tasted drones' honey and has come to associate with fierce and crafty natures who are able to provide for him all sorts of refinements and varieties of pleasure—then, as you may imagine, the change will begin of the oligarchical principle within him into the democratical?

Inevitably.

And as in the city like was help like, and the change was effected by an alliance from without assisting one division of the citizens, so too the young man is changed by a class of desires coming from without to assist the desires within him, that which is akin and alike again helping that which is akin and alike?

Certainly.

And if there be any ally which aids the oligarchical principle within him, whether the influence of a father or of kindred, advising or rebuking him, then there arises in his soul a faction and an opposite faction, and he goes to war with himself.

560

It must be so.

And there are times when the democratical principle gives way to the oligarchical, and some of his desires die, and others are banished; a spirit of reverence enters into the young man's soul and order is restored.

Yes, he said, that sometimes happens.

And then, again, after the old desires have been driven out, fresh ones spring up, which are akin to them, and because he their father does not know how to educate them, wax fierce and numerous.

Yes, he said, that is apt to be the way.

They draw him to his old associates, and holding secret intercourse with them, breed and multiply in him.

Very true.

At length they seize upon the citadel of the young man's soul, which they perceive to be void of all accomplishments and fair pursuits and true words, which make their abode in the minds of men who are dear to the gods, and are their best guardians and sentinels.

None better.

False and boastful conceits and phrases mount upwards and take their place.

They are certain to do so.

And so the young man returns into the country of

the lotus-eaters, and takes up his dwelling there in
the face of all men; and if any help be sent by his
friends to the oligarchical part of him, the aforesaid
vain conceits shut the gate of the king's fastness;
and they will neither allow the embassy itself to
enter, nor if private advisers offer the fatherly counsel of the aged will they listen to them or receive
them. There is a battle and they gain the day, and
then modesty, which they call silliness, is ignomini-
ously thrust into exile by them, and temperance,
which they nickname unmanliness, is trampled in
the mire and cast forth; they persuade men that
moderation and orderly expenditure are vulgarity
and meanness, and so, by the help of a rabble of evil
appetites, they drive them beyond the border.

Yes, with a will.

And when they have emptied and swept clean the
soul of him who is now in their power and who is
being initiated by them in great mysteries, the next
thing is to bring back to their house insolence and
anarchy and waste and impudence in bright array
having garlands on their heads, and a great company with them, hymning their praises and calling
them by sweet names; insolence they term breeding,
and anarchy liberty, and waste magnificence, and
impudence courage. And so the young man passes
out of his original nature, which was trained in the
school of necessity, into the freedom and libertinism
of useless and unnecessary pleasures.

Yes, he said, the change in him is visible enough.

After this he lives on, spending his money and
labor and time on unnecessary pleasures quite as
much as on necessary ones; but if he be fortunate,
and is not too much disordered in his wits, when
years have elapsed, and the heyday of passion is over
—supposing that he then re-admits into the city
some part of the exiled virtues, and does not wholly
give himself up to their successors—in that case he
balances his pleasures and lives in a sort of equi-
librium, putting the government of himself into the
hands of the one which comes first and wins the
turn; and when he has had enough of that, then
into the hands of another; he despises none of them
but encourages them all equally.

561

Very true, he said.

Neither does he receive or let pass into the fortress any true word of advice; if anyone says to him that some pleasures are the satisfactions of good and noble desires, and others of evil desires, and that he ought to use and honor some and chastise and master the others—whenever this is repeated to him he shakes his head and says that they are all alike, and that one is as good as another.

Yes, he said; that is the way with him.

Yes, I said, he lives from day to day indulging the appetite of the hour; and sometimes he is lapped in drink and strains of the flute; then he becomes a water-drinker, and tries to get thin; then he takes a turn at gymnastics; sometimes idling and neglecting everything, then once more living the life of a philosopher; often he is busy with politics, and starts to his feet and says and does whatever comes into his head; and, if he is emulous of anyone who is a warrior, off he is in that direction, or of men of business, once more in that. His life has neither law nor order; and this distracted existence he terms joy and bliss and freedom; and so he goes on.

Yes, he replied, he is all liberty and equality.

Yes, I said; his life is motley and manifold and an epitome of the lives of many;—he answers to the State which we described as fair and spangled. And many a man and many a woman will take him for their pattern, and many a constitution and many an example of manners is contained in him.

Just so.

Let him then be set over against democracy; he may truly be called the democratic man. 562

Let that be his place, he said.

Last of all comes the most beautiful of all, man and State alike, tyranny and the tyrant; these we have now to consider.

Quite true, he said.

Say then, my friend, In what manner does tyranny arise?—that it has a democratic origin is evident.

Clearly.

And does not tyranny spring from democracy in the same manner as democracy from oligarchy—I mean, after a sort?

How?

The good which oligarchy proposed to itself and the means by which it was maintained was excess of wealth—am I not right?

Yes.

And the insatiable desire of wealth and the neglect of all other things for the sake of money-getting was also the ruin of oligarchy?

True.

And democracy has her own good, of which the insatiable desire brings her to dissolution?

What good?

Freedom, I replied; which, as they tell you in a democracy, is the glory of the State—and that therefore in a democracy alone will the freeman of nature deign to dwell.

Yes; the saying is in everybody's mouth.

I was going to observe that the insatiable desire of this and the neglect of other things introduces the change in democracy, which occasions a demand for tyranny.

How so?

When a democracy which is thirsting for freedom has evil cupbearers presiding over the feast, and has drunk too deeply of the strong wine of freedom, then, unless her rulers are very amenable and give a plentiful draught, she calls them to account and punishes them, and says that they are cursed oligarchs.

Yes, he replied, a very common occurrence.

Yes, I said; and loyal citizens are insultingly termed by her slaves who hug their chains and men of naught; she would have subjects who are like rulers, and rulers who are like subjects: these are men after her own heart, whom she praises and honors both in private and public. Now, in such a State, can liberty have any limit?

Certainly not.

By degrees the anarchy finds a way into private houses, and ends by getting among the animals and infecting them.

How do you mean?

I mean that the father grows accustomed to descend to the level of his sons and to fear them, and the son is on a level with his father, he having no respect or reverence for either of his parents; and this is his freedom, and the metic is equal with the citizen and the citizen with the metic, and the stranger is quite as good as either.

Yes, he said, that is the way.

And these are not the only evils, I said—there are several lesser ones: In such a state of society the master fears and flatters his scholars, and the scholars despise their masters and tutors; young and old are all alike; and the young man is on a level with the old, and is ready to compete with him in word or deed; and old men condescend to the young and are full of pleasantry and gaiety; they are loth to be thought morose and authoritative, and therefore they adopt the manners of the young.

563

Quite true, he said.

The last extreme of popular liberty is when the slave bought with money, whether male or female, is just as free as his or her purchaser; nor must I forget to tell of the liberty and equality of the sexes in relation to each other.

Why not, as Aeschylus says, utter the word which rises to our lips?

That is what I am doing, I replied; and I must add that no one who does not know would believe, how much greater is the liberty which the animals who are under the dominion of man have in a democracy than in any other State; for truly, the she-dogs, as the proverb says, are as good as their she-mistresses, and the horses and asses have a way of marching along with all the rights and dignities of freemen; and they will run at anybody who comes in their way if he does not leave the road clear for them: and all things are just ready to burst with liberty.

When I take a country walk, he said, I often experience what you describe. You and I have dreamed the same thing.

And above all, I said, and as the result of all, see how sensitive the citizens become; they chafe impatiently at the least touch of authority and at length, as you know, they cease to care even for the laws, written or unwritten; they will have no one over them.

Yes, he said, I know it too well.

Such, my friend, I said, is the fair and glorious beginning out of which springs tyranny.

Glorious indeed, he said. But what is the next step?

The ruin of oligarchy is the ruin of democracy; the same disease magnified and intensified by liberty overmasters democracy—the truth being that the excessive increase of anything often causes a reaction in the opposite direction; and this is the case not only in the seasons and in vegetable and animal life, but above all in forms of government.

564

True.

The excess of liberty, whether in States or individuals, seems only to pass into excess of slavery.

Yes, the natural order.

And so tyranny naturally arises out of democracy, and the most aggravated form of tyranny and slavery out of the most extreme form of liberty?

As we might expect.

That, however, was not, as I believe, your question—you rather desired to know what is that disorder which is generated alike in oligarchy and democracy, and is the ruin of both?

Just so, he replied.

Well, I said, I meant to refer to the class of idle spendthrifts, of whom the more courageous are the leaders and the more timid the followers, the same whom we were comparing to drones, some stingless, and others having stings.

A very just comparison.

These two classes are the plagues of every city in which they are generated, being what phlegm and bile are to the body. And the good physician and lawgiver of the State ought, like the wise beemaster, to keep them at a distance and prevent, if possible, their ever coming in; and if they have anyhow found a way in, then he should have them and their cells cut out as speedily as possible.

Yes, by all means, he said.

Then, in order that we may see clearly what we are doing, let us imagine democracy to be divided, as indeed it is, into three classes; for in the first place freedom creates rather more drones in the democratic than there were in the oligarchical State.

That is true.

And in the democracy they are certainly more intensified.

How so?

Because in the oligarchical State they are disqualified and driven from office, and therefore they cannot train or gather strength; whereas in a democracy they are almost the entire ruling power, and while the keener sort speak and act, the rest keep buzzing about the bema and do not suffer a word to be said on the other side; hence in democracies almost everything is managed by the drones.

Very true, he said.

Then there is another class which is always being severed from the mass.

What is that?

They are the orderly class, which in a nation of traders is sure to be the richest.

Naturally so.

They are the most squeezable persons and yield the largest amount of honey to the drones.

Why, he said, there is little to be squeezed out of people who have little.

And this is called the wealthy class, and the drones feed upon them.

That is pretty much the case, he said.

565

The people are a third class, consisting of those who work with their own hands; they are not politicians, and have not much to live upon. This, when assembled, is the largest and most powerful class in a democracy.

True, he said; but then the multitude is seldom willing to congregate unless they get a little honey.

And do they not share? I said. Do not their leaders deprive the rich of their estates and distribute them among the people; at the same time taking care to reserve the larger part for themselves?

Why, yes, he said, to that extent the people do share.

And the persons whose property is taken from

them are compelled to defend themselves before the people as they best can?

What else can they do?

And then, although they may have no desire of change, the others charge them with plotting against the people and being friends of oligarchy?

True.

And the end is that when they see the people, not of their own accord, but through ignorance, and because they are deceived by informers, seeking to do them wrong, then at last they are forced to become oligarchs in reality; they do not wish to be, but the sting of the drones torments them and breeds revolution in them.

That is exactly the truth.

Then come impeachments and judgments and trials of one another.

True.

The people have always some champion whom they set over them and nurse into greatness.

Yes, that is their way.

This and no other is the root from which a tyrant springs; when he first appears above ground he is a protector.

Yes, that is quite clear.

How then does a protector begin to change into a tyrant? Clearly when he does what the man is said to do in the tale of the Arcadian temple of Lycaean Zeus.

What tale?

The tale is that he who has tasted the entrails of a single human victim minced up with the entrails of other victims is destined to become a wolf. Did you never hear it?

O yes.

And the protector of the people is like him; having a mob entirely at his disposal, he is not restrained from shedding the blood of kinsmen; by the favorite method of false accusation he brings them into court and murders them, making the life of man to disappear, and with unholy tongue and lips tasting the blood of his fellow citizen; some he kills and others he banishes, at the same time hinting at the abolition of debts and partition of lands: and after this, what will be his destiny? Must he not either perish at the hands of his enemies, or from being a man become a wolf—that is, a tyrant?

Inevitably.

This, I said, is he who begins to make a party against the rich?

The same.

After a while he is driven out, but comes back, in spite of his enemies, a tyrant full grown.

That is clear.

And if they are unable to expel him, or to get him condemned to death by a public accusation, they conspire to assassinate him.

Yes, he said, that is their usual way.

Then comes the famous request for a bodyguard, which is the device of all those who have got thus far in their tyrannical career—"Let not the people's friend," as they say, "be lost to them."

Exactly.

The people readily assent; all their fears are for him—they have none for themselves.

Very true.

And when a man who is wealthy and is also ac-cused of being an enemy of the people sees this, then, my friend, as the oracle said to Croesus, "By pebbly Hermus' shore he flees and rests not, and is not ashamed to be a coward."[23]

And quite right too, said he, for if he were, he would never be ashamed again.

But if he is caught he dies.

Of course.

And he, the protector of whom we spoke, is to be seen, not "larding the plain" with his bulk, but him-self the overthrower of many, standing up in the chariot of State with the reins in his hand, no longer protector, but tyrant absolute.

No doubt, he said.

And now let us consider the happiness of the man, and also of the State in which a creature like him is generated.

Yes, he said, let us consider that.

At first, in the early days of his power, he is full

[23] Herod. i. 55.

of smiles, and he salutes everyone whom he meets;
—he to be called a tyrant, who is making promises
in public and also in private! liberating debtors, and
distributing land to the people and his followers, and
wanting to be so kind and good to everyone!

Of course, he said.

But when he has disposed of foreign enemies by
conquest or treaty, and there is nothing to fear from
them, then he is always stirring up some war or
other, in order that the people may require a leader. 567

To be sure.

Has he not also another object, which is that they
may be impoverished by payment of taxes, and thus
compelled to devote themselves to their daily wants
and therefore less likely to conspire against him?

Clearly.

And if any of them are suspected by him of having notions of freedom, and of resistance to his
authority, he will have a good pretext for destroying
them by placing them at the mercy of the enemy;
and for all these reasons the tyrant must be always
getting up a war.

He must.

Now he begins to grow unpopular.

A necessary result.

Then some of those who joined in setting him up,
and who are in power, speak their minds to him
and to one another, and the more courageous of
them cast in his teeth what is being done.

Yes, that may be expected.

And the tyrant, if he means to rule, must get rid
of them; he cannot stop while he has a friend or an
enemy who is good for anything.

He cannot.

And therefore he must look about him and see
who is valiant, who is high-minded, who is wise, who
is wealthy; happy man, he is the enemy of them all,
and must seek occasion against them whether he will
or no, until he has made a purgation of the State.

Yes, he said, and a rare purgation.

Yes, I said, not the sort of purgation which the
physicians make of the body; for they take away
the worse and leave the better part, but he does
the reverse.

If he is to rule, I suppose that he cannot help himself.

What a blessed alternative, I said:—to be compelled to dwell only with the many bad, and to be by them hated, or not to live at all!

Yes, that is the alternative.

And the more detestable his actions are to the citizens the more satellites and the greater devotion in them will he require?

Certainly.

And who are the devoted band, and where will he procure them?

They will flock to him, he said, of their own accord, if he pays them.

By the dog! I said, here are more drones, of every sort and from every land.

Yes, he said, there are.

But will he not desire to get them on the spot?

How do you mean?

He will rob the citizens of their slaves; he will then set them free and enroll them in his bodyguard.

To be sure, he said; and he will be able to trust them best of all.

What a blessed creature, I said, must this tyrant be; he has put to death the others and has these for his trusted friends.

568

Yes, he said; they are quite of his sort.

Yes, I said, and these are the new citizens whom he has called into existence, who admire him and are his companions, while the good hate and avoid him.

Of course.

Verily, then, tragedy is a wise thing and Euripides a great tragedian.

Why so?

Why, because he is the author of the pregnant saying, "Tyrants are wise by living with the wise," and he clearly meant to say that they are the wise whom the tyrant makes his companions.

Yes, he said, and he also praises tyranny as godlike; and many other things of the same kind are said by him and by the other poets.

And therefore, I said, the tragic poets being

wise men will forgive us and any others who live
after our manner if we do not receive them into
our State, because they are the eulogists of tyranny.

Yes, he said, those who have the wit will doubtless forgive us.

But they will continue to go to other cities and
attract mobs, and hire voices fair and loud and
persuasive, and draw the cities over to tyrannies
and democracies.

Very true.

Moreover, they are paid for this and receive honor
—the greatest honor, as might be expected, from
tyrants, and the next greatest from democracies; but
the higher they ascend our constitution hill, the
more their reputation fails, and seems unable from
shortness of breath to proceed further.

True.

But we are wandering from the subject: Let us
therefore return and inquire how the tyrant will
maintain that fair and numerous and various and
ever-changing army of his.

If, he said, there are sacred treasures in the city,
he will confiscate and spend them; and in so far
as the fortunes of attainted persons may suffice, he
will be able to diminish the taxes which he would
otherwise have to impose upon the people.

And when these fail?

Why, clearly, he said, then he and his boon companions, whether male or female, will be maintained
out of his father's estate.

You mean to say that the people, from whom he
has derived his being, will maintain him and his
companions?

Yes, he said; they cannot help themselves.

But what if the people fly into a passion, and aver
that a grownup son ought not to be supported by
his father, but that the father should be supported
by the son? The father did not bring him into being,   569
or settle him in life, in order that when his son became a man he should himself be the servant of
his own servants and should support him and his
rabble of slaves and companions; but that his son
should protect him, and that by his help he might be
emancipated from the government of the rich and

aristocratic, as they are termed. And so he bids him and his companions depart, just as any other father might drive out of the house a riotous son and his undesirable associates.

By heaven, he said, then the parent will discover what a monster he has been fostering in his bosom; and, when he wants to drive him out, he will find that he is weak and his son strong.

Why, you do not mean to say that the tyrant will use violence? What! beat his father if he opposes him?

Yes, he will, having first disarmed him.

Then he is a parricide, and a cruel guardian of an aged parent; and this is real tyranny, about which there can be no longer a mistake: as the saying is, the people who would escape the smoke which is the slavery of freemen, has fallen into the fire which is the tyranny of slaves. Thus liberty, getting out of all order and reason, passes into the harshest and bitterest form of slavery.

True, he said.

Very well; and may we not rightly say that we have sufficiently discussed the nature of tyranny, and the manner of the transition from democracy to tyranny?

Yes, quite enough, he said.

Book IX (in Part)

Last of all comes the tyrannical man; about whom we have once more to ask, how is he formed out of the democratical? and how does he live, in happiness or in misery? 571

Yes, he said, he is the only one remaining.

There is, however, I said, a previous question which remains unanswered.

What question?

I do not think that we have adequately determined the nature and number of the appetites, and until this is accomplished the inquiry will always be confused.

Well, he said, it is not too late to supply the omission.

Very true, I said; and observe the point which I want to understand: Certain of the unnecessary pleasures and appetites I conceive to be unlawful; everyone appears to have them, but in some persons they are controlled by the laws and by reason, and the better desires prevail over them—either they are wholly banished or they become few and weak; while in the case of others they are stronger, and there are more of them.

Which appetites do you mean?

I mean those which are awake when the reasoning and human and ruling power is asleep; then the wild beast within us, gorged with meat or drink, starts up and having shaken off sleep, goes forth to satisfy his desires; and there is no conceivable folly or crime —not excepting incest or any other unnatural union, or parricide, or the eating of forbidden food— which at such a time, when he has parted company with all shame and sense, a man may not be ready to commit.

Most true, he said.

But when a man's pulse is healthy and temperate, and when before going to sleep he has awakened his rational powers, and fed them on noble thoughts and inquiries, collecting himself in meditation; after having first indulged his appetites neither too much nor too little, but just enough to lay them to sleep, and prevent them and their enjoyments and pains from interfering with the higher principle—which he leaves in the solitude of pure abstraction, free to contemplate and aspire to the knowledge of the unknown, whether in past, present, or future: when again he has allayed the passionate element, if he has a quarrel against anyone—I say, when, after pacifying the two irrational principles, he rouses up the third, which is reason, before he takes his rest, then, as you know, he attains truth most nearly, and is least likely to be the sport of fantastic and lawless visions.

572

I quite agree.

In saying this I have been running into a digression; but the point which I desire to note is that in all of us, even in good men, there is a lawless wild-beast nature, which peers out in sleep. Pray, consider whether I am right, and you agree with me.

Yes, I agree.

And now remember the character which we attributed to the democratic man. He was supposed from his youth upwards to have been trained under a miserly parent, who encouraged the saving appetites in him, but discountenanced the unnecessary, which aim only at amusement and ornament?

True.

And then he got into the company of a more refined, licentious sort of people, and taking to all their wanton ways rushed into the opposite extreme from an abhorrence of his father's meanness. At last, being a better man than his corruptors, he was drawn in both directions until he halted midway and led a life, not of vulgar and slavish passion, but of what he deemed moderate indulgence in various pleasures. After this manner the democrat was generated out of the oligarch?

Yes, he said; that was our view of him, and is so still.

And now, I said, years will have passed away, and you must conceive this man, such as he is, to have a son, who is brought up in his father's principles.

I can imagine him.

Then you must further imagine the same thing to happen to the son which has already happened to the father:—he is drawn into a perfectly lawless life, which by his seducers is termed perfect liberty; and his father and friends take part with his moderate desires, and the opposite party assist the opposite ones. As soon as these dire magicians and tyrant-makers find that they are losing their hold on him, they contrive to implant in him a master passion, to be lord over his idle and spendthrift lusts—a sort of monstrous winged drone—that is the only image which will adequately describe him.

Yes, he said, that is the only adequate image of him.

And when his other lusts, amid clouds of incense and perfumes and garlands and wines, and all the pleasures of a dissolute life, now let loose, come

573

buzzing around him, nourishing to the utmost the
sting of desire which they implant in his drone-like
nature, then at last this lord of the soul, having
Madness for the captain of his guard, breaks out
into a frenzy; and if he finds in himself any good
opinions or appetites in process of formation,[24] and
there is in him any sense of shame remaining, to
these better principles he puts an end, and casts
them forth until he has purged away temperance and
brought in madness to the full.

Yes, he said, that is the way in which the tyrannical man is generated.

And is not this the reason why of old love has
been called a tyrant?

I should not wonder.

Further, I said, has not a drunken man also the
spirit of a tyrant?

He has.

And you know that a man who is deranged, and
not right in his mind, will fancy that he is able to
rule, not only over men, but also over the gods?

That he will.

And the tyrannical man in the true sense of the
word comes into being when, either under the influence of nature, or habit, or both, he becomes
drunken, lustful, passionate? O my friend, is not
that so?

Assuredly.

Such is the man and such is his origin. And next,
how does he live?

Suppose, as people facetiously say, you were to
tell me.

I imagine, I said, at the next step in his progress,
that there will be feasts and carousals and revellings
and courtesans, and all that sort of thing; Love is
the lord of the house within him, and orders all the
concerns of his soul.

That is certain.

Yes; and every day and every night desires grow
up many and formidable, and their demands are
many.

[24] Or, "opinions or appetites such as are deemed to be good."

They are indeed, he said.

His revenues, if he has any, are soon spent.

True.

Then comes debt and the cutting down of his property.

Of course.

When he has nothing left, must not his desires, crowding in the nest like young ravens, be crying aloud for food; and he, goaded on by them, and especially by love himself, who is in a manner the captain of them, is in a frenzy, and would fain discover whom he can defraud or despoil of his property, in order that he may gratify them? 574

Yes, that is sure to be the case.

He must have money, no matter how, if he is to escape horrid pains and pangs.

He must.

And as in himself there was a succession of pleasures, and the new got the better of the old and took away their rights, so he being younger will claim to have more than his father and his mother, and if he has spent his own share of the property, he will take a slice of theirs.

No doubt he will.

And if his parents will not give way, then he will try first of all to cheat and deceive them.

Very true.

And if he fails, then he will use force and plunder them.

Yes, probably.

And if the old man and woman fight for their own, what then, my friend? Will the creature feel any compunction at tyrannizing over them?

Nay, he said, I should not feel at all comfortable about his parents.

But, O heavens! Adeimantus, on account of some new fangled love of a harlot, who is anything but a necessary connection, can you believe that he would strike the mother who is his ancient friend and necessary to his very existence, and would place her under the authority of the other, when she is brought under the same roof with her; or that, under like circumstances, he would do the same to his withered

old father, first and most indispensable of friends,
for the sake of some newly found blooming youth
who is the reverse of indispensable?

Yes, indeed, he said; I believe that he would.

Truly, then, I said, a tyrannical son is a blessing to
his father and mother.

He is indeed, he replied.

He first takes their property, and when that fails,
and pleasures are beginning to swarm in the hive of
his soul, then he breaks into a house, or steals the
garments of some nightly wayfarer; next he proceeds
to clear a temple. Meanwhile the old opinions which
he had when a child, and which gave judgment
about good and evil, are overthrown by those others
which have just been emancipated, and are now the
bodyguard of love and share his empire. These in
his democratic days, when he was still subject to the
laws and to his father, were only let loose in the
dreams of sleep. But now that he is under the dominion of Love, he becomes always and in waking
reality what he was then very rarely and in a dream
only; he will commit the foulest murder, or eat forbidden food, or be guilty of any other horrid act.
Love is his tyrant, and lives lordly in him and law-   575
lessly, and being himself a king, leads him on, as a
tyrant leads a State, to the performance of any reckless deed by which he can maintain himself and the
rabble of his associates, whether those whom evil
communications have brought in from without, or
those whom he himself has allowed to break loose
within him by reason of a similar evil nature in himself. Have we not here a picture of his way of life?

Yes, indeed, he said.

And if there are only a few of them in the State,
and the rest of the people are well disposed, they go
away and become the bodyguard or mercenary
soldiers of some other tyrant who may probably want
them for a war; and if there is no war, they stay at
home and do many little pieces of mischief in the
city.

What sort of mischief?

For example, they are the thieves, burglars, cut-
purses, foot-pads, robbers of temples, man-stealers

of the community; or if they are able to speak they turn informers, and bear false witness, and take bribes.

A small catalogue of evils, even if the perpetrators of them are few in number.

Yes, I said; but small and great are comparative terms, and all these things, in the misery and evil which they inflict upon a State, do not come within a thousand miles of the tyrant; when this noxious class and their followers grow numerous and become conscious of their strength, assisted by the infatuation of the people, they choose from among themselves the one who has most of the tyrant in his own soul, and him they create their tyrant.

Yes, he said, and he will be the most fit to be a tyrant.

If the people yield, well and good; but if they resist him, as he began by beating his own father and mother, so now, if he has the power, he beats them, and will keep his dear old fatherland or motherland, as the Cretans say, in subjection to his young retainers whom he has introduced to be their rulers and masters. This is the end of his passions and desires.

Exactly.

When such men are only private individuals and before they get power, this is their character; they associate entirely with their own flatterers or ready tools; or if they want anything from anybody, they in their turn are equally ready to bow down before them: they profess every sort of affection for them; but when they have gained their point they know them no more.

Yes, truly.

They are always either the masters or servants and never the friends of anybody; the tyrant never tastes of true freedom or friendship.

Certainly not.

And may we not rightly call such men treacherous?

No question.

Also they are utterly unjust, if we were right in our notion of justice?

Yes, he said, and we were perfectly right.

576

Let us then sum up in a word, I said, the character of the worst man: he is the waking reality of what we dreamed.

Most true.

And this is he who being by nature most of a tyrant bears rule, and the longer he lives the more of a tyrant he becomes.

That is certain, said Glaucon, taking his turn to answer. . . .

Outline of the Timaeus (Introductory Passages)

I. Introduction (17a–27b)
  A. Proem: the participants and the missing fourth guest (17a–b)
  B. Socrates and the best state in definition (17c–20c)
    1. he summarizes his previous account of the best constitution of citizens (17c–19b)
      a. division of labor (17c–d)
      b. nature, training, and property of guardians (17d–18b)
      c. women's natures (18c)
      d. offspring, mating and education of the rulers (18c–19b)
    2. the need to hear of the state in its conflicts (19b–20c)
      a. Socrates' desire to see how the state would act in conflict (19b–c)
      b. relative fitness of himself, poets, sophists, and the other speakers to describe this (19c–20c)
  C. Critias and the best state in action (20c–26c)
    1. the tale itself, originating from Solon (20c–25d)
      a. Solon as poet and as lawgiver (20c–21d)
      b. ancient knowledge of the Egyptians and the youth of Greek culture (21e–22c)
      c. explanation for this youthfulness (22c–23b)
      d. the earlier race of Athenians, their nature and nurture love of war and love of wisdom (23c–24e)
      e. the confederation of Atlantis and its defeat at hands of Athenians (24e–25d)
    2. Critias' recovery of his memory of the tale, which is true history (25d–26c)
  D. Program of the discourses (26c–27b)
    1. Critias: we will change Socrates' fable into truth (26c–e)
    2. Socrates: this is true discourse (26e–27a)
    3. Critias' order of the next three discourses projected (27a–b)
II. The discourse by Timaeus (27c–92c) (*Here omitted*)

TIMAEUS (SELECTION)

SOCRATES CRITIAS

TIMAEUS HERMOCRATES

Socrates. One, two, three; but where, my dear Timaeus, is the fourth of those who were yesterday my guests and are to be my entertainers today?

Timaeus. He has been taken ill, Socrates; for he would not willingly have been absent from this gathering.

Soc. Then, if he is not coming, you and the two others must supply his place.

Tim. Certainly, and we will do all that we can; having been handsomely entertained by you yesterday, those of us who remain should be only too glad to return your hospitality.

Soc. Do you remember what were the points of which I required you to speak?

Tim. We remember some of them, and you will be here to remind us of anything which we have forgotten: or rather, if we are not troubling you, will you briefly recapitulate the whole, and then the particulars will be more firmly fixed in our memories?

Soc. To be sure I will: the chief theme of my yesterday's discourse was the State—how constituted and of what citizens composed it would seem likely to be most perfect.

Tim. Yes, Socrates; and what you said of it was very much to our mind.

Soc. Did we not begin by separating the husbandmen and the artisans from the class of defenders of the State?

Tim. Yes.

Soc. And when we had given to each one that

single employment and particular art which was
suited to his nature, we spoke of those who were intended to be our warriors, and said that they were
to be guardians of the city against attacks from
within as well as from without, and to have no other
employment; they were to be merciful in judging
their subjects, of whom they were by nature friends,
but fierce to their enemies, when they came across
them in battle.

Tim. Exactly.

Soc. We said, if I am not mistaken, that the
guardians should be gifted with a temperament in
a high degree both passionate and philosophical; and
that then they would be as they ought to be, gentle
to their friends and fierce with their enemies.

Tim. Certainly.

Soc. And what did we say of their education?
Were they not to be trained in gymnastic, and music,
and all other sorts of knowledge which were very
proper for them?[1]

Tim. Very true.

Soc. And being thus trained they were not to consider gold or silver or anything else to be their own
private property; they were to be like hired troops,
receiving pay for keeping guard from those who
were protected by them—the pay was to be no more
than would suffice for men of simple life; and they
were to spend in common, and to live together in
the continual practice of virtue, which was to be
their sole pursuit.

Tim. That was also said.

Soc. Neither did we forget the women; of whom
we declared, that their natures should be assimilated
and brought into harmony with those of the men,
and that common pursuits should be assigned to
them both in time of war and in their ordinary life.

Tim. That, again, was as you say.

Soc. And what about the procreation of children?
Or rather was not the proposal too singular to be
forgotten? for all wives and children were to be in
common, to the intent that no one should ever know

---

[1] Or "which are akin to these"; or τούτοις may be taken with
ἐν ἅπασι.

his own child, but they were to imagine that they were all one family; those who were within a suitable limit of age were to be brothers and sisters, those who were of an elder generation parents and grandparents, and those of a younger, children and grandchildren.

Tim. Yes, and the proposal is easy to remember, as you say.

Soc. And do you also remember how, with a view of securing as far as we could the best breed, we said that the chief magistrates, male and female, should contrive secretly, by the use of certain lots, so to arrange the nuptial meeting, that the bad of either sex and the good of either sex might pair with their like; and there was to be no quarrelling on this account, for they would imagine that the union was a mere accident, and was to be attributed to the lot?

Tim. I remember.

Soc. And you remember how we said that the children of the good parents were to be educated, and the children of the bad secretly dispersed among the inferior citizens; and while they were all growing up the rulers were to be on the look-out, and to bring up from below in their turn those who were worthy, and those among themselves who were unworthy were to take the places of those who came up?

Tim. True.

Soc. Then have I now given you all the heads of our yesterday's discussion? Or is there anything more, my dear Timaeus, which has been omitted?

Tim. Nothing, Socrates; it was just as you have said.

Soc. I should like, before proceeding further, to tell you how I feel about the State which we have described. I might compare myself to a person who, on beholding beautiful animals either created by the painter's art, or, better still, alive but at rest, is seized with a desire of seeing them in motion or engaged in some struggle or conflict to which their forms appear suited; this is my feeling about the State which we have been describing. There are conflicts which all cities undergo, and I should like to hear someone tell of our own city carrying on a struggle against her neighbors, and how she went out to war in a becoming manner, and when at war showed by the greatness of her actions and the magnanimity of her words in dealing with other cities a result worthy of her training and education. Now I, Critias and Hermocrates, am conscious that I myself should never be able to celebrate the city and her citizens in a befitting manner, and I am not surprised at my own incapacity; to me the wonder is rather that the poets present as well as past are no better—not that I mean to depreciate them; but everyone can see that they are a tribe of imitators, and will imitate best and most easily the life in which they have been brought up; while that which is beyond the range of a man's education he finds hard to carry out in action, and still harder adequately to represent in language: I am aware that the Sophists have plenty of brave words and fair conceits, but I am afraid that being only wanderers from one city to another, and having never had habitations of their own, they may fail in their conception of philosophers and statesmen, and may not know what they do and say in time of war, when they are fighting or holding parley with their enemies. And thus people of your class are the only ones remaining who are fitted by nature and education to take part at once both in politics and philosophy. Here is Timaeus, of Locris in Italy, a city which has admirable laws, and who is himself in wealth and rank the equal of any of his fellow-citizens; he has held the most important and honorable offices in his own state, and, as I believe, has scaled the heights of all philosophy; and here is Critias, whom every Athenian knows to be no novice in the matters of which we are speaking; and as to Hermocrates, I am assured by many witnesses that his genius and education qualify him to take part in any speculation of the kind. And therefore yesterday when I saw that you wanted me to describe the formation of the State, I readily assented, being very well aware, that, if you only would, none were better qualified to carry the discussion further, and that when you had engaged our city in a suitable war, you of all men living could best exhibit her playing a fitting part.

20

When I had completed my task, I in return imposed this other task upon you. You conferred together and agreed to entertain me today, as I had entertained you, with a feast of discourse. Here am I in festive array, and no man can be more ready for the promised banquet.

Her. And we too, Socrates, as Timaeus says, will not be wanting in enthusiasm; and there is no excuse for not complying with your request. As soon as we arrived yesterday at the guest-chamber of Critias, with whom we are staying, or rather on our way thither, we talked the matter over, and he told us an ancient tradition, which I wish, Critias, that you would repeat to Socrates, so that he may help us to judge whether it will satisfy his requirements or not.

Crit. I will, if Timaeus, who is our other partner, approves.

Tim. I quite approve.

Crit. Then listen, Socrates, to a tale which, though strange, is certainly true, having been attested by Solon, who was the wisest of the seven sages. He was a relative and a dear friend of my great-grandfather, Dropides, as he himself says in many passages of his poems; and he told the story to Critias, my grandfather, who remembered and repeated it to us. There were of old, he said, great and marvelous actions of the Athenian city, which have passed into oblivion through lapse of time and the destruction of mankind, and one in particular, greater than all the rest. This we will now rehearse. It will be a fitting monument of our gratitude to you, and a hymn of praise true and worthy of the goddess, on this her day of festival.

21

Soc. Very good. And what is this ancient famous action of the Athenians, which Critias declared, on the authority of Solon, to be not a mere legend, but an actual fact?[2]

Crit. I will tell an old-world story which I heard from an aged man; for Critias, at the time of telling it, was as he said, nearly ninety years of age, and I was about ten. Now the day was that day of the

[2] Or "which, though unrecorded in history, Critias declared, on the authority of Solon, to be an actual fact?"

Apaturia which is called Registration of Youth, at which, according to custom, our parents gave prizes for recitations, and the poems of several poets were recited by us boys, and many of us sang the poems of Solon, which at that time had not gone out of fashion. One of our tribe, either because he thought so or to please Critias, said that in his judgment Solon was not only the wisest of men, but also the noblest of poets. The old man, as I very well remember, brightened up at hearing this and said, smiling: Yes, Amynander, if Solon had only, like other poets, made poetry the business of his life, and had completed the tale which he brought with him from Egypt, and had not been compelled, by reason of the factions and troubles which he found stirring in his own country when he came home, to attend to other matters, in my opinion he would have been as famous as Homer or Hesiod, or any poet.

And what was the tale about, Critias? said Amynander.

About the greatest action which the Athenians ever did, and which ought to have been the most famous, but, through the lapse of time and the destruction of the actors, it has not come down to us.

Tell us, said the other, the whole story, and how and from whom Solon heard this veritable tradition.

He replied:—In the Egyptian Delta, at the head of which the river Nile divides, there is a certain district which is called the district of Sais, and the great city of the district is also called Sais, and is the city from which King Amasis came. The citizens have a deity for their foundress; she is called in the Egyptian tongue Neith, and is asserted by them to be the same whom the Hellenes call Athene; they are great lovers of the Athenians, and say that they are in some way related to them. To this city came Solon, and was received there with great honor; he asked the priests who were most skillful in such matters, about antiquity, and made the discovery that neither he nor any other Hellene knew anything worth mentioning about the times of old. On one occasion, wishing to draw them on to speak of antiquity, he began to tell about the most ancient things in our part of the world—about Phoroneus, who is

called "the first man," and about Niobe; and after
the Deluge, of the survival of Deucalion and Pyrrha;
and he traced the genealogy of their descendants,
and reckoning up the dates, tried to compute how
many years ago the events of which he was speaking happened. Thereupon one of the priests, who
was of a very great age, said: O Solon, Solon, you
Hellenes are never anything but children, and there
is not an old man among you. Solon in return asked
him what he meant. I mean to say, he replied, that in
mind you are all young; there is no old opinion
handed down among you by ancient tradition, nor
any science which is hoary with age. And I will tell
you why. There have been, and will be again, many
destructions of mankind arising out of many causes;
the greatest have been brought about by the agencies
of fire and water, and other lesser ones by innumerable other causes. There is a story, which even you
have preserved, that once upon a time Phaëthon,
the son of Helios, having yoked the steeds in his
father's chariot, because he was not able to drive
them in the path of his father, burnt up all that was
upon the earth, and was himself destroyed by a
thunderbolt. Now this has the form of a myth, but
really signifies a declination of the bodies moving
in the heavens around the earth, and a great con-
flagration of things upon the earth, which recurs
after long intervals; at such times those who live
upon the mountains and in dry and lofty places are
more liable to destruction than those who dwell by
rivers or on the seashore. And from this calamity
the Nile, who is our never-failing savior, delivers
and preserves us. When, on the other hand, the gods
purge the earth with a deluge of water, the survivors
in your country are herdsmen and shepherds who
dwell on the mountains, but those who, like you, live
in cities are carried by the rivers into the sea.
Whereas in this land, neither then nor at any other
time, does the water come down from above on the
fields, having always a tendency to come up from
below; for which reason the traditions preserved
here are the most ancient. The fact is, that wherever
the extremity of winter frost or of summer sun does
not prevent, mankind exist, sometimes in greater,

sometimes in lesser numbers. And whatever happened 23
either in your country or in ours, or in any other
region of which we are informed—if there were
any actions noble or great or in any other way remarkable, they have all been written down by us of
old, and are preserved in our temples. Whereas just
when you and other nations are beginning to be
provided with letters and the other requisites of
civilized life, after the usual interval, the stream
from heaven, like a pestilence, comes pouring down,
and leaves only those of you who are destitute of
letters and education; and so you have to begin all
over again like children, and know nothing of what
happened in ancient times, either among us or among
yourselves. As for those genealogies of yours which
you just now recounted to us, Solon, they are no
better than the tales of children. In the first place
you remember a single deluge only, but there were
many previous ones; in the next place, you do not
know that there formerly dwelt in your land the fairest and noblest race of men which ever lived, and
that you and your whole city are descended from a
small seed or remnant of them which survived. And
this was unknown to you, because, for many generations, the survivors of that destruction died, leaving no written word. For there was a time, Solon,
before the great deluge of all, when the city which
now is Athens was first in war and in every way the
best governed of all cities, and is said to have performed the noblest deeds and to have had the fairest
constitution of any of which tradition tells, under
the face of heaven. Solon marveled at his words,
and earnestly requested the priests to inform him
exactly and in order about these former citizens.
You are welcome to hear about them, Solon, said
the priest, both for your own sake and for that of
your city, and above all, for the sake of the goddess
who is the common patron and parent and educator
of both our cities. She founded your city a thousand
years before ours,[3] receiving from the Earth and

---

[3] Observe that Plato gives the same date (9,000 years ago) for
the foundation of Athens and for the repulse of the invasion
from Atlantis. (Crit. 108 E).

Hephaestus the seed of your race, and afterwards she founded ours, of which the constitution is recorded in our sacred registers to be 8,000 years old. As touching your citizens of 9,000 years ago, I will briefly inform you of their laws and of their most famous action; the exact particulars of the whole we will hereafter go through at our leisure in the sacred registers themselves. If you compare these very laws with ours you will find that many of ours are the counterpart of yours as they were in the olden time. In the first place, there is the caste of priests, which is separated from all the others; next, there are the artificers, who ply their several crafts by themselves and do not intermix; and also there is the class of shepherds and of hunters,[4] as well as that of husbandmen; and you will observe, too, that the warriors in Egypt are distinct from all the other classes, and are commanded by the law to devote themselves solely to military pursuits; moreover, the weapons which they carry are shields and spears, a style of equipment which the goddess taught of Asiatics first to us, as in your part of the world first to you. Then as to wisdom, do you observe how our law from the very first made a study of the whole order of things, extending even to prophecy and medicine which gives health, out of these divine elements deriving what was needful for human life, and adding every sort of knowledge which was akin to them. All this order and arrangement the goddess first imparted to you when establishing your city; and she chose the spot of earth in which you were born, because she saw that the happy temperament of the seasons in that land would produce the wisest of men. Wherefore the goddess, who was a lover both of war and of wisdom, selected and first of all settled that spot which was the most likely to produce men likest herself. And there you dwelt, having such laws as these and still better ones, and excelled all mankind in all virtue, as became the children and disciples of the gods.

Many great and wonderful deeds are recorded of your state in our histories. But one of them ex-

---

[4] Reading τὸ τῶν θηρευτῶν.

ceeds all the rest in greatness and valor. For these histories tell of a mighty power which unprovoked made an expedition against the whole of Europe and Asia, and to which your city put an end. This power came forth out of the Atlantic Ocean, for in those days the Atlantic was navigable; and there was an island situated in front of the straits which are by you called the pillars of Heracles; the island was larger than Libya and Asia put together, and was the way to other islands, and from these you might pass to the whole of the opposite continent which surrounded the true ocean; for this sea which is within the Straits of Heracles is only a harbor, having a narrow entrance, but that other is a real sea, and the surrounding land may be most truly called a boundless continent. Now in this island of Atlantis there was a great and wonderful empire which had rule over the whole island and several others, and over parts of the continent, and, furthermore, the men of Atlantis had subjected the parts of Libya within the columns of Heracles as far as Egypt, and of Europe as far as Tyrrhenia. This vast power, gathered into one, endeavored to subdue at a blow our country and yours and the whole of the region within the straits; and then, Solon, your country shone forth, in the excellence of her virtue and strength, among all mankind. She was preeminent in courage and military skill, and was the leader of the Hellenes. And when the rest fell off from her, being compelled to stand alone, after having undergone the very extremity of danger, she defeated and triumphed over the invaders, and preserved from slavery those who were not yet subjugated, and generously liberated all the rest of us who dwell within the pillars. But afterwards there occurred violent earthquakes and floods; and in a single day and night of misfortune all your warlike men in a body sank into the earth, and the island of Atlantis in like manner disappeared in the depths of the sea. For which reason the sea in those parts is impassable and impenetrable, because there is a shoal of mud in the way; and this was caused by the subsidence of the island.

I have told you briefly, Socrates, what the aged

Critias heard from Solon and related to us. And when you were speaking yesterday about your city and citizens, the tale which I have just been repeating to you came into my mind, and I remarked with astonishment how, by some mysterious coincidence, you agreed in almost every particular with the narrative of Solon; but I did not like to speak at the moment. For a long time had elapsed, and I had forgotten too much; I thought that I must first of all run over the narrative in my own mind, and then I would speak. And so I readily assented to your request yesterday, considering that in all such cases the chief difficulty is to find a tale suitable to our purpose, and that with such a tale we should be fairly well provided.

And therefore, as Hermocrates has told you, on my way home yesterday I at once communicated the tale to my companions as I remembered it; and after I left them, during the night by thinking I recovered nearly the whole of it. Truly, as is often said, the lessons of our childhood make a wonderful impression on our memories; for I am not sure that I would remember all the discourse of yesterday, but I should be much surprised if I forgot any of these things which I have heard very long ago. I listened at the time with childlike interest to the old man's narrative; he was very ready to teach me, and I asked him again and again to repeat his words, so that like an indelible picture they were branded into my mind. As soon as the day broke, I rehearsed them as he spoke them to my companions, that they, as well as myself, might have something to say. And now, Socrates, to make an end of my preface, I am ready to tell you the whole tale. I will give you not only the general heads, but the particulars, as they were told to me. The city and citizens, which you yesterday described to us in fiction, we will now transfer to the world of reality. It shall be the ancient city of Athens, and we will suppose that the citizens whom you imagined, were our veritable ancestors, of whom the priest spoke; they will perfectly harmonize, and there will be no inconsistency in saying that the citizens of your republic are these ancient Athenians. Let us divide the subject among us, and

26

all endeavor according to our ability gracefully to execute the task which you have imposed upon us. Consider then, Socrates, if this narrative is suited to the purpose, or whether we should seek for some other instead.

Soc. And what other, Critias, can we find that will be better than this, which is natural and suitable to the festival of the goddess, and has the very great advantage of being a fact and not a fiction? How or where shall we find another if we abandon this? We cannot, and therefore you must tell the tale, and good luck to you; and I in return for my yesterday's discourse will now rest and be a listener.

Crit. Let me proceed to explain to you, Socrates, the order in which we have arranged our entertainment. Our intention is, that Timaeus, who is the most of an astronomer amongst us, and has made the nature of the universe his special study, should speak first, beginning with the generation of the world and going down to the creation of man; next, I am to receive the men whom he has created of whom some will have profited by the excellent education which you have given them; and then, in accordance with the tale of Solon, and equally with his law, we will bring them into court and make them citizens, as if they were those very Athenians whom the sacred Egyptian record has recovered from oblivion, and thenceforward we will speak of them as Athenians and fellow-citizens.

Soc. I see that I shall receive in my turn a perfect and splendid feast of reason. And now, Timaeus, you, I suppose, should speak next, after duly calling upon the Gods. . . .

Outline of the Critias

I. Preliminary (106a–108d)
  A. Timaeus (106a–b)
  B. Critias (106b–108a)
    1. need to ask indulgence (106b–107b)
    2. explanation (107b–e)
      a. all that we say must be imitations and representations
      b. we judge discourses in same way as paintings (107d–e)
    3. to the account of humans to be given just now we must grant indulgence (107e–108a)
  C. Socrates: we shall grant you indulgence (108a–b)
  D. Hermocrates (108b–c)
  E. Critias: I call upon Memory, the god (108c–d)
II. The account of Athens and Atlantis (108e–121c)
  A. Proem (108e–109a)
    1. summary of what was said (in the *Timaeus*) of the sinking of Atlantis by earthquakes following a war 9,000 years ago (108e–109a)
    2. program of the account to come (109a)
  B. The account (109b–121c)
    1. Athens (109b–112e)
      a. origin of crafts and husbanding (109b–110c)
        i. the gods and goddesses took over the places of the earth according to lot, not strife (109b)
        ii. then they reared us, to be their cattle and nurslings, not through our bodies by force but through our souls, by persuasion (109b–c)
        iii. Hephaestus and Athene, agreeing on wisdom and crafts, planted men of virtue as native to the soil (109c–d)
        iv. the names of these citizens are preserved, but not their deeds (109d–110a)
      b. the military class was separated by divine heroes and lived apart (110c–112e)
        i. it was supplied with its needs for sustenance

CRITIAS

CRITIAS

HERMOCRATES

TIMAEUS

SOCRATES

Timaeus. How thankful I am, Socrates, that I have arrived at last, and, like a weary traveller after a long journey, may be at rest! And I pray the being who always was of old, and has now been by me revealed, to grant that my words may endure in so far as they have been spoken truly and acceptably to him; but if unintentionally I have said anything wrong, I pray that he will impose upon me a just retribution, and the just retribution of him who errs is that he should be set right. Wishing, then, to speak truly in future concerning the generation of the gods, I pray him to give me knowledge, which of all medicines is the most perfect and best. And now having offered my prayer I deliver up the argument to Critias, who is to speak next according to our agreement.[1]

Critias. And I, Timaeus, accept the trust, and as you at first said that you were going to speak of high matters, and begged that some forbearance might be shown to you, I too ask the same or greater forbearance for what I am about to say. And although I very well know that my request may appear to be somewhat ambitious and discourteous, I must make it nevertheless. For will any man of sense deny that you have spoken well? I can only attempt to show that I ought to have more indulgence than you, because my theme is more difficult; and I shall argue that to seem to speak well of the gods to men is

106

107

[1] Tim. 27 A.

far easier than to speak well of men to men: for the inexperience and utter ignorance of his hearers about any subject is a great assistance to him who has to speak of it, and we know how ignorant we are concerning the gods. But I should like to make my meaning clearer, if you will follow me. All that is said by any of us can only be imitation and representation. For if we consider the likenesses which painters make of bodies divine and heavenly, and the different degrees of gratification with which the eye of the spectator receives them, we shall see that we are satisfied with the artist who is able in any degree to imitate the earth and its mountains, and the rivers, and the woods, and the universe, and the things that are and move therein, and further, that knowing nothing precise about such matters, we do not examine or analyze the painting; all that is required is a sort of indistinct and deceptive mode of shadowing them forth. But when a person endeavors to paint the human form we are quick at finding out defects, and our familiar knowledge makes us severe judges of anyone who does not render every point of similarity. And we may observe the same thing to happen in discourse; we are satisfied with a picture of divine and heavenly things which has very little likeness to them; but we are more precise in our criticism of mortal and human things. Wherefore if at the moment of speaking I cannot suitably express my meaning, you must excuse me, considering that to form approved likenesses of human things is the reverse of easy. This is what I want to suggest to you, and at the same time to beg, Socrates, that I may have not less, but more indulgence conceded to me in what I am about to say. Which favor, if I am right in asking, I hope that you will be ready to grant.

108

Socrates. Certainly, Critias, we will grant your request, and we will grant the same by anticipation to Hermocrates, as well as to you and Timaeus; for I have no doubt that when his turn comes a little while hence, he will make the same request which you have made. In order, then, that he may provide himself with a fresh beginning, and not be compelled to say the same things over again, let him understand that the indulgence is already extended by anticipation to him. And now, friend Critias, I will announce to you the judgment of the theater. They are of opinion that the last performer was wonderfully successful, and that you will need a great deal of indulgence before you will be able to take his place.

Hermocrates. The warning, Socrates, which you have addressed to him, I must also take to myself. But remember, Critias, that faint heart never yet raised a trophy; and therefore you must go and attack the argument like a man. First invoke Apollo and the Muses, and then let us hear you sound the praises and show forth the virtues of your ancient citizens.

Crit. Friend Hermocrates, you, who are stationed last and have another in front of you, have not lost heart as yet; the gravity of the situation will soon be revealed to you; meanwhile I accept your exhortations and encouragements. But besides the gods and goddesses whom you have mentioned, I would specially invoke Mnemosyne; for all the important part of my discourse is dependent on her favor, and if I can recollect and recite enough of what was said by the priests and brought hither by Solon, I doubt not that I shall satisfy the requirements of this theater. And now, making no more excuses, I will proceed.

Let me begin by observing first of all, that nine thousand was the sum of years which had elapsed since the war which was said to have taken place between those who dwelt outside the pillars of Heracles and all who dwelt within them; this war I am going to describe. Of the combatants on the one side, the city of Athens was reported to have been the leader and to have fought out the war; the combatants on the other side were commanded by the kings of Atlantis, which, as I was saying, was an island greater in extent than Libya and Asia, and when afterwards sunk by an earthquake, became an impassable barrier of mud to voyagers sailing from hence to any part of the ocean. The progress of the history will unfold the various nations of barbarians and families of Hellenes which then existed, as they successively appear on the scene; but I must describe first of all Athenians of that day, and their enemies who fought with them, and then the respective powers and governments of the two kingdoms. Let us give the precedence to Athens.

In the days of old the gods had the whole earth distributed among them by allotment.[2] There was no quarrelling; for you cannot rightly suppose that the gods did not know what was proper for each of them to have, or, knowing this, that they would seek to procure for themselves by contention that which more properly belonged to others. They all of them by just apportionment obtained what they wanted, and peopled their own districts; and when they had peopled them they tended us, their nurselings and possessions, as shepherds tend their flocks, excepting only that they did not use blows or bodily force, as shepherds do, but governed us like pilots from the stern of the vessel, which is an easy way of guiding animals, holding our souls by the rudder of persuasion according to their own pleasure;—thus did they guide all mortal creatures. Now different gods had their allotments in different places which they set in order. Hephaestus and Athene, who were brother and sister, and sprang from the same father, having a common nature, and being united also in the love of philosophy and art, both obtained as their common portion this land, which was naturally adapted for wisdom and virtue; and there they implanted brave children of the soil, and put into their minds the order of government; their names are preserved, but their actions have disappeared by reason of the destruction of those who received the tradition, and the lapse of ages. For when there were any survivors, as I have already said, they were men who dwelt in the mountains; and they were ignorant of the art of writing, and had heard only the names of the chiefs of the land, but very little about their actions. The names they were willing enough to give to their children; but the virtues and the laws of their predecessors, they knew only by obscure traditions; and as they themselves and

[2] Cp. Polit. 271 ff.

their children lacked for many generations the necessaries of life, they directed their attention to the supply of their wants, and of them they conversed, to the neglect of events that had happened in times long past; for mythology and the inquiry into antiquity are first introduced into cities when they begin to have leisure,[3] and when they see that the necessaries of life have already been provided, but not before. And this is the reason why the names of the ancients have been preserved to us and not their actions. This I infer because Solon said that the priests in their narrative of that war mentioned most of the names which are recorded prior to the time of Theseus such as Cecrops, and Erechtheus, and Erichthonius, and Erysichthon, and the names of the women in like manner. Moreover, since military pursuits were then common to men and women, the men of those days in accordance with the custom of the time set up a figure and image of the goddess in full armor, to be a testimony that all animals which associate together, male as well as female, may, if they please, practice in common the virtue which belongs to them without distinction of sex.

Now the country was inhabited in those days by various classes of citizens;—there were artisans, and there were husbandmen, and there was also a warrior class originally set apart by divine men. The latter dwelt by themselves, and had all things suitable for nurture and education; neither had any of them anything of their own, but they regarded all that they had as common property; nor did they claim to receive of the other citizens anything more than their necessary food. And they practiced all the pursuits which we yesterday described as those of our imaginary guardians. Concerning the country the Egyptian priests said what is not only probable but manifestly true, that the boundaries were in those days fixed by the Isthmus, and that in the direction of the continent they extended as far as the heights of Cithaeron and Parnes; the boundary line came down in the direction of the sea, having the district of Oropus on the right, and with the river Asopus as

[3] Cp. Arist. Metaphys, I. i, § 16.

the limit on the left. The land was the best in the world, and was therefore able in those days to support a vast army, raised from the surrounding people. Even the remnant of Attica which now exists may compare with any region in the world for the variety and excellence of its fruits and the suitableness of its pastures to every sort of animal, which proves what I am saying; but in those days the country was fair as now and yielded far more abundant produce. How shall I establish my words? and what part of it can be truly called a remnant of the land that then was? The whole country is only a long promontory extending far into the sea away from the rest of the continent, while the surrounding basin of the sea is everywhere deep in the neighborhood of the shore. Many great deluges have taken place during the nine thousand years, for that is the number of years which have elapsed since the time of which I am speaking; and during all this time and through so many changes, there has never been any considerable accumulation of the soil coming down from the mountains, as in other places, but the earth has fallen away all round and sunk out of sight. The consequence is, that in comparison of what then was, there are remaining only the bones of the wasted body, as they may be called, as in the case of small islands, all the richer and softer parts of the soil having fallen away, and the mere skeleton of the land being left. But in the primitive state of the country, its mountains were high hills covered with soil, and the plains, as they are termed by us, of Phelleus were full of rich earth, and there was abundance of wood in the mountains. Of this last the traces still remain, for although some of the mountains now only afford sustenance to bees, not so very long ago there were still to be seen roofs of timber cut from trees growing there, which were of a size sufficient to cover the largest houses; and there were many other high trees, cultivated by man and bearing abundance of food for cattle. Moreover, the land reaped the benefit of the annual rainfall, not as now losing the water which flows off the bare earth into the sea, but, having an abundant supply in all places, and receiving it into her-

self and treasuring it up in the close clay soil, it
let off into the hollows the streams which it absorbed
from the heights, providing everywhere abundant
fountains and rivers, of which there may still be observed sacred memorials in places where fountains
once existed; and this proves the truth of what I
am saying.

Such was the natural state of the country, which
was cultivated, as we may well believe, by true husbandmen, who made husbandry their business, and
were lovers of honor, and of a noble nature, and had
a soil the best in the world, and abundance of water,
and in the heaven above an excellently attempered
climate. Now the city in those days was arranged on
this wise. In the first place the Acropolis was not as
now. For the fact is that a single night of excessive   112
rain washed away the earth and laid bare the rock;
at the same time there were earthquakes, and then
occurred the extraordinary inundation, which was
the third before the great destruction of Deucalion.
But in primitive times the hill of the Acropolis extended to the Eridanus and Ilissus, and included the
Pnyx on one side, and the Lycabettus as a boundary
on the opposite side of the Pnyx, and was all well
covered with soil, and level at the top, except in one
or two places. Outside the Acropolis and under the
sides of the hill there dwelt artisans, and such of
the husbandmen as were tilling the ground near; the
warrior class dwelt by themselves around the temples
of Athene and Hephaestus at the summit, which
moreover they had enclosed with a single fence like
the garden of a single house. On the north side they
had dwellings in common and had erected halls for
dining in winter, and had all the buildings which
they needed for their common life, besides temples,
but there was no adorning of them with gold and
silver, for they made no use of these for any purpose;
they took a middle course between meanness and
ostentation, and built modest houses in which they
and their children's children grew old, and they
handed them down to others who were like themselves, always the same. But in summertime they left
their gardens and gymnasia and dining halls, and
then the southern side of the hill was made use of by

them for the same purpose. Where the Acropolis now is there was a fountain, which was choked by the earthquake, and has left only the few small streams which still exist in the vicinity, but in those days the fountain gave an abundant supply of water for all and of suitable temperature in summer and in winter. This is how they dwelt, being the guardians of their own citizens and the leaders of the Hellenes, who were their willing followers. And they took care to preserve the same number of men and women through all time, being so many as were required for warlike purposes, then as now—that is to say, about twenty thousand. Such were the ancient Athenians, and after this manner they righteously administered their own land and the rest of Hellas; they were renowned all over Europe and Asia for the beauty of their persons and for the many virtues of their souls, and of all men who lived in those days they were the most illustrious. And next, if I have not forgotten what I heard when I was a child, I will impart to you the character and origin of their adversaries. For friends should not keep their stories to themselves, but have them in common.

Yet, before proceeding further in the narrative, I ought to warn you, that you must not be surprised if you should perhaps hear Hellenic names given to foreigners. I will tell you the reason of this: Solon, who was intending to use the tale for his poem, inquired into the meaning of the names, and found that the early Egyptians in writing them down had translated them into their own language, and he recovered the meaning of the several names and when copying them out again translated them into our language. My great-grandfather, Dropides, had the original writing, which is still in my possession, and was carefully studied by me when I was a child. Therefore if you hear names such as are used in this country, you must not be surprised, for I have told how they came to be introduced. The tale, which was of great length, began as follows:—

I have before remarked in speaking of the allotments of the gods, that they distributed the whole earth into portions differing in extent, and made for

themselves temples and instituted sacrifices. And Poseidon, receiving for his lot the island of Atlantis, begat children by a mortal woman, and settled them in a part of the island, which I will describe. Looking towards the sea, but in the center of the whole island, there was a plain which is said to have been the fairest of all plains and very fertile. Near the plain again, and also in the center of the island at a distance of about fifty stadia, there was a mountain not very high on any side. In this mountain there dwelt one of the earth-born primeval men of that country, whose name was Evenor, and he had a wife named Leucippe, and they had an only daughter who was called Cleito. The maiden had already reached womanhood, when her father and mother died; Poseidon fell in love with her and had intercourse with her, and breaking the ground, inclosed the hill in which she dwelt all round, making alternate zones of sea and land larger and smaller, encircling one another; there were two of land and three of water, which he turned as with a lathe, each having its circumference equidistant every way from the center, so that no man could get to the island, for ships and voyages were not as yet. He himself, being a god, found no difficulty in making special arrangements for the center island, bringing up two springs of water from beneath the earth, one of warm water and the other of cold, and making every variety of food to spring up abundantly from the soil. He also begat and brought up five pairs of twin male children; and dividing the island   114
of Atlantis into ten portions, he gave to the firstborn of the eldest pair his mother's dwelling and the surrounding allotment, which was the largest and best, and made him king over the rest; the others he made princes, and gave them rule over many men, and a large territory. And he named them all; the eldest, who was the first king, he named Atlas, and after him the whole island and the ocean were called Atlantic. To his twin brother, who was born after him, and obtained as his lot the extremity of the island towards the pillars of Heracles, facing the country which is now called the region of Gades in that part of the world, he gave the name

which in the Hellenic language is Eumelus, in the
language of the country which is named after him,
Gadeirus. Of the second pair of twins he called one
Ampheres, and the other Evaemon. To the elder of
the third pair of twins he gave the name Mneseus,
and Autochthon to the one who followed him. Of the
fourth pair of twins he called the elder Elasippus,
and the younger Mestor. And of the fifth pair he
gave to the elder the name of Azaes, and to the
younger that of Diaprepes. All these and their
descendants for many generations were the inhabitants and rulers of divers islands in the open sea;
and also, as has been already said, they held sway
in our direction over the country within the pillars
as far as Egypt and Tyrrhenia. Now Atlas had a
numerous and honorable family, and they retained
the kingdom, the eldest son handing it on to his
eldest for many generations; and they had such an
amount of wealth as was never before possessed by
kings and potentates, and is not likely ever to be
again, and they were furnished with everything which
they needed, both in the city and country. For because of the greatness of their empire many things
were brought to them from foreign countries, and
the island itself provided most of what was required
by them for the uses of life. In the first place, they
dug out of the earth whatever was to be found there,
solid as well as fusile, and that which is now only a
name and was then something more than a name,
orichalcum, was dug out of the earth in many parts
of the island, being more precious in those days than
anything except gold. There was an abundance of
wood for carpenter's work, and sufficient maintenance for tame and wild animals. Moreover, there
were a great number of elephants in the island; for   115
as there was provision for all other sorts of animals,
both for those which live in lakes and marshes and
rivers, and also for those which live in mountains
and on plains, so there was for the animal which is
the largest and most voracious of all. Also whatever
fragrant things there now are in the earth, whether
roots, or herbage, or woods, or essences which distill
from fruit and flower, grew and thrived in that land;
also the fruit which admits of cultivation, both the

dry sort, which is given us for nourishment and any
other which we use for food—we call them all by
the common name of pulse, and the fruits having a
hard rind, affording drinks and meats and ointments,
and good store of chestnuts and the like, which
furnish pleasure and amusement, and are fruits
which spoil with keeping, and the pleasant kinds of
dessert, with which we console ourselves after dinner, when we are tired of eating—all these that
sacred island which then beheld the light of the sun,
brought forth fair and wondrous and in infinite
abundance. With such blessings the earth freely furnished them; meanwhile they went on constructing
their temples and palaces and harbors and docks.
And they arranged the whole country in the following manner:—

First of all they bridged over the zones of sea
which surrounded the ancient metropolis, making a
road to and from the royal palace. And at the very
beginning they built the palace in the habitation of
the god and of their ancestors, which they continued
to ornament in successive generations, every king
surpassing the one who went before him to the utmost of his power, until they made the building a
marvel to behold for size and for beauty. And beginning from the sea they bored a canal of three
hundred feet in width and one hundred feet in depth
and fifty stadia in length, which they carried through
to the outermost zone, making a passage from the
sea up to this, which became a harbor, and leaving
an opening sufficient to enable the largest vessels to
find ingress. Moreover, they divided at the bridges
the zones of land which parted the zones of sea,
leaving room for a single trireme to pass out of one
zone into another, and they covered over the channels so as to leave a way underneath for the ships;
for the banks were raised considerably above the
water. Now the largest of the zones into which a
passage was cut from the sea was three stadia in
breadth, and the zone of land which came next of
equal breadth; but the next two zones, the one of
water, the other of land, were two stadia, and the
one which surrounded the central island was a stadium only in width. The island in which the palace

was situated had a diameter of five stadia. All this including the zones and the bridge, which was the sixth part of a stadium in width, they surrounded by a stone wall on every side, placing towers and gates on the bridges where the sea passed in. The stone which was used in the work they quarried from underneath the center island, and from underneath the zones, on the outer as well as the inner side. One kind was white, another black, and a third red, and as they quarried, they at the same time hollowed out double docks, having roofs formed out of the native rock. Some of their buildings were simple, but in others they put together different stones, varying the color to please the eye, and to be a natural source of delight. The entire circuit of the wall, which went round the outermost zone, they covered with a coating of brass, and the circuit of the next wall they coated with tin, and the third, which encompassed the citadel, flashed with the red light of orichalcum. The palaces in the interior of the citadel were constructed on this wise:—in the center was a holy temple dedicated to Cleito and Poseidon, which remained inaccessible, and was surrounded by an enclosure of gold; this was the spot where the family of the ten princes first saw the light, and thither the people annually brought the fruits of the earth in their season from all the ten portions, to be an offering to each of the ten. Here was Poseidon's own temple which was a stadium in length, and half a stadium in width, and of a proportionate height, having a strange barbaric appearance. All the outside of the temple, with the exception of the pinnacles, they covered with silver, and the pinnacles with gold. In the interior of the temple the roof was of ivory, curiously wrought everywhere with gold and silver and orichalcum; and all the other parts, the walls and pillars and floor, they coated with orichalcum. In the temple they placed statues of gold: there was the god himself standing in a chariot—the charioteer of six winged horses—and of such a size that he touched the roof of the building with his head; around him there were a hundred Nereids riding on dolphins, for such was thought to be the number of them by the men of those days. There were also in the interior of the temple other images which had been dedicated by private persons. And around the temple on the outside were placed statues of gold of all the descendants of the ten kings and of their wives, and there were many other great offerings of kings and of private persons, coming both from the city itself and from the foreign cities over which they held sway. There was an altar too, which in size and workmanship corresponded to this magnificence, and the palaces, in like manner, an- 117 swered to the greatness of the kingdom and the glory of the temple.

In the next place, they had fountains, one of cold and another of hot water, in gracious plenty flowing; and they were wonderfully adapted for use by reason of the pleasantness and excellence of their waters.[4] They constructed buildings about them and planted suitable trees; also they made cisterns, some open to the heavens, others roofed over, to be used in winter as warm baths: there were the kings' baths, and the baths of private persons, which were kept apart; and there were separate baths for women, and for horses and cattle, and to each of them they gave as much adornment as was suitable. Of the water which ran off they carried some to the grove of Poseidon, where were growing all manner of trees of wonderful height and beauty, owing to the excellence of the soil, while the remainder was conveyed by aqueducts along the bridges to the outer circles; and there were many temples built and dedicated to many gods; also gardens and places of exercise, some for men, and others for horses in both of the two islands formed by the zones; and in the center of the larger of the two there was set apart a race-course of a stadium in width, and in length allowed to extend all around the island, for horses to race in. Also there were guard-houses at intervals for the guards, the more trusted of whom were appointed to keep watch in the lesser zone, which was nearer the Acropolis; while the most trusted of all had houses given them within the citadel, near the persons of the kings. The docks were full of triremes and naval

---

[4] Reading ἑκατέρον πρὸς τὴν χρῆσιν.

stores, and all things were quite ready for use. Enough of the plan of the royal palace.

. Leaving the palace and passing out across the three harbors, you came to a wall which began at the sea and went all round; this was everywhere distant fifty stadia from the largest zone or harbor, and enclosed the whole, the ends meeting at the mouth of the channel which led to the sea. The entire area was densely crowded with habitations; and the canal and the largest of the harbors were full of vessels and merchants coming from all parts, who, from their numbers, kept up a multitudinous sound of human voices, and din and clatter of all sorts night and day.

I have described the city and the environs of the ancient palace nearly in the words of Solon, and now I must endeavor to represent to you the nature and arrangement of the rest of the land. The whole country was said by him to be very lofty and precipitous on the side of the sea, but the country immediately about and surrounding the city was a level plain, itself surrounded by mountains which descended towards the sea; it was smooth and even, and of an oblong shape, extending in one direction three thousand stadia, but across the center inland it was two thousand stadia. This part of the island looked towards the south, and was sheltered from the north. The surrounding mountains were celebrated for their number and size and beauty, far beyond any which still exist, having in them also many wealthy villages of country folk, and rivers, and lakes, and meadows supplying food enough for every animal, wild or tame, and much wood of various sorts, abundant for each and every kind of work.

I will now describe the plain, as it was fashioned by nature and by the labors of many generations of kings through long ages. It was for the most part rectangular and oblong, and where falling out of the straight line followed the circular ditch. The depth, and width, and length of this ditch were incredible, and gave the impression that a work of such extent, in addition to so many others, could never have been artificial. Nevertheless I must say what I was told.

It was excavated to the depth of a hundred feet, and its breadth was a stadium everywhere; it was carried round the whole of the plain, and was ten thousand stadia in length. It received the streams which came down from the mountains, and winding round the plain and meeting at the city, was there let off into the sea. Further inland, likewise, straight canals of a hundred feet in width were cut from it through the plain, and again let off into the ditch leading to the sea: these canals were at intervals of a hundred stadia, and by them they brought down the wood from the mountains to the city, and conveyed the fruits of the earth in ships, cutting transverse passages from one canal into another, and to the city. Twice in the year they gathered the fruits of the earth—in winter having the benefit of the rains of heaven, and in summer the water which the land supplied by introducing streams from the canals.

As to the population, each of the lots in the plain had to find a leader for the men who were fit for military service, and the size of a lot was a square of ten stadia each way, and the total number of all the lots was sixty thousand. And of the inhabitants of the mountains and of the rest of the country there was also a vast multitude, which was distributed among the lots and had leaders assigned to them according to their districts and villages. The leader was required to furnish for the war the sixth portion of a war chariot, so as to make up a total of ten thousand chariots; also two horses and riders for them, and a pair of chariot horses without a seat, accompanied by a horseman who could fight on foot carrying a small shield, and having a charioteer who stood behind the man-at-arms to guide the two horses; also, he was bound to furnish two heavy armed soldiers, two archers, two slingers, three stone-shooters and three javelin-men, who were light-armed, and four sailors to make up the complement of twelve hundred ships. Such was the military order of the royal city—the order of the other nine governments varied, and it would be wearisome to recount their several differences.

As to offices and honors, the following was the arrangement from the first. Each of the ten kings in his own division and in his own city had the absolute control of the citizens, and, in most cases, of the laws, punishing and slaying whomsoever he would. Now the order of precedence among them and their mutual relations were regulated by the commands of Poseidon which the law had handed down. These were inscribed by the first kings on a pillar of orichalcum, which was situated in the middle of the island, at the temple of Poseidon, whither the kings were gathered together every fifth and every sixth year alternately, thus giving equal honor to the odd and to the even number. And when they were gathered together they consulted about their common interests, and inquired if anyone had transgressed in anything, and passed judgment, and before they passed judgment they gave their pledges to one another on this wise:—There were bulls who had the range of the temple of Poseidon; and the ten kings, being left alone in the temple, after they had offered prayers to the god that they might capture the victim which was acceptable to him, hunted the bulls, without weapons, but with staves and nooses; and the bull which they caught they led up to the pillar and cut its throat over the top of it so that the blood fell upon the sacred inscription. Now on the pillar, besides the laws, there was inscribed an oath invoking mighty curses on the disobedient. When therefore, after slaying the bull in the accustomed manner, they had burnt its limbs, they filled a bowl of wine and cast in a clot of blood for each of them; the rest of the victim they put in the fire, after having purified the column all round. Then they drew from the bowl in golden cups, and pouring a libation on the fire, they swore that they would judge according to the laws on the pillar, and would punish him who in any point had already transgressed them, and that for the future they would not, if they could help, offend against the writing on the pillar, and would neither command others, nor obey any ruler who commanded them, to act otherwise than according to the laws of their father Poseidon. This was the prayer which each of them offered up for himself and for his descendants, at the same time drinking and dedicating the cup

120

out of which he drank in the temple of the god; and after they had supped and satisfied their needs, when darkness came on, and the fire about the sacrifice was cool, all of them put on most beautiful azure robes, and, sitting on the ground, at night, over the embers of the sacrifices by which they had sworn, and extinguishing all the fire about the temple, they received and gave judgment, if any of them had an accusation to bring against anyone; and when they had given judgment, at daybreak they wrote down their sentences on a golden tablet, and dedicated it together with their robes to be a memorial.

There were many special laws affecting the several kings inscribed about the temples, but the most important was the following: They were not to take up arms against one another, and they were all to come to the rescue if anyone in any of their cities attempted to overthrow the royal house; like their ancestors, they were to deliberate in common about war and other matters, giving the supremacy to the descendants of Atlas. And the king was not to have the power of life and death over any of his kinsmen unless he had the assent of the majority of the ten.

Such was the vast power which the god settled in the lost island of Atlantis; and this he afterwards directed against our land for the following reasons, as tradition tells: For many generations, as long as the divine nature lasted in them, they were obedient to the laws, and well-affectioned towards the god, whose seed they were; for they possessed true and in every way great spirits, uniting gentleness with wisdom in the various chances of life, and in their intercourse with one another. They despised everything but virtue, caring little for their present state of life, and thinking lightly of the possession of gold and other property, which seemed only a burden to them; neither were they intoxicated by luxury; nor did wealth deprive them of their self-control; but they were sober and saw clearly that all these goods are increased by virtue and friendship with one another, whereas by too great regard and respect for them, they are lost and friendship with them. By such reflections and by the continuance in them of

121

a divine nature, the qualities which we have described grew and increased among them; but when the divine portion began to fade away, and became diluted too often and too much with the mortal admixture, and the human nature got the upper hand, they then, being unable to bear their fortune, behaved unseemly, and to him who had an eye to see, grew visibly debased, for they were losing the fairest of their precious gifts; but to those who had no eye to see the true happiness, they appeared glorious and blessed at the very time when they were full of avarice and unrighteous power. Zeus, the god of gods, who rules according to law, and is able to see into such things, perceiving that an honorable race was in a woeful plight, and wanting to inflict punishment on them, that they might be chastened and improve, collected all the gods into their[5] most holy habitation, which, being placed in the center of the world, beholds all created things. And when he had called them together, he spake as follows:—[6]

[5] Reading αὐτῶν.
[6] The fragment *Critias* thus breaks off in the middle of a sentence.

SELECTED BIBLIOGRAPHY

I. ENGLISH TRANSLATIONS

Benjamin Jowett, trans., *The Dialogues of Plato* (Oxford: At the Clarendon Press, 4th ed., 1953). 4 vols.

This edition has been heavily edited by D. J. Allan and H. E. Dale, and is of considerable worth, being closer to the Greek than is the third edition. Jowett's analyses and introductions (pruned) remain. The third edition translations, with marginal summaries but without the other material, are to be found in a two-volume edition frequently reprinted by Random House, New York. This is still satisfactory, and has been a standby for generations. The Letters are not included in either edition.

The Dialogues of Plato (Cambridge: Harvard University Press, Loeb Classical Library, various dates).

Most of the translations have been done by W. R. M. Lamb, Harold Fowler, and R. G. Bury, and are of uneven value, but the great merit of this edition is its inclusion of the Greek texts on facing pages. For a student seriously interested in Plato this is virtually a necessary item of equipment.

Edith Hamilton and Huntington Cairns, eds., *Plato: The Complete Dialogues* (New York: Bollingen Books, 1958).

An admirable one-volume collection of translations by various hands, chiefly those in the Loeb Library series. Clever book designing has made it possible to include more material than is to be found in the two-volume Random House collection.

II. GENERAL STUDIES

THE BOOKS and articles devoted to various aspects of Plato's work, at every level of precision and scholarly learning, would occupy an enormous library. What follows is a list of a few books of outstanding general interest, together with a book or two devoted to explaining each of many of the major dialogues. All books are in English, most of them are still (1973) in print, and many of them are in paperback. It goes without saying that a plurality—no, a great majority—maintain and develop points of view regarding Plato that are quite different from my own.

There are easier introductory books on Plato than these, and there are many pocket editions of translations of dialogues which can be picked up on book counters, so those are not included here. Platonic studies, along with standard textbooks of philosophic history, tend to squeeze Plato into a very narrow mold.

Sir Ernest Barker, *The Political Thought of Plato and Aristotle* (New York: Dover Publications, 1959).
    A treatment that sets a high standard.
Robert S. Brumbaugh, *Plato's Mathematical Imagination* (Bloomington: Indiana University Press, 1954).
    A careful study of the Platonic images derived from mathematics and incorporated into the dialectic. An important book, though not always an easy one.
Ronald S. Crane, ed., *Critics and Criticism, Ancient and Modern* (Chicago: University of Chicago Press, 1952).
    Contains Richard McKeon's "Concept of Imitation in Antiquity" and "The Philosophic Bases of Art and Criticism," parts of which are devoted to insightful interpretations of Plato's theory of art.
Raphael Demos, *The Philosophy of Plato* (New York: Charles Scribner's Sons, 1939; reprinted by Octagon Books 1966).
    An intelligent attempt to restate Plato in terms of such topics as the receptacle, the doctrines surrounding ideas, being, appearance, art, beauty, etc. One of the best books to cut across the dialogues, except for its failure to deal with the many mathematical aspects of Plato's thinking.

Guy Cromwell Field, *Plato and His Contemporaries* (London: Methuen, 1930).

Fairly rich in information, this does not pretend to be a study of the philosophy itself. Perhaps the best single work on "background."

Warner Fite, *The Platonic Legend* (New York: Charles Scribner's Sons, 1934).

Fite has valiantly attempted to call a spade a spade but in so doing has ignored virtually all philosophical significances in the dialogues, and has made Plato's remarks that are illuminated by these dialogues into little more than scurrilities.

Paul Friedländer, *Plato*, trans. Hans Meyerhoff (New York: Pantheon Books, Vol. I, 1958, Vol. II, 1965, Vol. III, 1969).

The first volume is a very thoughtful, informative, and rather unusual book on Plato as a whole. A multitude of valuable references. The second and third volumes deal separately with the individual dialogues.

Georges Maximilien Antoine Grube, *Plato's Thought* (Boston: The Beacon Press, 1958).

A treatment of eight leading concepts in the dialogues. Humanistic in emphasis.

Ronald Bartlett Levinson, *In Defense of Plato* (Cambridge: Harvard University Press, 1953).

Levinson attempts to rescue Plato from his modern detractors, and does so with a prodigious flow of erudition and elegant writing. Levinson is best on the individual statements.

W. Lutoslawski, *The Origin and Growth of Plato's Logic* (London: Longmans, Green, and Co., 1897).

One of the first serious attempts to establish an order in the dialogues by appeal to stylistic statistics. The philosophy tends to disintegrate in the process.

Karl R. Popper, *The Open Society and its Enemies*, Vol. I, *The Spell of Plato* (New York: Harper & Row, 4th ed., 1962). Paperback.

A long, learned, yet curiously poorly informed attack upon Plato's social philosophy, by an unsympathetic contemporary critic.

Gilbert Ryle, "Plato," article in *The Encyclopedia of Philosophy* (New York: The Machmillan Co., 1967).

A more substantial contribution than the same author's *Plato's Progress*. Useful summaries.

Gilbert Ryle, *Plato's Progress* (New York: Cambridge University Press, 1968).

A learned but strange little book, reducing much in Plato's philosophy to very questionable biographical speculations.

Richard Robinson, *Plato's Earlier Dialectic*, 2nd ed. (New York: Oxford University Press, 1953).

A serious study of several problems contained in a half-dozen dialogues. Robinson is rigid in his adherence to the written words, and misses the invisible connections between them, but this is a worthwhile inquiry nevertheless.

Paul Shorey, *The Unity of Plato's Thought* (Hamden, Connecticut: Archon, Shoe String Press, 1968). A reprint.

This was one of the first important books in opposition to the developmental theory; it seeks to find a solid body of doctrine at the core of all of Plato's work, but in so doing removes most of the philosophical subtleties.

Paul Shorey, *What Plato Said* (Chicago: University of Chicago Press, 1933).

A large volume of uneven worth. Shorey is perceptive—sometimes—in ethics, art, and science. His interpretation suffers from a belligerent dogmatism. Very useful references. A paperback edition of 1965 abridges the general discussion and notes, but retains the summaries of all the dialogues.

Herman L. Sinaiko, *Love, Knowledge and Discourse in Plato: Dialogue and Dialectic in Phaedrus, Republic, Parmenides* (Chicago: University of Chicago Press, 1965).

A significant, thoughtful account of the dialectic, restricted in range but intensive and perceptive in its treatment.

Julius Stenzel, *Plato's Method of Dialectic*, D. J. Allan, trans. (Oxford: At the University Press, 1929). Reprinted 1964.

A much referred-to book, which touches frequently upon the historical order of the texts.

J. A. Stewart, *The Myths of Plato*, G. R. Levy, ed. (Carbondale: Southern Illinois University Press, 1960).

A work of considerable value. Stewart sets each myth in its presumed connections with other literary and religious documents, but in general ignores the philosophic problems. The book has been well edited for modern readers.

A. E. Taylor, *Plato, The Man and his Work* (London: Methuen, 1949).

This is the sixth edition of one of the best expositions of Plato, dialogue by dialogue. The book is erudite but humane, and makes relatively few errors in its attempt to steer between systematization and informalism.

Theodore Tracy, *Physiological Theory and the Doctrine of the Mean in Plato and Aristotle* (Chicago: Loyola University Press, 1969).

A careful examination of the texts, comparing these two philosophers in regard to their ethical and biological theories.

Eric Voegelin, *Plato* (Baton Rouge: Louisiana State University Press, 1966). Paperback reprint of the first half of Voegelin's *Plato and Aristotle*.

Overwritten in places, and with a slightly excessive existentialist cast, this is still an indispensable book for the interpretation of the *Republic*, the *Laws*, and a few other dialogues.

Encyclopedia Britannica articles on Plato by Lewis Campbell (11th ed.) and A. E. Taylor (14th ed.).
General articles which manage to compress much valuable information into relatively short space.

III. SOME INDIVIDUAL DIALOGUES

APOLOGY

The Apology of Plato, with a revised text and English notes, and a digest of Platonic idioms, by Rev. James Riddell (Oxford: Clarendon Press, 1867).

A schoolbook edition, but extremely useful nevertheless for the history of law and rhetoric in relation to Plato.

EPISTLES

Glenn R. Morrow, *Plato's Epistles*, translation with critical essays and notes (Indianapolis: Bobbs-Merrill Co., 1962).

A revised version of the same author's *Studies in the Platonic Epistles*

EUTHYDEMUS

Rosamond Kent Sprague, *Plato's Use of Fallacy: A Study of the Euthydemus and Some Other Dialogues* (London: Routledge and Kegan Paul, 1962).

The "other dialogues" are the *Theaetetus, Cratylus,* and *Hippias Minor.* The account of *The Euthydemus* is a useful study.

GORGIAS

E. R. Dodds, *Plato: Gorgias: A Revised Text with Introduction and Commentary* (Oxford: At the Clarendon Press, 1959).

An elaborate scholarly edition; most of the notes are philological rather than philosophical.

LAWS

Glenn R. Morrow, *Plato's Cretan City, A Historical Interpretation of the Laws* (Princeton: Princeton University Press, 1960).

A very important book. The author sets detail after detail of the proposed legislation in a context of Greek political and cultural history.

MENO

R. S. Bluck, *Plato's Meno, With Introduction and Commentary.* (Cambridge: At the University Press, 1961).

A serious study, partly historical, partly philological, and partly philosophical.

Alexander Sesonske and Noel Fleming, eds., *Plato's Meno: Text and Criticism* (Belmont, California: Wadsworth Publishing Co., 1965).

Jowett translation, followed by half a dozen critical essays by various hands.

PARMENIDES

Francis MacDonald Cornford, *Plato and Parmenides: Parmenides' Way of Truth and Plato's Parmenides,* translated with an Introduction and Running Commentary (London: Routledge and Kegan Paul, 1939).

Translation and straightforward commentary.

Robert S. Brumbaugh, *Plato on the One: The Hypotheses in the "Parmendie."* (New Haven: Yale University Press, 1961).

Philosophically exciting treatment of the last two thirds of the *Parmenides.* A fine book.

PHAEDO

R. S. Bluck, *Plato's Phaedo* (New York: Library of Liberal Arts, no date).

A translation and commentary which raises many important issues.

R. M. Hackforth, *Plato's Phaedo* (New York: Library of Liberal Arts, no date).

A smooth-flowing translation, with commentary.

PHAEDRUS

Josef Pieper, *Enthusiasm and Divine Madness: On the Platonic Dialogue Phaedrus,* trans. Richard and Clara Winston (New York: Harcourt, Brace and World, 1964).

A short, imaginative book containing some worthwhile suggestions.

PHILEBUS

Plato, *Philebus,* R. G. Bury, ed. (Cambridge: At the University Press, 1897).

A good standard text, with introduction and notes.

R. Hackforth, *Plato's Examination of Pleasure: A Translation of the Philebus, with Introduction and Commentary* (Cambridge: At the University Press, 1958). Also published in paperback by Liberal Arts Press.

Hackforth makes some good points, though the main design of the dialogue seems to elude him.

A. E. Taylor, *Philebus and Epinomis,* Klibansky, Calogero, and Lloyd, eds. (London: Thomas Nelson, 1956).

Translation and notes. Taylor is always erudite and honest, but his British idealism occasionally stands in his way.

REPUBLIC

James Adam, *The Republic of Plato* (Cambridge: At the University Press, 1929).

This work is in two volumes, and has recently been reprinted. It is a standard text, and contains valuable notes, most of them on philological matters.

Plato, *The Republic,* with an English translation by Paul Shorey (Cambridge: Harvard University Press, 1935). 2 vols.

This edition of the text is in the Loeb Classical Library, and as with all volumes in that series, has Greek and English on facing pages. Shorey's notes and introduction are not, as a rule, philosophically perceptive, but he keeps up a running gunfight with all his learned opponents, and this is often amusing. The translation is colloquial, but quite accurate.

Francis M. Cornford, trans. *The Republic* (Oxford: At the University Press, 1941).

An edition that ignores the customary division into ten books, and arranges the text (in the same order, of course) under quite different topical headings. The question-and-answer conversations are reduced to straight exposition wherever possible, which means that many hints on interpretation are destroyed in the process. Useful outline and summaries nevertheless.

Bernard Bosanquet, *A Companion to Plato's Republic for English Readers* (London: Rivington's, 2nd ed., 1925).

Helpful commentary.

Richard Lewis Nettleship, *Lectures on the Republic of Plato,* G. R. Benson, ed. (New York: Macmillan & Co., 1929). Reprinted as a paperback, 1964.

. Useful. Nettleship was more sensitive to humanistic than scientific aspects of the text.

Neville Richard Murphy, *The Interpretation of Plato's Republic,* (New York: Oxford, 1951).

A very able set of connected essays aimed chiefly at the problems of morals and politics.

Allan Bloom, trans., *The Republic of Plato,* with notes and an interpretive essay (New York: Basic Books, 1968).

Bloom is determined to make a very literal translation, which is the only defensible policy for serious scholarship. Brilliant notes and interpretive essay.

STATESMAN

J. B. Skemp, trans., *Plato's Statesman,* with translation, introduction and notes (New Haven: Yale University Press, 1952).

Skemp is at home in the physics as well as the other phases of Plato's philosophy, and his notes are always interesting. The translation is easy and a trifle loose, but it is clear. This is a significant contribution to scholarship.

SYMPOSIUM

Stanley Rosen, *Plato's Symposium* (New Haven: Yale University Press, 1968).

A very intelligent book, with certain shortcomings nevertheless. Full commentary containing many important insights.

THEAETETUS AND SOPHIST

Francis M. Cornford, trans., *Plato's Theory of Knowledge: the Theaetetus and Sophist,* with introduction and a running commentary (New York: Humanities Press, 1961).

Clear, but with some axes to grind. Valuable in spite of this.

TIMAEUS

A. E. Taylor, *A Commentary on Plato's Timaeus* (Oxford: At the University Press, 1928).

Without doubt the most exhaustive treatment of the *Timaeus* ever written. Excellent account of individual doctrines and their historical antecedents, together with a highly dubious interpretation of the dialogue as a whole.

Francis M. Cornford, trans., *Plato's Cosmology: The Timaeus of Plato*, with a running commentary (New York: Harcourt Brace and Co., 1937).

Cornford seeks to correct what he takes to be a "heresy" on Taylor's part, and reunifies the *Timaeus*. The work is more perspicuous though less historically informative than Taylor's massive *Commentary*.

THE LAUREL CLASSICAL DRAMA SERIES

This new series presents outstanding contemporary translations in an eminently readable paperbound format. The Aeschylus collection, for example, features translations by George Thomson, Professor of Greek at Birmingham University, England, and noted scholar and translator. The general editor for the series is Robert W. Corrigan, Professor of Drama, New York University.

SOPHOCLES   75c

Antigone
Oedipus the King
Electra
Philoctetes

EURIPIDES   75c

Medea
Hippolytus
Alcestis
The Bacchae

AESCHYLUS   60c

The Oresteia Trilogy:
Agamemnon, Choepho-
roe, and Eumenides
Prometheus Bound

GREEK COMEDY   75c

Aristophanes
Lysistrata
The Birds
Peace
Menander
The Grouch

ROMAN DRAMA   75c

Plautus
The Menaechmi
The Merchant

Terence
Phormio
The Brothers

Seneca
Medea

as well as Horace's
essay *Ars Poetica*
The Plutus

If you cannot obtain copies of these titles from your local bookseller, just send the price (plus 15c per copy for handling and postage) to Dell Books, Post Office Box 1000, Pinebrook, N. J. 07058.